Dreamweaver® CS3 For Dummies®

D0727665

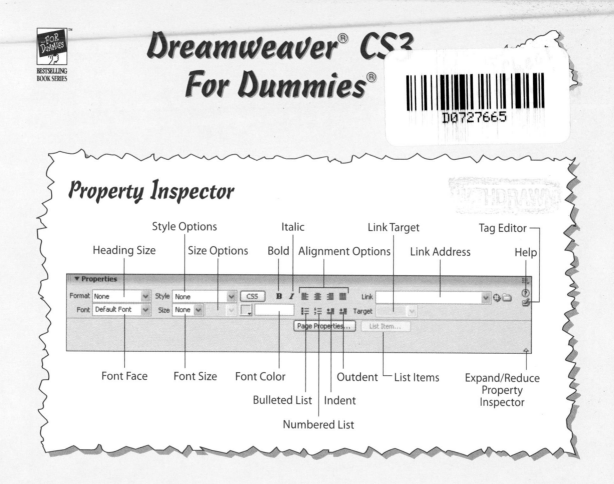

Property Inspector

- Heading Size
- Style Options
- Size Options
- Italic
- Bold
- Alignment Options
- Link Target
- Link Address
- Tag Editor
- Help
- Font Face
- Font Size
- Font Color
- Outdent
- List Items
- Expand/Reduce Property Inspector
- Bulleted List
- Indent
- Numbered List

Table Properties

- Name
- Columns in Table
- Space between Cell and Border
- Space between Cells
- Table Alignment
- Style Options
- Table
- Rows in Table
- Width
- Clear Column Widths
- Clear Row Heights
- Convert to Percent
- Background Color
- Border Color
- Table Border
- Convert to Pixels
- Background Color Picker
- Border Color Picker
- Background URL

BESTSELLING
BOOK SERIES

Dreamweaver® CS3 For Dummies®

Cheat Sheet

Image Properties

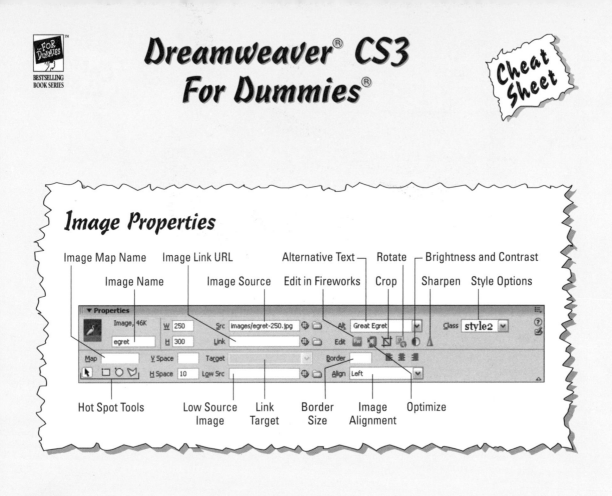

Image Map Name — Image Link URL — Alternative Text — Rotate — Brightness and Contrast

Image Name — Image Source — Edit in Fireworks — Crop — Sharpen — Style Options

Hot Spot Tools — Low Source Image — Link Target — Border Size — Image Alignment — Optimize

Common Insert Bar

Insert Link — Insert Anchor — Insert Image — Insert Date — Apply Template

Insert E-mail Link — Insert Table — Insert Media — Insert Comment — Tag Chooser

Wiley, the Wiley Publishing logo, For Dummies, the Dummies Man logo, the For Dummies Bestselling Book Series logo and all related trade dress are trademarks or registered trademarks of John Wiley & Sons, Inc. and/or its affiliates. All other trademarks are property of their respective owners.

Copyright © 2007 Wiley Publishing, Inc. All rights reserved. Item 1490-2.
For more information about Wiley Publishing, call 1-800-762-2974.

For Dummies: Bestselling Book Series for Beginners

Dreamweaver® CS3

FOR

DUMMIES®

by Janine Warner

BICENTENNIAL
1807
WILEY
2007
BICENTENNIAL

Wiley Publishing, Inc.

Dreamweaver® CS3 For Dummies®

Published by
Wiley Publishing, Inc.
111 River Street
Hoboken, NJ 07030-5774

www.wiley.com

Copyright © 2007 by Wiley Publishing, Inc., Indianapolis, Indiana

Published by Wiley Publishing, Inc., Indianapolis, Indiana

Published simultaneously in Canada

No part of this publication may be reproduced, stored in a retrieval system or transmitted in any form or by any means, electronic, mechanical, photocopying, recording, scanning or otherwise, except as permitted under Sections 107 or 108 of the 1976 United States Copyright Act, without either the prior written permission of the Publisher, or authorization through payment of the appropriate per-copy fee to the Copyright Clearance Center, 222 Rosewood Drive, Danvers, MA 01923, (978) 750-8400, fax (978) 646-8600. Requests to the Publisher for permission should be addressed to the Legal Department, Wiley Publishing, Inc., 10475 Crosspoint Blvd., Indianapolis, IN 46256, (317) 572-3447, fax (317) 572-4355, or online at http://www.wiley.com/go/permissions.

Trademarks: Wiley, the Wiley Publishing logo, For Dummies, the Dummies Man logo, A Reference for the Rest of Us!, The Dummies Way, Dummies Daily, The Fun and Easy Way, Dummies.com, and related trade dress are trademarks or registered trademarks of John Wiley & Sons, Inc. and/or its affiliates in the United States and other countries, and may not be used without written permission. Dreamweaver is a registered trademark of Adobe Systems Incorporated in the United States and/or other countries. All other trademarks are the property of their respective owners. Wiley Publishing, Inc., is not associated with any product or vendor mentioned in this book.

LIMIT OF LIABILITY/DISCLAIMER OF WARRANTY: THE PUBLISHER AND THE AUTHOR MAKE NO REPRESENTATIONS OR WARRANTIES WITH RESPECT TO THE ACCURACY OR COMPLETENESS OF THE CONTENTS OF THIS WORK AND SPECIFICALLY DISCLAIM ALL WARRANTIES, INCLUDING WITHOUT LIMITATION WARRANTIES OF FITNESS FOR A PARTICULAR PURPOSE. NO WARRANTY MAY BE CREATED OR EXTENDED BY SALES OR PROMOTIONAL MATERIALS. THE ADVICE AND STRATEGIES CONTAINED HEREIN MAY NOT BE SUITABLE FOR EVERY SITUATION. THIS WORK IS SOLD WITH THE UNDERSTANDING THAT THE PUBLISHER IS NOT ENGAGED IN RENDERING LEGAL, ACCOUNTING, OR OTHER PROFESSIONAL SERVICES. IF PROFESSIONAL ASSISTANCE IS REQUIRED, THE SERVICES OF A COMPETENT PROFESSIONAL PERSON SHOULD BE SOUGHT. NEITHER THE PUBLISHER NOR THE AUTHOR SHALL BE LIABLE FOR DAMAGES ARISING HEREFROM. THE FACT THAT AN ORGANIZATION OR WEBSITE IS REFERRED TO IN THIS WORK AS A CITATION AND/OR A POTENTIAL SOURCE OF FURTHER INFORMATION DOES NOT MEAN THAT THE AUTHOR OR THE PUBLISHER ENDORSES THE INFORMATION THE ORGANIZATION OR WEBSITE MAY PROVIDE OR RECOMMENDATIONS IT MAY MAKE. FURTHER, READERS SHOULD BE AWARE THAT INTERNET WEBSITES LISTED IN THIS WORK MAY HAVE CHANGED OR DISAPPEARED BETWEEN WHEN THIS WORK WAS WRITTEN AND WHEN IT IS READ.

For general information on our other products and services, please contact our Customer Care Department within the U.S. at 800-762-2974, outside the U.S. at 317-572-3993, or fax 317-572-4002.

For technical support, please visit www.wiley.com/techsupport.

Wiley also publishes its books in a variety of electronic formats. Some content that appears in print may not be available in electronic books.

Library of Congress Control Number: 2007924226

ISBN: 978-0-470-11490-2

Manufactured in the United States of America

10 9 8 7 6 5 4 3 2 1

WILEY

About the Author

Janine Warner is a bestselling author, journalist, and Internet consultant.

Since 1995, she's written and coauthored more than a dozen books about the Internet, including *Creating Family Web Sites For Dummies* and *Teach Yourself Dreamweaver Visually*.

She's also the host of a series of training videos on Web design for Total Training, a pioneer in innovative video-based training. Her first video on Dreamweaver has won two industry awards, and excerpts of her videos are features at both Microsoft.com and Adobe.com.

An award-winning journalist, her articles and columns have appeared in a variety of publications, including *The Miami Herald*, *Shape Magazine*, and the Pulitzer Prize-winning *Point Reyes Light* newspaper. She also writes a regular column about Dreamweaver for *Layers Magazine*.

Janine is a popular speaker at conferences and events throughout the United States and abroad, and she's taught online journalism courses at the University of Southern California Annenberg School for Communication and the University of Miami.

Warner is a special guest reporter for the consumer technology show Into Tomorrow (a syndicated program that reaches more than one million weekly listeners), and she has been a featured guest on television news and technology programs on ABC, NBC, and TechTV.

Warner has extensive Internet experience working on large and small Web sites. From 1994 to 1998, she ran Visiontec Communications, a Web design business in Northern California, where she worked for a diverse group of clients including Levi Strauss & Co., AirTouch International, Beth's Desserts, and many other small and medium-size businesses.

In 1998, she joined The Miami Herald as their Online Managing Editor. A year later, she was promoted to Director of New Media and managed a team of designers, programmers, journalists, and sales staff. She left that position to serve as Director of Latin American Operations for CNET Networks, an international technology media company.

Warner earned a degree in journalism and Spanish from the University of Massachusetts, Amherst, and spent the first several years of her career in Northern California as a reporter and editor.

To learn more, visit www.JCWarner.com.

Dedication

To all those who dare to dream about the possibilities of the Web: May this book make your work easier so you can make those dreams come true.

Author's Acknowledgments

I love teaching Web design because it's so much fun to see what everyone creates on the Internet. Most of all, I want to thank all the people who have read my books or watched my videos over the years and gone on to create Web sites. You are my greatest inspiration. Thank you, thank you, thank you.

Thanks to my love, David LaFontaine, whose patience and support have kept me fed, loved, and entertained. Thanks also to Duce, Yuki, and Faust.

Thanks to Frank Vera, a skilled programmer who deserves credit for revising the three most complex chapters in this book, Chapters 13, 14, and 15, and helping me test the dynamic database features in Dreamweaver.

Thanks to Web designers Mariana Davi Cheng (DaviDesign.com), Susie Gardner (HopStudios.com), Sheila Castelli (DigitalCottage.com), and Anissa Thompson (Anissat.com), who designed many of the Web sites featured in the examples in this book.

Thanks to the entire editorial team: Travis Smith for his superb tech editing; Susan Pink for catching the details and improving the prose; and Bob Woerner for shepherding this book through the development and publishing process.

Over the years, I've thanked many people in my books — family, friends, teachers, and mentors — but I have been graced by so many wonderful people now that no publisher will give me enough pages to thank them all. So let me conclude by thanking everyone who has ever helped me with a Web site, a book, or any other aspect of writing and Internet research, just so I can go to sleep tonight and know I haven't forgotten anyone.

Publisher's Acknowledgments

We're proud of this book; please send us your comments through our online registration form located at www.dummies.com/register/.

Some of the people who helped bring this book to market include the following:

Acquisitions, Editorial, and Media Development

Project Editor: Susan Pink

(Previous Edition: Rebecca Huehls)

Acquisitions Editor: Bob Woerner

Technical Editor: Travis Smith

Editorial Manager: Jodi Jensen

Media Development Specialists: Angela Denny, Kate Jenkins, Steven Kudirka, Kit Malone

Media Development Coordinator: Laura Atkinson

Media Project Supervisor: Laura Moss

Media Development Manager: Laura VanWinkle

Media Development Associate Producer: Richard Graves

Editorial Assistant: Amanda Foxworth

Sr. Editorial Assistant: Cherie Case

Cartoons: Rich Tennant (www.the5thwave.com)

Composition Services

Project Coordinator: Heather Kolter

Layout and Graphics: Claudia Bell, Carl Byers, Joyce Haughey, Barbara Moore, Laura Pence, Rashell Smith, Ronald Terry

Proofreaders: John Greenough

Indexer: Aptara

Anniversary Logo Design: Richard Pacifico

Publishing and Editorial for Technology Dummies

    Richard Swadley, Vice President and Executive Group Publisher

    Andy Cummings, Vice President and Publisher

  Mary Bednarek, Executive Acquisitions Director

    Mary C. Corder, Editorial Director

Publishing for Consumer Dummies

    Diane Graves Steele, Vice President and Publisher

    Joyce Pepple, Acquisitions Director

Composition Services

    Gerry Fahey, Vice President of Production Services

    Debbie Stailey, Director of Composition Services

Contents at a Glance

Table of Contents

Part II: Appreciating Web Design Options 125

Chapter 5: Cascading Style Sheets 127

Part III: Making It Cool with Multimedia and JavaScript 263

Introduction

· ·

*I*n the ten-plus years that I've been writing about Web design, I've seen many changes — from the early days (before Dreamweaver even existed) when you could create only simple pages with HTML 1.0, to the elaborate designs you can create with Dreamweaver today using XHTML, CSS, JavaScript, multimedia, and more.

If you're not sure what those acronyms mean yet, don't worry. I remember what it was like to learn all this stuff, too, so I designed this book to introduce you to the basic concepts. But I also want to prepare you for the ever-changing world of Web design, so I show you how to use Dreamweaver to create Web sites that take advantage of the latest advances in Web technologies, such as CSS and XHMTL.

One of the challenges of Web design today is that Web pages are not only displayed on different kinds of computers but are also being downloaded to computers with monitors that are as big as wide-screen televisions and as small as cell phones. As a result, creating Web sites that look good to all visitors is a lot more complex than it used to be, and standards have become a lot more important. That's why you find out not only how to use all the great features in Dreamweaver but also how to determine which of those features will best serve your goals and your audience.

About This Book

I designed *Dreamweaver CS3 For Dummies* to help you find the answers you need when you need them. You don't have to read this book cover to cover, and you certainly don't have to memorize it. Consider this a quick study guide and a reference you can return to. Each section stands alone, giving you easy answers to specific questions and step-by-step instructions for common tasks.

Want to find out how to change the background color in Page Properties, design styles to align images, or add an interactive photo gallery with the Swap Image behavior? Jump right in and go directly to the section that most interests you. And don't worry about getting sand on this book if you do take it to the beach or coffee spilled on the pages if you bring it with you to breakfast — I promise it won't complain!

What's New in Dreamweaver CS3?

Dreamweaver's high-end features make it the preferred choice for professional Web designers, and its easy-to-use graphical interface makes it popular among novices and hobbyists as well. With each new version, Dreamweaver has become more powerful and feature rich, but this upgrade is arguably the most dramatic, with the following new features:

- ✔ **Better integration with Photoshop, Flash, and other design programs.** Some of the coolest improvements to Dreamweaver CS3 are due to the fact that Macromedia (the company that created all previous versions of Dreamweaver) was acquired by Adobe (a company well-known for creating other popular programs, including Photoshop, Illustrator, and InDesign). As a result, programs that used to belong to Macromedia, including Fireworks and Flash, are now fully integrated with programs created by Adobe, such as Photoshop and Acrobat. And that means you can now work much more efficiently with this popular collection of tools, creating graphics in Photoshop and moving them into Dreamweaver with cut-and-paste ease. If you're an experienced Photoshop user, you may already be familiar with Adobe's Bridge program, which makes it easy to share images and other files among programs. With CS3, the Bridge now supports files from a wide collection of programs, including Dreamweaver.

- ✔ **Enhanced CSS support.** Other enhancements to Dreamweaver CS3 include better CSS support and new CSS features and templates. Creating Web sites with Cascading Style Sheets is by far the best option today. That's why so many of the improvements to Dreamweaver are related to CSS and why I've dedicated more of this book than ever to the best strategies for creating styles and CSS layouts.

- ✔ **A built-in device emulator.** When it comes to testing your Web designs, one of the most exciting additions to Dreamweaver CS3 is the new device emulator (shown at the end of in Chapter 2). Adobe Device Central comes with a collection of emulators that let you see how your pages will look when displayed in a variety of cell phone brands and models, and you can add more emulators as they become available.

- ✔ **Advances in dynamic site development.** The most advanced features in Dreamweaver CS3 are designed to help you create database-driven Web sites using a broad range of technologies. Whether you prefer

PHP, ColdFusion, ASP, or any of several other options, you can use Dreamweaver to create these kinds of advanced site technologies. If you're still not sure how dynamic sites work or their advantages, you'll find an introduction to database development in Chapter 13 and instructions for defining data sources, displaying data in Web pages, and building master pages in Chapters 13 and 15.

Using Dreamweaver on a Mac or PC

Dreamweaver works almost identically on Macintosh or Windows computers. In these two figures, you see the same Web page opened in design view on a Mac and a PC. To keep screenshots consistent throughout this book, I've used a computer running Windows XP. However, I've tested the program on both platforms, and whenever there is a difference in how a feature works, I indicate that difference in the instructions.

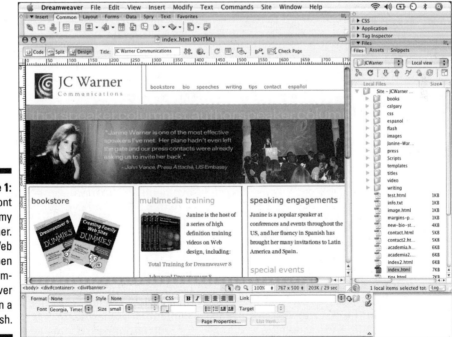

Figure 1: The front page of my JCWarner.com Web site open in Dreamweaver CS3 on a Macintosh.

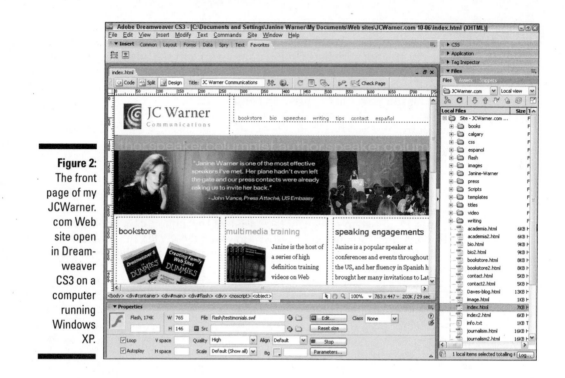

Figure 2:
The front
page of my
JCWarner.
com Web
site open
in Dream-
weaver
CS3 on a
computer
running
Windows
XP.

Conventions Used in This Book

Keeping things consistent makes them easier to understand. In this book, those consistent elements are *conventions*. Notice how the word *conventions* is in italics? That's a convention I use frequently. I put new terms in italics and then define them so that you know what they mean.

When I type URLs (Web addresses) or e-mail addresses within regular paragraph text, they look like this: `www.jcwarner.com`. Sometimes, however, I set URLs off on their own line, like this:

```
www.jcwarner.com
```

That's so you can easily spot them on a page if you want to type them into your browser to visit a site. I also assume that your Web browser doesn't require the introductory `http://` for Web addresses. If you use an older browser, remember to type this before the address (also make sure you include that part of the address when you're creating links in Dreamweaver).

Even though Dreamweaver makes knowing HTML code unnecessary, you may want to wade into HTML waters occasionally. I include HTML code in this book when I think it can help you better understand how things work in design view. Sometimes it's easier to remove or edit a tag in code view than design view. When I do provide examples, such as the following code which links a URL to a Web page, I set off the HTML in the same monospaced type as URLs:

```
<A HREF="http://www.jcwarner.com">Janine's Web Site</A>
```

When I introduce you to a new set of features, such as options in a dialog box, I set these items apart with bullets so that you can see that they're all related. When I want you to follow instructions, I use numbered steps to walk you through the process.

What You're Not to Read

If you're like most of the Web designers I know, you don't have time to wade through a thick book before you start working on your Web site. That's why I wrote *Dreamweaver CS3 For Dummies* in a way that makes it easy for you to find the answers you need quickly. You don't have to read this book cover to cover. If you're in a hurry, go right to the information you need most and then get back to work. If you're new to Web design, or you want to know the intricacies of Dreamweaver, skim through the chapters to get an overview and then go back and read what's most relevant to your project in greater detail. Whether you are building a simple site for the first time or working to redesign a complex site for the umpteenth time, you'll find everything you need in these pages.

Foolish Assumptions

Although Dreamweaver is designed for *professional* developers, I don't assume you're a pro — at least not yet. In keeping with the philosophy behind the *For Dummies* series, this book is an easy-to-use guide designed for readers with a wide range of experience. Being interested in Web design and wanting to create a Web site is key, but that desire is all that I expect from you.

If you're an experienced Web designer, *Dreamweaver CS3 For Dummies* is an ideal reference for you because it gets you working quickly with this program, starting with basic Web page design features and progressing to more advanced options. If you're new to Web design, this book walks you through all you need to know to create a Web site, from creating a new page to publishing your finished project on the Web.

How This Book Is Organized

To ease you through the learning curve associated with any new program, I organized *Dreamweaver CS3 For Dummies* to be a complete reference. This section provides a breakdown of the five parts of the book and what you can find in each one. Each chapter walks you through the features of Dreamweaver step by step, providing tips and helping you understand the vocabulary of Web design as you go along.

Part I: Creating Great Web Sites

Part I introduces you to the basic concepts of Web design as well as the main features of Dreamweaver. In Chapter 1, I give you an overview of the many approaches to Web design, so you can best determine how you want to build your Web site before you get into the details of which features in Dreamweaver are best suited to any particular design approach. In Chapter 2, I start you on the road to your first Web site, including creating a new site, importing an existing site, creating new Web pages, applying basic formatting, and setting links. To make this chapter more interesting and help you see how all these features come together, I walk you through creating a real Web page as I show you how the features work.

In Chapter 3, we move onto graphics, with an introduction to creating graphics for the Web, an overview of the differences in formats (GIFs, JPEGs, and PNG files), and detailed instructions for adding and positioning graphics in your pages. In Chapter 4, you discover Dreamweaver's testing and publishing features, so you can start uploading pages to the Internet as soon as you're ready. If you work with a team of designers, you may be especially interested in the Check In/Out feature, which makes it easier to manage a site when several people are working together. You'll also find instructions for using integrated e-mail for communicating with other team members.

Part II: Appreciating Web Design Options

Chapter 5 provides an overview of how Cascading Style Sheets work and how they can save you time. CSS has become *the* way to create page designs and manage formatting on Web pages, and these features have been nicely improved in Dreamweaver CS3. In this chapter, you find descriptions of the style definition options available in Dreamweaver as well as instructions for creating and applying styles. In Chapter 6, I take you further into CSS, introducing you to the power of `<div>` tags and how to create CSS layouts. Here you'll find instructions for working with Dreamweaver's Layers features, as well as how to create centered CSS designs and fluid layouts.

In Chapter 7, you discover how to use HTML table features. In Chapter 8, you find all you need to know about designing a site with frames and iframes. (This chapter also includes tips about when frames are useful and why they should sometimes be avoided.)

In Chapter 9, I introduce you to some of my favorite Dreamweaver features, including sophisticated template capabilities, that enable you to create more consistent designs and make global updates across many pages at once. I also cover Dreamweaver's Library items, which can be used to place and update commonly used elements, such as navigation bars or copyright tags.

Part III: Making It Cool with Multimedia and JavaScript

In Part III you discover how cool your site can look when you add interactive image features, audio, video, and Flash. In Chapter 10, you find instructions for creating an interactive photo gallery with the Swap Image behavior, as well as how to use other features in Dreamweaver's Behaviors panel, including the Open New Browser behavior. In Chapter 11, you find out what it takes to add multimedia to your Web pages, including how to insert as well as create links to a variety of file types — from Flash to video and audio files. In Chapter 12, I cover Dreamweaver's HTML form options, which you can use to add feedback forms, surveys, and much more.

Part IV: Working with Dynamic Content

Part IV features three chapters that cover the most advanced features in Dreamweaver CS3. Chapter 13 is designed to help you understand how database-driven Web sites work and why they have become so important on the Web. In Chapter 14, you discover how to add dynamic content to your pages, define data sources, display recordsets, and take advantage of Dreamweaver CS3's new Spry features. And in Chapter 15, you pull it all together and find out how to build master pages, create pages to search databases, and test your work with a live connection.

Part V: The Part of Tens

Part V features three quick references to help you develop the best Web sites possible. Chapter 16 provides a collection of online resources where you can register domain names and find hosting services, as well as a few services that can help you take care of more advanced challenges, such as setting up an e-commerce system. In Chapter 17, you find ten design tips to help you get the most out of Dreamweaver, and Chapter 18 showcases ten Web sites created with Dreamweaver to give you an idea of what's possible and inspire you in your own Web projects.

Icons Used in This Book

When I want to point you toward something you can download for your use, I use this icon.

This icon points you toward valuable resources on the Web.

This icon reminds you of an important concept or procedure that you'll want to store away in your memory banks for future use.

This icon signals technical stuff that you may find informative and interesting but that isn't essential for using Dreamweaver. Feel free to skip over this information.

This icon indicates a tip or technique that can save you time and money — and a headache — later.

This icon warns you of any potential pitfalls — and gives you the all-important information on how to avoid them.

Where to Go from Here

If you want to get familiar with the latest in Web design strategies and options, don't skip Chapter 1, which is designed to help guide you through the many ways to create Web sites today. If you're ready to dive in and build a basic Web site right away, jump ahead to Chapter 2. If you want to find out about a specific trick or technique, consult the Table of Contents or the index; you won't miss a beat as you work to make those impossible Web design deadlines. Most of all, I wish you great success in all your Web projects!

Part I
Creating Great Web Sites

The 5th Wave   By Rich Tennant

"I have to say I'm really impressed with the interactivity on this car wash Web site."

In this part . . .

In Part I, you find an introduction to Web design and an overview of the many ways you can create a Web site in Dreamweaver. Chapter 1 compares different layout techniques and provides an introduction to the toolbars, menus, and panels that make up Dreamweaver's interface.

In Chapter 2, you dive right into setting up a Web site, creating a Web page and adding text, images, and links. In Chapter 3, you find an introduction to Web graphics and tips for using Photoshop to optimize images in GIF, PNG, and JPEG formats. And Chapter 4 covers testing and publishing features, so you can make sure that everything works before you put your site online.

Chapter 1

The Many Ways to Design a Web Page

*W*eb design is an art and a science. I think that's what makes it so hard. Most of us don't have the artistic talent to create great Web designs, the science and math skills to develop all the technical elements, and the understanding of interface design and usability that make a Web site easy to use and intuitive to navigate. But you need all those skills to create a great Web site. That's why most of the best Web sites were created by a team of people with many different specialties.

In the early days, Web design was relatively easy — and vanilla boring. You could combine images and text, but that was about it; no complex layouts, no fancy fonts, and certainly no multimedia or animation.

Over the years, Web design has evolved into an increasingly complex field and Dreamweaver has evolved with it, adding new features that go way beyond the basics of combining a few words and images.

When I first started learning to creating Web sites in the mid 1990s, it was easy to learn and easy to teach others how to do it. More than 10 years and a dozen books later, it's a lot more complex, and I've come to realize that one of the first things you have to understand about Web design is that there isn't just one way to create a Web site anymore.

Today, you can find out how to design simple Web sites with HTML in a matter of hours or you can spend years developing the advanced programming skills it takes to create complex Web sites like the ones you see at Amazon.com or MSNBC.

For everything in between, Dreamweaver is the clear choice among professional Web designers as well as among a growing number of people who want to build sites for their hobbies, clubs, families, and small businesses.

But before we dive into the details about how you create a Web page in Dreamweaver, I think it's helpful to start by introducing the many ways you can create a Web site. The more you understand about the various approaches to Web design, the better you can appreciate your options.

Comparing Web Designs

Throughout this book, you find chapters covering a variety of aspects of Web design, from the basics of creating a page and adding images and links to more complex concepts such as creating rollover effects and pop-up windows with Dreamweaver's behaviors, which use JavaScript to create advanced interactive features.

You also find a few chapters that explore different page layout techniques. You can create Web designs using HTML tables, frames, or Cascading Style Sheets. You can even use these different technologies in combination. The next few sections are designed to help you understand the differences in these approaches before you decide which one is best for your Web site.

Appreciating the advantages of CSS

Today, the W3C, which sets standards for the Internet, recommends CSS for nearly every aspect of Web design. That's because the best CSS designs are accessible, flexible, and adaptable. Also, the fact that they follow standards has become increasingly important over the years.

If everyone who designed Web sites and everyone who created the browsers that displayed them followed the same standards, we'd have a much better Internet today. Unfortunately, over the years Web technology has evolved but Web browsers haven't always displayed the features of Web sites in the same way. As a result, the same Web page can look quite different from one browser to another, especially in older browsers. (You find more about browser differences and testing your designs in Chapter 4.)

Today, there is a growing movement among some of the best designers in the world to get everyone to follow the same standards, create Web sites with CSS, and make sure they are accessible to everyone.

When Web designers talk about *accessibility,* they mean creating a site that can be accessed by anyone who might ever visit your pages — and that includes people with limited vision who use special browsers (often called screen readers) that *read* Web pages aloud, as well as many others who use specialized browsers for a variety of other reasons.

If you work for a university, a nonprofit, a government agency, or a similar organization, you may be required to create accessible designs. But even if you're not required to use CSS or to design for accessibility, it's still good practice. That's why Dreamweaver CS3 includes so many CSS features and a collection of predesigned CSS layouts like the one I used to create the site design shown in Figure 1-1. You find instructions for creating CSS layouts like this one in Chapter 6.

One of the big advantages of CSS is that it lets you separate content from design. For example, instead of formatting every headline in your site as 24-point Arial bold, you can create a style for the `<h1>` tag and use it to format all your headlines. Then if you decide later that you want all your headlines to use the Garamond font instead of Arial, you need to change the style for the `<h1>` tag only once in the style sheet and it automatically applies every-where you've used that style.

Figure 1-1:
This site was designed using one of Dream-weaver's CSS layouts.

Separating content from design also enables you to create different style sheets for different audiences and devices. In the future this is likely to become even more important as a growing number of people view Web pages on everything from giant flat-screen monitors to tiny cell phone screens like the one shown in Figure 1-2. One of the coolest additions to Dreamweaver CS3 is Device Central, where you can preview your page designs in a variety of handheld devices and cell phones to see just how different they can look when displayed on these small screens.

As you get more advanced with CSS, you can create multiple style sheets for the same Web page. For example, you can create one that's ideally suited to a small screen like the one shown in Figure 1-2, another that works best when the page is printed, and yet another designed with a larger font size for anyone who may have a trouble reading the small print that is so common on Web pages.

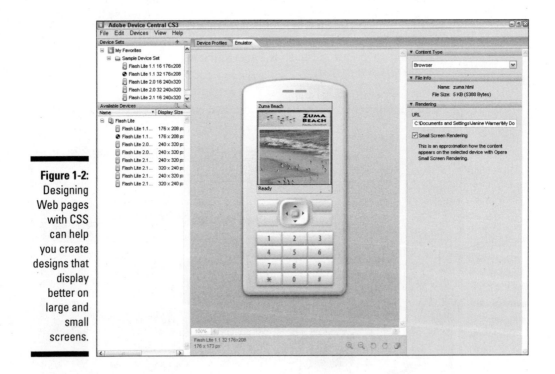

Figure 1-2: Designing Web pages with CSS can help you create designs that display better on large and small screens.

Reviewing old-school designs

Although CSS is by far the best option for creating Web designs today, many sites on the Web were created using tables to control the layout, like the one shown in Figure 1-3. Old-school sites like this one were created using the HTML table tag. To help you appreciate how this page was created, I altered the original design to display the table borders, although most designers turn off table borders when using them to create layouts like this.

Because you can merge and split table cells, you can control the layout of a page, positioning text and images more or less where you want them. And if you set the table border to 0 (instead of 10 as I did here to show you the borders), you can hide the table so that it doesn't interfere with the design.

In Chapter 7, you find an introduction to Dreamweaver's Table features and tips for creating accessible table designs by including the table header tag in all your tables. You can even combine CSS with tables to create more streamlined designs.

Figure 1-3: In the old days, the only way you could create a complex Web page design was by using a HTML table like the one shown here to control the placement of text and images.

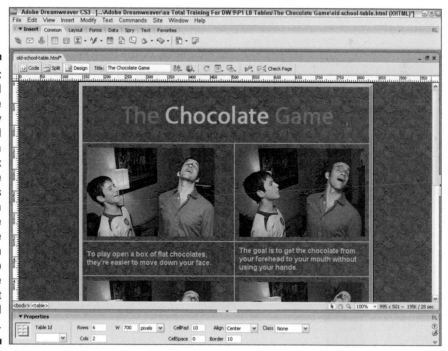

Although I recommend that you redesign sites like the one shown in Figure 1-3 with CSS and `<div>` tags, as you'll find out how to do in Chapter 6, I do understand that many designers still find it easier to create layouts with tables, and not everyone has time to redesign their Web sites right away. I have to admit, I've been guilty of leaving sites online designed with tables long after I learned better myself. So in the chapter on tables, I show you how to use Dreamweaver's features to create a page layout like the one in Figure 1-3, as well as how best to create tables for displaying tabular data like the content you'd find in a spreadsheet.

Although tables are no longer recommended for page layouts, they are still considered the best way to format data like the order page from the artist site shown in Figure 1-4.

Considering frame options

In Chapter 8 you find instructions for creating Web sites that use frames, like the family site shown in Figure 1-5. Many designers make a face much like the one my niece is displaying in the photo in Figure 1-5 because they think Frames are a terrible way to design Web sites.

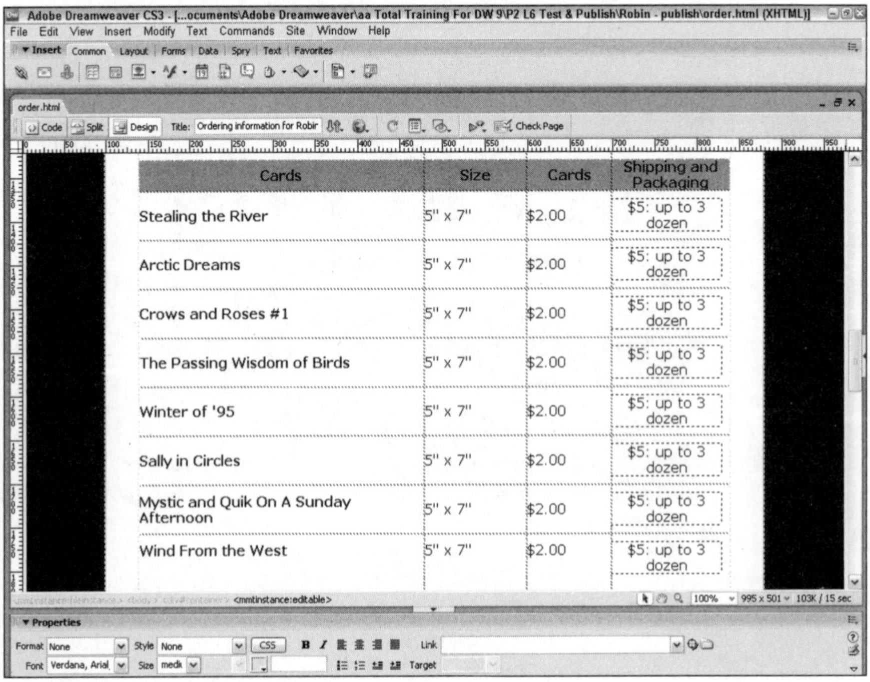

Figure 1-4: Tables are still considered the best way to display tabular data like the information on this order page.

Cards	Size	Cards	Shipping and Packaging
Stealing the River	5" x 7"	$2.00	$5: up to 3 dozen
Arctic Dreams	5" x 7"	$2.00	$5: up to 3 dozen
Crows and Roses #1	5" x 7"	$2.00	$5: up to 3 dozen
The Passing Wisdom of Birds	5" x 7"	$2.00	$5: up to 3 dozen
Winter of '95	5" x 7"	$2.00	$5: up to 3 dozen
Sally in Circles	5" x 7"	$2.00	$5: up to 3 dozen
Mystic and Quik On A Sunday Afternoon	5" x 7"	$2.00	$5: up to 3 dozen
Wind From the West	5" x 7"	$2.00	$5: up to 3 dozen

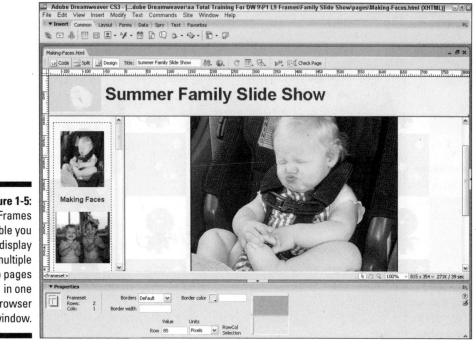

Figure 1-5:
Frames
enable you
to display
multiple
Web pages
in one
browser
window.

Frames have a bad rep, and there are some compelling reasons why they're not used much anymore. But frames still have their place on the Web, so I've included a chapter on the basics of using Dreamweaver's frame features to create pages like the one in Figure 1-5 that display multiple Web pages in one browser window.

Creating dynamic Web sites

When you use Dreamweaver's most advanced features, you can create Web sites (like the one shown in Figures 1-6 and 1-7) which connect to a database and display content dynamically on a Web page.

What's happening behind the scenes of a site like the one at www.PowerYoga. com gets complicated fast, but one of the advantages of using this kind of technology is that you can create a Web page like the one in Figure 1-7 and make it easy for anyone to enter data, like the details for a new event, even if they don't know how to use Dreamweaver. If you've used Dreamweaver's programming features, such as PHP or ASP, to set up a system that saves that data into a database automatically, you can then serve the contents of the form back to the live site on a page like the one shown in Figure 1-6, which includes a long list of events and retreats.

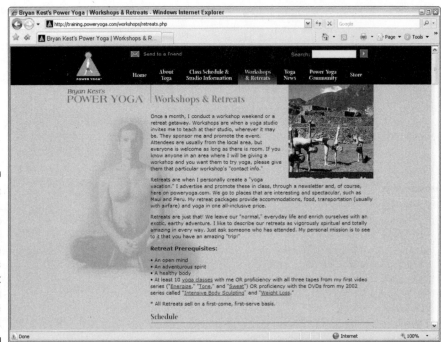

Figure 1-6:
PowerYoga.
com is a
dynamic
Web site
that displays
content
from a
database
using PHP.

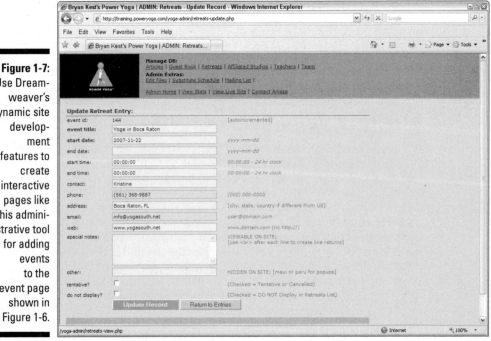

Figure 1-7:
Use Dream-
weaver's
dynamic site
develop-
ment
features to
create
interactive
pages like
this admini-
strative tool
for adding
events
to the
event page
shown in
Figure 1-6.

In Figure 1-7, you see an administrative tool that was designed to make it easy for someone who works at Power Yoga to update this section of the site without having to know HTML or even Dreamweaver, but you could also use this technology to create an online discussion board or any other system that collects data in one page and then uses that data to determine what is displayed on another page.

That's how the most advanced sites on the Web do things like remind you of the last book you searched for or keep track of your order as you select products in an online shopping cart. Although I can't cover all these advanced features in this book, you find an introduction to creating database-driven Web sites in Chapters 13, 14, and 15.

One other thing I feel compelled to mention at this point is that most of the big, complicated Web sites in the world were created by a team of developers, not just one person. In the case of the Power Yoga site, the design was created by Kathy McCarthy and the programming that makes all the dynamic features work was created by my friend Anissa Thompson. And that's part of why Christine Fang, the Managing Director who runs Power Yoga, is able to update the training section by herself using a Web browser, even though she knows only a little HTML.

Understanding Browser Differences

Another thing that's important to understand before you start creating Web pages is that no matter how carefully you create your designs, your pages will never look exactly the same to every possible visitor to your site. That's because one of the greatest advantages of the Web is also one of the biggest challenges. HTML was created to share information in a way that could be displayed on every computer on the planet. Unfortunately, not all those computers use the same browsers, or the same fonts, or the same-sized monitors. On top of that, a lot of older Web browsers are out there, and they can't display the latest Web features. And even the newer browsers don't all display the same features the same way.

As a result, although you have more design control today than ever before, and the capability to create more interesting Web sites, you also have more challenges if you want your pages to look good to everyone who might visit your site. My best advice is to test, test, test, and then ask your friends to test your pages some more. If you want to play it safe, the simpler your page design, the more likely it will look the same, or at least similar, to all your visitors.

If you want to create more interesting designs, and you want to reach the broadest possible audience, pay special attention to Dreamweaver's browser preview and compatibility features and be prepared to look for more advanced books and training programs when you finish with this one. Entire books and Web sites are dedicated to creating layouts that work on a variety of computers and browsers.

Because you're reading this book, I assume you are relatively new to Web design or looking for a refresher course and a chance to update your skills with CSS and the new features in Dreamweaver CS3, so I begin with the basics. In the next sections of this chapter, you find a few tips and suggestions for planning a Web site. At the end of this chapter, you find an introduction to Dreamweaver's interface.

Over the course of the nearly 400 pages that follow, you find a variety of approaches to Web design, from old-school techniques like tables and frames to the newest and most advanced features like CSS and multimedia.

Developing a New Site

In a nutshell, building a Web site involves creating individual pages and linking them to other pages. You need to have a home page (the first page visitors will see when they arrive at your URL) and that page needs to bring them into the rest of the pages of the site, usually with links to each of the main sections of the site. Those pages, in turn, link to subsections that can then lead to deeper subsections.

A big part of planning a Web site is determining how to divide the pages of your site into sections and how those sections should link to one another. Dreamweaver makes creating pages and setting links easy, but how you organize the pages is up to you.

If you're new to this, you may think you don't need to worry much about how your Web site will grow and develop. Think again. All good Web sites grow, and the bigger they get, the harder they are to manage. Planning the path of growth for your Web site before you begin can make a tremendous difference later. Neglecting to think about growth is probably one of the most common mistakes among new designers. This becomes even more serious when more than one person is working on the same site. Without a clearly established site organization and some common conventions for tasks such as naming files, confusion reigns.

Managing your site's structure

Managing the structure of a Web site has two sides: the side that users see, which depends on how you set up links, and the behind-the-scenes side, which depends on how you organize files and folders.

What the user sees

The side that the user sees is all about navigation. When users arrive at your home page, where do you direct them? How do they move from one page to another in your site? A good Web site is designed so that users navigate easily and intuitively and can make a beeline to the information most relevant to them. As you plan, make sure that users can

- ✔ Access key information easily from more than one place in the site
- ✔ Move back and forth easily between pages and sections
- ✔ Return to main pages and subsections in one step

Setting links is easy in Dreamweaver; the challenge is to make sure that those links are easy for visitors to follow.

What's behind the scenes

The second side to managing your Web site structure happens behind the scenes (where your users can't see the information, but you want some kind of organizational system to remember what's what). Before you get too far into building your site with Dreamweaver, spend some time thinking about the management issues involved in keeping track of all the files you create for your site. *Files* are all the images, HTML pages, animations, sound files, and anything else you put in your Web site.

Once your Web site grows past a handful of pages, organizing them in separate folders or directories can help you keep track. Fortunately, Dreamweaver makes this easy by providing a Files panel, shown in Figure 1-8, where you can see all the files of your site and even move and rename files and folders. (You find detailed instructions for organizing the files and folders in a Web site in Chapters 2 and 4.)

Under construction? No hard hats here!

All good Web sites are under construction — always. It's the nature of the Web. But build your site in such a way that you can add pages when they're ready instead of putting up placeholders. Don't greet your viewers with a guy in a yellow hat who seems to say, "You clicked this link for no good reason. Come back another day, and maybe we'll have something for you to see." Instead of creating "Under Construction" placeholders, create directory structures that make adding new pages later easy. You can let readers know that new things are coming by putting notices on pages that already have content — a message like "Come here next Thursday for a link to something even cooler" is a great idea. But never make users click a link and wait for a page to load, only to find that nothing but a guy with a hard hat is waiting for them.

Preparing and planning a Web site

One of the most common mistakes new Web designers make is plunging into developing a site without thinking through all their goals, priorities, budget, and design options. The instinct is to simply start creating pages, throw them all into one big directory, and then string stuff together with links. Then, when designers finally test the site out on an audience, they're often surprised when users say the site is hard to navigate and they can't find what they want.

Save yourself some grief by planning ahead, and you stand a much better chance of creating an attractive Web site that's easy to maintain and update.

Visualizing your site

Before you get too far into building Web pages, take some time to plan your site and think about its structure and organization. A good place to begin is by answering the following questions:

- ✔ What do you want to accomplish with your Web site? (What are your goals and objectives?)
- ✔ Who is your target audience?
- ✔ Who will be working on your site? How many developers do you have to manage?
- ✔ How will you create or collect the text and images you need for your site?
- ✔ How will you organize the files in your site?
- ✔ Will you include multimedia files such as Flash, audio, or video?
- ✔ Will you want interactive features such as a feedback form or chat room?
- ✔ What kind of navigation system will you have for your site (that is, how can you make it easy for visitors to move from one page or section to another in your site)?
- ✔ How will you accommodate growth and further development of the site? (Good Web sites always grow over time.)

Taking the time to get clear on your goals and objectives is time well spent. It can help you set the tone for a successful Web project from the beginning and ensure you spend your precious time, money, and energy on the elements and features that matter most.

Preparing for development

One of the first things many professional Web designers do when they're working on a new site with a group or a company is hold a brainstorming session with a few key people who understand the mission for the Web site. The purpose of this session is to come up with proposed sections and features for the site, what should be included, and how the site should be organized. A good brainstorming session is a nonjudgmental free-for-all — a chance for everyone involved to share all the ideas they can think of, whether realistic or not.

Not discrediting ideas at the brainstorming stage is important. Often an unrealistic idea leads to an innovation that no one may have thought of otherwise, especially when you're working on the Internet, where the best ideas are almost always new ones.

After a brainstorming session like this, you'll probably have a long list of possible features to develop into your site. Your next challenge is to edit that list to the most important ones and then plan your course of development to ensure that everything will work well together when you're finished.

Customizing the Workspace in Dreamweaver CS3

Dreamweaver can seem a bit overwhelming at first. It has so many features, and they are spread out in so many panels, toolbars, and dialog boxes that you can easily get lost. If you prefer to understand by poking around, have at it (and feel free to skip ahead to the next chapter, where you start building your first Web page right away). If you want a tour before you get started, the last few sections of this chapter introduce you to the interface and are designed to give you a quick overview of the features in this powerful program.

When you launch Dreamweaver, the Start screen appears in the main area of the program (and reappears anytime you don't have a file open unless you close it permanently by selecting the Don't Show Again option). From the Start screen, you can choose to create a new page from one of the many Dreamweaver predesigned sample files, or you can create a new blank page by selecting HTML from the Create New options in the middle column. When you select HTML, Dreamweaver creates a new blank HTML page in the main *workspace,* as shown in Figure 1-8.

You build HTML pages, templates, style sheets, and other files in the workspace, which consists of a main window that shows the page you're working on surrounded by a number of panels and menus that provide tools you can use to design and develop your pages. The Dreamweaver workspace consists of the following basic components: the menu bar (at the very top), the Insert bar (just below it), the Document window (the main area of the screen, just below the Insert bar), the Property inspector (at the bottom of the screen), and the vertical docking panels (to the right of the Document window) that expand and collapse as needed. More detailed descriptions of each of these follows.

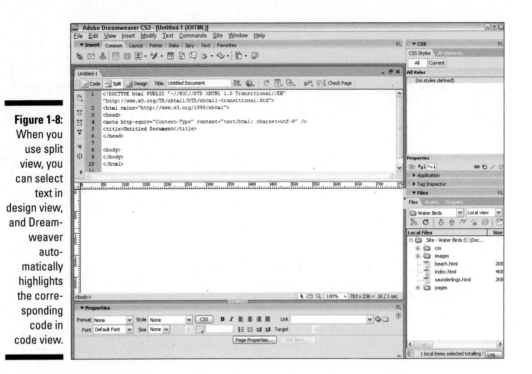

Figure 1-8:
When you
use split
view, you
can select
text in
design view,
and Dream-
weaver
auto-
matically
highlights
the corre-
sponding
code in
code view.

Dreamweaver has two main program layout settings: the designer layout, shown in Figure 1-8, and the coder layout, which places the panels on the left side of the screen instead of the right side. You can change layouts by choosing Window➪Workspace Layout and then choosing Coder or Designer.

The Document window

The big, open section in the main area of the workspace is the Document window, which is where you work on new and existing pages. If you use the Designer interface in design view, you see your page as it would appear in a Web browser. If you want to see the HTML code behind your page, click the Code button at the top of the work area. Choose the Split button to see the HTML code and design view simultaneously (which you can see in Figure 1-8).

Customizing the interface

The docking panels, palettes, and bars in Dreamweaver provide easy access to most of the program's features, and you can drag these elements around the screen. You can also close any panels on the right by clicking the tiny Options icon in the top right of each panel and choosing Close Panel from the drop-down list. (The Options icon looks like three bullet points with lines next to them and a little arrow underneath, and it's really, really small.) You can also close all the panels at once by choosing Window➪Hide Panels (or by clicking the arrow in the middle of the row of panels). If you want to open a panel, select it from the Window menu. For example, to open the CSS Styles panel, choose Window➪CSS Styles.

The Insert bar

The Insert bar, located at the top of the screen, includes seven *subcategories*, each with a different set of icons representing common features. Click the small arrow to the right of the name to access the drop-down list and switch from the buttons of one subcategory to the buttons for another. The options are

- **Common bar:** Displays icons for many of the most common features, including links, tables, and images.

- **Layout bar:** Displays div, table, and frame options essential for creating page layouts.

- **Forms bar:** Features the most common form elements, such as radio buttons and boxes.

- **Data bar:** Displays options for building dynamic Web pages powered by database material.

- **Spry bar:** Features a collection of widgets that combines HTML, CSS, and JavaScript to create interactive page elements.

- **Text bar:** Displays common text-formatting features, including paragraphs, breaks, and lists.

- **Favorites bar:** Enables you to right-click (Windows) or Control+click (Mac) to add any of the icons from any of the other Insert bar options to create your own collection of favorite features.

At the end of the drop-down list is Show as Tabs option, which enables you to display the names of the Insert bars as tabs across the top of the screen, as shown in Figure 1-9.

Figure 1-9:
The
Common
Insert bar
provides
access for
forms,
tables,
images,
and more.

The Property inspector

The Property inspector is docked at the bottom of the workspace in Dreamweaver. If you prefer it at the top of the screen, you can drag it to the top and it will lock into place; but I rather like that it's handy, yet out of the way, at the bottom of the screen.

The Property inspector displays the *properties,* or options, for any selected element on a page, and it changes based on what's selected. For example, if you click an image, the Property inspector displays image properties. If you click a Flash file, it displays Flash properties. Figure 1-10 shows the image options displayed in the Property inspector, including height and width, alignment, and link settings.

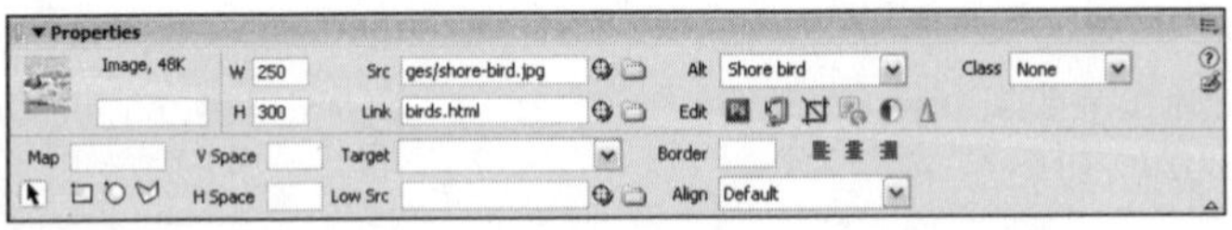

Figure 1-10:
The
Property
inspector
displays the
attributes
of any
selected
element,
such as an
image
shown here.

At the bottom-right corner of the Property inspector, you see a small arrow. Click this arrow (or double-click in any open inspector space) to reveal additional attributes that let you control more advanced features, such as the image map options when a graphic is selected.

The docking panels

The docking panels are located to the right of the work area when you choose designer layout, as shown in Figure 1-11, or on the left if you choose coder layout. You can move the panels anywhere on the screen by clicking and dragging them.

The docking panels display a variety of important features in Dreamweaver, including all the files and folders in a site in the Files panel and Cascading Style Sheets in the CSS panel. You can open and close panels by clicking the small arrow to the left of each panel's name. To display more panels, select the panel name from the Window menu. To hide all the visible panels at once, click the tab with the small arrow in the middle of the row of panels.

Figure 1-11:
Panels
provide
easy access
to all the
files, styles,
and many
other assets
in a Web
site.

The menu bar

Like most programs you've used, the menu at the top of the screen provides easy access to most program features, including the options you find in the Insert bar, Property inspector, and panels, as well as a few others that are available only from the menu.

The status bar

The status bar, at the bottom of the Document window, includes a number of useful details about the page that's open in the program, as well as access to a number of useful features. On the right side of the status bar are tool icons that control the on-screen display of your document. On the left end, you find the Tag selector, which features a collection of HTML tags that change depending on your cursor's location on the page. The tags indicate how elements on your page are formatted. If you click a tag in the Tag selector, you can select the tag and everything it contains in the main Document window, a handy feature for making precise selections in Dreamweaver.

The more you use Dreamweaver, the more you are likely to appreciate the capability to customize its features. Remember that you can always change the workspace to better suit the way you like to work, and you can easily alter Dreamweaver's preference settings using the Preferences dialog box shown in Figure 1-12 by choosing Edit⇨Preferences on a Windows computer, or Dreamweaver⇨Preferences if you're using a Mac.

Figure 1-12: You can change how Dreamweaver creates code, displays elements, and manages accessibility options.

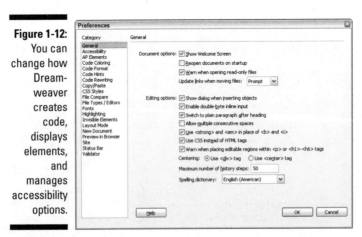

Chapter 2

Opening and Creating Sites in Dreamweaver

*I*f you're ready to dive in and start building a Web site, you've come to the right place. If you're working on an existing site and need to make changes, this is also the place to start because in this chapter you discover an important preliminary step — the site definition process, which enables Dreamweaver to keep track of the images and links in your site. After you've completed the site setup process, you're ready to create Web pages, insert text and images, set links, and more. But whatever you do, don't skip this first step.

Although you can use Dreamweaver without doing this initial site definition, you run the risk of breaking links when you upload your site, and many of Dreamweaver's features, such as automated link checking and the Library, won't work at all.

Setting Up a New or Existing Site

The first thing to understand about the site definition process is that you need to store all your site's resources in one local root folder on your hard drive and identify the folder in Dreamweaver. That's because all the elements of your site must remain in the same relative location on your hard drive as they are on your Web server in order for your links, images, and other elements to work properly.

Building and publishing a Web site

As a general rule, you should first create a Web site on your computer's hard drive, where you can test the site before it is visible on the Internet. Then when you're ready to publish the completed site, you transfer it to a Web server. A *Web server* is a computer with a permanent connection to the Internet and special software that enables it to communicate with Web browsers such as Internet Explorer and Firefox. You find detailed instructions for publishing a Web site in Chapter 4.

As you go through the site definition process, you can create a new folder on your hard drive and designate that as your local root folder or you can identify an existing folder.

The Site Definition dialog box, where you define a site, also contains Dreamweaver's file transfer features, including its FTP (File Transfer Protocol) capabilities. For now, we'll skip those (as well as Dreamweaver's other publishing and site management features) to keep things simple. In Chapter 4, however, you find detailed instructions for using these features as well as instructions for downloading an existing Web site hosted on a remote server.

FTP is a common method of copying files to and from computers connected across a network, such as the Internet. FTP is the protocol you'll probably use to send your Web pages to your Web server when you're ready to publish your site on the Web.

Defining a Web site in Dreamweaver

If the site definition process seems a little confusing at first, don't worry; it's a quick, relatively painless process, and you have to do it only once for each site. Just trust me; don't skip this preliminary step.

Whether you are creating a new site or working on an existing site, the following steps walk you through the process of defining a root site folder.

1. **Choose Site⇨New Site.**

   The Site Definition dialog box appears, as shown in Figure 2-1.

2. **Click the Advanced tab.**

   The Advanced window appears. If you prefer, you can use the Basic wizard that steps you through the setup process, but I find it faster and easier to view all the options at once using the Advanced tab.

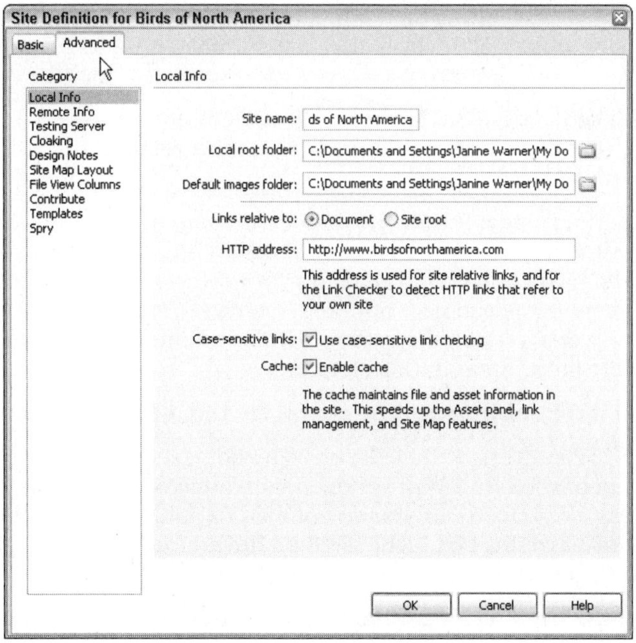

Site Definition for Birds of North America

Basic | Advanced

Category | Local Info

Local Info
Remote Info
Testing Server
Cloaking
Design Notes
Site Map Layout
File View Columns
Contribute
Templates
Spry

Site name: ds of North America

Local root folder: C:\Documents and Settings\Janine Warner\My Do

Default images folder: C:\Documents and Settings\Janine Warner\My Do

Links relative to: ⦿ Document ◯ Site root

HTTP address: http://www.birdsofnorthamerica.com

This address is used for site relative links, and for
the Link Checker to detect HTTP links that refer to
your own site

Case-sensitive links: ☑ Use case-sensitive link checking

Cache: ☑ Enable cache

The cache maintains file and asset information in
the site. This speeds up the Asset panel, link
management, and Site Map features.

OK | Cancel | Help

Figure 2-1:
The Site
Definition
dialog box
enables you
to set up a
new or
existing
Web site in
Dream-
weaver.

3. **In the Category box on the left, make sure that the Local Info category is selected.**

4. **In the Site Name text box, type a name for your site.**

   You can call your site whatever you like; this name is used only to help you keep track of your sites. Many people work on more than one site in Dreamweaver, and this feature enables you to keep track of them by name. The name you enter here appears in the drop-down list in the Files panel and in the Manage Sites dialog box. You use this list to select the site you want to work on when you open Dreamweaver. In the example shown in Figure 2-1, I named the new site "Birds of North America."

5. **Click the Browse icon next to the Local Root Folder text box to locate the folder on your hard drive that you want to serve as the main folder for all the files in your Web site.**

   If you're working on a new site, create a new folder and designate that as the location of your site in Dreamweaver. If you're working on an existing site, select the folder that contains the files for that site.

6. **Specify the Default Images folder by entering the location or using the Browse icon to locate it.**

   You do not have to identify an images folder, but it's another way Dreamweaver helps keep track of things for you. If you store images in more than one folder, I still recommend that you identify a main image folder. If you're setting up a new site, you can create a new folder inside your site folder and identify that as your images folder, even if it is empty.

7. **For Links Relative To, leave the Document option selected unless you know that you want your links to be set up relative to the root of your site.**

This setting controls how the path is set in links. If you're working on a site with other developers and you're not sure, check with your colleagues. If you're working alone on your own site, Links Relative to Document is the simplest option to manage. (You can learn more about relative versus root links in the sidebar, "Creating relative, root, and absolute links," later in this chapter.)

8. **In the HTTP Address text box, type the URL of your Web site.**

The HTTP address is the URL, or Web address, that your site will have when published on a Web server. If you do not yet know the Web address for your site or you do not plan to publish it on a Web server, you can leave this box blank. Include the http:// at the beginning, and a / at the end.

9. **Select the Use Case-Sensitive Link Checking box.**

Unless you know for sure that you don't have to worry about the case of your filenames, checking this box means Dreamweaver will ensure that the case matches for all your site's links (which many Web hosting services require).

10. **Select the Enable Cache option.**

Dreamweaver creates a local cache of your site to quickly reference the location of files in your site. The local cache speeds up many site management features of the program and takes only a few seconds to create.

11. **Click OK to close the Site Definition dialog box and save your settings.**

If the folder you selected as your local site folder already contains files or subfolders, they are automatically cached and all the files and folders in your site are displayed in the Files panel, as you see in Figure 2-2.

If you haven't checked the Enable Cache option, a message box appears asking whether you want to create a cache for the site.

Editing and managing multiple sites

You can define as many sites as you like in Dreamweaver and change from one site to another by selecting the site name in the Files panel. To load a different site into the Files panel, use the drop-down arrow next to the site name and choose the name of the site you want to display.

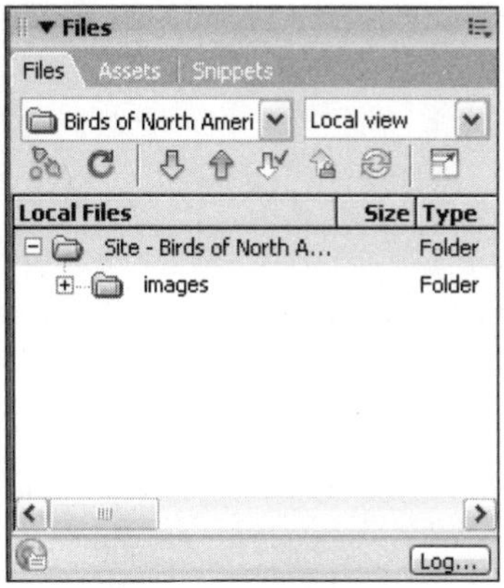

Figure 2-2:
When site setup is complete, the files and folders in an existing site are displayed in the Files panel.

In Figure 2-3, I'm selecting the Digital Family site from a list of defined sites. It is always best to have the site you're working on selected in the Files panel.

Figure 2-3:
You can define multiple sites and change the active site by selecting its name in the Files panel.

Once you've completed the site definition process covered in the preceding exercise, you can make changes and additions to a site definition by choosing Site⇨Manage Sites, selecting the name of the site in the Manage Sites dialog box, and then clicking the Edit button. The defined site is then opened in the Site Definition dialog box, where you can make changes to any of the settings.

In Figure 2-4, I selected the Birds of North America site to edit. You can use this dialog box to define a new site, remove an existing site, duplicate a site, and import or export a site. Note that when you remove a site from the Manage Sites dialog box, you do not delete the site's files or folders from your hard drive.

Figure 2-4:
You can edit
any site
definition by
selecting it
in the
Manage
Sites dialog
box and
clicking the
Edit button
to open
the Site
Definition
dialog box.

Manage Sites

Birds of North America
Digital Family
HardNewsInc
JCWarner
SCUBA Site
Water Birds

New...
Edit...
Duplicate
Remove
Export...
Import...

Done
Help

Creating New Pages

Every Web site begins with a single page. Visitors are first greeted by the front page — or *home page* — of your site, and that's usually a good place to start building. Dreamweaver makes creating new pages easy: When the program opens, you are greeted by a Start Screen with shortcuts to many handy features for creating new pages in a variety of formats.

If you want to create a simple, blank Web page, choose HTML from the Create New list in the middle column (see Figure 2-5). If you are creating a dynamic site, choose ColdFusion, PHP, or one of the ASP options. (If you don't even know what those options mean, you probably won't need to use them yet, but you can find some information about these advanced options in Chapters 13, 14, and 15.)

Get in the habit of saving new Web pages in your main Web site folder as soon as you create them, even though they are still blank. As you create links or add images to your pages, Dreamweaver needs to be able to identify the location of your page. Although Dreamweaver will set temporary links until your page is saved, it's always best to save a page first.

You can create a new page from the Start Screen or by using the New Document window available from the File menu, as you see in the following the steps. If you prefer not to use the Start Screen, you can turn it off by selecting the Don't Show Again box in the bottom-left corner.

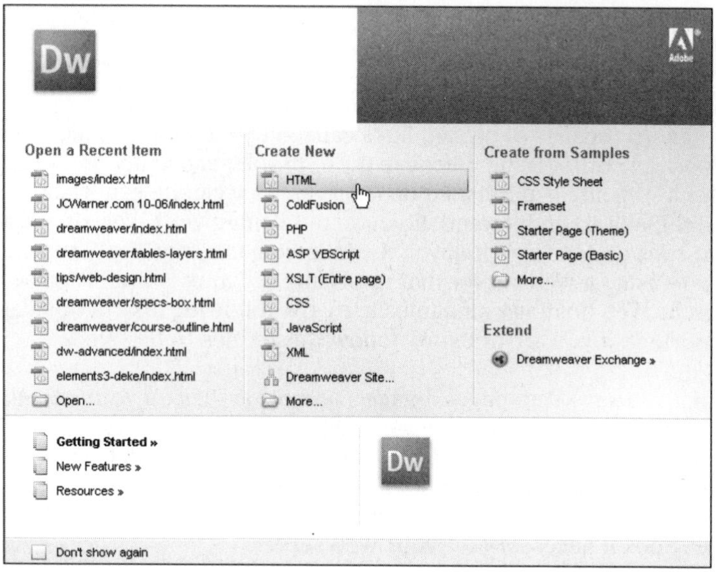

Figure 2-5:
The Start
Screen
provides
a list of
shortcuts
for creating
new files or
opening
existing
pages in
Dream-
weaver.

Open a Recent Item
- images/index.html
- JCWarner.com 10-06/index.html
- dreamweaver/index.html
- dreamweaver/tables-layers.html
- tips/web-design.html
- dreamweaver/specs-box.html
- dreamweaver/course-outline.html
- dw-advanced/index.html
- elements3-deke/index.html
- Open...

Create New
- HTML
- ColdFusion
- PHP
- ASP VBScript
- XSLT (Entire page)
- CSS
- JavaScript
- XML
- Dreamweaver Site...
- More...

Create from Samples
- CSS Style Sheet
- Frameset
- Starter Page (Theme)
- Starter Page (Basic)
- More...

Extend
- Dreamweaver Exchange »

Getting Started »
New Features »
Resources »

Don't show again

Follow these steps to create a new page using the New Document window:

1. **Choose File⇨New.**

   The New Document window opens.

2. **From the left side of the screen, select Blank Page.**

3. **From the Page Type list, select HTML, and then choose Create.**

4. **Choose File⇨Save to save your page.**

   You find many other options in the Dreamweaver New Document
   window, including a wide range of predesigned templates. For now, let's
   start with a simple blank page. You find instructions for working with
   templates in Chapter 9.

It's also good practice to add a page title right away. It's an easy detail to
forget, and pages on the Web look bad when they are titled "Untitled document." You can add a page title by changing the text in the Title box at the
top of the workspace. The page title won't appear in the main part of your
Web page, but it does appear at the top of a browser window, usually just to
the right or left of the name of the browser. The page title is also the text that
appears in a user's list of Favorites or Bookmarks. And perhaps even more
important, many search engines give special priority to the words that
appear in the title of a Web page.

Naming Web Pages

Over the years, I have received more e-mail messages from panicked Web designers because of broken links caused by filename conflicts than about almost any other issue. Because these problems usually don't occur until after a Web site is published on a server, they can be especially confusing and difficult to understand. If you're publishing your Web site to a Web server that runs on Mac or Windows, the following may not apply to you; but if you're using a Web server that runs Unix or Linux (which is what many commercial Web hosting companies use), the following instructions are especially important. If you are not sure, follow these rules to be safe.

When you save Web pages, images, and other files on your site, the first rule is to include an extension at the end to identify the file type (such as .html for HTML files or .gif for GIF images). Dreamweaver automatically adds the .html file extension to the end of HTML files (which works for most Web servers), but you can change the extensions in Dreamweaver's preference dialog box if necessary for your Web server.

Filenames are especially important in Web sites because they are included in the HTML code when you set links. The rules are easy: Don't use spaces or special characters in the name. For example you shouldn't name a Web page with an apostrophe, such as cat's page.html. If you want to separate words, you can use the underscore (_) or the hyphen (-). For example, cat-page.html is a fine filename. Numbers are okay in most cases and capital letters don't generally matter, as long as the filename and the code in the link match.

What can be misleading about these filename restrictions is that links with spaces and special characters work just fine when you test pages on a Mac or PC computer, but the software programs used on many of the Web servers on the Internet don't understand spaces or special characters in links. Thus, links that don't follow these rules may get broken when you publish the site to a Web server.

Another confusing rule, and one of the most important, is that the main page (or the *front page)* of your Web site must be called index.html or default. html, depending on your Web server. That's because most servers are set up to serve the index.html page first. To be sure what to name the main page of your site, you should check with your service provider or system administrator. (Some servers are set up to handle home.html, or default.asp for dynamic sites, but most commercial service providers serve index.html before any other page in any folder on a site.) The rest of the pages in your site can be named anything you like, as long as the names don't include any spaces or special characters (except the dash or underscore).

Designing your first page

Many people are pleasantly surprised by how easily they can create a basic Web page in Dreamweaver.

If you're ready to plunge right in, create a page and click to insert your cursor at the top of the blank page. (See the previous section, "Creating New Pages," if you need to start from the beginning.) Type some text on the page, anything you like; you just need something to get started. In the example in Figure 2-6, I've typed the text "A Great Egret Hunts Prey in Northern California." I'll use this as a headline in the simple page I'm creating.

In this chapter, I stick with the most basic formatting options. In Chapter 5, you find detailed instructions for going beyond these basic formatting options by creating Cascading Style Sheets to control and manage formatting.

Creating a headline

One of the most common text formatting options is to use the collection of heading tags. In HTML, there are many advantages to using heading tags (<h1>, <h2>, and so forth) to format text that serves as a title or headline. That's because heading tags are designed to be displayed in relative sizes, with <h1> the largest, <h2> smaller, <h3> smaller still, and so on through <h6>. That's valuable because no matter what the default text size is for a Web page (and text sizes can vary because of things such as browser settings and computer platform), any text formatted with an <h1> tag will always be larger than text formatted with <h2>.

Many search engines also give priority to keywords in text formatted with an <h1> tag because it is perceived to be the most important text on a page.

To format text with a heading style, follow these steps:

1. **Highlight the text you want to format.**

2. **In the Property inspector, at the bottom of the page, use the drop-down arrow in the Format field to select a style (see Figure 2-6).**

   When heading tags are applied, the text automatically changes to display the formatting in design view.

Although Dreamweaver's design view provides a good preview of how text, images, and other elements should look when viewed in a Web browser (such as Firefox or Internet Explorer), the page display varies from browser to browser depending on the browser settings and the operating system used to display the page.

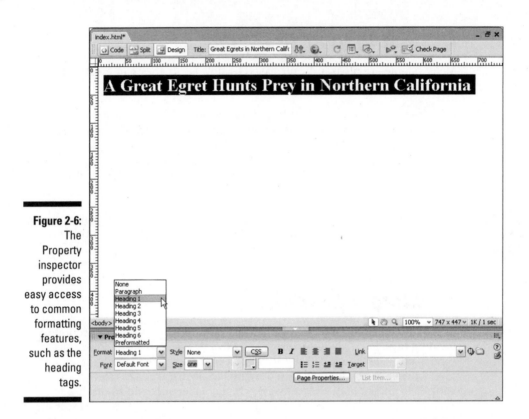

Figure 2-6:
The
Property
inspector
provides
easy access
to common
formatting
features,
such as the
heading
tags.

In general, I find the Property inspector the easiest way to apply basic formatting, but some people prefer using the Text menu. Both achieve the same results, except the Property inspector features font sizes (listed as sizes 9 through 36 and xx-small through xx-large) and the Text menu offers only the capability to increase or decrease font size.

Changing fonts and text sizes

You can change the font and the size of the text for the entire page or for any selected text on a page. You find instructions for changing font options for an entire page in the following section, "Changing Page Properties." To change the font face or size for a selected section of text, follow these steps:

1. **Highlight the text you want to change.**

2. **In the Font drop-down list, at the bottom of the work area, select a collection of fonts, as shown in Figure 2-7.**

The selected text changes to the first font in the collection of fonts you selected (unless that font is not available on your hard drive). You can also choose the Edit Font list option and use any font, but beware that the font you apply is displayed on your visitors' computers only if that font is on their hard drives. (See the "Why so many fonts?" sidebar for more about how this works.)

3. In the Size drop-down list, specify the size for your text.

Font sizes in HTML are different from the font sizes you may be used to using in a word processing or image program. Your size options are more limited, and you have the added choices of small, x-small, and so on. The numbered font sizes work much like those you may be used to, but they offer less flexibility to users of your site. When you set the size using the settings, which include *small*, *medium*, or *large*, the text is displayed according to the settings of the user's browser. You'll find more about font sizes in Chapter 5, where I cover creating text styles with CSS.

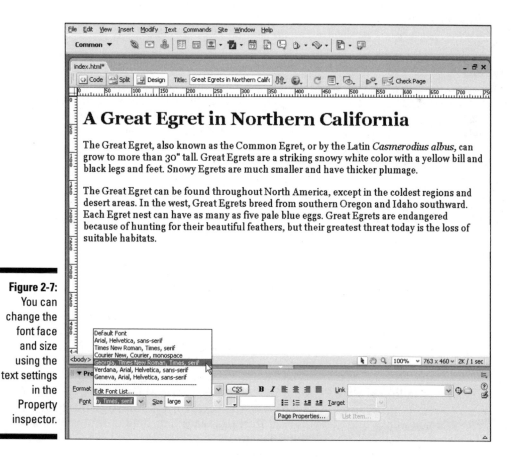

Figure 2-7:
You can change the font face and size using the text settings in the Property inspector.

Why so many fonts?

Although you can specify any font you want for text on your Web pages, you don't have complete control over how that font appears on your visitor's computer. That's because the font you apply is displayed properly only if your visitors have the same font on their hard drives. To help ensure that your text appears as you intend, Dreamweaver offers collections of common fonts, grouped together in families, such as Arial, Helvetica, sans-serif, Georgia, Times New Roman, Times, and serif.

Here's how it works. When you apply a collection of fonts like these, the browser displays the formatted text in the first font available in the font list. For example, if you choose the font collection that starts with Georgia and your visitors don't have Georgia, the text is displayed in Times New Roman; if they don't have that font, either, the text is displayed in Times; and if they don't even have Times, the browser looks for another serif font. (In case you're not familiar with font terms, *serif* describes fonts, such as Times, that have those little curly things on the edges of letters; *sans serif* means no curly things, which is what you get with a font such as Arial.)

You can create your own font collections by selecting the Edit Font List option from the bottom of the Font field in the Property inspector and using the Edit Font List dialog box. Use the plus and minus buttons at the top of the Edit Font List dialog box to add or remove a font collection. To add fonts to a collection, select the font name from the bottom right of the dialog box and use the arrow to add it to a font list.

The only way to ensure that text appears in the font you want is to create the text in a graphic in a program such as Photoshop or Fireworks and then insert the graphic with the text into your page. That's not a bad option for special text, such as banners or logos; but it's usually not a good option for all your text because graphics take longer to download than text and are harder to update later.

You find many more text formatting options in the Property inspector, such as bold and italic. Go ahead, experiment a little; you can always undo your formatting choices or change them again if you don't like the way they look.

Adding paragraphs and line breaks

When you create page designs for the Web, you must work within many limitations that may be confusing at first, even if they serve a purpose. How you create paragraph and line breaks is a good example.

If you are working in design view in Dreamweaver and press the Enter key (Windows) or the Return key (Mac), Dreamweaver inserts a Paragraph, or <p>, tag in the code, which creates a line break followed by a blank line. If you want a line break without the extra blank line, hold down the Shift key and press Return or Enter; Dreamweaver inserts the <br /> tag into the code, creating a single line break.

Inserting text from another program

Dreamweaver gives you many options for maintaining formatting when you copy and paste text from another program. You can change the default for how Dreamweaver handles formatting when you choose Edit⇨Paste and alter the Preferences in the Copy/Paste category. And you can choose Edit⇨Paste Special to have all the options available each time you paste new content. Here are your four options:

✔ **Text only:** Dreamweaver strips any formatting and inserts plain text.

✔ **Text with structure:** Dreamweaver includes paragraphs, lists, tables, and other structural formatting options.

✔ **Text with structure plus basic formatting:** Dreamweaver includes structural formatting

as well as basic formatting, such as bold and italic

✔ **Text with structure plus full formatting:** In addition to the previous options, Dreamweaver includes formatting created by style sheets in programs such as Microsoft Word.

✔ **Retain line breaks:** Line breaks are preserved, even if you don't keep other formatting options.

✔ **Clean up Word paragraph spacing:** The option addresses a common problem with the way Microsoft Word's paragraph spacing is converted when content is pasted into an HTML file.

If you want to add a lot of space, you'll need to use some other formatting option because by default most Web browsers condense extra spacing created by the paragraph or break tags and remove the extra space when the page is displayed in the browser. You'll have greater design control and more consistent results if you use CSS to create your page layouts. (I cover CSS in Chapters 5 and 6.)

If you are working in code view and add space using the Enter or Return key, you add blank space within the code, but you will not affect the display of the page in design view or how it will look in a browser.

Adding images

Now for the fun part. Adding an image to your Web page may seem almost magical at first because it is so simple with Dreamweaver. The challenge with Web graphics is not adding them to your pages but creating good-looking images that load quickly in your viewer's browser. You need another program, such as Photoshop or Fireworks, to create, convert, and edit images. Dreamweaver just lets you place the images on your page.

For more information on finding and creating images, as well as keeping file sizes small, see Chapter 3. For now, I assume that you have a GIF or JPEG image file ready and that you want to insert your image into your page. The two most common image formats you can use on your Web page are GIF and JPEG (which is often shortened to JPG), but the PNG file is increasingly used today because it is superior to the GIF format. But beware: PNG is not fully supported in older versions of Internet Explorer. For the exercise that follows, you can use any image in GIF, JPEG, or PNG format.

If you don't have an image handy, you can download free images from my Web site at www.DigitalFamily.com/free. (You find instructions for downloading the free images on the site).

Before inserting an image into a Web page, it's good practice to save the image inside your local root folder (the one you should have identified in the site definition process described in the "Defining a Web site in Dreamweaver" section, earlier in this chapter). Saving your image in your Web site's local root folder is important because you need to keep Web pages and images in the same location relative to each other in your Web site or you risk broken image links when you publish your site to a server. If you insert an image into a page that is not saved in the local root folder, Dreamweaver will display a warning and offer to copy the image into your local root folder as it inserts the image into the page.

Many designers create a folder called *images* so they can keep all their image files in one place. If you are working on a very large site, you may want to create an images folder within each of the main subfolders of your site to better organize your files. The thing to remember is that if you move a page or image to another folder after you place the image on your page, you risk breaking the link between the page and the image.

To avoid breaking links or image references, always use the Files panel to move or rename files. When you do so, Dreamweaver automatically fixes your links. If you move or rename a file or folder outside Dreamweaver, the links will break. You find more detailed instructions on managing and fixing links in Chapter 4.

Okay, assuming you've saved your page and the image you want to link is saved within your main Web site folder (or you're ready to let Dreamweaver copy it into your local root folder for you), you're ready to follow these steps to add an image on your Web page:

1. **Click to place your cursor on the page where you want to add the image.**

   I inserted my cursor under the headline at the beginning of the first paragraph.

You can't just place your cursor anywhere on a blank page and insert an image where you want it. This is not a limitation of Dreamweaver; it's a restriction caused by how HTML is displayed on a Web page. By default, all images, text, and other elements are inserted starting at the top-left corner. To create more complex layouts, you'll need to position elements with CSS (the most highly recommended option, which is covered in Chapter 6), or with an HTML table (covered in Chapter 7) or a layer (also covered in Chapter 6).

 2. **Click the Image icon, located in the Common Insert bar at the top of the work area and choose Image from the drop-down list.**

    The Select Image Source dialog box opens, displaying files and folders on your hard drive.

 3. **Navigate to the folder that has the image you want to insert and double-click to select the image you want to insert into your page.**

    If you have Accessibility options turned on in Preferences (the default), the Image Tag Accessibility Attributes dialog box appears. It is good practice to always add alternate text in this dialog box. To do so, simply enter text in the Alternate Text field. You can type any text in this field, but it is meant to provide a description of the image. Alternate text will not appear on your Web page unless the image is not visible, but it will appear in Internet Explorer when a user holds the cursor over the image. Alternate text is also important for Web surfers who use browsers that "read" Web pages to them, such as those with limited vision. For this reason, Alternate text is required for accessibility compliance. A long description is considered optional under most accessibility guidelines. You can also add or edit alternate text in the Property inspector.

 4. **Click OK.**

    The image automatically appears on the Web page.

 5. **Click to select the image on your Web page.**

    Image options are automatically displayed in the Property inspector at the bottom of the page.

 6. **Use the Property inspector to specify image attributes, such as alignment, spacing, and Alternate text.**

    In the example shown in Figure 2-8, I've set the alignment to Left, using the align option at the very bottom right of the Property inspector. That's how I got the text to wrap to the right of the image. I've also added 10 pixels of space using the H Space field to create a margin between the image and the text.

If you use CSS, you can create more precise formatting options. For example, H Space inserts space on both the left and right sides of an image. Using CSS, you can create a style that applies margin space on any or all sides of an image.

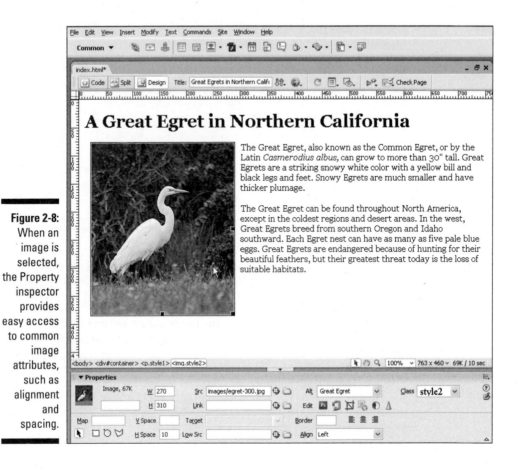

Figure 2-8:
When an image is selected, the Property inspector provides easy access to common image attributes, such as alignment and spacing.

With an image selected, the Property inspector enables you to specify many attributes for an image. Table 2-1 describes those attributes. If you don't see all the attributes listed in the table on your screen, click the triangle in the bottom-right corner of the Property inspector to reveal all the image options.

Table 2-1		Image Attributes in the Property Inspector
Abbreviation	*Attribute*	*Function*
Image	N/A	Specifies the file size.
Image Name	Name	Identifies image uniquely on the page — an important detail if you use behaviors or other scripts that are triggered by the image.
Map	Map Name	Assigns a name to an image map. All image maps require a name.

Abbreviation	Attribute	Function
Hotspot tools	Image Map Coordinates	Use the Rectangle, Oval, and Polygon icons to create image map hotspots for links. (See Chapter 5 to find out how to create an image map.)
W	Width	Dreamweaver automatically specifies the width of the image based on the actual size of the image dimensions.
H	Height	Dreamweaver automatically specifies the height of the image based on the actual size of the image dimensions.
Src	Source	Required. The *source* is the filename and path from the current document to the desired image. Dreamweaver automatically sets this when you insert the image.
Link	Hyperlink	This field shows the address or path if the image links to another page. (For more about linking, see "Setting Links" later in this chapter.)
Alt	Alternate Text	The words you enter are displayed if the image doesn't appear on your viewer's screen because images are turned off in the user's browser. Alt text is especially important for search engines and browsers used by the blind to read Web pages.
Edit	Icons for Fireworks, Optimize, Crop, Resample, Brightness and Contrast, and Sharpen	Click the Fireworks icons to launch Fireworks. Use any of the other icons to make other minor alterations to an image in Dreamweaver.
V Space	Vertical Space	Measured in pixels, this setting inserts blank space above and below the image.
H Space	Horizontal Space	Measured in pixels, this setting inserts blank space to the left and right of the image.

(continued)

Table 2-1 *(continued)*

Abbreviation	Attribute	Function
Target	Link Target	Use this option when the image appears in a page where you want to control the target, such as when a page is part of an HTML frameset or when you want a link to open a new window. The Target specifies the frame into which the linked page opens. I cover creating frames and how to set links in frames in Chapter 7.
Low Src	Low Source	This option enables you to link two images to the same place on a page. The Low Source image loads first and, after the rest of the page loads, it is replaced by the primary image. You may find this option especially useful when you have a large image size because you can set a smaller image (such as a stretched black-and-white version) as the Low Source, which appears while the main image downloads. The combination of two images in this way creates the illusion of a simple animation.
Border	Image Border	Measured in pixels, this attribute enables you to put a border around an image. I nearly always set the image border to 0 (zero) when using an image as a link to prevent the image from being surrounded by a border with link colors.
Align	Alignment	This option enables you to align the image. Text automatically wraps around images aligned to the right or left. The other options, including Baseline, Top, and Middle, control how text or other elements align next to the image. The alignment icons control the entire paragraph containing the image, and align the text left, right, or center.
Class	CSS Setting	The Class field enables you to apply any class styles defined in Dreamweaver. To use this option, select any element in the workspace and then select any class style you want to apply from the drop-down list.

Creating multiple pages to set links

Creating a new page to start a Web site may seem obvious, but consider this: You may want to create a bunch of new pages before you get too far in your development, and you may even want to start organizing the new pages in sub-directories before you have anything on them. Doing so enables you to organize the structure of your site before you start setting links. After all, you can't link to a page that doesn't exist. If you plan to have five links on your front page to other pages in your site, go ahead and create those other pages, even if you don't put anything on them yet.

For example, say you're creating a site for your department at a big company. You're likely to want a few main pages, such as a page about your staff, another about what you do, and a third with general information and resources. At this initial stage, you could create four pages — one for the front page of the site and three others for each of the subsections. Name the front page `index.html` and name the other pages `staff.html`, `about.html`, and `general.html`. With these initial pages in place, you benefit from having an early plan for organizing the site, and you can start setting links more easily among the main pages of your site. See Chapter 4 for more tips on Web site planning and managing and testing links.

Although you can resize an image in Dreamweaver by clicking and dragging the edge of the image or by changing the Height and Width values in the Property inspector, I don't recommend you change an image size this way. Changing the height and width in the Property inspector won't actually change the size of the image, just the way it appears on the page. That's a problem for two reasons. First, using this option to make an image look larger or smaller can make the image look distorted. Second, using this option to make an image look smaller requires your visitor to download a larger file than necessary.

You can use Dreamweaver's Cropping tool in the Property inspector to crop an image, but doing so changes the image file permanently. For more precise image-editing options, use an image editor such as Fireworks or Photoshop. In Chapter 3 you find instructions for optimizing images for the Web in Photoshop.

Setting Links

Dreamweaver is truly a dream when it comes to setting links. The most important thing to keep in mind is that a link is essentially an address (a URL) that tells a viewer's browser what page to go to when the viewer clicks the text or image containing the link.

If the page you want to link to is within your Web site, you can create a *relative link* that includes a path describing how to get from the current page to the linked page. A relative link doesn't need to include the domain name of the site, just instructions for a browser to get from one page within your site to another. Here's an example of what the code looks like for the relative link from the home page on my Web site at www.JCWarner.com to the main page in the books section, which is contained in a folder called books:

```
<A HREF="books/index.html">Janine's Books</A>
```

If you select the Root option instead of Relative in the Site Definition dialog box, this address would begin with a forward slash (as you see here) instructing the browser to begin at the root level:

```
<A HREF="/books/index.html">Janine's Books</A>
```

Because my Web server is set up to deliver any page named index.html first, no matter what folder it's inside of, I gain an advantage when I name the main page of a subdirectory index.html. Here's the advantage. If I had named this page books.html, then to get to this page on my Web site, you'd have to enter www.JCWarner.com/books/books.html into a browser. With the main page named index, you can simply type www.JCWarner.com/books into a browser and get to the same page. (This works similarly on servers that are set up to deliver default.html).

If you link to a page on a different Web site, you need to create an absolute, or external, link. An *absolute link* includes the full Internet address of the other site. Here's an example of what the code would look like behind an absolute link if you created a link from your site to the books page on my site:

```
<A HREF="http://www.jcwarner.com/books/index.html">Janine's Books</A>
```

Note that because I named the main page index.html, you could leave out the filename and use the shortened address http://www.jcwarner.com/books. And if all that HREF code stuff looks like Greek to you, don't worry. The following section shows you how Dreamweaver sets links like this for you so you don't even have to look at this code if you don't want to. (But I do think it's helpful to have a little understanding of what's happening behind the scenes.)

Linking pages within your Web site

Linking from one page to another page in your Web site is easy. The most important thing to remember is to save your pages in your site's root folder (as described in the "Defining a Web site in Dreamweaver" section, previously in the chapter) before you start setting links. Here's how you create a link from one page in a Web site to another:

1. **In Dreamweaver, open the page where you want to create a link.**

2. **Select the text or image that you want to serve as the link (meaning the text or image that a user will click to trigger the link).**

   Click and drag to highlight text or click once to select an image. In this example, I've selected the text *Great Egret* and I'm linking it to a page named `egret.html` located in the same folder.

3. **Click the Link icon in the Common Insert bar, at the top of the workspace.**

   Alternatively, you can set a link using the Link field in the Property inspector.

4. **In the Hyperlink dialog box (see Figure 2-9), click the Browse icon to the right of the Link drop-down list.**

   The Select File dialog box opens.

Figure 2-9:
The
Hyperlink
dialog box
includes a
number of
link settings
including
Targeting
options.

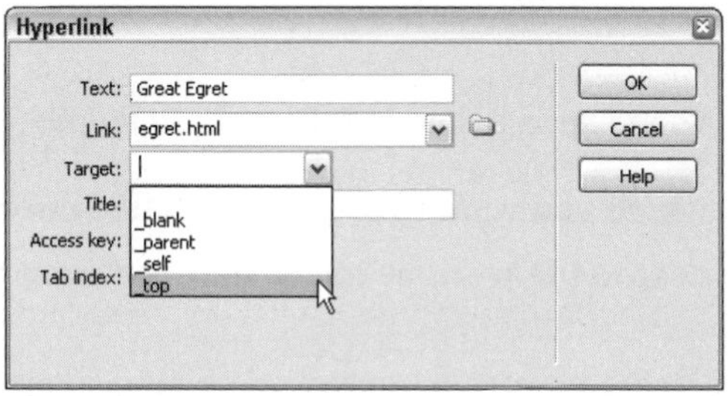

5. **Click the filename to select the page that you want your image or text to link to, and then click OK (Windows) or Choose (Mac).**

   The link is automatically set and the dialog box closes. If you haven't already saved your page, a message box opens explaining that you can create a relative link only after you save the page. It's always best to save the page you're working on before you set links. Note that, to test your links, you have to view your page in a browser, a process covered in the "Previewing Your Page in a Browser" section, later in this chapter.

You can use the Target field in the Hyperlink dialog box shown in Figure 2-9 to "target" where your linked page will open. For example, the _top option causes the linked page to open in a new browser window. The other options are most important when working with Frames, which are covered in Chapter 8.

Setting links to named anchors within a page

If you like to create really long pages, using anchor links to break up navigation within the page is a good idea. A *named anchor link,* often called a *jump link,* enables you to set a link to a specific part of a Web page. You can use a named anchor to link from an image or text string on one page to another place on the same page, or to link from one page to a specific part of a different page. To create a named anchor link, you first insert a named anchor in the place that you want to link to, and then use that anchor to direct the browser to that specific part of the page when a viewer follows the link.

Suppose that you want to set a link from the word *Convertible* at the top of a page to a section lower on the page that starts with the headline *Convertible Sports Cars.* You first insert a named anchor at the *Convertible Sports Cars* headline. Then you link the word *Convertible* from the top of the page to that anchor.

To insert a named anchor and set a link to it, follow these steps:

1. **Open the page on which you want to insert the named anchor.**

2. **Place your cursor next to the word or image that you want to link to on the page.**

   You don't need to select the word or image; you just need a reference point that appears when the link is selected. For this example, I placed the cursor to the left of the headline *Convertible Sports Cars.*

3. **Choose Insert⇨Named Anchor.**

   The Insert Named Anchor dialog box appears.

4. **Enter a name for the anchor.**

   You can name anchors anything you want (as long as you don't use spaces or special characters). Just make sure that you use a different name for each anchor on the same page. Then be sure that you remember what you called the anchor, because you have to either type the anchor name to set the link or select it from the drop-down list in the Hyperlink dialog box, as you see in Step 8. In this example, I chose *convertible* as the anchor name because it's easy for me to remember.

5. **Click OK.**

   The dialog box closes, and a small anchor icon appears on the page where you inserted the anchor name. You can move an anchor name by clicking the anchor icon and dragging it to another location on the page.

   If you're curious about what this named anchor looks like in HTML, here's the code that appears before the headline in my example:

   ```
   <A NAME="convertible"></A>
   ```

6. **To set a link to the named anchor location, select the text or image that you want to link from.**

   You can link to a named anchor from anywhere else on the same page or from another page. In my example, I linked from the word *Convertible* that appears at the top of the page to the anchor I made next to the headline.

7. **Click the Link icon in the Common Insert bar, at the top of the screen.**

8. **In the Hyperlink dialog box, use the small arrow to the right of the Link box to select the anchor.**

   Alternatively, you can set a jump link using the Property inspector by typing a pound sign (#) followed by the anchor name.

   You can also select the text and drag a line from the Point to File icon (next to the Link text box) to the anchor icon. The anchor name automatically appears in the Link box, saving you from typing the name.

   In my example, I typed **#convertible** in the Link text box. The HTML code for this line looks like this:

   ```
   <A HREF="#convertible">Convertible</A>
   ```

   If you want to link to an anchor named *convertible* on another page with the filename `coolcars.html`, you type **coolcars.html#convertible** in the Link text box.

Linking to another Web site

Linking to a page on another Web site — called an *external link* — is even easier than linking to an internal link. All you need is the URL of the page to which you want to link, and you're most of the way there.

To create an external link, follow these steps:

1. **In Dreamweaver, open the page from which you want to link.**

2. **Select the text or image that you want to act as a link.**

3. In the Link text box in the Property inspector, type the URL of the page you want your text or image to link to.

The link is set automatically. In the example in Figure 2-10, I created a link using the photograph of the egret to the California Nature Conservancy Web site at www.nature.org.

Although, you don't have to type the http:// or even the www. at the beginning of a Web site address to get to a site in most browsers, you must always use the full URL, including the http://, when you create an external link in HTML. Otherwise, the browser can't find the correct external site address and the visitor will probably end up on an error page.

Figure 2-10: To set a link to another Web site, highlight the text or image you want to link and type the URL in the Link text box.

Setting a link to an e-mail address

Another common link option goes to an e-mail address. Visitors can send you messages easily with e-mail links. I always recommend that you invite visitors to contact you because they can point out mistakes in your site and give you valuable feedback about how you can further develop your site. Setting a link to an e-mail address is just as easy as setting a link to another Web page. All you need to know is the e-mail address you want to link to and what text or image you want to use when you set the link.

 To create an e-mail link, select the text you want to link and then click on the E-mail link icon in the Common Insert bar. In the Email Link dialog box, enter the e-mail address in the Link field and then click OK. If you want to use an image as an e-mail link, you must select the image in the main work area and then enter the e-mail link into the Link field of the Property inspector.

When you create an e-mail link using the Link field in the Property inspector, the e-mail links must begin with the code `mailto:` (no `//`). For example, if you were to type a link to my e-mail address into the Property inspector, you'd need to type **mailto:janine@jcwarner.com**. Here's what the full line of code behind that e-mail link would look like:

```
<A HREF="mailto:janine@jcwarner.com">Send a message to Janine</A>
```

 When visitors to your Web site click an e-mail link, their computer systems automatically launches their e-mail program and create a blank e-mail message to the specified e-mail address. This is a cool trick, but it can be disconcerting to your users if they don't expect it to happen, and it won't work if they don't have e-mail programs on their computers. That's why I always try to let users know when I use an e-mail link. For example, instead of just linking the words *Contact Janine,* I link the words *E-mail Janine.* Even better, I often link the actual e-mail address.

When you create an e-mail link on a Web page that will be displayed on the public Internet, you open yourself to spammers, some of whom use automated programs to "lift" e-mail addresses off Web pages. That's why many sites don't include e-mail links, but instead use text such as *Send e-mail to Janine at jcwarner.com.* You can also use a form to get around this potential problem. By setting up a form with a script that delivers the form's contents to an e-mail address, you can shield your e-mail address from spammers while still making it easy for visitors to your site to send comments. You find instructions for creating forms in Chapter 12.

Changing Page Properties

You can change many individual elements on a page in the Property inspector, but if you want to make changes that affect the entire page, such as changing the background color of the entire page or changing the way links and text are formatted, you need to use the Page Properties dialog box.

As you see in Figure 2-11, the Page Properties dialog box includes a list of categories on the left. Each of these reveals different page options. Some of these options are covered in other parts of the book, such as the Tracing Image feature (Chapter 5), and the Background Image feature (Chapter 3). For now, to keep things simple, this section focuses only on changing the background and text colors available from the Appearance category, shown in Figure 2-11, and the options in the Links category.

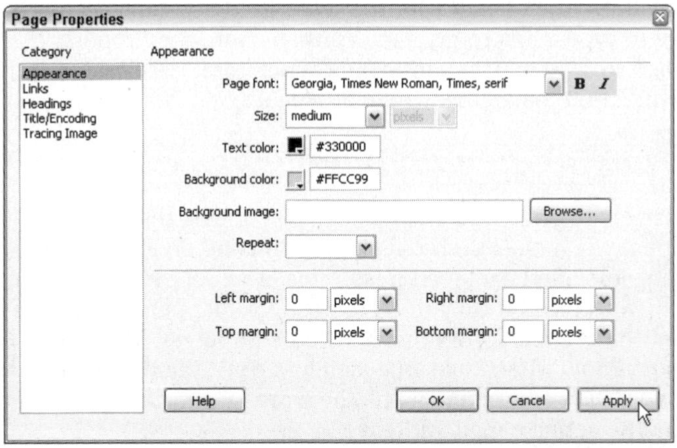

Figure 2-11:
The
Appearance
category in
the Page
Properties
dialog box
enables you
to change
text colors,
font face,
font size,
background,
and
margins.

Page Properties	
Category	**Appearance**
Appearance	Page font: Georgia, Times New Roman, Times, serif **B** *I*
Links	Size: medium
Headings	Text color: #330000
Title/Encoding	Background color: #FFCC99
Tracing Image	Background image: Browse...
	Repeat:
	Left margin: 0 pixels Right margin: 0 pixels
	Top margin: 0 pixels Bottom margin: 0 pixels
	Help OK Cancel Apply

Although you can apply global settings, such a text size and color, in the Page Properties dialog box, you can override those settings with other formatting options in specific instances. For example, you could set all your text to Helvetica in Page Properties and then change the font for an individual headline to Arial using the Font field in the Property inspector.

To change the font settings, the background and text colors, and the page margins for an entire page, follow these steps:

1. **Choose Modify➪Page Properties.**

   The Appearance category of the Page Properties dialog box appears (refer to Figure 2-11).

2. **In the Page Font drop-down list, specify the fonts you want for the text on your page.**

   In this example, I set the font face to the collection that begins with the Georgia font. If you don't specify a font, your text appears in the font specified in your user's browser, which is usually Times.

3. **If you want all the text on your page to appear bold or italic, click the B or I, respectively, to the right of the Page Font drop-down list.**

   If you select one of these options, all your text appears bold or italic in the page.

4. **In the Size drop-down list, specify the font size you want for the text on your page.**

   Again, you can override these settings for any text on the page.

5. **Click the Text Color swatch box to reveal the color palette. Choose any color you like.**

   The color you select fills the color swatch box but will not change the text color on your page until you click the Apply or OK button.

6. **Click the Background Color swatch box to reveal the color palette. Choose any color you like.**

   The color you selected fills the color swatch box. The color does not fill the background until you click the Apply or OK button.

7. **If you want to insert a graphic or photograph into the background of your page, click the Browse button next to the Background Image box and select the image in the Select Image Source dialog box.**

   When you insert a background image it automatically repeats or tiles across and down the page unless you choose the no-repeat option from the Repeat drop-down list or use CSS to further define the display.

8. **Use the margin options at the bottom of the dialog box to change the left, right, top, or bottom margins of your page.**

   Entering 0 in all four of these fields removes the default margin settings that automatically add margin space at the top and left of a Web page, enabling you to create designs that begin flush with the edge of a browser.

9. **Click the Apply button to see how the colors look on your page.**

10. **Click OK to finish and close the Page Properties dialog box.**

When you change the background, text, or link colors, make sure the colors look good together and that your text is still readable. As a general rule, a light background color works best with dark text color and vice versa.

To change the link color and underline options, follow these steps:

1. **Choose Modify⇨Page Properties.**

   The Page Properties dialog box appears.

2. **In the Category list, select the Links option.**

   The Links category is displayed, as shown in Figure 2-12.

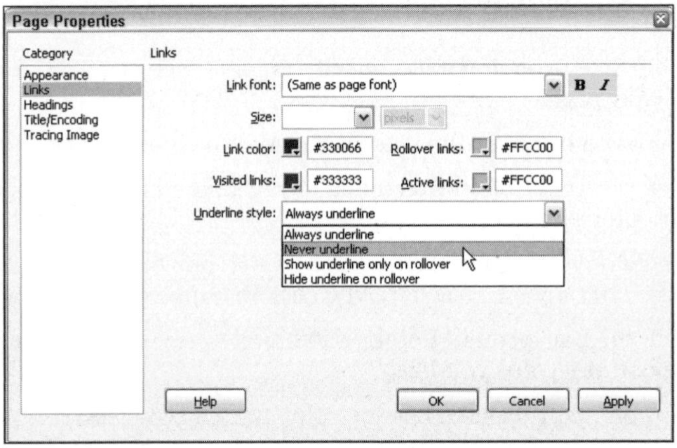

Figure 2-12:
The Links category enables you to change link colors and remove the underline.

3. **Specify the font face and size you want for the links on your page.**

   If you don't specify a font, your links appear in the same font and size specified for the text of your document.

4. **To the right of the Link Font drop-down list, click the B or I if you want all the links on your page to appear bold or italic, respectively.**

   If you select one of these options, all your links appear bold or italic unless you specify other formatting in the page.

5. **Specify a color for any or all link options.**

   The color you selected is applied to links on your page based on the link state. There are four link states, and all can be displayed in the same or different colors:

   Link Color: This option controls the color in which a link appears when it is first displayed on a page.

   Visited Links: This option controls the color of links that a visitor has already clicked (or visited).

   Rollover Links: A link changes to this color when a user rolls a cursor over the link (also known as *hovering*).

   Active Links: A link changes to this color briefly while a user is actively clicking it.

6. **In the Underline drop-down list, specify whether you want your links underlined.**

   By default, all links on a Web page appear underlined in a browser, but many designers find the underline distracting and prefer to turn off underlining by selecting Never Underline. You can also choose Show Underline Only on Rollover to make the underline appear when a user moves a cursor over a link. Hide Underline on Rollover causes the underline to disappear when a user moves a cursor over a link.

7. **Click the Apply button to see how the changes appear on your page.**

8. **Click OK to finish and close the Page Properties dialog box.**

When you change formatting options in the Page Properties dialog box, Dreamweaver automatically creates styles corresponding to these settings and saves them in the CSS styles panel, as shown in Figure 2-13. I cover Dreamweaver's CSS panel in detail in Chapters 5 and 6.

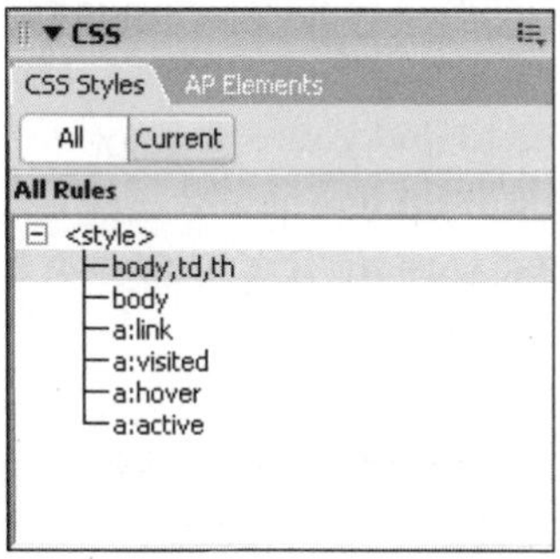

Figure 2-13:
When you specify formatting options in the Page Properties dialog box Dream-weaver auto-matically creates styles that appear in the CSS panel.

> ▼ CSS
> CSS Styles   AP Elements
> All   Current
> **All Rules**
> ⊟ <style>
>   — body,td,th
>   — body
>   — a:link
>   — a:visited
>   — a:hover
>   — a:active

Adding Meta Tags for Search Engines

If you've heard of Meta tags, you probably associate them with search engines, and you'd be right. Meta tags are used for a variety of things, but the most common use is to provide special text that doesn't appear on your page but is read by crawlers, bots, and other programs that scour the Web cata-loging and ranking Web pages for Yahoo!, Google, and a long list of other search-related sites.

Some search engines read the Meta tags for keyword tags and descriptions. The first enables site designers to include a list of keywords they would like used to make their Web site a match when someone types the same keywords into a search engine. Unfortunately, Meta keywords have been so abused by Web designers attempting to mislead visitors about the true content of their Web pages that most search engines ignore the Meta keyword tag. Some search engines continue to recognize Meta keywords, however, and it shouldn't hurt your ranking with any search engines if you use this Meta tag.

The Meta description tag is more widely used and is definitely worth using. This tag is designed to let you include a written description of your Web site and is often used by search engines as the brief description that appears in search results pages. If you don't include your own text in a Meta description tag, many search engines use the first several words that appear on your front page or some other collection of text from your page, usually based on formatting or placement on the page. Depending on your design, the first few words may not be the best description of your site, and you'll be better served by including your own Meta description.

Follow these steps to fill in the Meta description tag:

1. **Open the page where you want to add a Meta description.**

   You can use Meta descriptions on any or all pages on your Web site. (Many people using search engines to find your site may end up directly at internal pages if the content matches the search.)

2. **Choose Insert➪HTML➪Head Tags➪Description, as shown in Figure 2-14.**

   The Description dialog box appears.

3. **In the Description text box, enter the text you want for your page description.**

   Don't add any HTML to the text in this box.

4. **Click OK.**

   The description text you entered is inserted into the Head area at the top of the page in the HTML code. Meta content does not appear in the body of the page.

If you want to add keywords, repeat Steps 1 through 4, choosing Insert➪HTML➪Head Tags➪Keywords in Step 2.

Figure 2-14:
Many
search
engines use
the text
entered into
the Meta
description
field as the
description
of your Web
page in
search
results.

Previewing Your Page in a Browser

Although Dreamweaver displays Web pages much like a Web browser, not all interactive features work in Dreamweaver. To test links, for example, you need to preview your work in a Web browser.

The simplest way to preview your work is to save the page you are working on and then click the Preview/Debug in Browser icon located at the top-right of the workspace (it looks like a small globe). You can also choose File➪ Preview in a Browser.

When you install Dreamweaver, it automatically finds all the browsers installed on your computer and sets them up so that you can easily select them to preview your pages. It's always a good practice to test your pages in more than one Web browser because page display can vary. How many browsers you test your pages on depends on the audience you expect to visit your Web site, but most good Web designers test their pages on at least the latest two or three versions of Internet Explorer and Firefox. It's also good practice to preview your pages on both Macintosh and Windows computers because the page display might differ.

If you install more browsers on your computer, you can add them to the Browser Preview list by choosing Edit➪Preferences (Dreamweaver➪ Preferences on a Mac) and then choosing Preview in Browser from the Category list. Click the plus sign at the top of the screen to add a browser and then navigate your hard drive to select the installed browser to add to the list. Alternatively, you can click the globe icon at the top of the workspace and choose Edit Browser List.

One of the newest and most exciting additions to Dreamweaver CS3 is the device emulator, shown in Figure 2-15. Adobe Device Central features an impressive list of cell phone brands and models, and you can add more emulators as they become available. Essentially, the device emulator makes it easy for you to see how your Web pages will look when displayed on a cell phone or other device.

To use this feature, open the page you want to test and choose File➪ Preview➪Device Central. When you double-click the name from the Device List on the left, the Web page is automatically displayed in the corresponding emulator in the main area of the dialog box. It's never been easier to test how your Web pages will look when displayed on a cell phone.

Figure 2-15: Adobe Device Central is a new emulator included in Dreamweaver CS3 to make it easy to test your Web pages in a variety of cell phones and other devices.

Chapter 3

Adding Graphics

• •

In This Chapter

▶ Creating and optimizing images for the Web

▶ Buying royalty-free images

▶ Aligning images

▶ Image editing

▶ Including a background image

▶ Using image maps

• •

*N*o matter how great the writing may be on your Web site, the graphics always get people's attention first. And the key to making a good first impression is to use images that look great, download quickly, and are a good fit with the design of your Web site.

If you're familiar with using a graphics-editing program, such as Adobe Photoshop or Fireworks, to create graphics for the Web, you're a step ahead. If not, you find pointers throughout this chapter on how to convert images for the Web, what image formats to use, and how to optimize images for faster download times.

If your images are already in GIF or JPEG format and ready for the Web, you can jump ahead to the "Inserting Images on Your Pages" section, where you find out how to place and align images, create image maps, and use an image as a background. You also discover some of Dreamweaver's built-in image-editing features, which enable you to crop images and even adjust contrast and brightness without ever launching an external image-editing program.

Comparing Adobe Web graphics programs

Most professional designers strongly prefer Adobe Photoshop, although I have to say I've been impressed with Photoshop Elements, which is a "light" version but offers many of the same features for a fraction of the cost. (If you're designing images for print, you need Photoshop; but for the Web, Elements is a surprisingly complete, low-cost alternative.) For vector-based graphics (a good choice for illustrations), Adobe Illustrator is the favorite.

The following is a list of the most popular image-editing programs on the market today. Unless otherwise indicated, all the following image programs are available for both Mac and Windows:

✔ **Adobe Fireworks (`www.adobe.com/fireworks`):** Fireworks was one of the first image-editing programs designed to create and edit Web graphics. Originally created by Macromedia, the program is now part of the Adobe Web Suite and is fully integrated with Dreamweaver. Fireworks gives you everything you need to create, edit, and output Web graphics, all in one well-designed product.

✔ **Adobe Photoshop (`www.adobe.com/photoshop`):** Adobe calls Photoshop the "camera of the mind." This is unquestionably the most popular image-editing program on the market and a widely used standard among graphics professionals.

With Photoshop, you can create original artwork, correct color in photographs, retouch photographs, scan images, and so much more. Photoshop has a wealth of powerful painting and selection tools in addition to special effects and filters to create images that go beyond what you can capture on film or create with other illustration programs. In previous versions, Photoshop came bundled with a program called Image Ready, a companion program designed for Web graphics. In CS3, those Web features are included in Photoshop. And thanks to the acquisition of Macromedia, Photoshop is now fully integrated with Dreamweaver as well.

✔ **Adobe Photoshop Elements (`www.adobe.com/elements`):** If you're not designing images for print and don't need all the bells and whistles offered in the full-blown version of Photoshop, Photoshop Elements is a remarkably powerful program — for about a sixth of the cost of Photoshop. If you're a professional designer, you will be best served by Photoshop CS3. But if you're a hobbyist or small business owner and want to create good-looking images without the high cost and learning curve of a professional graphics programs, Elements is a great deal and well suited to creating Web graphics.

Creating and Optimizing Web Graphics

The most important thing to keep in mind when creating images for the Web is that you want to *optimize* your images to keep your file sizes as small as possible. You can optimize images using compression techniques or color reduction.

How you optimize an image depends on how the image was created and whether you want to save it as a JPEG or a GIF. You find instructions for optimizing GIFs and JPEGs with Photoshop in the next section, but first you should know that no matter what program, format, or optimization technique you choose, the biggest challenge is finding the best balance between small file size and good image quality. Essentially, the more you reduce colors or compress an image, the worse it looks but the faster it downloads.

Choosing the best image format

One of the most common questions about images for the Web concerns when to use GIF and when to use JPEG. Table 3-1 provides the simple answer.

Table 3-1	Image Formats for the Web
Format	**Best Use**
GIF	For line art (such as one- or two-color logos), simple drawings, animations, and basically any image that has no gradients or blends. GIF is also the best format for images that you want displayed with a transparent background.
PNG	PNG generally produces better-looking images with smaller file sizes than GIF for the same kinds of limited-color images. Just beware that really old browsers such as IE 3 don't support the PNG format and that even newer browsers such as IE 4, 5, and 6 have problems with full PNG alpha channel support.
JPEG	Colorful, complex images (such as photographs), images containing gradients or color blends, and any other images with millions of colors.

Saving images for the Web

You can convert images from any format, including TIF, BMP, and PSD, into the GIF, PNG, and JPEG formats. And you can optimize images that are already in GIF, PNG, or JPEG format to further reduce their file sizes for faster download over the Internet.

You can use many programs to create Web graphics, but one of the best and easiest to use is Photoshop. Under the File menu in Photoshop (and Photoshop Elements), you'll find the Save for Web option. (In Photoshop CS3, the option is Save for Web & Devices.) Fireworks provides a similar feature, but to help you appreciate how file conversion works, I include a few instructions for converting Web graphics right away. Although the dialog boxes are different in different programs, the basic options for compressing and reducing colors are the same.

It's always best to use the highest quality image possible when you are editing, so take care of resizing and any other editing before you optimize your images for the Web and always go back to the higher resolution image if you want to do further editing.

In the Save for Web dialog box, you can preview your image and select your optimization settings, choosing the format, amount of compression, and color options. You can view the same image in multiple panes to make it easy to compare the original image with optimized versions at different settings.

Below the original image preview, you see the filename and file size of the original image. Below each of the optimized image previews, you see the effects of the optimization settings specified when that preview was selected, including the format, the settings, and the new file size and estimated download time. Download time is calculated using an estimated Internet connection. You can change the setting by right-clicking (Option-clicking on a Mac) the file size and optimization time text.

When you use the Save for Web feature, Photoshop creates a new copy of your image using the settings you specified and leaves the original unchanged in the main Photoshop workspace.

Optimizing JPEG images in Photoshop

The JPEG format is the best choice for optimizing continuous-tone images such as photographs and images with many colors or gradients. When you optimize a JPEG, you specify how much compression should be applied, a process that makes the file size of the image smaller.

If you have a digital photograph or another image that you want to prepare for the Web, follow these steps to optimize and save it in Photoshop. If you're using another image program, the process is similar although the specific steps may vary:

1. **With the image open in Photoshop, choose File⇨Save for Web & Devices (or File ⇨Save for Web).**

   The Save for Web & Devices dialog box appears.

2. **Click the arrow to open the Optimized File Format drop-down list on the right side of the dialog box and choose JPEG (see Figure 3-1).**

3. **Set the compression quality.**

   Use the preset options: Low, Medium, High, Very High, or Maximum from the pull-down list. Or use the slider just under the Quality field to make more precise adjustments. Lowering the quality reduces the file size and makes the image download more quickly, but if you lower this number too much, the image will look blurry and blotchy.

JPEG settings

Optimized File
Format list

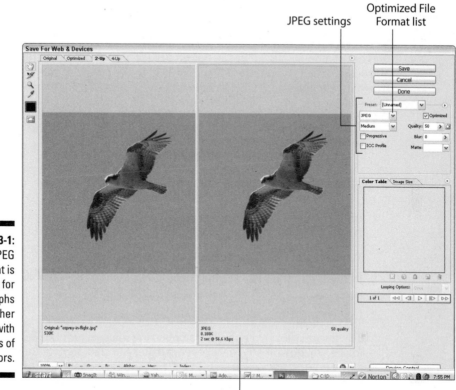

Figure 3-1:
The JPEG
format is
best for
photographs
and other
images with
millions of
colors.

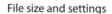

File size and settings

Photoshop uses a compression scale of 0 to 100 for JPEGs in this dialog window, with 0 the lowest possible quality (the highest amount of compression and the smallest file size) and 100 the highest possible quality (the least amount of compression and the biggest file size). Low, Medium, and High represent compression values of 10, 30, and 60, respectively.

4. If you want to make the image focus softer, use the Blur settings.

5. Click Save.

The Save Optimized As dialog box opens.

6. Enter a name for the image and save it into the images folder in your Web site folder.

Photoshop saves the optimized image as a copy of the original and leaves the original open in the main Photoshop work area.

Repeat these steps for each image you want to optimize as a JPEG.

Optimizing GIF images in Photoshop

If you're working with a graphic, such as a logo, cartoon character, or drawing that can be displayed in 256 colors or less, you should use the GIF format and reduce the total number of colors used in the image as much as possible to reduce the file size. To help make up for the degradation in image quality that can happen when colors are removed, GIF uses a trick called dithering. *Dithering* involves alternating pixels in a checkerboard-like pattern to create subtle color variations, even with a limited color palette. The effect can smooth the edges in an image and make it appear that the image uses more colors than it does.

To convert an image to a GIF in Photoshop, follow these steps:

1. **With the image open in Photoshop, choose File⇨Save for Web & Devices (or File ⇨Save for Web).**

   The Save for Web & Devices dialog box appears.

2. **In the Optimized File Format drop-down list on the right side of the screen, choose GIF, as shown in Figure 3-2.**

3. **In the Colors box, select the number of colors.**

   The fewer colors you use, the smaller the file size and the faster the image will download. For an even smaller file size, reduce the number to 4 or 8 colors, but be careful. The ideal number depends on your image; if you go too far, you'll lose details and the image will look terrible.

4. **If you want to maintain a transparent area in your image, select the Transparency option.**

   Any area of the image that was transparent when you created the image in the editor appears transparent in the preview window. If you don't have a transparent area in your image, this setting will have no effect.

   Transparency is a good trick for making text or another part of an image appear to float on a Web page because the transparent background doesn't appear on the Web page. You can select transparency as a background option in the New File dialog box when you create a new image.

5. **Leave the other settings unchanged.**

   The remainder of the settings in this dialog box can be left at their defaults in Photoshop.

6. **Click Save.**

   The Save Optimized As dialog box opens.

7. **Enter a name for the image and save it into your local root folder.**

Repeat these steps for each image you want to prepare for your site.

File size and settings   GIF settings   Optimized File Format list

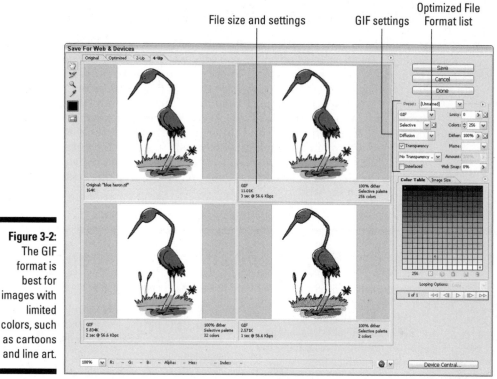

Figure 3-2:
The GIF format is best for images with limited colors, such as cartoons and line art.

Illustration by Tom McCain

Trial and error is a great technique in the Save for Web & Devices dialog box. In each of the three preview windows displaying optimized versions of the Blue Heron cartoon image in Figure 3-2, I used fewer and fewer colors, which reduced the file size. The version in the top left is the original, which has a file size of 164K. Reducing the image to 256 colors dramatically reduced the file size to 11K, but made little noticeable change to the image, as you see in the top right. In the bottom left, the image is reduced to 32 colors, which brought the size down to 5.8K, but still made little change to the image. In the bottom right, I reduced it to 2 colors, and although it's hard to tell in the black-and-white reproduction in this book, the image quality suffered dramatically. Because it is displayed in only two colors, it lost the original blue color of the bird and the green in the grass at its feet. In this last case, the small savings in file size is clearly not worth the loss of image quality.

How small is small enough?

After you know how to optimize GIFs and JPEGs and appreciate the goal of making them as small as possible, you may ask, "How small is small enough?" The answer is mostly subjective — remember that the larger your graphics files, the longer people have to wait for them to download before they can see them. You may have the most beautiful picture of Mount Fuji on the front page of your Web site, but if it takes forever to download, most people aren't going to be patient enough to wait to see it. Also remember that when you build pages with multiple graphics, you have to consider the cumulative download time of all the graphics on the page. Even if each individual image is a small file size, they can add up. Unlike most things in life, smaller is definitely better on the Web.

Buying royalty-free clip art and photographs

If you don't want the hassle of creating your own images (or if you lack the artistic talent), you may be happy to find that many sources of clip art are available. Royalty-free images, which include clip art and photographs, are generally sold for a one-time fee that grants you all or most of the rights to use the image. (Read the agreement that comes with any art you purchase to make sure that you don't miss any exclusions or exceptions. For example, you may have to pay extra to use an image for commercial purposes.) You can find a wide range of CD-ROMs and Web sites full of clip art, photographs, and even animations that you can use on your Web site. (Speaking of animations, nowadays you can even find Web sites that sell Flash files, animations, buttons, and other artistic elements that you can edit and integrate into your Web site. For more info on how to add multimedia to your Web site, see Chapter 11.) Many professional designers buy clip art images and then alter them in an image program — such as Adobe Fireworks, Adobe Illustrator, or Adobe Photoshop — to tailor them for a specific project or to make the image more distinct.

Here are some clip art suppliers:

- **Getty Images, Inc. (www.gettyimages.com):** Getty Images is the largest supplier of royalty-free digital imagery on the Web, specializing in photographs and illustrations of a wide variety of subjects, including film footage. Pay for images and footage as you go.

- **Photos.com (www.photos.com):** Photos.com is a subscription-based service for royalty-free stock photography and photo objects. A 1- to 12-month subscription gives you unlimited access and use of its collection.

- **iStockphoto.com (www.istockphoto.com):** An innovative variation of the fee-for-use model, iStockphoto lets you trade your own photographs for stock images.

- **Web Promotion (www.webpromotion.com):** A great source for animated GIFs and other Web graphics. Artwork on this site is free provided you create a link back to Web Promotion on your Web site, or you can buy the artwork for a small fee.

Most Web pros consider anything from about 75K to 150K a good maximum *cumulative* size for all the elements on a given page. With the increasing popularity of DSL and cable modems, many Web sites are starting to become a bit more graphics heavy and go beyond that size limit. However, anything over 150K is pushing the limits, especially if you expect people with dialup modems (56K and under) to stick around long enough to view your pages.

To make determining the total file size of the images on your page easy, Dreamweaver includes this information in the status bar of the current Document window, as shown in Figure 3-3. This number indicates the total file size of all the images and HTML on your page as well as the expected download time at a given connection speed. (You can set your own connection speed by choosing Edit➪Preferences➪Status Bar➪Connection Speed. On a Mac, choose Dreamweaver➪Preferences➪Status Bar➪Connection Speed).

Figure 3-3:
The Dreamweaver status bar indicates the total file size of all elements on a page and the estimated download time.

Total download size

Estimated download time

Inserting Images in Dreamweaver

Dreamweaver makes placing images on your Web pages easy and provides a variety of ways to do so, including choosing Insert⇨Image, clicking the Image icon in the Common Insert bar and selecting an image using the Insert image dialog box, or simply clicking an image name in the Files list panel and dragging it onto the page.

To place an image on a Web page, follow these steps:

1. **Open an existing page or choose File⇨New to create a new page.**

2. **Make sure you save your page before inserting an image by choosing File⇨Save and saving it to your main site folder.**

3. **Click to place your cursor where you want to insert the image on the page.**

 4. **Click the Image icon on the Common Insert bar at the top of the work area (the icon looks like a small tree) or choose Insert⇨Image.**

   The Select Image Source dialog box appears.

5. **Browse to locate the image you want to insert.**

   Choose Thumbnails from the View menu, as shown in Figure 3-4, to see a preview of the images in the Select Image Source dialog box. You also see a preview of any selected image on the right side of the dialog box if you're using the Windows operating system. (The Mac doesn't have an image preview option.)

6. **To insert the image, double-click it or click once and then click OK.**

   The image automatically appears on the page.

When you insert an image file onto a page, you create a reference to the image from the page. The underlying code looks much like it does when you create a link from one page to another and then include the path from the image to the page. As a result, if your images and the pages they are linked to are not in the same relative location on your hard drive as they are on your server, you break the reference to your images and they will not appear on your pages. (Instead, you get that ugly broken image icon.) The best way to make sure that your images and files stay where they're supposed to in relation to one another is to save all your images in your local root folder (or in a subfolder within that folder) and make sure they are located in the same folder or subfolder on your Web server. You find more information about creating and identifying a local root folder at the beginning of Chapter 2.

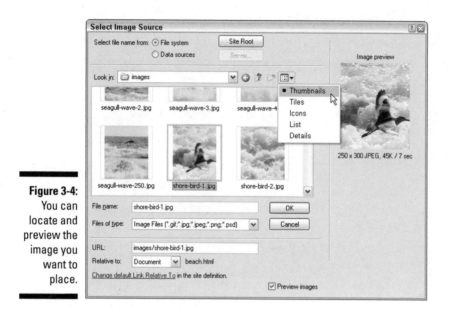

Figure 3-4:
You can
locate and
preview the
image you
want to
place.

Aligning Images on a Page

After you place an image on your Web page, you may want to center or align it so that text can wrap around it. In the following two sections — "Centering an image" and "Aligning an image with text wrapping" — you find the steps to accomplish both these goals using basic HTML. In Chapters 5 and 6, you find instructions for aligning and positioning images using CSS, which provides more precise design options.

Centering an image

To center an image on a page, follow these steps:

1. **Click to select the image that you want to center.**

   The Property inspector changes to display the image properties.

2. **From the icons for alignment options in the Property inspector, shown in Figure 3-5, click the Align Center icon.**

   The image automatically moves to the center of the page.

Figure 3-5:
Use the
alignment
tools in the
Property
inspector to
center an
image.

Align center icon

You may have noticed the Align drop-down list in the Property inspector has left and right alignment options but no center option. In HTML there is no center option for the image tag, but when you use the Align center icon in the Property inspector, you can add a center align option to any tag that surrounds the image, usually the paragraph, or <p>, tag. You can also create a CSS style that will serve to center an image by setting the left and right margins to default. You learn more about creating styles in Chapters 5 and 6.

Aligning an image with text wrapping

To align an image to the right of a page and wrap text around it on the left, follow these steps:

1. **Insert the image immediately to the left of the first line of the text (see Figure 3-6).**

   The easiest way to do this is to place the cursor just before the first letter of text; then choose Insert➪Image or click the Image icon in the Common Insert bar.

Figure 3-6:
To wrap text around an image, first place the image immediately to the left of the text with no spaces between the text and image.

If you want the text to wrap, don't put spaces or line breaks between the image and the text.

2. **Click to select the image.**

   The Property inspector changes to display the image attribute options.

3. **In the Property inspector, choose Right from the Align drop-down list.**

   The image aligns to the right, and the text automatically wraps around it as shown in Figure 3-7.

To align the image to the left of the page with text wrapping around on the right, follow Steps 1 and 2, but choose Left from the Align drop-down list instead of Right in Step 3.

Figure 3-7:
The Align
drop-down
list in the
Properties
panel aligns
an image.

To prevent text from running up against an image, click the image, find V and H spacing in the Property inspector, and enter the amount of space you want (the space is measured in pixels). Five to ten pixels is usually enough to prevent the text from bumping up against its edge. If you want to add space to only one side of an image, it's a bit more complicated, but you can more precisely control spacing with CSS (covered in Chapters 5 and 6).

Creating complex designs with images

The alignment options available in HTML enable you to align your images vertically or horizontally, but you can't do both at once. Also, the alignment options don't really enable you to position images in relation to one another or in relation to text with much precision. For example, if you try to center an image positioned up against a text block, the text gets centered, too. One way to get around this limitation is to create HTML tables and then combine and merge cells in the table to control positioning. This old-school but still common technique is covered in Chapter 7. A better options it to use Cascading Style Sheets (see Chapters 5 and 6) to create layout and alignment styles to control the positioning of all elements on a page following the latest standards.

Image Editing in Dreamweaver

The image-editing features in Dreamweaver enable you to make minor changes to images inside Dreamweaver without opening Fireworks or Photoshop or any other graphics-editing program. These tools are available from the Property inspector when an image is selected (see Figure 3-8).

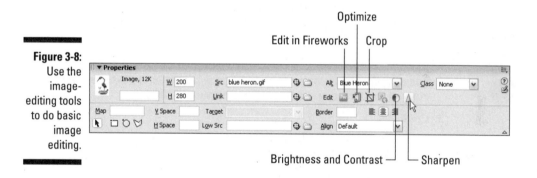

Figure 3-8:
Use the image-editing tools to do basic image editing.

You also find two buttons that enable you to easily move an image between Dreamweaver and Fireworks to make editing images easy. The Edit button launches Fireworks and opens the selected image in the main window of the program. The integration between these programs means that when you save changes to the image in Fireworks, they are automatically reflected in the page in Dreamweaver. A new button, just to the right of the Edit button, is designed to make optimizing an image in Fireworks fast and easy. Chapter 10 covers the Edit in Fireworks and Optimize in Fireworks features in greater detail.

Before you get carried away editing your images, remember that Dreamweaver is primarily a Web-page-creation application and not really designed to edit graphics. Although these tools can be useful, they shouldn't take the place of doing serious work on your graphics in a graphics application, such as Fireworks or Photoshop.

When you do use the tools for cropping, adjusting brightness and contrast, and sharpening an image, beware that you are changing the actual image (not just a copy of it). Make sure you're happy with these changes before you save the page you're working on. You can use the undo feature in Dreamweaver to revert back several steps, but after you save the page, you can't undo changes to an image. To protect your original image, save a copy before editing it.

Cropping an image

Essentially, cropping an image is trimming it. To crop a graphic or photo, follow these steps:

1. **In the Document window, select the image you'd like to crop by clicking it.**

   The Property inspector changes to display the image's properties.

2. **Click the Crop icon (labeled in Figure 3-8).**

   A dialog box appears warning you that cropping will change the original image.

   Don't make the change if you're concerned about keeping the entire image available. If you're concerned, the best thing to do is to make a copy of the image and apply your cropping to the copy.

3. **Click OK.**

   A solid crop line with handles at the sides and corners appears over the image, as shown in Figure 3-9.

4. **Click and drag the handles to outline the area of the image you want to keep.**

   Any part of the image outside the crop line (and shaded) will be deleted when the crop is completed.

5. **Double-click inside the box, or press Enter (Return on a Mac).**

   The image is cropped.

You can undo cropping by choosing Edit⇨Undo. However, after you save the page, changes permanently apply to the image and cannot be undone.

Adjusting brightness and contrast

Adjusting an image's *brightness* allows you to change the overall amount of light in an image. *Contrast* controls the difference between the light and dark areas of an image.

Solid crop line

Figure 3-9:
Define the
area to crop
by dragging
the edges of
the cropping
tool outline.

Using Dreamweaver's editing tools will permanently alter the image when the page is saved. If you're concerned, the best thing to do is to make a copy of the image and make your adjustments to the copy.

To adjust brightness and contrast, follow these steps:

1. **In the Document window, select the image you want to alter.**

   The Property inspector shows the image properties.

2. **Click the Brightness and Contrast icon (labeled in Figure 3-8).**

   A dialog box appears, indicating that the changes you make are made to the original file.

3. **Click OK.**

   The Brightness/Contrast dialog box appears.

4. **Use the sliders to adjust the brightness and contrast settings of the image.**

Make sure to select the Preview check box if you want to see how the changes affect the image as you move the sliders around.

5. Click OK.

The settings take effect permanently when you save the page.

Sharpening an image

When you apply *sharpening* to an image, you increase the distinction between areas of color. The effect can be one of increased definition to the shapes and lines in an image.

Using Dreamweaver's editing tools will permanently alter the image when the page is saved. If you're concerned, the best thing to do is to make a copy of the image and make your adjustments to the copy.

To sharpen an image, follow these steps:

1. In the Document window, select the image you want to sharpen.

The Property inspector shows the image properties.

2. Click the Sharpen icon (labeled in Figure 3-8).

A dialog box appears, indicating that your change is made to the original file.

3. Click OK.

The Sharpen dialog box appears.

4. Use the slider to adjust the sharpness of the image.

Make sure you select the Preview check box if you want to see how the changes affect the image as you move the slider.

5. Click OK.

The image is sharpened and changes are made permanently when you save changes to the page.

Optimizing images in Dreamweaver

Dreamweaver CS3 includes an Optimize icon that you can use to convert an image to the GIF, PNG, or JPEG format and optimize it by reducing the colors or increasing the compression, much as you can do in Photoshop or Fireworks. To use this feature, simply select any image and then click the Optimize icon in the Property inspector. (Hint: it looks like a C-clamp.)

Dreamweaver's editing tools permanently alter the image when the page is saved. If you're concerned, copy the image and make changes to the copy.

To optimize an image in Dreamweaver, follow these steps:

1. **In the Document window, select the image you want to optimize.**

   The Property inspector shows the image properties.

2. **Click the Optimize icon (labeled in Figure 3-8).**

   A dialog box appears, indicating that your change is made to the original file.

3. **Click OK.**

   The Image Preview dialog box appears, as shown in Figure 3-10.

Figure 3-10: Optimize an image here.

4. **In the Format drop-down list, select the image format you want.**

   You can select from Gif, JPEG, or PNG format.

5. **If you choose JPEG, use the slider next to Quality to select the level of compression. If you choose Gif or PNG, choose the number of colors desired.**

   The image is altered based on the settings you specify.

You can also change other settings in the Image Preview dialog window, such as transparency settings for the GIF format, much as you would in Photoshop or Fireworks.

Inserting a Background Image

Background images can add depth and richness to a page design by adding color and fullness. Used cleverly, a background image helps create the illusion that the entire page is one large image while still downloading quickly and efficiently. The trick is to use an image with a small file size that creates the impression of a large image. One way this works on the Web is to use the default settings for a background image, which cause the image to *tile* (repeat) across and down the page (see Figure 3-11).

Beware that certain backgrounds (such as the one shown in Figure 3-11) can make it difficult to read text placed on top. Choose your background images carefully and make sure your background and your text have plenty of contrast — reading on a computer screen is hard enough.

Figure 3-11: This background example shows how an image repeats across and down a page when inserted into the background using the default HTML settings.

Using CSS, you can have far greater control over the display of a background image. When you create a CSS background style you can insert a background image that does not repeat or that repeats only across the Y axis or down the X axis of the page. When you insert an image using Dreamweaver's Page Properties feature, as shown in Figure 3-12, you can use the Repeat drop-down menu to specify how the image repeats on the page, and Dreamweaver automatically creates a background style for the page with these settings. If you use the CSS Definition dialog box to further edit the background options in the body style, you can also specify where the background image is displayed on a page. (You find more on CSS background options in Chapter 5).

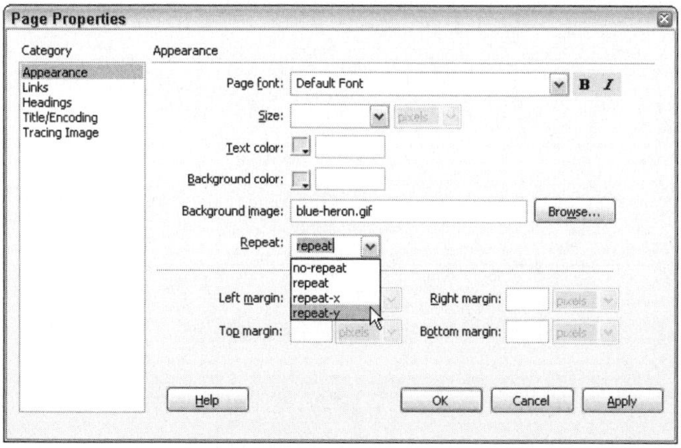

Figure 3-12:
Settings control how a background image is repeated or not repeated on a page.

Creating Image Maps

Image maps are popular on the Web because they enable you to create hot spots in an image and link them to different URLs. A common use of an image map is with a geographic map, such as a map of the United States, that links to different locations, depending on the section of the map selected. For example, if you have a national bank and want customers to find a local branch or ATM machine easily, you can create hot spots on an image map of the United States and then link each hot spot to a page listing banks in that geographic location.

Dreamweaver makes creating image maps easy by providing a set of simple drawing tools that enable you to create hot spots and set their corresponding links. To create an image map, follow these steps:

1. **Place the image you want to use as an image map on your page.**

2. **Select the image.**

   The image properties are displayed in the Property inspector.

3. **To draw your hot spot, choose a shape tool from the image map tools in the lower-left of the Property inspector (labeled in Figure 3-13).**

   The shape tools (a rectangle, a circle, and an irregular polygon) allow you to draw regions on your images, called *hot spots,* each with a specific link.

4. **With a shape tool selected, click and drag over an area of the image that you want to make *hot* (link to another page).**

   Here's how the different hot spot tools work:

   • **Rectangle:** As you click and drag, a light blue highlight appears around the region that you're making hot; this highlighted area indicates the active region. If you need to reposition the hot area, select the Pointer hotspot tool (labeled in Figure 3-13) and then select and move the region to the location you want. You can also resize the hot spot by clicking and dragging any of the corners.

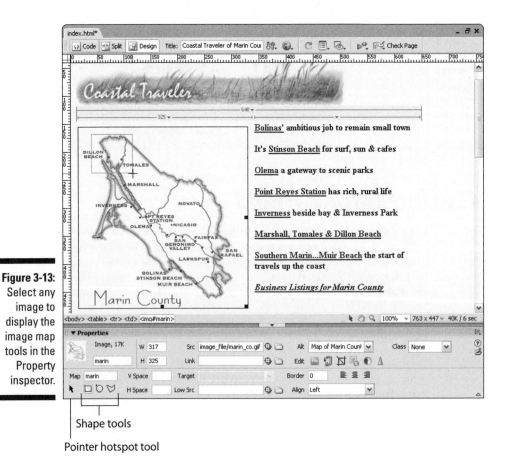

Figure 3-13:
Select any image to display the image map tools in the Property inspector.

Shape tools

Pointer hotspot tool

- **Circle:** The Circle tool works much like the Rectangle tool — just click and drag. To resize a circle hot spot, select the Pointer hotspot tool, and click and drag one of the small square boxes on its edges.

- **Polygon:** The Polygon tool functions a little bit differently than do the other two tools. To make a polygon selection, you click the tool once for each point of the polygon shape you want to draw. The shape automatically connects the points as you click. When you're finished, switch to another map tool or click outside the image. You can change the size of the polygon or move any of its points by using the Pointer hotspot tool.

5. **To link a selected hot area:**

   a. **Click the Browse icon, next to the Link text box (at the top of the Property inspector).**

   The Select File dialog box opens.

   b. **Browse to find the HTML file that you want to link to the hot spot on your image.**

   c. **Double-click the file to which you want to link.**

   The hot spot links to the selected page and the Select File dialog box automatically closes.

   You can also type the path directly in the Link text box.

6. **To add more hot spots, choose an image and a shape tool, and repeat Steps 4 and 5.**

7. **To give your image map a name, type a name in the Map text field, just above the shape tools.**

   Giving your map (and all the hot spots it includes) a name helps to distinguish it in the event that you have multiple image maps on the same page. You can call the map anything you want, as long as you don't include spaces or special punctuation.

   When you finish, all your image map hot spots are indicated by a light blue highlight.

At any time, you can go back and edit the image map. Simply click and highlight the blue region on your image and drag the edges to resize the hot spot or enter a new URL to change the link.

Chapter 4

Managing, Testing, and Publishing a Site

After you've built your Web site, you'll probably want to publish it on the Web. But before you go live with your site, I recommend that you take a little time to test your pages using Dreamweaver's many testing features, which I cover at the beginning of this chapter.

At the end of this chapter, you find instructions for using Dreamweaver's site management features, which are designed to help teams of designers work better together. These include the Check In/Out feature, which prevents two people from working on the same page on a site — an important feature if you want to make sure that one designer doesn't overwrite the work of another. And believe me, you want to do everything you can to prevent this situation.

If you're anxious to get your site online, jump ahead to midway through this chapter, where you find instructions for using Dreamweaver's publishing features in the "Publishing a Site to a Web Server" section.

If you want to work more on the design of your site before you move onto testing and publishing, feel free to skip ahead to the CSS chapters and other more advanced chapters that follow. You can always come back to this chapter when you're ready to put your work online.

If you're looking for information about Web hosting services and domain registration sites, you find recommendations and tips for choosing the best hosting and domain services in Chapter 16.

Testing Your Site in Different Browsers

One of the more confusing and frustrating aspects of Web design is that you can create a page design that looks great in Dreamweaver and test it in a browser to confirm that it looks fine, only to discover later that it looks terrible in a different browser. Web pages can look different from one browser to another for many reasons, but it all boils down to this: Browsers display Web pages differently because HTML and other Web technologies have evolved dramatically over the years, and not all browser makers have designed their programs to display Web design features, such as HTML and CSS, in the same way.

Today, dozens of browsers are in use on the Web, not counting the different versions of each browser. For example, at the time of this writing, Internet Explorer 7 is the newest release from Microsoft, but a significant percentage of Web users have not yet upgraded and are still using IE 6 or earlier versions. Similarly, browser companies such as Firefox and Safari have now created a number of versions that are still in use on the Web.

Add to that the differences between Macintosh and Windows computers. For example, the same font size can appear smaller on a Macintosh than on a PC, and image colors can vary from one computer to another. In addition, the same Web page may look very different on a 21-inch monitor than it does on a 15-inch monitor.

As a result, the same Web page can look very different to the many people who visit a Web site. For example, Figure 4-1 shows a Web page in Internet Explorer and Figure 4-2 shows the same page in Firefox. The kinds of differences you see in these two browsers can become even more pronounced in older browsers and on different size monitors.

This challenging aspect of Web design is at the root of many of the limitations and complications of creating good Web sites. But with patience, testing, and an understanding of the tags and styles that are most problematic, you can create great Web sites that look good to most, if not all, of the people who visit your Web site.

Figure 4-1:
A Web page
in Internet
Explorer.

Figure 4-2:
The same
Web page
but this time
displayed in
Firefox.

In the example shown in Figures 4-1 and 4-2, the design is created using the HTML `<div>` tag to separate each of the elements and create columns on the page. CSS styles position the elements in the `<div>` tags on the page and add margin spacing and padding. Because that spacing is not displayed the same in Firefox as it is in Internet Explorer in the examples shown in these figures, the display is different from one browser to another, and the right column is forced down below the middle column in Figure 4-2. (You find out more about using `<div>` tags and CSS to create page layouts and a few tips about how to avoid this common problem in Chapter 6.)

Understanding browser differences

Entire books and Web sites are dedicated to the differences among browsers, especially when it comes to CSS. Although I can't possibly cover all these differences here, I do provide instructions for using Dreamweaver features that can help you manage this type of design challenge, such as the Preview in Browser feature covered in Chapter 2. The best way to test your work is to view your pages in a selection of browsers.

Getting your pages to look exactly the same across every browser in use on the Web is difficult to impossible, unless you're willing to use only the simplest and most basic HTML formatting options or create multiple copies of the same page, each designed for the unique display settings of the different browsers that may be used to display your page. Most designers create a page that looks as good as possible on as many browsers as they consider important, even if the page doesn't look exactly the same on all browsers.

Which browsers you should design for depends on your audience. If you have the luxury of having good log files or visitor statistics, you may be able to get a list of the browsers (and even the browser versions) used by visitors to your site. For example, you may be able to determine that 50 percent of your audience uses Firefox, 40 percent uses Internet Explorer, and 10 percent uses Safari. With that in mind, you may decide that you want to optimize your pages for display in Firefox, make sure they look almost if not equally good in Internet Explorer, and make sure the content is at least readable and accessible in Safari.

If you want to create complex page designs using CSS and want your pages to look as good as possible on as many browsers as possible, a number of hacks and workarounds have been developed by Web designers to help ensure pages look good to a broad audience. Some of these tricks are relatively simple; others are extraordinarily complex.

Because these kinds of problems are so common, especially when you use CSS, Adobe has launched a special section of its Web site dedicated to helping Web designers share ideas and strategies for designing with CSS. You'll find these tips and tricks in the Adobe CSS Advisor section. Just visit `adobe.com/go/cssadvisor` and search for *CSS Advisor*.

If you know that your visitors will be using only one browser — for example, if you're designing a corporate intranet and can require that all employees use the same browser — your design work will be much simpler. Some public Web site designers resort to putting a note on the front page of a site advising anyone who visits that the pages display best in a particular browser. Although that may be warranted in some cases, I don't recommend it because you risk losing many potential visitors.

Using Dreamweaver's Browser Compatibility feature

To help you test your pages for possible problems in different Web browsers, Dreamweaver includes a Browser Compatibility feature. To test a Web page, open the page in Dreamweaver and choose File➪Check Page➪Browser Compatibility. You can also access this feature by clicking the drop-down arrow next to Check Page at the top right of the workspace. Any recognized conflicts are displayed in a report at the bottom of the workspace.

You can specify which browsers and browser versions you want to target by clicking the small menu icon at the top-right corner of the Browser Compatibility Check dialog box (the cursor is hovering over it in Figure 4-3). You can also access the Browser Settings from the Check Page drop-down list. When you select Browse Settings, the Target Browsers dialog box appears, as you see in Figure 4-3.

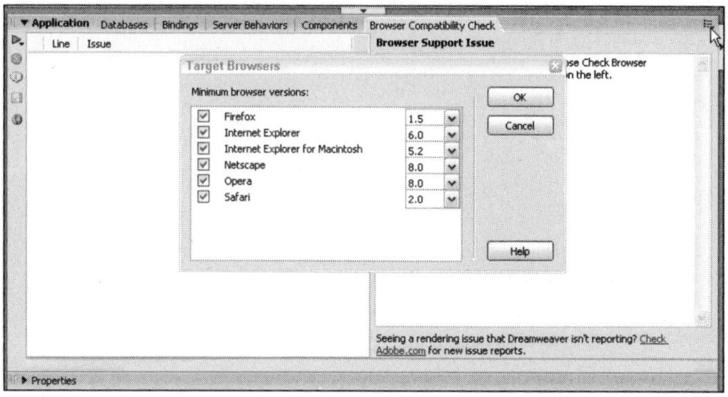

Figure 4-3: Specify the browsers and versions you want to target when you run a browser compatibility check.

Testing Your Work with the Site Reporting Features

Before you put your site online for the world to see, checking your work using the Dreamweaver Site Reporting feature is a good idea. You can create a variety of reports and even customize them to identify problems with external links, redundant and empty tags, untitled documents, and missing Alt text. You can easily miss things — especially when you work on a tight deadline — and what you miss can cause real problems for your viewers.

Before Dreamweaver added this great new feature, finding these kinds of mistakes was a tedious and time-consuming task. Now you can run a report that identifies these errors for you and use Dreamweaver to correct mistakes across your entire site automatically.

Follow these steps to produce a Site Report of your entire Web site:

1. **In the drop-down list at the top of the Files panel, select the site name. In the list that appears, select the site you want to work on.**

   Your site appears in the Files panel list only if you've completed the Site setup process covered in Chapter 2.

2. **Make sure all your open documents are saved by choosing File⇨ Save All.**

3. **Choose Site⇨Reports.**

   The Reports dialog box appears (see Figure 4-4).

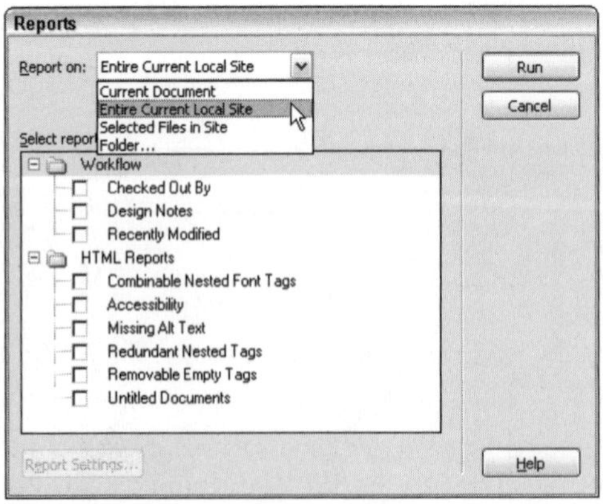

Figure 4-4: You can select any and all options, and you can run reports on a single page or the entire site.

Reports
Report on: Entire Current Local Site ▾
Current Document
Entire Current Local Site
Selected Files in Site
Folder...
Select repor

Run
Cancel

Workflow
  ☐ Checked Out By
  ☐ Design Notes
  ☐ Recently Modified
HTML Reports
  ☐ Combinable Nested Font Tags
  ☐ Accessibility
  ☐ Missing Alt Text
  ☐ Redundant Nested Tags
  ☐ Removable Empty Tags
  ☐ Untitled Documents

Report Settings...
Help

4. **In the Report On drop-down list, choose Entire Current Local Site.**

   You can also choose to check only a single page by opening the page in Dreamweaver and then choosing Current Document in the Report On drop-down list. You can also run a report on selected files or on a particular folder. If you choose Selected Files, you must have already selected the pages you want to check in the Files panel.

5. **In the Select Reports section, select the reports you want.**

   Table 4-1 describes the kind of report you get with each option. You can select as many reports as you want.

   TIP

   The Workflow options in the Select Reports section are available only if you already enabled Check In/Out in the Remote Info section of the Site Definition dialog box and selected Maintain Design Notes in the Design Notes section of the Site Definition dialog box's Advanced tab. You can read more about the Site Definition dialog box in Chapter 2 and more about Design Notes and the Check In/Out in the "Making the Most of Dreamweaver's Site Management Features" section, later in this chapter.

6. **Click the Run button to create the report(s).**

   If you haven't already done so, you may be prompted to save your file, define your site, or select a folder. (See Chapter 2 for more information on defining a site in Dreamweaver.)

   The Results panel appears, as shown in Figure 4-5, displaying a list of problems found on the site. You can sort the list by different categories (filename, line number, or description) by clicking the corresponding column headings.

Properties
Results
Search
Reference
Validation
Browser Compatibility Check
Link Checker
Site Reports
FTP Log
Server Debug
File
Line
Description
tips\web-design.html 289 Warning: Missing "alt" attribute
tips\photoshop\index.html 288 Warning: Missing "alt" attribute
tips\photoshop\index.html 288 Warning: Missing "alt" attribute
tips\family-faq.html 244 Warning: Redundant nested tag: <STRONG>
tips\family-faq.html 243 Warning: Redundant nested tag: <STRONG>
Complete.

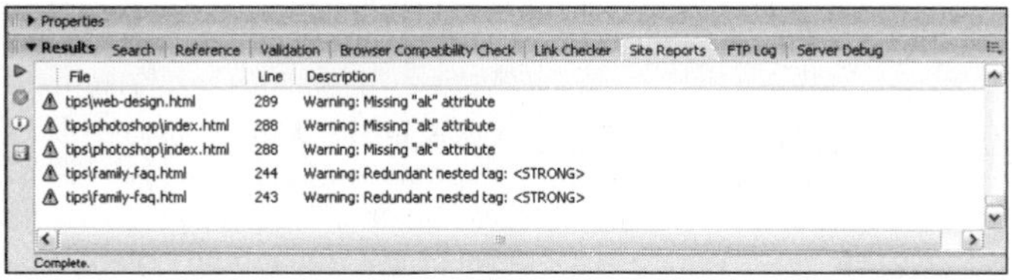

Figure 4-5: The Results panel displays a list of problems on your site.

7. **Double-click any item in the Results panel to open the corresponding file in the Document window.**

   You can also right-click (Windows) or Control+click (Mac) on any line of the report and choose More Info to find additional details about the specific error or condition.

8. **Use the Property inspector or another Dreamweaver feature to correct the identified problem and then save the file.**

Table 4-1	Site Report Options
Report Name	*What It Does*
Checked Out By	Lists files checked out of the site and identifies the person who checked them out.
Design Notes	Lists Design Notes used in the site.
Recently Modified	List files that have been edited within a specified time period. You can set the time period for the report by selecting the Recently Modified check box and then clicking the Report Settings button at the bottom of the dialog box.
Combinable Nested Font Tags	Lists all instances where you can combine nested tags. For example, `<font color="#000000"><font size="2">Great Web Sites You Should Visit</font></font>` is listed because you can simplify the code by combining the two font tags into `<font color="#000000" size="2">Great Web Sites You Should Visit</font>`.
Accessibility	Lists possible accessibility issues in a wide variety of categories. To specify what this report checks, select the Accessibility check box and then click the Report Settings button at the bottom of the dialog box.
Missing Alt Text	Lists all the image tags that do not include Alt text. Alt text is a text description for an image tag included in the HTML code as an alternative if the image is not displayed. Alt text is important to anyone who uses a special browser that reads Web pages.
Redundant Nested Tags	Lists all places where you have redundant nested tags. For example, `<h1>Good headlines <h1>are harder to write</h1> than you might think</h1>` is listed because you can simplify the code by removing the second `<h1>` tag to make the code look like this: `<h1>Good headlines are harder to write than you might think</h1>`.

Report Name	What It Does
Removable Empty Tags	Lists the empty tags on your site. Empty tags can occur when you delete an image, text section, or other element without deleting all the tags applied to the element.
Untitled Documents	Lists filenames that don't have a title. The `title` tag is easy to forget because it does not appear in the body of the page. The `title` tag specifies the text that appears at the very top of the browser window and also the text that appears in the Favorites list when someone bookmarks a page. You can enter a title for any page by entering text in the title field just above the work area or in the title field in the Page Properties dialog box.

Finding and Fixing Broken Links

If you're trying to rein in a chaotic Web site, or if you just want to check a site for broken links, you'll be pleased to discover the Check Links feature. You can use Check Links to verify the links in a single file or an entire Web site, and you can use it to automatically fix all the referring links at once.

Here's an example of what Check Links can do. Assume that someone on your team (because you would never do such a thing yourself) changed the name of a file from `new.htm` to `old.htm` without using the Files panel or any of Dreamweaver's automatic link update features. Maybe this person changed the name using another program or simply renamed it in Explorer (Windows) or the Finder (Mac). Changing the filename was easy, but what this person may not have realized is that if he or she didn't change the links to the file when the file was renamed, the links are now broken.

If only one page links to the file that your clueless teammate changed, fixing the broken link isn't such a big deal. As long as you remember what file the page links from, you can simply open that page and use the Property inspector to reset the link the same way you created the link in the first place. (You can find out all the basics of link creation in Chapter 2.)

But many times, a single page in a Web site is linked to many other pages. When that's the case, fixing all the link references can be time-consuming, and forgetting some of them is all too easy. That's why the Check Links feature is so helpful. First, it serves as a diagnostic tool that identifies broken links throughout the site (so you don't have to second-guess where someone may have changed a filename or moved a file). Then it serves as a global fix-it tool. You can use the Check Links dialog box to identify the page a broken link should go to, and Dreamweaver automatically fixes all links referring to that page. The following section walks you through this cool process.

If you are working on a dynamic, database-driven site or if your site was altered with programming that was performed outside Dreamweaver, the Check Links feature may not work properly. This feature works best for sites with static HTML pages

Checking for broken links

To check a site for broken links, follow these steps:

1. **In the drop-down list at the top of the Files panel, select the site name. In the list that appears, select the site you want to work on.**

   Link checking works only for sites listed in the Dreamweaver Site dialog box. For more information about the Site dialog box and how to set up a new site or import an existing one, see Chapter 2.

2. **Choose Site➪Check Links Sitewide.**

   The Link Checker tab opens in the Results panel at the bottom of the page, just under the Property inspector, as shown in Figure 4-6. The tab displays a list of internal and external links. The tab also lists any pages, images, or other items not linked from any other page in the site. (Dreamweaver calls these *orphans*.) Unused images can waste space on your server, so this list is handy if you want to clean up old images or other elements you no longer use on the site.

   Most service providers limit the amount of space on your server and charge extra if you exceed that limit. You can save valuable server space by deleting unused files, especially if they are image or multimedia files. But remember, just because you delete them from your hard drive doesn't mean they are deleted from the server. Make sure you remove them from the Remote Site window in the Files panel as well as the Local Site panel. (For more on using FTP and synchronization to update or delete files on your server, see the section, "Publishing Your Site to a Web Server," later in this chapter.)

Fixing broken links

Broken links are one of the worst problems you can have on a Web site. After you identify a broken link in a site, you should fix it as soon as possible.

Nothing turns off visitors faster than clicking a link and getting a `File Not Found` error page. Fortunately, Dreamweaver makes fixing broken links simple by providing quick access to files with broken links and automating the process of fixing multiple links to the same file.

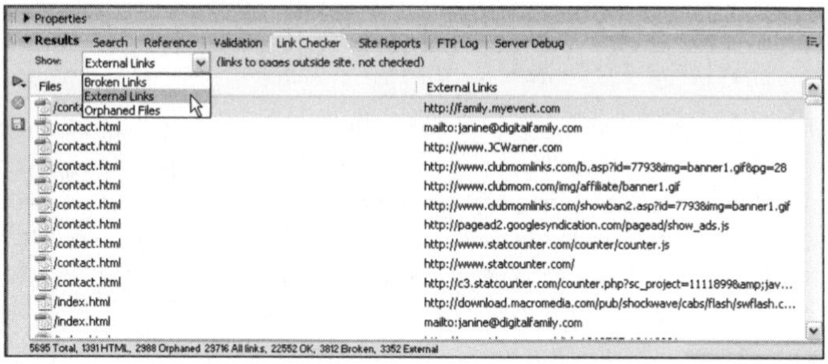

Figure 4-6:
The report can be organized by broken links, external links, and orphans (unused files).

After using the Link Checker tab described in the preceding section to identify broken links, follow these steps to use the Results panel to fix them:

1. **With the Results panel open at the bottom of the page, double-click a filename that Dreamweaver identified as a broken link.**

   The page and its corresponding Property inspector opens. The Results panel remains visible.

2. **Select the broken link or image on the open page.**

   In Figure 4-7, a broken image was selected and is being fixed by using the Property inspector to find the correct image name.

3. **In the Property inspector, click the folder icon to the right of the Src text box to identify the correct image file.**

   (Alternatively, you can type the correct filename and path in the text box instead of using the browse option to find the correct image.) The Select Image Source dialog box appears. You fix links to pages just as you fix links to images, except you type the name of the correct file into the Link text box or click the folder icon next to it to find the file in your site folder.

4. **Click to select the filename of the correct image or file and then click OK.**

   The link automatically changes to reflect the new filename and location. If you replace an image, the image file reappears on the page.

If the link that you correct appears in multiple pages and you fix the link using the broken link's Results panel, Dreamweaver prompts you with a dialog box asking whether you want to fix the remaining broken link references to the file. Click the Yes button to automatically correct all other references. Click the No button to leave the other files unchanged.

Finding files by their addresses

If you're not sure where you saved a file or what you called it, but you can get to it with your browser, you can determine the filename and location by looking at the URL in the browser's address bar. Each folder in a Web site is included in the address to a page within that folder. Folder names are separated by the forward slash, /, and each filename can be distinguished because it includes an extension. For example, the address to the page displayed in the figure tells me that the file is named `dw8fd.html` and is located in a folder called `dreamweaver`, which is a subfolder of a folder called `books`.

Similarly, you can identify the name and location of any image you are viewing on a Web page. If you're using Internet Explorer, place your cursor over the image and right-click (Windows) and then choose Properties. The Properties dialog box includes the specific URL of the image, which has the name and folder (path). In this example, the image is named `DW8FD-cover-sm.gif` and is stored in a folder named `images` inside a folder named dreamweaver inside a folder named books. If you're using the Safari browser on a Mac, it works a little differently. Control+click an image and choose Open Image in New Window. In the new window, the image URL appears in the location bar.

Element Properties

Image Properties

Location:	http://www.digitalfamily.com/books/dreamweaver/images/DW8FD-cover-sm.gif
Width:	112px
Height:	144px
Size of File:	7.75 KB (7940 bytes)
Alternate text:	Dreamweaver 8 For Dummies

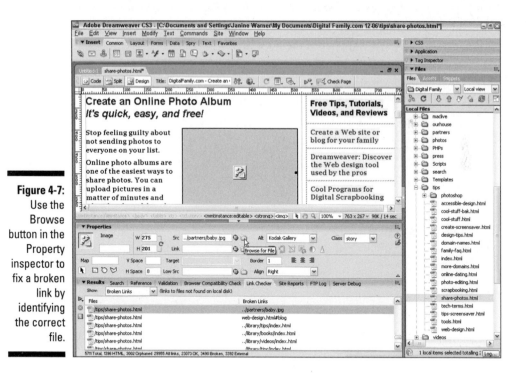

Figure 4-7:
Use the Browse button in the Property inspector to fix a broken link by identifying the correct file.

Changing and moving linked files

Dreamweaver includes a variety of tools that help you manage the files and folders within a site without breaking links. You can use the Files panel to rename and rearrange files and folders, as well as create new folders, all with drag-and-drop ease.

You need to define your site for Dreamweaver's Files panel features to work. If you haven't already defined your site, turn to the instructions at the beginning of Chapter 2.

To rename or rearrange files, follow these steps:

1. **If it's not already active, select the site you want to work on in the drop-down list at the top of the Files panel, as shown in Figure 4-8.**

   When you select a site by clicking the site name, the folders and files in that site appear in the Files panel.

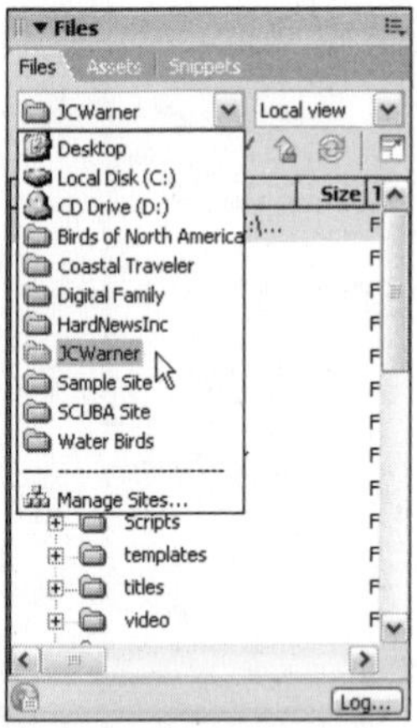

Figure 4-8:
You can select any defined site in the Files panel.

2. **To open and close folders in the Files panel, use the plus (+) and minus (–) signs, respectively.**

3. **In the Files panel, select the file or folder you want to move or rename or both.**

4. **To move a selected file or folder:**

   a. **Drag the selected file or group of files into a folder.**

   Dreamweaver automatically changes all the related links. The Files panel works much like the Explorer window on a PC or the Finder on a Mac, except Dreamweaver tracks and fixes links when you move files through the Files panel. By contrast, if you move or rename site files or folders in the Finder or Explorer, you break any links set to or from those files.

When you move a linked file into a new folder in Dreamweaver, the Update Files dialog box appears with a list of links that need to be updated, as shown in Figure 4-9.

b. To adjust the links, choose Update. If you choose Don't Update, any links to or from that file are left unchanged.

5. **To rename a selected file:**

   a. Click twice on any filename or folder name.

   b. When a box appears around the name, edit it just as you would a name in the Finder or Explorer. Then press Enter (Return on a Mac).

   Again you're prompted with the Update Files dialog box to update any links affected by the filename change.

   c. Choose Update to adjust the links.

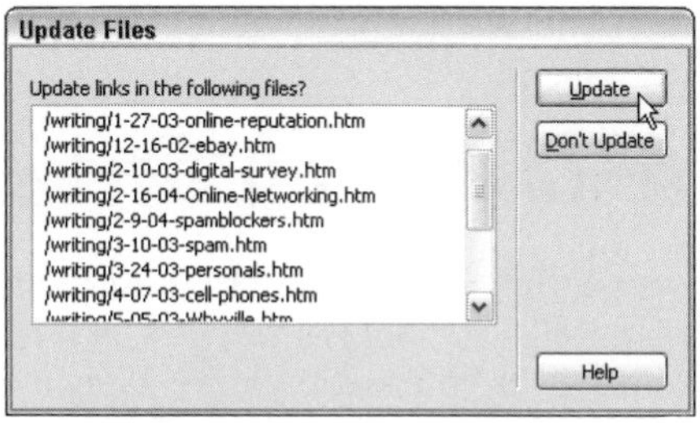

Figure 4-9:
The Update
Files dialog
box lists all
files that will
be changed
during the
update
process.

Update Files

Update links in the following files?

/writing/1-27-03-online-reputation.htm
/writing/12-16-02-ebay.htm
/writing/2-10-03-digital-survey.htm
/writing/2-16-04-Online-Networking.htm
/writing/2-9-04-spamblockers.htm
/writing/3-10-03-spam.htm
/writing/3-24-03-personals.htm
/writing/4-07-03-cell-phones.htm
/writing/5-05-03-Whyville.htm

Update
Don't Update
Help

Making global changes to links

If you want to globally change a link to point at a new URL or to some other page on your site, you can use the Change Link Sitewide option to enter the new URL and change every reference automatically. You can use this option to change any kind of link, including mailto, ftp, and script links. For example, if an e-mail address that you use throughout your site changes, you can use this feature to fix it automatically — a real timesaver. You can use this feature also when you want a string of text to link to a different file than it currently does. For example, you can change every instance of the words *Enter this month's contest* to link to /contest/january.htm instead of /contest/december.htm throughout your Web site.

To change a collection of links using the Change Link Sitewide feature, follow these steps:

1. **Make sure the site you want to work on is displayed in the Files panel.**

   See the preceding exercise for instructions on selecting a site.

2. **Choose Site⇨Change Link Sitewide.**

   The Change Link Sitewide dialog box appears.

4. **Enter the old address and then enter the new address, or click the Browse button to identify files where you want to change the links.**

   You can use this feature to change any link, including e-mail links, links from one page to another within a site, or links to a different Web site.

5. **Click OK.**

   Dreamweaver updates any documents that include the specified links.

Any changes you make to links using Dreamweaver's automated link features occur only on the local version of your site on your hard drive. Make sure you upload all affected files to your Web server to ensure that all changes are included on your published site. To automatically reconcile changes on your local and remote sites, use Dreamweaver's Synchronize Files feature, which is described later in this chapter.

Publishing Your Site to a Web Server

After you create your Web site, test it, and are ready to publish it on the Web, it's time to put Dreamweaver's publishing tools to work. Which features you use depends on the kind of Web server you use. If you're using a commercial service provider, you'll most likely need Dreamweaver's FTP features, which are covered in detail in the following section.

To access Dreamweaver's publishing tools:

1. **Choose Site⇨Manage Sites.**

   The Manage Sites dialog box opens.

2. **In the list of defined sites, select the site you want to publish and then click the Edit button.**

   The Site Definition dialog box opens. If you have not already defined your site, refer to the instructions for this important initial site setup process at the beginning of Chapter 2.

3. **Select the Advanced tab from the top of the Site Definition dialog box.**

   The Advanced options appear instead of the Site Definition wizard available on the Basic tab.

4. **In the Category list, select the Remote Info category.**

5. **Click the drop-down arrow to the right of the Access box (see Figure 4-10) and select the publishing option that is best suited to your Web server and development environment.**

   As you can see in Figure 4-10, Dreamweaver provides five Access options:

   - **None:** Select this option if you are not uploading your site to a server or if are not yet ready to fill in these settings.

   - **FTP:** Select this option to use Dreamweaver's built-in File Transfer Protocol features, which are covered in detail in the following section. These are the settings you're most likely to need if you're using a commercial Web hosting service.

   - **Local/Network:** Select this option if you are using a Web server on a local network, such as your company or university server. For specific settings and requirements, check with your system administrator.

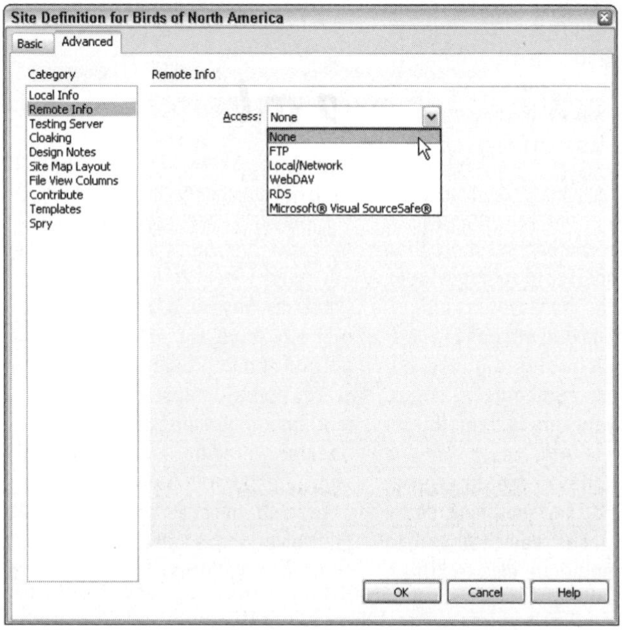

Figure 4-10:
The Remote
Info
category
has many
options for
publishing a
Web site.

- **WebDAV (Web-based Distributed Authoring and Versioning):** Select this option if you are using a server with the WebDAV protocol, such as Microsoft IIS.

- **RDS (Rapid Development Services):** Select this option if you are using ColdFusion on a remote server.

- **Microsoft Visual SourceSafe:** Select this option if you are using Microsoft Visual SourceSafe. Note this option is available only in Windows.

Setting up Web server access for FTP

To make your life simpler, Dreamweaver incorporates FTP capability so that you can easily upload your pages to a remote Web server. The FTP options include features that can help you keep track of changes you make to files on your hard drive and ensure that they match the files on your Web server.

Protecting yourself with clever passwords

An extraordinary number of people use the same word for their user IDs and passwords. That may seem like a good idea because it's easy to remember, but it's also the easiest password for someone to guess if they find (or guess) your user ID and want to break into your system.

If you want to make it harder for someone to break into your computer system, use more than just a name or a common word (using a pet's name is also a popular password choice). Adding punctuation and mixing the case in your password makes it much harder to guess, but not necessarily harder to remember if you're clever. For example, if your dog is named Spot and you live at 44 Maple, you could add the number to your dog's name to create a great password such as spot44. The goal is to come up with a password that is easy for you to remember but hard for someone else to guess,

even if they use a software program designed to try random names and common words from the dictionary as passwords.

Add a random capital letter, and you make it even harder to guess. For example, sPoT44 would be an even more challenging password to crack. (Assuming the password system on your Web server is case-sensitive, and most are.) Oh, and don't leave your password on a sticky note next to your computer, unless you want anyone who walks into your home or office to have access to your system. Also be careful about throwing notes with written passwords away (dumpster diving is a tried-and-true method for stealing passwords). E-mail can also be intercepted or discovered, so it's best not to share passwords through e-mail if you're concerned about security. Good old-fashioned telephone service is still one of the best options for sharing passwords.

To upload your site using FTP, you need the following information from your Web hosting service:

- ✔ FTP host name
- ✔ Path for the Web directory (this is optional but useful)
- ✔ FTP login
- ✔ FTP password

To access the FTP features in Dreamweaver:

1. Follow the steps in the preceding section, choosing FTP in Step 5.

   The dialog box in Figure 4-11 appears.

2. **In the FTP Host text box, type the hostname of your Web server.**

   It should look something like `ftp.host.com` or `shell.host.com` or `ftp.domain.com`, depending on your server. (In my example, I used `ftp.techytranslator.com`.)

3. **In the Host Directory text box, type the directory on the remote site in which documents visible to the public are stored (also known as the *site root*).**

   It should look something like `public_html/` or `www/htdocs/`. Again, this depends on your server.

4. **In the Login and Password text boxes, type the login name and password, respectively, required to gain access to your Web server. If you check the Save box, Dreamweaver stores the information and automatically supplies it to the server when you connect to the remote site.**

   This is your unique login and password information that provides you access to your server.

   Click the Test button to make sure you've entered everything correctly. If there are no problems, Dreamweaver responds with a box saying `Dreamweaver connected to your Web server successfully.`

5. **Select the Use Passive FTP or Use Firewall option only if your service provider or site administrator instructs you to do so.**

   If you aren't on a network but you do use a commercial service provider, you should not need to select either option.

6. **Click OK to save your Web Server Info settings and close the Site Definition dialog box.**

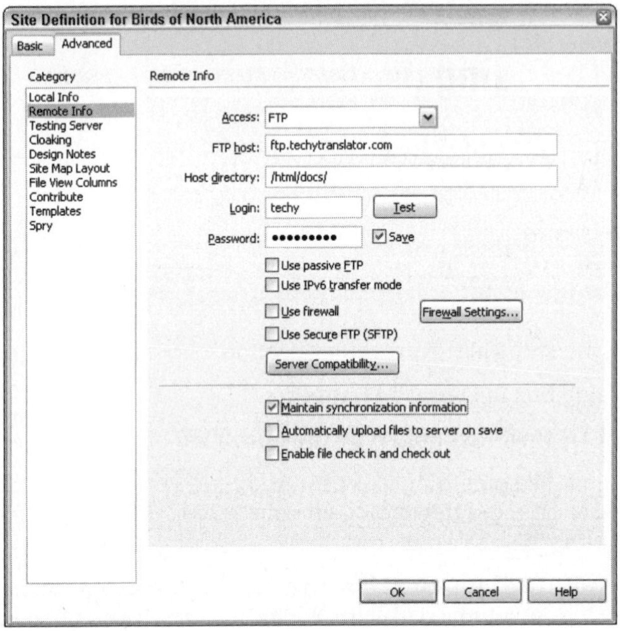

Figure 4-11:
If you're
using a
commercial
Web hosting
service,
you'll need
to specify
the FTP
settings to
upload your
site using
Dream-
weaver.

If you prefer to use a dedicated FTP program instead of Dreamweaver's built-in features, you can download FTP programs for the Mac and PC at the following Web addresses:

- ✔ A popular FTP program for the PC with the unusual name of WS_FTP, can be downloaded from www.ipswitch.com.
- ✔ Another popular Windows program, Cute FTP, can be downloaded from www.cuteftp.com.
- ✔ If you use a Macintosh computer, popular options are Fetch, available for download at www.fetchsoftworks.com, and Transmit, available for download at www.panic.com/transmit.

Putting your Web site online

Now that your site is set up, it's time to upload pages on your server and retrieve them by using the built-in FTP capabilities of Dreamweaver.

Downloading an existing Web site

If you want to work on an existing Web site and you don't already have a copy of it on your local computer's hard drive, you can use Dreamweaver to download any or all the files in the site so that you can edit the existing pages, add new pages, or use any of Dreamweaver's other features to check links and manage the site's further development. The first step is to get a copy of the site onto your computer by downloading it from the server.

To download an existing Web site, follow these steps:

1. **Create a new folder on your computer to store the existing site.**

2. **Specify this folder as the local root folder for the site with Dreamweaver's site setup features.**

   Check out Chapter 2 for information on defining a site, if you're not sure how to do this.

3. **Set up the Remote Info dialog box.**

   I explain how to do this in the "Setting up Web server access for FTP" section.

4. **Connect to the remote site by clicking the Connects to Remote Host button, which looks like the ends of two cables, in the Files panel.**

5. **Click the Get Files button, which looks like a down arrow, to download the entire site to your local drive.**

Sometimes your Web host has files on the remote server that you don't need to download. If you want to download only specific files or folders from the site, select those files or folders in the Remote Site pane of the Files panel and click the Get Files button. Dreamweaver automatically duplicates some or all of the remote site's structure, meaning the folders in the site but not all the files within them, and places the downloaded files in the correct part of the site hierarchy. Re-creating the folder structure on your local computer is important because Dreamweaver needs to know the location of the files as they relate to other parts of the site to set links properly. The safest option is to download the entire site; but if you are working on a large Web project, downloading a part and duplicating the structure enables you to work on a section of the site without downloading all of it.

If you are working on only one page or section of a site, you should generally choose to include *dependent files*, meaning any files linked from those pages, to ensure that links are set properly when you make changes.

6. **After you download the site or specific files or folders, you can edit them as you do any other file in Dreamweaver.**

To transfer files between your hard drive and a remote server, follow these steps:

1. **Make sure you have defined your site (as described in the beginning of Chapter 2), the site you want to upload is open and displayed in the Files panel, and you have used all the FTP settings described in the previous section.**

2. In the top left of the Files panel, click the Connects to Remote Host icon.

If you're not already connected to the Internet, the Connects to Remote Host icon starts your dialup connection. If you have trouble connecting this way, try establishing your Internet connection as you usually do to check e-mail or surf the Web, and then return to Dreamweaver and click the Connects to Remote Host icon after establishing your Internet connection. When your computer is online, Dreamweaver should have no trouble establishing an FTP connection with your host server automatically.

If you still have trouble establishing a connection to your Web server, refer to the preceding section, "Setting up Web server access for FTP," and make sure that you specified the server information correctly. If you still have trouble, contact your service provider or site administrator to ensure you have all the correct information for connecting to your server. Getting all this information set up correctly the first time can be tricky, and each service provider is different.

After you establish the connection, the directories on your server appear in the Files panel. You can move between views in this panel by choosing from the drop-down list at the top right, (visible in Figure 4-12). The main options are Local View, which displays files on your local hard drive, and Remote View, which displays files on the server.

Expand/Collapse

Get files   Put files

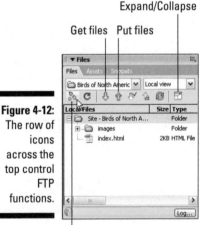

Figure 4-12:
The row of
icons
across the
top control
FTP
functions.

Connects to remote host

3. To *upload* a file (transfer a file from your hard drive to your Web server), select the file from the Local View panel (which displays the files on your hard drive) and click the Put Files icon (the up arrow) in the Files panel.

The files are automatically copied to your server when you transfer them. You can select multiple files or folders to be transferred simultaneously.

After you upload files to you server, test your work by using a Web browser to view them online. Sometimes things that look and work fine on your computer (such as links) won't work on the server.

4. **To** *download* **files or folders (transfer files or folders from your Web server to your hard drive), select the files or folders from the Remote View panel (which displays the files on your server) and click the Get Files button (the down arrow) in the Files panel.**

The files are automatically copied to your hard drive when you transfer them. Be aware that when you copy files to or from your server, the files you're transferring overwrite the files already at the destination. Dreamweaver notifies you about the overwriting if it notices you're replacing a new file with an old one, but it isn't always able to correctly assess the proper time differences. When the transfer is complete, you can open the files on your hard drive.

You can see both the remote and local views simultaneously by clicking the Expand/Collapse icon on the far right side of the Files panel (labeled in Figure 4-12). To collapse this Site dialog box and return the Files panel to the side of the screen again, click the Expand/Collapse icon again.

The arrows with the check mark and the little lock at the top of the Files panel are for the Check In/Out feature, which enables you to keep track of who is working on a site and prevent more than one person making changes to the same page. These features are covered in the "Using Check In and Check Out" section, later in this chapter.

Synchronizing Local and Remote Sites

One of the most valuable features in Dreamweaver's FTP options is the capability to automatically synchronize the files on your hard drive with the files on your server. This is cool because it helps you keep track of which pages you've edited and ensure that they have been updated on the server. This may not matter much to you the first time you upload your site, or if you have only a few pages in your site. But if you have a large site and make frequent updates, this feature is a wonderful way to make sure all the changes you make get to your server. Dreamweaver also confirms which files are updated after you complete the synchronization.

Follow these steps to synchronize your Web site:

1. **Make sure the site you want to work on is selected and displayed in the Files panel.**

2. **Click the Connects to Remote Host icon, in the top left of the Files panel, to log on to your remote site.**

3. **Click the Expand/Collapse icon (labeled in Figure 4-12) to expand the dialog box and view the remote and local sites simultaneously.**

   The Site dialog box displays both the remote and local views of the site. (To collapse this dialog box, click the Expand/Collapse icon again.)

4. **Choose Site⇨Synchronize Sitewide.**

   The Synchronize Files dialog box appears.

5. **In the Synchronize drop-down list, choose whether to synchronize the Entire Site or Selected Files Only.**

6. **In the Direction drop-down list, choose which option you want to use to copy the files:**

   • **Put Newer Files to Remote:** This option copies the most recently modified files from your local site to the remote site. Click the Delete Remote Files Not on Local Drive box if you want those files removed from your Web site.

   • **Get Newer Files from Remote:** This option copies the most recently modified files from your remote site to the local site. Click the Delete Local Files Not on Remote Server box if you want to remove those files from your local copy.

   • **Get and Put Newer Files:** This option updates both the local and remote sites with the most recent versions of all the files.

7. **Make sure the Delete Remote Files Not on Local Drive box is not selected.**

   Be careful of this feature. As a general rule, I recommend you leave it unchecked because you may have folders and files on the server, such as log files, that do not exist on your hard drive, and you don't want to delete them inadvertently.

8. **Click the Preview button.**

   The Site FTP dialog box displays the files that are about to be changed.

   Now you have the option to verify the files you want to delete, put, and get. If you don't want Dreamweaver to alter a file, deselect it from the Site FTP dialog box now, or forever live with the consequences.

9. **Click OK.**

   All approved changes are automatically made, and Dreamweaver updates the Site FTP dialog box with the status.

10. **When the synchronization finishes, you can choose to save or not save the verification information to a local file.**

    I recommend you choose to save the verification information because it can be handy if you want to review your changes after synchronization is complete.

Be careful of the Delete Remote Files Not on Local Drive option, especially if you have special administrative pages, such as stats files, which are often added to your server space by your service provider to track traffic on your site.

Setting Cloaking Options

The Dreamweaver Cloaking option enables you to exclude folders or files from all site operations, meaning they won't be uploaded to the live site when you're synchronizing or batching files back and forth. This feature is handy if you have sections of a site that you want to save but don't want visible to your viewers. For example, if you have a special holiday folder that you don't want visible during the rest of the year, you can use the Cloaking feature to save it locally, with the assurance that no one can accidentally publish the files with Dreamweaver until you uncloak them and publish them in December.

To use the Cloaking feature, follow these steps:

1. **Choose Site➪Manage Sites.**

2. **Select the site you want to work on and then click Edit.**

    The Site Definition dialog box appears.

3. **In the Category list on the left, select the Cloaking category.**

4. **Select the Enable Cloaking box.**

5. **If you want to cloak files of a certain type, select the Cloak Files Ending With box and enter the extension(s) in the text field, as shown in Figure 4-13.**

    For example, if you want to cloak any original Photoshop files that may be saved in your local root folder so they don't upload and take up space on your server, enter the .psd extension. If you want to cloak more than one file type, separate each file extension with a space. Do not use a comma or other delimiter.

6. **Click OK to close the Site Definition dialog box and then click the Done button in the Define Sites dialog box to close it.**

    Files matching the extensions specified, if any, are now cloaked.

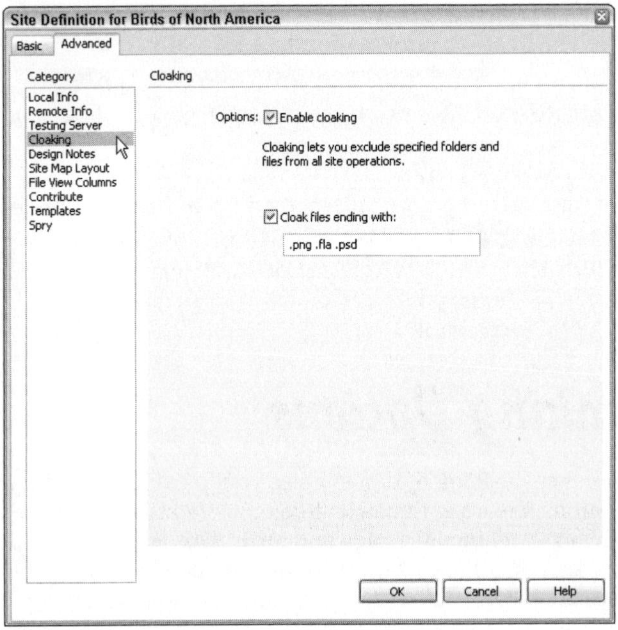

Figure 4-13:
The
Cloaking
feature
enables you
to specify
files or
folders that
you don't
want
transferred
to your
server.

7. **If you want to manually cloak specific folders, select the folders in the Files tab of the Files panel.**

   You can't cloak individual files, for reasons known only to the Dreamweaver programmers.

8. **Right-click (Windows) or Control+click (Mac) and select Cloaking⇨Cloak.**

To uncloak files or folders, repeat Steps 4 through 8 and select Uncloak from the shortcut menu. You can also use these steps to uncloak all the files in your current site, disable cloaking in the site, and change the cloaking settings.

Editing Web pages online

If you're an experienced Web designer and just want to make quick changes to a site or use the FTP features to access files on a server without doing the site setup steps, Dreamweaver does enable you to use these features without completing site setup. To access FTP features and set them up quickly, choose Site⇨Manage Sites and then choose New⇨FTP & RDS Server from the Manage Sites dialog box. This shortcut enables you to work directly on your server using FTP & RDS Server; however, Dreamweaver does not manage link checking, and none of the other site management features work.

If you disable cloaking for all files, any manual cloaking choices you've made are lost, even if you enable cloaking again later.

Making the Most of Dreamweaver's Site Management Features

In the following sections, you'll find descriptions and instructions for using more of the options available from the Site Definition dialog box, including Design Notes, Check In/Out, and integrated e-mail. If you're the only person working on a Web site, you probably don't need the features described in this section because they are intended for use on sites developed by a team of people who need to communicate with each other and make sure they don't overwrite each other's work.

Using a testing server

The Testing Server option enables you to specify a development server, a necessary step if you are creating a Web site using the Dreamweaver dynamic page-creation features for developing sites using PHP, ASP, or ColdFusion. You find more information about using these options in Chapters 13, 14, and 15.

Using Check In and Check Out

The Check In/Out feature is designed to keep people from overwriting each other's work when more than one person is working on the same Web site (a valuable feature if you want to keep peace among all the members of your Web design team). When a person working on the Web site checks out a file, other developers working on the site are unable to make changes to that file. When you check out a file, a green check mark appears next to the filename in the Files panel. If someone else checks out a file, you see a red check mark next to the filename.

To use the Check In/Out feature, select the Enable File Check In and Check Out option at the bottom of the Remote Info dialog box. The dialog box expands to expose other options. If you want files checked out whenever they are opened, select the Check Out Files When Opening option (see Figure 4-14).

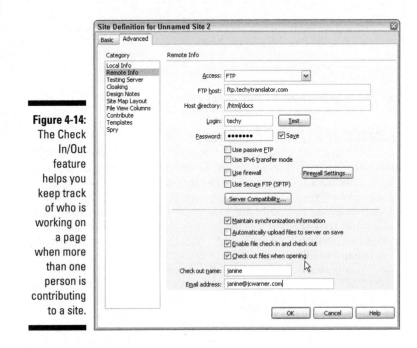

Figure 4-14:
The Check In/Out feature helps you keep track of who is working on a page when more than one person is contributing to a site.

Using this feature, you can track which files a particular person is working on. But if you want to use this tracking mechanism, select the Check Out Files When Opening option and then fill in the name you want associated with the files (presumably your name or nickname) in the Check Out Name field and then include your e-mail address in the Email Address field. (The Email Address field is needed for Dreamweaver's integration with e-mail, which facilitates communication among developers on a site. See the next section for more information about integrated e-mail.)

Keeping the peace with version control

Version control systems enable you to better manage changes and prevent different team members from overwriting each other's work. If you already use these programs, you'll be glad to know that you can integrate both Visual SourceSafe and systems that use the Web DAV protocol with Dreamweaver. This way, you can take advantage of the Dreamweaver site management features and still protect your code development process. If you don't know about these programs, visit the Microsoft site (http://msdn.microsoft.com/ssafe/) to find out more about Visual SourceSafe. For more on Web DAV, visit www.webdav.org.

Staying in touch with integrated e-mail

Dreamweaver features integrated e-mail as another handy tool for collaborative Web design when you use the Dreamweaver Check In/Out tool (described in the preceding section). With the e-mail program you already use, integrated e-mail gives you easy access to the e-mail addresses of other members of your team.

When you work on a site with a team of people, finding that someone else has already checked out the page you want to work on is common. Until that person checks the file back in, doing the work you need to do to the page is impossible. In the Dreamweaver Site Definition dialog box, each developer types his or her e-mail address with the Check In/Out feature. Then, when you find that someone else has the page you need, you can easily fire off an e-mail asking that person to check it back in so you can work on it, just by clicking that person's name in the Files window. (I find bribes can be more effective than threats, especially when you bribe with chocolate or free movie passes.)

Developers on your team can use the following steps to associate their e-mail addresses with their version of Dreamweaver as part of the Check In/Out setup:

1. **Choose Site⇨Manage Sites.**

   The Manage Sites dialog box opens.

2. **Select the site you want to work on and then click the Edit button.**

   The Site Definition dialog box opens.

3. **Click the Advanced tab.**

4. **In the Category list on the left, choose Remote Info.**

   The Remote Info page appears (refer to Figure 4-14).

5. **Select the Enable File Check In and Check Out check box.**

6. **Select the Check Out Files When Opening check box.**

7. **In the Check Out Name text box, enter your name.**

   Nicknames are okay as long as everyone on the team knows your silly name.

8. **In the Email Address text box, enter your e-mail address.**

9. **Click OK to save your changes. Click the Done button in the Manage Sites dialog box.**

   The Manage Sites dialog box closes.

Using Design Notes

If you sometimes forget the details of your work or neglect to tell your colleagues important things about the Web site you're all working on, the Dreamweaver Design Notes feature may save you some grief.

Design Notes are ideal if you want to hide sensitive information from visitors, such as pricing structures or creative strategies, but make it available to members of your development team. Information saved as a Design Note in Dreamweaver can travel with any HTML file or image, even if the file transfers from one Web site to another or from Fireworks to Dreamweaver.

Essentially, Design Notes enable you to record information (such as a message to another designer on your team) and associate it with a file or folder. Design Notes work a lot like the *comment tag* (HTML code that enables you to embed in a page text that won't appear in a browser) but with a bit more privacy. Unlike the comment tag, which is embedded directly in the HTML code of a page (and can be seen if someone views the source code behind a page on the Web), Design Notes are never visible to your visitors. The only way for a visitor to view Design Notes is to deliberately type the path to your notes subdirectory and view the notes files directly. You can even explicitly block this from being allowed, but only if you have administrative access to your server. To be even more secure, you can keep the notes on your hard drive and prevent them from ever being uploaded to your server — though, of course, your team members won't see your witty remarks.

To access the Design Notes page, choose Design Notes in the Category list in the Site Definition dialog box (see Figure 4-15). The settings on this page enable you to control how Dreamweaver uses Design Notes:

- **Maintain Design Notes:** Select this option to ensure that the Design Note remains attached to the file when you upload, copy, or move it.

- **Upload Design Notes for Sharing:** Choose this option to include Design Notes when you send files to the server via FTP.

- **Clean Up:** Use the Clean Up button, also shown in Figure 4-15, to delete any Design Notes that are not associated with any files in the site.

When you create graphics in Adobe Fireworks, you can save a Design Note for each image file that is also available in Dreamweaver. To use this integrated feature, create a Design Note in Fireworks and associate it with the image. Then when you save the Fireworks image to your local Web site folder, the Design Note goes with it. When you open the file in Dreamweaver, the Design Note appears when you right-click the image (Control+click on the Mac). This feature is a great way for graphic designers to communicate with other members of the Web development team.

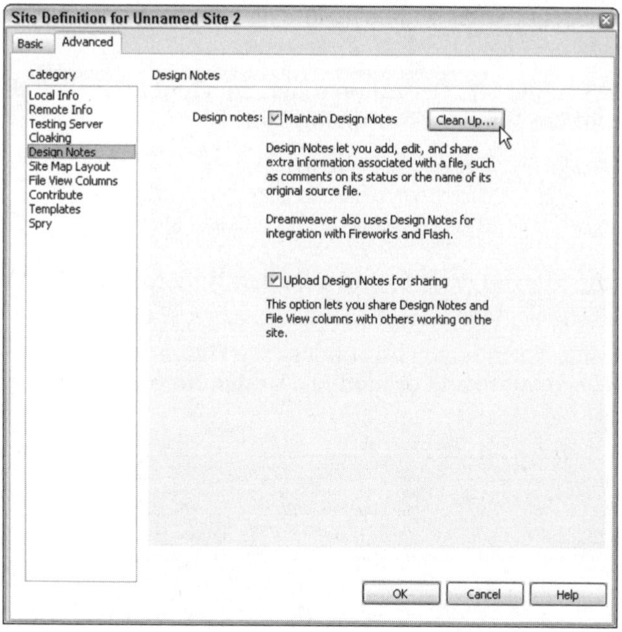

Figure 4-15:
You can include Design Notes when sending files to the Web server.

To activate the Design Notes feature, follow these steps:

1. **Choose Site⇨Manage Sites.**

   The Manage Sites dialog box opens.

2. **Select the site you want to work on and then click the Edit button.**

   The Site Definition dialog box opens.

3. **Select the Advanced tab.**

4. **In the Category list at the left, choose Design Notes.**

   The Design Notes page appears (refer to Figure 4-15).

5. **Select the Maintain Design Notes option.**

   With this option selected, whenever you copy, move, rename, or delete a file, the associated Design Notes file is also copied, moved, renamed, or deleted with it.

6. **If you want your Design Notes to be sent with your files when they are uploaded to your server, select the Upload Design Notes for Sharing option.**

   If you're making notes only to yourself and don't want them to be associated with the page when you upload it to the server, deselect this option and the Design Notes will be maintained locally but not uploaded with your file.

   7. **Click OK in the Site Definition dialog box and then click the Done button in the Manage Sites dialog box.**

      The Manage Sites dialog box closes.

To add Design Notes to a document, follow these steps:

   1. **Open the file you want to add a Design Note to and then choose File⇨Design Notes.**

      The Design Notes dialog box opens (see Figure 4-16). You need to have a file checked out to add or modify a Design Note, but not to read a note.

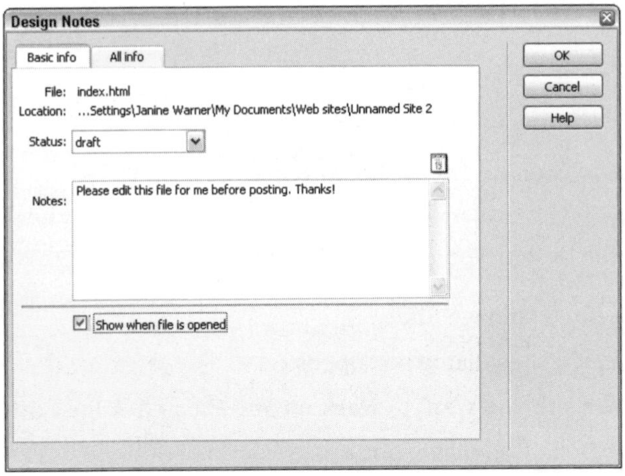

Figure 4-16:
Design Notes make it easy to add messages to documents, images, and even entire folders.

   2. **In the Status drop-down list box, choose the status of the document.**

      Your options are Draft, Revision 1, Revision 2, Revision 3, Alpha, Beta, Final, and Needs Attention. You can choose any status, and you should set a policy with your design team about what each status means and how you use these options to manage your development.

   3. **In the Notes text box, type your comments.**

   4. **If you want to insert the current local date, click the Insert Date icon, which is just above the Notes text box.**

      The current date is inserted automatically.

      You can also select the Show When File Is Open check box. If this box is selected, the Design Notes appear whenever the file is opened so that they can't be missed.

5. **Click the All Info tab.**

   You can add other information that may be useful to developers of your site. For example, you can name a key designer (in the Name field) and define the value as the name of that person or the priority of the project (in the Value field). You may also define a field for a client or the type of file that you commonly use.

6. **Click the plus (+) button to add a new information item; click the minus (–) button to remove a selected item.**

7. **Click OK to save the notes.**

   The notes you entered are saved to a subfolder named *notes* in the same location as the current file. The filename is the document's filename plus the extension .mno. For example, if the filename is art.htm, the associated Design Notes file is named art.htm.mno. Design Notes are indicated in Site View by a small yellow icon that looks like a cartoon bubble.

Activating Site Map Layout

If you have trouble keeping track of all the files in your Web site and how they link to one another, you're not alone. As Web sites get larger and larger, this task becomes increasingly daunting. That's why Dreamweaver includes a Site Map Layout feature — to help you keep track of the structure and hierarchy of your site. This is not a site map (like those you often see on Web sites) that links to the main pages of a site. The Dreamweaver Site Map Layout is never visible to your visitors; it's a site management feature designed to help you visually manage the files and folders in your site.

To create a site map from the Site Map Layout page, follow these steps:

1. **Choose Site⇨Manage Sites.**

   The Manage Sites dialog box opens.

2. **Select the name of the site you want to work on.**

3. **Click the Edit button.**

   The Site Definition dialog box opens.

4. **Make sure the Advanced tab at the top of the Site Definition dialog box is selected and the Advanced options are visible.**

5. **In the Category list on the left, select Site Map Layout.**

   The Site Map Layout options appear on the right side of the Site Definition dialog box, as shown in Figure 4-17.

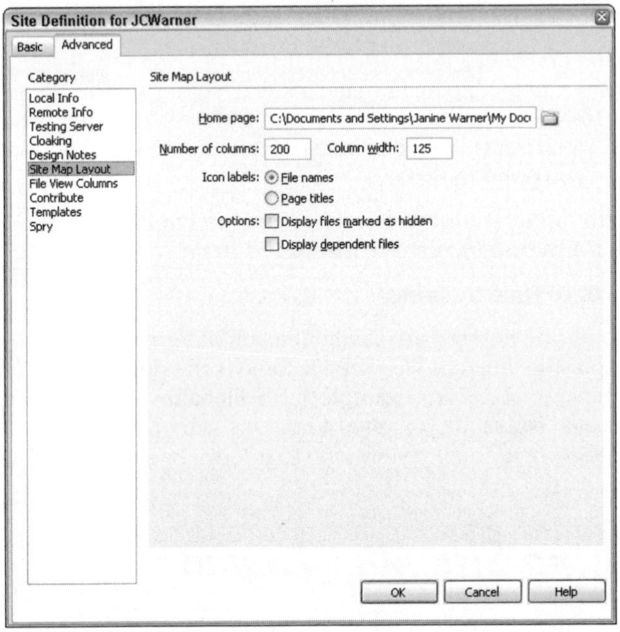

Figure 4-17:
The Site
Map Layout
options
enable you
to specify
how the
Site Map
navigation
window
appears.

6. **Click the Browse icon next to the Home Page text box and browse to find the main folder of your Web site. Note: If you already filled out the Local Info page for your site, this field is already filled in.**

   This text box specifies the location of the home page of the Web site and the main site folder. This information is essential because it shows Dreamweaver where the Web site begins and ends.

7. **Specify the number of columns you want to display per row in the site map.**

   If you're not sure what you want for these settings, start with the default value of 200. You can always come back and change these settings later if you don't like the spacing of the icons in your site map.

8. **In the Column Width text box, set the width of the site map's columns in pixels.**

   Again, start with the default value of 125 if you're not sure of the width.

9. **In the Icon Labels section, select the File Names or Page Titles option if you want the filename or the page title, respectively, as the label for each page in the site map.**

   You can manually edit the displayed filename or page title after you generate the site map.

10. **In the Options section, you can choose to hide certain files, meaning they won't be visible in the Site Map window.**

    If you select the Display Files Marked as Hidden option, files you have marked as hidden appear in italic in the site map. If you select the Display Dependent Files option, all dependent files in the site's hierarchy appear. A *dependent file* is an image or other non-HTML content that the browser loads when loading the main page.

11. **Click OK.**

    The site map is generated automatically.

12. **To view the Site Map, open the Files panel on the right side of the screen and select Map View from the drop-down list in the top-right corner.**

    (In Figure 4-18 the drop-down list is displayed on the left because the Files panel has been expanded.) The site map appears in the Files panel using icons to represent each file and link in the site.

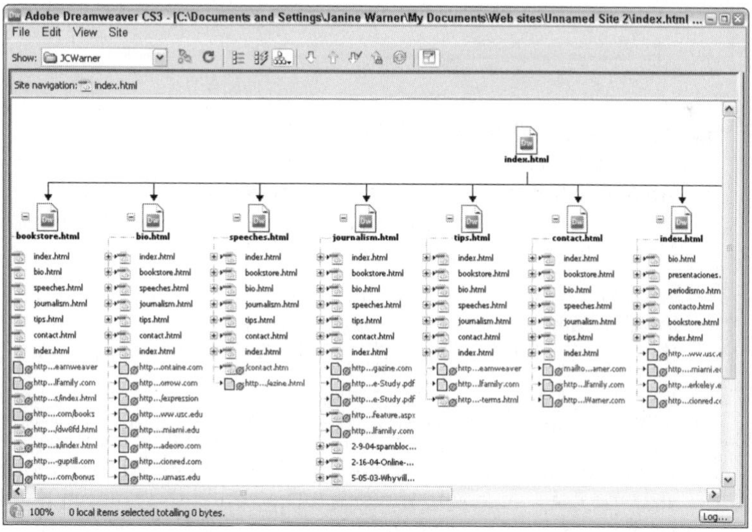

Figure 4-18: The site map provides a visual reference to the structure, hierarchy, and links in a Web site.

Using the File View Columns option

You can use the File View Columns category in the Site Definition dialog box (see Figure 4-19) to customize how file and folder options appear in the expanded Files panel. This can be useful for sorting or grouping files in novel ways — for example, by adding a *section*, *department*, *season*, or *version* column.

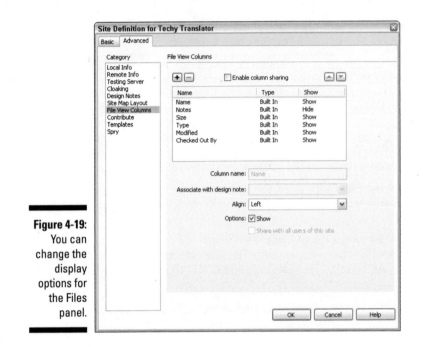

Figure 4-19:
You can
change the
display
options for
the Files
panel.

You can customize File View Columns in the following ways:

- You can add up to 10 new columns by clicking the small plus sign at the top of the dialog box and entering the name, association, and alignment of each new column.

- You can reorder or realign the order in which columns appear by selecting the name of the column and then clicking the up or down arrow in the top right of the dialog box to move it up or down the list.

- You can hide any columns except the filename column by selecting the column name and clicking to remove the check mark in the Show box.

- You can designate which (if any) columns are shared with other developers who have access to the site by selecting the column name and clicking to remove the check mark in the Enable Column Sharing check box.

- You can delete any of the custom columns (you can not delete default columns) by selecting the column name and clicking the minus sign at the top of the dialog box.

- You can rename custom columns as you would edit a filename.

- You can associate Design Notes with custom columns by selecting the column name and using the drop-down list next to Associate with Design Note.

Enabling Contribute features

Adobe Contribute is a program that was created so that people who don't know much about Web design can easily contribute to a Web site. Think of Contribute as sort of a Dreamweaver Light, except it doesn't work very well as a stand-alone program. Contribute was designed to work on sites designed in Dreamweaver, and a number of features have been carefully integrated to make that collaboration work smoothly. If you're working with other developers of a site who use Contribute, make sure you select the box next to Enable Contribute Compatibility in the Contribute category of the Site Definition dialog box.

Remembering Your History

You can keep track of what you're doing and even replay your steps with the History panel. The History panel also lets you undo one or more steps and create commands to automate repetitive tasks.

To open the History panel, shown in Figure 4-20, choose Window⇨History. As soon as you open a file, the History panel starts automatically recording your actions as you do work in Dreamweaver. You can't rearrange the order of steps in the History panel, but you can copy them, replay them, and undo them. Don't think of the History panel as an arbitrary collection of commands; think of it as a way to view the steps you've performed, in the order in which you performed them. This is a great way to let Dreamweaver do your work for you if you have to repeat the same steps over and over. It's also a lifesaver if you make a major mistake and want to go back one or more steps in your development work.

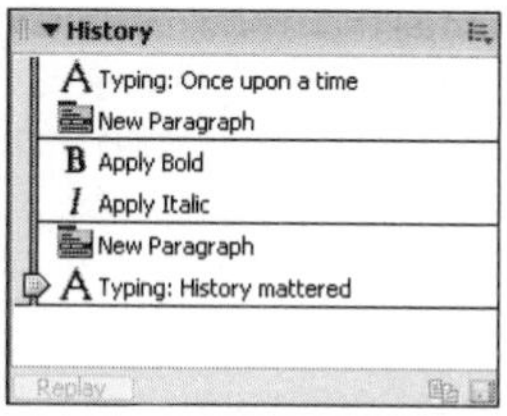

Figure 4-20:
The History panel keeps track of what you do, making undoing and repeating your steps easy.

```
▼ History                          ≣
   A  Typing: Once upon a time
   🖼 New Paragraph
   B  Apply Bold
   I  Apply Italic
   🖼 New Paragraph
⇨ A  Typing: History mattered

 Replay                        🗎 🗑
```

Repeating your steps with Recorded Commands

You can automate repeat tasks using Dreamweaver's Recorded Commands feature, available from the Commands menu. Simply start the record option, execute any series of actions in Dreamweaver, stop, and save them. Then you just replay the recording to repeat the actions automatically. To use the Recorded Commands option, choose Commands⇨Start Recording and then carefully execute a series of steps that you want to be able to repeat. When you complete the steps you want to record, choose Commands⇨Stop Recording and name the command to save it. To play the actions back, choose Commands⇨Play Recorded Command and select your new command. Then kick back and watch the action; or better yet, take a break and get out of your office for a change.

Here's a rundown of how you can put the History panel to use:

- ✔ **To copy steps you already executed:** Use the Copy Steps option as a quick way to automate steps you want to repeat. You can even select steps individually, in case you want to replay some (but not all) actions exactly as you did them.

- ✔ **To replay any or all steps displayed in the History panel:** Highlight the steps you want to replay and click the Replay button at the bottom of the History panel.

- ✔ **To undo the results of the replayed steps:** Choose Edit⇨Undo Replay Steps.

- ✔ **To apply steps to a specific element on a page:** Highlight that element in the Document window before selecting and replaying the steps. For example, if you want to apply bold and italic formatting to just a few words on a page, you can replay the steps that applied bold and italics to selected text.

You can also set the number of steps displayed in the History panel by choosing Edit⇨Preferences (Windows) or Dreamweaver⇨Preferences (Mac) and selecting General from the Category list on the left. The default is 50 steps, more than enough for most users. The higher the number, the more memory the History panel uses.

Using the Quick Tag Editor

If you're one of those developers who likes to work in the Dreamweaver WYSIWYG editing environment but still wants to look at the HTML tags once in a while, you'll love the Quick Tag Editor.

The Quick Tag Editor, as the name implies, lets you quickly access HTML tags and enables you to modify, add, or remove an HTML tag without opening the HTML Source window. That means that while you're in the middle of working on a page in design view, you can view the HTML tag you are working on without switching over to code view. You can use the Quick Tag Editor to insert HTML, edit an existing tag, or wrap new tags around a selected text block or other element.

The Quick Tag Editor opens in one of three modes — Edit, Insert, or Wrap — depending on what you selected on the page before you launched the editor. Use the keyboard shortcut Ctrl+T (Windows) or ⌘+T (Mac) to change modes while the Quick Tag Editor is open.

You can enter or edit tags in the Quick Tag Editor just as you would in code view, without having to switch back and forth between code view and design view. To enter or edit tags in the Quick Tag Editor, follow these steps:

1. **With the document you want to edit open, select an element or text block.**

   If you want to add new code, simply click anywhere in the file without selecting text or an element.

2. **Choose Modify⇨Quick Tag Editor.**

   You can also press Ctrl+T (Windows) or ⌘+T (Mac).

   The Quick Tag Editor opens in the mode that is most appropriate for your selection, as shown in Figure 4-21. For example, if you click an image or formatted text, it displays the current tag so that you can edit it. If you don't select anything or if you select unformatted text, the Quick Tag Editor opens with nothing in it, and you can enter the code you want to add. Press Ctrl+T (⌘+T) to switch to another mode.

   If you want to edit an existing tag, go to Step 3. If you want to add a new tag, skip to Step 4.

3. **If you selected an element formatted with multiple HTML tags or a tag with multiple attributes, press Tab to move from one tag, attribute name, or attribute value to the next. Press Shift+Tab to move back to the previous one.**

   If you aren't sure about a tag or attribute, pause for a couple of seconds and a drop-down list appears automatically, offering you a list of all the tags or attributes available for the element you are editing. If this Hints list doesn't appear, choose Edit⇨Preferences⇨Code Hints (Windows) or Dreamweaver⇨Preferences⇨Code Hints (Mac) and make sure that the Enable Code Hints option is selected.

4. **To add a new tag or attribute, simply type the code into the Quick Tag Editor.**

   You can use the Tab and arrow keys to move the cursor where you want to add code. You can keep the Quick Tag Editor open and continue to edit and add attribute names and values as long as you like.

5. **To close the Quick Tag Editor and apply all your changes, press Enter (Windows) or Return (Mac).**

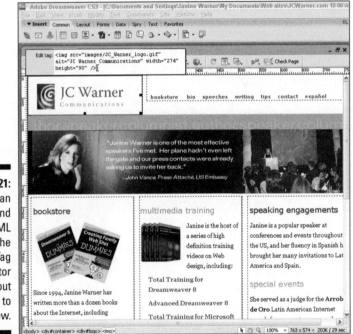

Figure 4-21:
You can view and edit HTML tags in the Quick Tag Editor without switching to code view.

Part II
Appreciating Web Design Options

The 5th Wave · By Rich Tennant

"Just how accurately should my Web site reflect my place of business?"

In this part . . .

The best way to create standards-based, accessible Web designs is with Cascading Style Sheets (CSS). This part introduces you to the power and advantages of CSS, but you'll also find instructions for working with tables and frames, which are still viable approaches to Web design.

In Chapter 5, you find an introduction to CSS and a review of the CSS features in Dreamweaver. In Chapter 6, you move on to creating CSS layouts, using div tags and other block-level elements to create accessible, flexible designs.

In Chapter 7, you find out how to create tables, split and merge cells, and use table attributes. In Chapter 8, you get an introduction to frames and discover how targeting makes it possible to open a link in a specific part of the page. And in Chapter 9, you discover how Dreamweaver's templates can make creating Web pages faster and save you even more time if you ever have to redesign your pages.

Chapter 5

Cascading Style Sheets

• •

• •

*W*ant to add a little style to your pages? *Cascading Style Sheets (CSS)* is the way to create Web sites today if you want to follow the latest standards and develop Web sites that are accessible, flexible, and designed to work on a wide range of devices.

The concept of creating styles has been around since long before the Web. Desktop publishing programs, such as Adobe InDesign, and even word processing programs, such as Microsoft Word, have long used styles to manage the formatting and editing of text on printed pages. Using styles in a word processor, you could create styles for common features such as headlines, subheads, and captions. In print design, styles are great timesavers because they enable you to combine a collection of formatting options, such as Arial, bold, italic, and centered, into one style and then apply all those options at once to any selected text in your document using a single style. When you use styles this way in print, you also have the advantage that if you change a style, you can apply the change everywhere you've used that style.

On the Web, you can do all that and more with CSS because you can use styles sheets for a lot more than just text formatting. In addition to creating styles for things such as headlines, you can use CSS to create styles that align images to the left or right side of a page, add padding around text or images, and change background and link colors. You also have the option of creating style sheets that apply only to the page you are working on or to create style sheets that are separate documents and can be applied to many pages in the same site. Using this approach, you can make changes across any or all pages in a Web site simply by altering the styles in an external style sheet. Because you can create multiple style sheets for the same page, CSS is rapidly becoming the preferred method of designing Web pages among most professional Web designers.

If you haven't jumped on the CSS bandwagon yet, this chapter is designed to help you appreciate the benefits of CSS, introduce you to Dreamweaver's CSS, and show you how to create and apply styles. In Chapter 6, you find instructions for using CSS to control the position of elements and create page layouts by combining HTML <div> tags and styles.

Introducing Cascading Style Sheets

One of the most powerful aspects of CSS is the way you can use it to make global style changes across an entire Web site. Suppose, for example, that you create a style for your headlines by redefining the <h1> tag to create large, blue, bold headlines. Then one fine day you decide that all your headlines should be red instead of blue. If you aren't using CSS, changing all your headlines could be a huge undertaking — a matter of opening every Web page in your site and making changes to the font tags around your headlines. But if you are using CSS, you can simply change the style sheet, and voila! Your headlines all turn red automatically. If you ever have to redesign your site (and believe me, every good site goes through periodic redesigns), you can save hours or even days of work if you have created your design with CSS.

CSS has many other advantages and a remarkably broad scope. The following partial list shows some of what you can do with CSS:

✔ Make global changes anywhere a style is applied simply by changing the original style.

✔ Create multiple styles for the same page. For example, you can create one style for print and another that uses a large text size for anyone who has trouble reading small print on the Web.

✔ Create styles for commonly used elements, such as headlines, captions, and sidebars to create a more consistent design and speed the development process.

✔ Define styles that align and position elements, including images, tables, and <div> tags.

✔ Define font sizes in fixed or relative sizes using percentages, pixels, picas, points, inches, millimeters, ems, and exs (described in the sidebar, "Understanding CSS size options," later in this chapter).

✔ Add and remove borders around images, tables, <div> tags, and more.

✔ Alter the display of existing HTML tags, such as the unordered list tag, which you can redefine to appear in a browser as a horizontal or vertical list with or without bullets. You can also replace standard HTML bullets with a variety of other bullet styles or an image.

✔ Change link colors, remove link underlining, and create mouseover effects using text links.

Understanding the basics of styles

When you create a CSS rule, you essentially define an element, either by redefining an existing HTML tag or by creating and naming a new style. You can name a style anything you like as long as you don't use spaces or special characters and you follow a few simple rules about how different kinds of selectors are created.

Once you've created a CSS definition, such as .imagecaption, you can apply that style to an element in your Web page, such the text under a photo, and a browser will format the text or other element based on the definition you created in the style sheet.

Many people find CSS confusing at first. If you're starting to feel baffled at this point, hang in there. Once you read about the basic concepts and start creating and applying styles yourself, it all starts to make a lot more sense.

Understanding style selectors

You can create a number of different kinds of styles or selectors. Each has different naming restrictions and purposes. These are the most common options:

✔ Class selectors, which must begin with a period and can be used as many times as you like on any page.

✔ ID selectors, which begin with a # (pound sign) and can be used only once per page. (Dreamweaver groups ID selectors in the Advanced category.)

✔ Tag selectors, which redefine existing HTML tags and must exactly match the HTML tag. For example, if you redesign the <h3> tag, you must name the style H3, not a variation like heading3.

✔ You can also create contextual styles that are combinations of these style types and enable you to define rules for a style that appear only when a style is contained within another style on the same page. (You find more information about contextual styles in Chapter 6.)

Understanding style sheet options

You also have the option of creating internal, external, or inline styles. If you create internal styles, or styles that apply only to the document you are working on, they are created and stored in the <HEAD> area at the top of the HTML page.

If you save your styles in an external style sheet, they are stored in a separate file with a .css extension. External style sheets can be attached to any Web page in much the same way as you link one Web page to another. You can attach the same style to many pages, and you can attach multiple style sheets to the same page.

Inline styles are created within a document at the place that a style is used and only apply to the element they are attached to in the document.

No matter how you create your styles, each style definition, or *rule,* contains a *selector* and a *declaration.* The selector identifies the name and type of style; for example, the selector would be something like H1, or #container, or .caption. The declaration defines the style and describes its properties, such as bold or blue.

Looking at the code behind the scenes

If you prefer not to look at HTML and CSS code, you'll appreciate that if you work in design view you never *have* to look at the code. That said, I find it helpful to have a general understanding of the code behind the scenes to better understand how and why CSS works the way it does.

The following examples show what the CSS code would look like in Dreamweaver for a class style called .imagecaption — defined as small, bold, and italic with the font face Times — and a redefined HTML tag H1 — defined as large, bold, and formatted with the font face Arial.

```
.imagecaption {
        font-family: "Times New Roman", Times, serif;
        font-size: small;
        font-style: italic;
        font-weight: bold;
}
H1 {
        font-family: Arial, Helvetica, sans-serif;
        font-size: large;
}
```

Creating page layouts with CSS

CSS is a great alternative to plain old HTML when it comes to formatting text. But the formatting fun doesn't stop there! Besides helping you to style text, CSS can be used to create complex layouts with styles that control the placement and alignment of every element on the page. In Chapter 7 you find detailed instructions for creating CSS layouts and using style options such as floats and positioning to create flexible, adaptable page designs.

When you apply a style, like the preceding .imagecaption style, to an element in your Web page, such as the text that appears under a photo, the HTML code looks something like this:

```
<p class=".imagecaption">This text is formatted with the
        caption style.</p>
```

In this example, the style .imagecaption was applied to the paragraph tag (p>) that was already surrounding the text; but this same style could have been applied to a <div> tag, a <span> tag, or to any other HTML tag that was already associated with the text.

When you redefine a style, like the <h1> tag, you simply use that existing tag to apply the style. In this case, formatting the text with the <h1> tag is all that is needed to apply the defined style to a headline because when a browser reads the new definition for H1 in the style sheet, it formats any text surrounded by <h1> tags with those rules. Thus, the code for a headline formatted with the <h1> tag would look like this, whether or not you redefined the <h1> tag with a CSS rule:

```
<h1>This headline is formatted with the H1 tag.</h1>
```

If you happen to know some CSS already, and you're advanced enough to be able to hand-code CSS or HTML, you'll be interested in a cool feature named code hints, which offer autocomplete options for filling in code. Code hints work only in code view. To use them, simply start typing the code and Dreamweaver's code hints will help fill in the details, such as close tags, for you. You can change code hint options in the preferences dialog box available from Edit ⇨ Preferences (Dreamweaver⇨Preferences on a Mac). You can also display the list of code hints by pressing Ctrl+spacebar (⌘+spacebar on the Mac).

Creating Styles in Dreamweaver

When you start creating and using Cascading Style Sheets, you use one of the most complex and advanced Dreamweaver features. Consequently, creating style sheets takes a little more time to grasp than does applying basic HTML tags and modifying their attributes. Still, Dreamweaver makes defining style sheets much easier than writing them by hand.

To help you get the hang of using Dreamweaver to create style sheets, you find detailed descriptions of all the panels and dialog boxes that define CSS rules later in this chapter in the "Working with the CSS Panel" section.

Defining a new style

Using styles to format text in Dreamweaver is a relatively simple process. First you define a style, and then, as you see in the following exercise, you apply it to an element on the page. This first exercise walks you through the process of creating a class style that can be applied to text. In this example, you'll create a class style called .imagecaption and then, in the next exercise, you'll use it to format the text under a photo.

As you go through the steps to create a new style in Dreamweaver, you may be surprised by the number of options in the many panels and dialog boxes available for creating CSS. As you explore the possibilities, remember that you can leave attributes unspecified if you don't want to use them. For example, if you're creating a style for a headline and you don't specify a font, the browser uses the default page font.

To define a new style, create a new document or open an existing HTML file, and follow these steps:

1. **Choose Text➪CSS Styles➪New.**

   The New CSS Rule dialog box appears, as shown in Figure 5-1.

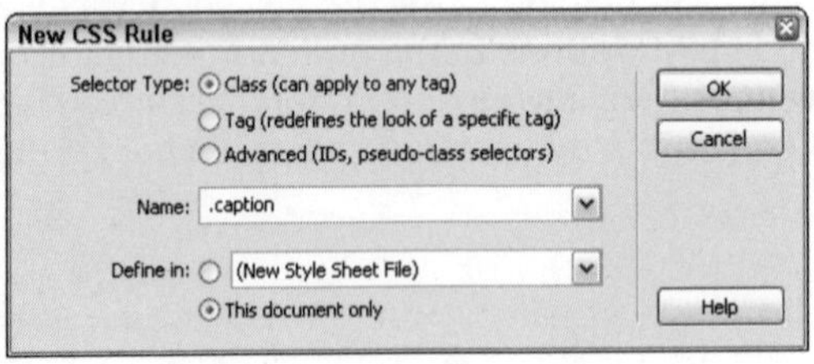

Figure 5-1:
The New
CSS Rule
dialog box.

New CSS Rule

Selector Type: ⦿ Class (can apply to any tag)
○ Tag (redefines the look of a specific tag)
○ Advanced (IDs, pseudo-class selectors)

Name: .caption

Define in: ○ (New Style Sheet File)
⦿ This document only

OK
Cancel
Help

2. **Choose a Selector Type.**

   For this example, choose Class.

   When you create a new style, you must first specify which type of style you are creating. Select the radio button that corresponds with the type of style you want to create. You can choose:

   - **Class:** Creates a class style that can be applied to any element on a page and can be used multiple times on the same page. You can name a class style anything you like, as long as you don't use spaces or punctuation. Class style names must begin with a period (.). If you select the class option and neglect to enter a period at the beginning of the name, Dreamweaver adds one for you. Once created, class styles are available from the Class drop-down list in the Property inspector.

   - **Tag:** Redefines any *existing* HTML tag. In this case, you're creating a new style that will override the existing rules for the selected tag or add additional formatting to an existing tag rule. When you alter an existing tag, you change the way all instances of that HTML tag appear throughout your page, unless you use the Advanced option to redefine a tag within another style.

   - **Advanced:** Creates an ID style, a contextual style, or any other advanced style option. ID styles must begin with a pound sign (#) and can be used only once per page. Contextual styles specify that the display of one style requires the context of the other. (In Chapter 6, you find instructions for creating contextual styles).

3. **In the Name field, select an existing HTML tag from the drop-down list or type a new name for the style.**

   For this example, type **.imagecaption**.

   The name you enter depends on which option you select in Step 2. The drop-down list provides a collection of HTML tags that you can select and redefine if you want to create a tag style. If you want to redefine an existing tag and selected the Tag option, you must select a tag from the drop-down list. If you choose the Class option, you should enter a name that begins with a period and includes no other spaces or special characters. If you choose the Advanced option and want to create an ID style, you should enter # at the beginning of the name.

4. **In the Define In area, select This Document Only to create an internal style sheet.**

   An internal style sheet affects only the current page. When you select this option, the style will be created and added to the top of the HTML page in the `<head>` section. If you choose the first radio button, you can select any existing external style sheet from the drop-down list or create a new style sheet by selecting the radio button and leaving (New Style Sheet File) displayed in the field.

5. **Click OK.**

   The CSS Rule Definition dialog box opens,.

6. **Choose a Category from the left of the CSS Rule Definition dialog box.**

   For this example, choose the Type category, as shown in Figure 5-2. (For a detailed description of each of the categories, refer to the "Comparing CSS Rule Options" section, later in this chapter.)

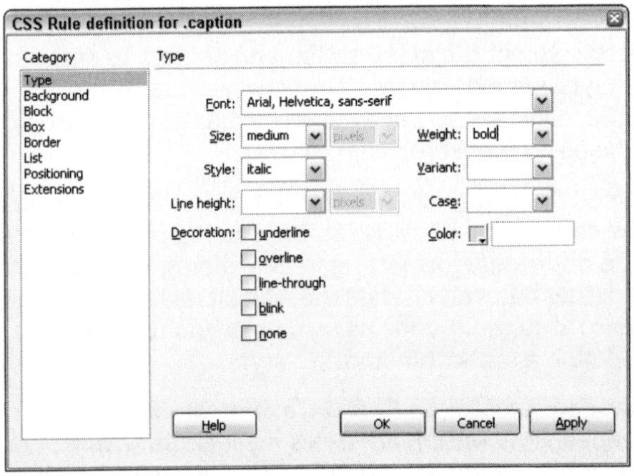

Figure 5-2:
The Type
category of
the CSS
Rule
Definition
dialog box.

7. **In the Font field, choose a Font List collection from the drop-down list or enter the name of a font.**

   For this example, I chose Arial, Helvetica, san serif. To use a font that isn't included, choose the Edit Font List option from the drop-down list and create a new font list using your own fonts.

   Dreamweaver includes predesigned font lists that are designed for optimal display on Web pages. The biggest challenge when it comes to using less common fonts is that a browser can display a font in the text of a page only if the font is installed on the user's computer. If a user doesn't have the font, the browser searches for the next font in the font list. If the user doesn't have any of the fonts specified, the browser's default font is used to display the text. By specifying multiple fonts, you have a better chance that your text appears the way you intend. If you want to use an unusual font for a logo or other special text, your best option is to create a graphic or Flash file and insert that file into the page instead of using formatted text.

8. **In the Size drop-down list, choose the size you want for your caption style.**

   For this example, I chose Medium. You can specify text sizes in pixels, picas, mm, and several other measurements. For an explanation of options, see the sidebar "Understanding CSS size options," later in this chapter.

9. **In the Style drop-down list, choose a font style.**

   In this example, I chose italic.

10. **In the Weight drop-down list, chose a weight.**

    For this example, I chose bold.

11. **Click the color well and choose a color for the style.**

    Sticking to the default color swatches in the color well (the square icon) is certainly the quickest way to choose a color, but you can also create custom colors by clicking the icon that looks like a rainbow-colored globe in the upper-right corner of the color well and selecting a color from the System Color Picker. For this example, I left the color set to the default, which is black in most browsers.

12. **Click OK.**

    As you see in Figure 5-3, the new style is added to the CSS panel. If the style doesn't appear, click the plus sign (+) (or triangle on the Mac) next to the `<style>` tag to reveal the rules in the current style.

When you create a class style, like the .imagecaption style in this example, it is also added to the class drop-down list in the Property inspector, as you will see in the following exercise.

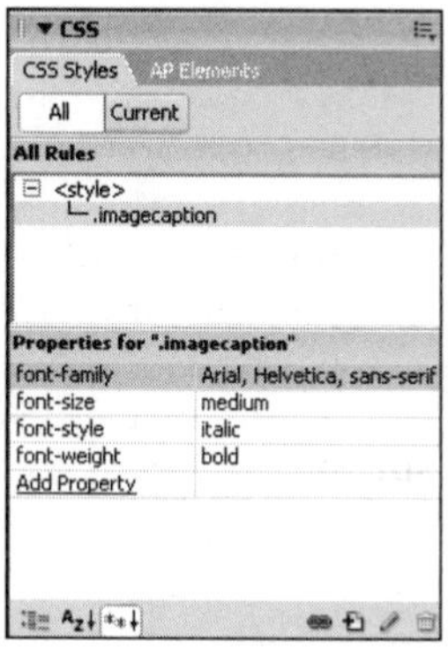

Figure 5-3:
The CSS Styles panel showing a class style named .image caption.

Applying styles in Dreamweaver

Defining custom styles in Dreamweaver is the time-consuming part. Applying them after you define them is the timesaving part. How you apply a style depends on the kind of style you've created. If you've redesigned an existing tag, you simply format the text or other element with that tag and the new style is automatically associated with that tag. If you create a class style, such as the caption style created in the preceding lesson, you can apply it by simply selecting the text or other element you want to affect and choosing the style from the Class field in the Property inspector (as you see in this exercise).

To apply a style in Dreamweaver, follow these steps:

1. **Open an existing document or create a new one and add some text or an image. Highlight the text or other element to which you want to apply a style.**

2. **In the Property inspector, click the Style pop-up menu to reveal the list of styles associated with the document and select the one you want.**

   Notice that Dreamweaver provides a preview of the style by formatting the name in the drop-down list based on the specified options in the style definition. When you choose a style, the selected text or other element automatically changes in the Document window to reflect the application of the style. If Figure 5-4 you see the caption style created in the previous exercise applied to the text below the image in this page.

Figure 5-4:
To apply a class style, select the text or other element in the main workspace and then choose the style from the Style field in the Property inspector.

TIP

Another way to apply a style to a highlighted text selection is by choosing the name of the style from the menu you see when you choose Text⇨CSS Styles or when you right-click (Control+click on the Mac) the selected text and choose the style from the resulting pop-up menu. The method you choose depends on your own preferences. I like to use the Property inspector because it's the only method that allows you to preview the way the style appears before applying it.

Removing styles in Dreamweaver

To remove a style from a selected text block or other element, select the element and choose the None option in the Style drop-down list in the Property inspector. You can also remove a style or any HTML tag using the Tag selector, as shown in Figure 5-5.

Figure 5-5:
You can use the Tag selector at the bottom left of the Dreamweaver workspace to remove a style or tag.

Redefining HTML tags

When you create a class style, as you saw in the preceding section, you create a completely new style with its own unique name and any rules that you defined in the CSS Rule Definition dialog box.

In contrast, when you redefine an existing HTML tag, you begin with all the formatting options associated with that tag — such as the bold settings already included in a header tag. Any options you specify in the CSS Rule Definition dialog box are added to the style of the tag or replace the existing formatting created by the tag if there is a conflict. For example, in the exercise that follows, I redefine the <h1> tag by changing the headline font to Garamond instead of the browser's default font, but I don't need to make bold part of the style definition because it is already included in the style for an <h1> tag.

When you redefine an existing HTML tag, you don't need to apply the style for the formatting to change. You simply apply the HTML tag, and the style definition settings are applied at the same time.

You may ask "Why would I redefine the <h1> tag instead of just creating a new headline style as a class style?" or "What's the best scenario for using each of these options?" In the preceding section, you find out how to create a new style class that you can *selectively* apply to any block of text on your page, but there are times when using an existing HTML tag is better. Heading styles are especially important because they are well recognized on the Web as an indicator of the most important text on a page.

Many search engines place a higher priority on keywords that appear in an <h1> tag than on any other text on the page. As a result, you can improve search engine ranking by placing important text in the <h1> tag. By redefining the style of an <h1> tag you can get the benefits of the <h1> tag and still change the formatting of the text to look however you prefer.

To redefine an HTML tag such as the <h1> tag, follow these steps:

1. **Choose Text⇨CSS Styles⇨New to create a new CSS rule.**

   Alternatively you can right-click (Option-click on a Mac) anywhere in the CSS panel and choose New or you can click the New CSS Rule icon at the bottom right of the CSS panel. The icon looks like a small plus (+) sign.

2. **In the Selector Type area, select the Tag option.**

   Notice that when you select the Tag option, the name of the Name text box at the top changes to Tag.

3. **Click the Tag pop-up menu to reveal a comprehensive list of HTML tags and choose the tag you want from this list (see Figure 5-6).**

   If you're unsure of the meaning of any of these HTML tags, consult the Reference panel, available by choosing Window⇨Reference.

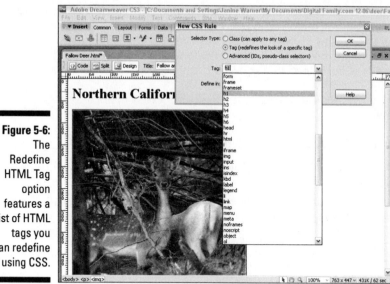

Figure 5-6:
The
Redefine
HTML Tag
option
features a
list of HTML
tags you
can redefine
using CSS.

4. In the Define In box, select the This Document Only option to create an internal style sheet.

If you prefer, you can choose the New Style Sheet File option to create a new external style sheet as you create the style, or you can use the drop-down list to select any existing style sheet already attached to the page and add the new style to it.

5. Click the OK button, and then use the CSS style definition categories to define the new tag style.

For this example, I redefined the <h1> tag to use the Garamond font instead of the default browser font and changed the size to Large.

Be aware that when you redefine an existing HTML tag, any text you have already formatted with that tag changes to reflect the new definition. If you want to be able to use the same tag with different style definitions, you can create contextual styles, as described in Chapter 7.

Changing link styles

If you're like many designers, you probably don't like the underline to appear under all linked text. You'll be happy to discover how easy it is to remove that underline and change the color and other style options for the links in your Web pages.

Although you can change link styles by redefining the anchor tag using the CSS Rule Definition dialog box covered in the previous two exercises, the easiest way to alter link styles for an entire page is to change them in the Page Properties dialog box. When you use this option, Dreamweaver automatically creates all the corresponding styles and adds them to the CSS panel.

To change hyperlink styles using the Page Properties dialog box, follow these steps:

1. **Choose Modify⇨Page Properties.**

   Alternatively, you can click the Page Properties button in the Property inspector. The Page Properties dialog box appears.

2. **Select the Links category on the left of the Page Properties dialog box, as shown in Figure 5-7.**

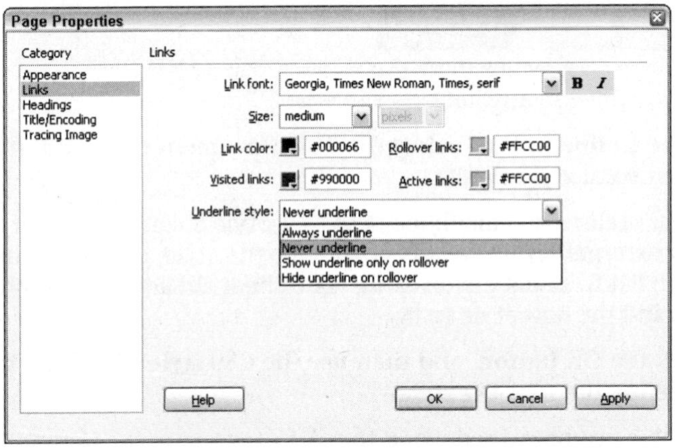

Figure 5-7:
You can use the Links category to change the style definitions for all four hyperlink states.

Page Properties

Category	Links
Appearance	
Links	Link font: Georgia, Times New Roman, Times, serif **B** *I*
Headings	Size: medium pixels
Title/Encoding	Link color: #000066 Rollover links: #FFCC00
Tracing Image	Visited links: #990000 Active links: #FFCC00
	Underline style: Never underline
	Always underline
	Never underline
	Show underline only on rollover
	Hide underline on rollover

Help   OK   Cancel   Apply

3. **Specify a font face and size or leave these fields blank to use the default text settings for the page.**

   If you don't want to change the font size or face of your linked text, it's best to leave these options blank; then if you change the text settings for the page, you won't risk having specified conflicting settings for your links.

4. **Specify colors for each of the hyperlink states by clicking in the corresponding color well and selecting a color from the color dialog box.**

   You can change any link color settings. If you do not specify a link color, the browser will use the default link color. Here's an explanation of each of the four link states:

Link color: The color in which your links appear when the page is first loaded and the linked page has not yet been visited by the browser. The corresponding HTML tag is `<a:link>`.

Visited Links: The color in which your links appear after a browser has already viewed the linked page. The corresponding HTML tag is `<a:visited>`.

Rollover Links: The color a link changes to as a user rolls a cursor over a link. The corresponding HTML tag is `<a:hover>`.

Active Links: The color a link changes to as a user is actively clicking a link. The corresponding HTML tag is `<a:active>`.

5. **In the Underline Style list, select a style.**

   Many designers prefer to remove the underline that automatically appears under linked text by choosing Never Underline, as you see in Figure 5-7.

6. **Click OK.**

   The Page Properties dialog box closes, the style settings are automatically applied to any links on the page, and the new styles are added to the CSS panel.

To view link styles and test links, you have to preview your page in a Web browser. It's good practice to test link settings in a browser when you make changes like the ones in the preceding exercise. Take a look at how your links now appear and how they interact with the user when you trigger the rollover color and other options. Remember that any styles you create in this way affect *all* links on your page unless you specifically apply a different class style to the individual link that overrides the redefined tag style or you create a contextual style using the advanced options covered in Chapter 7.

Creating advanced styles

Dreamweaver lumps a number of style types into the *advanced selector* category. If you want to create ID styles, for example, you'll need to select the Advanced option in the New CSS Rule dialog box. ID styles and contextual styles, which often include ID styles, are covered in detail in Chapter 7.

Managing conflicting styles

Be careful when you apply more than one style to the same element (something that's easier to do than you may realize). This advice holds true for CSS styles as well as style attributes applied via HTML, such as font-styling properties. The styles may conflict, and because browsers aren't consistent in the way in which they display styles, the results can be inconsistent and undesirable.

For the most part, the latest versions of Firefox and Internet Explorer display all attributes applied to any element, even if they're from different style rules, as long as the styles don't conflict. If they do conflict, browsers prioritize styles depending on how the styles have been defined and the order in which they appear. The method for determining this priority is what cascading is all about.

The term *cascading* refers to the way in which multiple styles can apply to — or cascade over — the same element on a page. Because multiple styles can affect the same element, CSS has many rules to help prevent conflicts. These rules determine the priority each style should receive as a browser interprets styles. Style priorities are organized in a hierarchical order and work in a kind of a top-down fashion, similar to the way water cascades over rocks as it flows down a stream.

To help you better understand how styles cascade, consider this example. You can create a style for an entire page by redefining the <body> tag, the HTML tag that surrounds all the content displayed in the main window of a browser. So, for example, you could redefine the <body> tag with a rule that makes the default font for all text on your page Arial. Then you could redefine the <h1> tag with a rule that makes your headlines Garamond. And then the browser would have to determine how to display your headline based on this conflicting information. Should the headline be Arial because the page font is set to Arial in the body style or should it be Garamond because that's the font in the h1 style?

To resolve this kind of conflict, CSS follows a hierarchy that can get rather complicated, but one of the simplest things to remember is that the closer a style is to an element, or the more specifically a style defines an element, the higher that style's priority. So, as you might imagine, the headline style overrides the page style because it more specifically defines the style of the headline than the body style, which applies to the entire page.

CSS selectors also follow a hierarchy. Styles created with ID selectors are given priority over styles created with class, and both are given higher priority than styles that use the Tag selector to redefine existing HTML tags. When styles have the same priority, which is highest comes down to which style most specifically applies to an element.

Another basic guideline is that CSS rules get the highest priority, followed by HTML presentation attributes (for example, align, color, face, and bgcolor), followed by the browser default settings (font type and font size, for example). CSS rules always get the highest priority in any scenario. But within CSS, internal style sheets have priority over external style sheets, and inline styles, which are styles defined within the line of HTML code where the tag appears, get the highest priority.

Editing an existing style

You can change the attributes of any style after you have created it by editing its style definitions. This is where some of the biggest advantages of Cascading Style Sheets come into play. You can make global changes to a page or even to an entire Web site by changing a style you applied to multiple elements through the use of an external style sheet. Be aware, however, that everything you defined with that style changes when you make your edit, which also makes it possible to accidentally change the style of elements on many pages at once.

You can also create new styles by duplicating an existing style and then altering it. Then, you can apply that new style without affecting elements that are already formatted on your pages with the original version of the style.

To edit an existing style, follow these steps:

1. **Open the CSS panel by selecting Window⇨CSS Styles.**

2. **Click to select the name of an existing style in the CSS panel.**

   The corresponding definition settings are displayed in the CSS Properties panel below it.

3. **Click to select any of the settings in the CSS Properties panel and edit them.**

   Alternatively, you can double-click the name of any style in the CSS panel to launch the CSS Rule Definition dialog box and edit the style there.

4. **Click OK to close the CSS Rule Definition dialog box and automatically apply the style changes.**

   If you edit a style definition in the CSS Properties panel, the changes are automatically applied as soon as you press the Return or Enter key or click outside the formatting field in the panel.

Comparing CSS Rule Options

When you choose to make a new style and select one of the three style options in the New CSS Rule dialog box, the CSS Rule Definition dialog box opens. You can define a wide variety of attribute options, which in CSS are referred to as *rules*. This dialog box includes eight categories, each with multiple options you can use to define various rules to apply as part of your CSS declaration. In this section, you find a general overview of the options in each of these eight categories.

You don't have to specify any of the options in any category when you create a new style. In fact, usually you select only a few properties for each style. Any options you leave blank retain the browser's default settings. For example, if you don't specify a text color, the text displays as black or whatever the default color is in the browser.

Some options in the CSS Rule Definition dialog box aren't supported by all current browsers and are included for future compatibility. Some other CSS properties aren't displayed in these dialog boxes because they are not commonly supported.

The Type category

As you see in the exercises earlier in this chapter, the Type category features a collection of options that control the display of text in your pages. With the Type category selected (see Figure 5-8), you have the following formatting options:

- ✔ **Font:** Specifies a font, font family, or series of families. You can add fonts to the list by choosing Edit Font List in the drop-down list.

- ✔ **Size:** Defines the size of the text. You can choose a specific numeric size or a relative size. Use the drop-down arrow to select from a list of options including pixels, picas, and percentages. For more on size options, see the sidebar "Understanding CSS size options."

- ✔ **Style:** Enables you to choose whether the text appears as normal, italic, or oblique. (Italic and oblique are rarely different in a Web browser, so stick with italic unless you have a specific reason not to.)

- ✔ **Line Height:** Enables you to specify the height of a line on which the text is placed (graphic designers usually call it *leading*).

- ✔ **Decoration:** Enables you to specify whether text is underlined, overlined (the line appears over the text rather than under it), or displayed with a strikethrough. You can also choose Blink, which makes the text flash on and off, or None, which removes all decorative effects.

Use the Decoration options sparingly, if at all. Links are automatically underlined, so if you underline text that isn't a link, you risk confusing viewers. Overlined and strikethrough text can be hard to read. Use these options only if they enhance your design. And by all means, resist the blink option; it's distracting and can make the screen difficult to read. (Overline and blink don't appear in the Document window; you must preview your page in a Web browser to see these effects.)

✔ **Weight:** Enables you to control how bold the text appears by using a specific or relative boldness option.

✔ **Variant:** Enables you to select a variation of the font, such as small caps. Unfortunately, this attribute isn't supported by most browsers; for example, if you specify small caps the text may simply display in all caps.

✔ **Case:** Enables you to globally change the case of selected words, making them all uppercase or lowercase or with initial caps.

✔ **Color:** Defines the color of the text. You can use the color well (the square icon) to open a Web-safe color palette in which you can select predefined colors or create custom colors.

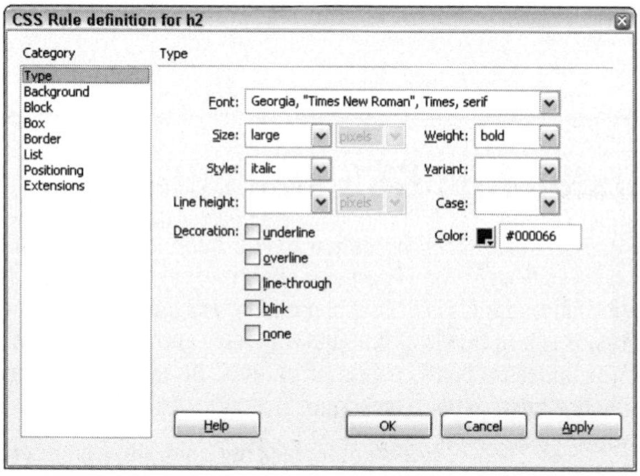

Figure 5-8:
The Type category in the CSS Rule Definition dialog box.

After you select the Type options for your style sheet, click OK to save the settings.

The Background category

The Background category in the CSS Rule Definition dialog box (see Figure 5-9) enables you to specify a background color or image for a style and to control how the background will be displayed on the page. You can use background style settings for any block-level element of your Web page. For example, you can alter the <body> tag and include background settings that apply to the entire page, or you can create a class style with background settings and apply the style to a table cell or a <div> tag. As you see in Chapter 7, you can also alter background settings for ID tags.

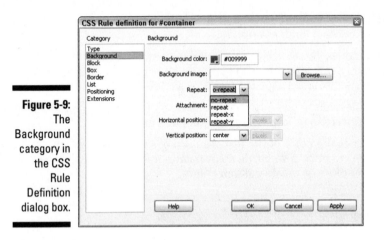

Figure 5-9:
The
Background
category in
the CSS
Rule
Definition
dialog box.

Understanding CSS size options

One of the more confusing aspects of CSS is that there are so many ways to specify sizes for fonts and other elements. A common option is to use point sizes or pixel sizes. If you're familiar with print, this may be the most familiar option, but it's not necessarily the best, especially if you're designing with accessibility in mind.

A better option is to use relative sizes, such as the small, medium, and large sizes. The advantage is that the font size adjusts based on your visitor's settings while maintaining its relative relationship so that text formatted as large will display larger than text formatted as small, no matter what the default font size. This enables you to maintain the hierarchy of text elements on a page, which gives your user control over how large the text is displayed.

Once you've set a font size for the page, you can use percentages to make text larger or smaller,

relative to the base size, by choosing a percentage option. For example, if you set the page font to medium, you can define the text in a caption style as 90% and your caption text would appear at 90% of the default text size for medium.

Another size option is em, which is named after the letter *M*. When you use em as a measurement of size, the size is based on the font size of the letter *M* in the font face and size of the displayed text. The ex option is similar, but it's based on the size of a small *x*. These two sizes are popular for line spacing because the spacing is adjusted relative to the displayed text size. This can get confusing, but em and ex work similarly to percentages and are even better at adapting to different user settings.

You can choose from these options:

- **Background Color:** Specifies the background color of an element such as a table. You can use the color well to open a Web-safe color palette in which you can select predefined colors or create custom colors.

- **Background Image:** Enables you to select a background image as part of the style definition. Click the Browse button to select the image.

- **Repeat:** Determines how and whether the background image tiles across and down the page. In all cases, the image is cropped if it doesn't fit behind the element. The Repeat options are

  - **No Repeat:** The background is displayed once at the beginning of the element.

  - **Repeat:** The background image repeats vertically and horizontally behind the element.

  - **Repeat-x:** The background repeats horizontally, but not vertically, behind the element.

  - **Repeat-y:** The background repeats vertically, but not horizontally, behind the element.

- **Attachment:** This property determines how the background behaves when the page is scrolled.

  - **Fixed:** The background remains glued to one place in the viewing area and does not scroll out of sight even when the Web page is scrolled.

  - **Scroll:** The background scrolls along with the Web page. This is the default behavior for backgrounds.

- **Horizontal Position:** Allows you to align the image left, center, or right, or to set a numeric value to determine the horizontal placement of the background. You can use horizontal positioning only when the background doesn't repeat.

- **Vertical Position:** Allows you to align the image top, center, or bottom, or to set a numeric value to determine the vertical placement of the background. You can use vertical positioning only when the background doesn't repeat.

The Block category

The Block category (see Figure 5-10) defines the spacing and alignment settings for tags and attributes.

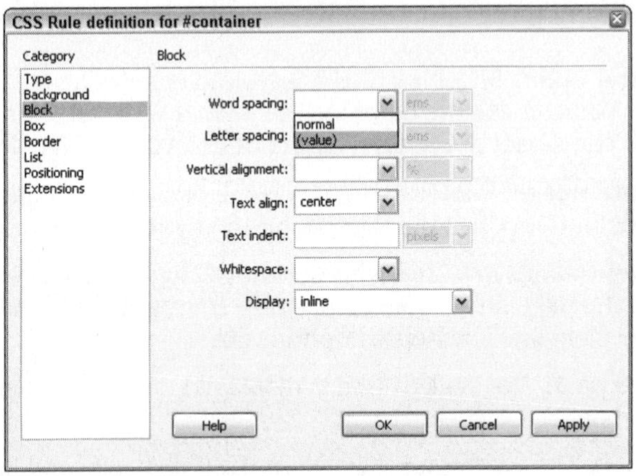

Figure 5-10:
The Block
category in
the CSS
Rule
Definition
dialog box.

You can choose from these options:

- ✓ **Word Spacing:** Defines the amount of white space inserted between words in points, millimeters (mm), centimeters (cm), picas, inches, pixels, ems, and exs.

- ✓ **Letter Spacing:** Defines the amount of white space inserted between letters in points, millimeters (mm), centimeters (cm), picas, inches, pixels, ems, and exs.

- ✓ **Vertical Alignment:** Aligns inline elements such as text and images in relation to the elements that surround them. Note that you may have to preview the page in a browser to see these effects. Your options are baseline, sub, super, top, text-top, middle, bottom, and text-bottom, or you can set a numeric value.

- ✓ **Text Align:** Enables you to left, right, center, or justify your text.

- ✓ **Text Indent:** Specifies how far the first line of text is indented. Negative numbers are allowed if you want the first line to stick out.

- ✓ **Whitespace:** Tells the browser how to handle line breaks and spaces within a block of text. Your options are Normal, Pre (for preformatted), and Nowrap.

- ✓ **Display:** Indicates how to render an element in the browser. You can hide an element by choosing None.

The Box category

The Box category (see Figure 5-11) defines settings for tags and attributes that control the placement and appearance of elements on the page. As you see in Chapter 7, these settings are especially important for creating page layouts using CSS.

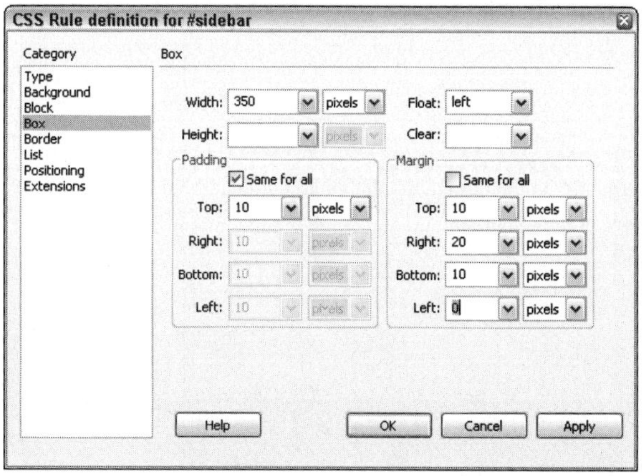

Figure 5-11:
The Box
category in
the CSS
Rule
Definition
dialog box.

You can use the Box category properties to set positioning and spacing issues for box-level tags such as the table, list, and <div> tags:

- **Width, Height:** Enables you to specify a width and height that you can use in styles you apply to images, <div> tags, or any other element that can have its dimensions specified. You can use pixels, points, inches, centimeters, millimeters, picas, ems, exs, or percentages for your measurements.

- **Float:** Enables you to align a boxed element to the left or right so that other elements, such as text, wrap around it.

- **Clear:** Prevents floating content from overlapping an area to the left or right, or to both sides.

- **Padding:** Sets the amount of space around an element to its edge. You can set padding separately for the top, right, bottom, and left. Padding is measured in pixels, points, inches, centimeters, millimeters, picas, ems, exs, and percentages.

- **Margin:** Sets the amount of space between the edge of an element and other elements on the page. You can set the margin separately for the top, right, bottom, and left. Padding is measured in pixels, points, inches, centimeters, millimeters, picas, ems, exs, and percentages.

The Border category

The Border category defines settings — such as width, color, and style — for the borders of box elements on a page. As you see in Figure 5-12, you can specify border settings on all four sides of an element or create borders only on one, two, or three sides of an element. Using this technique, you can use the border settings to create dividing lines and other kinds of borders.

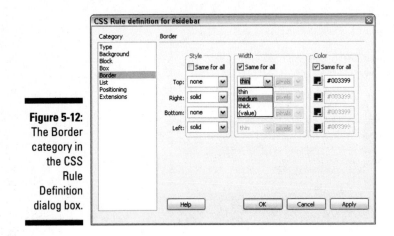

Figure 5-12:
The Border
category in
the CSS
Rule
Definition
dialog box.

The List category

The List category defines settings, such as bullet size and type, for list tags. You can specify whether bullets are disc, circle, square, decimal, lower-roman, upper-roman, upper-alpha, lower-alpha, or none (see Figure 5-13). If you want to use a custom bullet, you can use the Browse button to locate an image to be used as the bullet. You can control the location of the list bullet in relation to the list item. In Chapter 7, you find instructions for redefining the unordered list tag to create rollover effects for links, a popular option for creating navigation rows and other collections, or lists, of links.

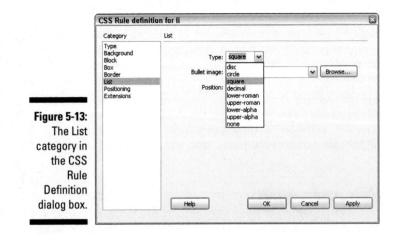

Figure 5-13:
The List
category in
the CSS
Rule
Definition
dialog box.

The Positioning category

The Positioning category (see Figure 5-14) enables you to alter the way elements are positioned on a page. As you see in Chapter 7, positioning can dramatically change the way block-level elements appear in a browser. Block-level elements include table, list, header, paragraph, and `<div>` tags. For example, AP Divs in Dreamweaver are simply `<div>` tags that use absolute positioning to place elements in a specific part of a page.

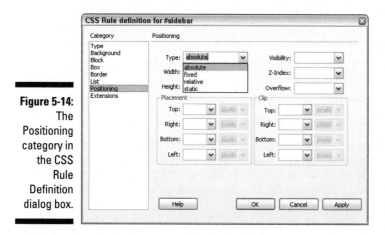

Figure 5-14: The Positioning category in the CSS Rule Definition dialog box.

To understand how positioning works, it's important to know that positioning is always determined relative to something else, such as another element on the page or the browser window. How you set up positioning depends on where your element is on the page and whether the element is inside another element, such as a `<div>` tag. Here are the Positioning options:

✔ **Type:** Enables you to specify the position of an element, such as a `<div>` tag as absolute, relative, fixed, or static:

  • **Absolute:** Uses the top and left coordinates to control the position of an element relative to the upper-left corner of the browser window or the upper-left corner of an element that contains the element. (For example, the positioning of an AP Div contained within another AP Div is based on the position of the first AP Div.)

  • **Fixed:** Positions an element relative to the top-left corner of the browser. The content of an element using fixed positioning will remain constant even if the user scrolls down or across the page.

- **Relative:** Uses a position relative to the point where you insert the element into the page or relative to its container.

- **Static:** By default, all HTML elements that can be positioned are static, which simply places the content at its location within the flow of the document.

✔ **Visibility:** Enables you to control whether the browser displays the element. You can use this feature, combined with a scripting language such as JavaScript, to dynamically change the display of elements. Visibility is used to create a number of effects on a page because you can control when something is seen or not seen. For example, you can cause an element to appear on a page only when a user clicks a button and then make it disappear when the button is clicked again. The options are

- **Inherit:** The element has the visibility of the element in which it is contained. This is the default.

- **Visible:** The element is displayed.

- **Hidden:** The element isn't displayed.

✔ **Width, Height:** Enables you to specify a width and height that you can use in styles you apply to images, AP Divs, or any other element that can have its dimensions specified. You can use pixels, points, inches, centimeters, millimeters, picas, ems, exs, or percentages for your measurements.

✔ **Z-Index:** Controls the position of an element, such as an AP Div, on the Z coordinate, which is how it stacks in relation to other elements on the page. Higher-numbered elements overlap lower-numbered elements.

✔ **Overflow:** Tells the browser how to display the contents of an element if the element doesn't contain the entire contents. (This option does not currently appear in the Dreamweaver Workspace.)

- **Visible:** Forces the element to increase in size to display all its contents. The element expands downward and to the right.

- **Hidden:** Cuts off the contents of the element that don't fit. This option doesn't provide scroll bars.

- **Scroll:** Adds scroll bars to the element regardless of whether the contents exceed the element's size.

- **Auto:** Makes scroll bars appear only when the element's contents exceed its boundaries. (This feature does not currently appear in the Dreamweaver workspace.)

✔ **Placement:** Defines the size and location of an element within its containing element. For example, you can set the right edge of the element to line up with the right edge of the element that contains it. You can use pixels, points, inches, centimeters, millimeters, picas, ems, exs, or percentages for your measurements.

✔ **Clip:** When the content of an element overflows the space allotted and you set the Overflow property to scroll or auto, you can set the clip settings to specify which part of the element is visible by controlling which part of the element is cropped if it doesn't fit in the display area.

The Extensions category

Extensions (see Figure 5-15) include filters and cursor options:

✔ **Pagebreak:** Inserts a point in a page where a printer sees a page break. This option allows you to control the way the document is printed.

✔ **Cursor:** Defines the type of cursor that appears when a user moves the cursor over an element.

✔ **Filter:** Enables you to apply to elements special effects such as drop shadows and motion blurs. These are visible only in Microsoft Internet Explorer.

Figure 5-15:
The Extensions category in the CSS Rule Definition dialog box.

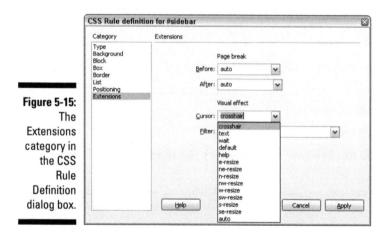

Using External Style Sheets

The first part of this chapter focuses on using CSS only in the context of internal style sheets. Internal style sheet information is stored in the HTML code of the document you're working on and applies to only the current document. If you want to create styles you can share among documents, you need to use external style sheets. External style sheets enable you to create styles you can apply to pages throughout a Web site by storing the style sheet information in a separate text page that can be linked to from any HTML document.

External style sheets (also called *linked style sheets*) are where you can realize the greatest time savings with CSS. You can define styles for common formatting options used throughout an entire site, such as headlines, captions, and even images, which makes applying multiple formatting options to elements fast and easy. Big news- and magazine-type Web sites often use external style sheets because they need to follow a consistent look and feel throughout the sites, even when many people are working on the same site. Tying styles to HTML tags via an external style sheet is a foolproof way of making sure that everyone creating content for your Web site ends up with pages that look the same. Using external style sheets also makes global changes easier because when you change the external style sheet, you globally change every element to which you applied the style throughout the site.

Creating an external style sheet

You create external style sheets almost exactly the same way you create internal style sheets, except that external style sheets need to be saved as separate files. When you use Dreamweaver to create an external style sheet, Dreamweaver automatically links the style sheet to the page you're working on. You can then link it to any other Web page in which you want to apply the style definitions.

To create an external style sheet as you create a new style, follow these steps:

1. **Choose Text⇨CSS Styles⇨New.**

   The New CSS Rule dialog box appears.

2. **Select from the Selector Type category the type of style you want to create.**

   The three options — Class, Tag, and Advanced — are described in detail in the "Understanding style selectors or types" section, earlier in this chapter.

3. **Fill out the Name field or select an option from the Tag or Selector fields, depending on which selector type you chose in Step 2.**

4. **In the Define In area, select (New Style Sheet File).**

   This is how you create an external style sheet instead of an internal style.

5. **Click OK.**

   The Save Style Sheet File As dialog box opens.

6. **Select a location in which to save the style sheet file.**

   Note that you should save the style sheet in the root folder of your Web site and upload it to your Web server when you publish the site. (For more information on the root folder and how to define a site in Dreamweaver, see Chapter 2.)

7. **Name the file and be sure to use a `.css` extension to identify your file as a style sheet.**

   Dreamweaver automatically adds the `.css`; just make sure you don't delete it.

8. **Click Save.**

   The CSS Rule Definition dialog box opens.

9. **Define the new style rule specifying all formatting options you want applied with the new style.**

10. **Click OK to save the new style and close the dialog box.**

    Your new style is saved to your external style sheet and made available to link to any of the files in your Web site.

Linking to an external style sheet

After you set up an external style sheet, you may want to link it to additional Web pages. Begin by opening the page to which you want to attach the style sheet, and then follow these steps:

1. **Choose Window⇨CSS Styles.**

   The CSS panel appears.

2. **Click the Attach Style Sheet icon in the CSS panel (the first button in the lower-right area).**

   The Attach External Style Sheet dialog box appears (shown in Figure 5-16), prompting you to select the location of the external style sheet.

3. **Use the Browse button to locate the CSS file in your site folder.**

   You can also enter a URL if you want to use a remote CSS file located on another Web site, but it is most common to use a style sheet contained within the Web site you are working on. Either way, Dreamweaver automatically sets the link to the style sheet for you, includes the style sheet link code at the top of the HTML file, and applies the styles to the page.

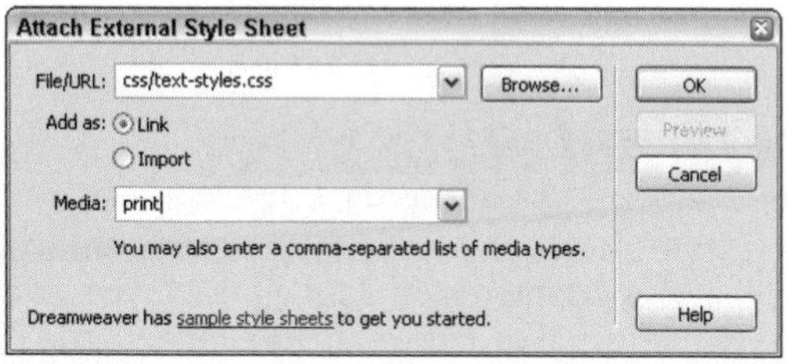

Figure 5-16:
The Attach
External
Style Sheet
dialog box.

Attach External Style Sheet

File/URL: css/text-styles.css Browse... OK

Add as: ⦿ Link   Preview

⦾ Import   Cancel

Media: print

You may also enter a comma-separated list of media types.

Dreamweaver has sample style sheets to get you started. Help

4. **Select the Link or Import option.**

   You can attach a style sheet to an HTML file by linking to it; importing is intended to allow one style sheet to refer to another.

5. **In the Media drop-down list, choose an option.**

   Using the Media list, you can specify the intended use for the style sheet. For example, if you've created a style sheet that formats your page for printing, select the print option on this menu. You can leave this option blank if you are attaching a style sheet to control the way the page will appear in a browser.

6. **Click OK.**

   The dialog box closes, and the external CSS file is automatically linked to the page. Any styles you have defined in the external style sheet appear in the CSS panel under the name of the style sheet, and styles are automatically applied to the page (see Figure 5-17).

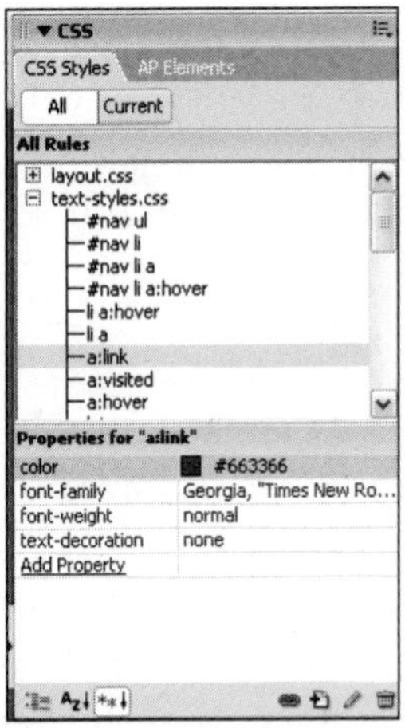

Figure 5-17:
External style sheets linked to the current document appear in the CSS Styles panel.

You can attach multiple style sheets to the same HTML page. For example, you can save all your text styles in one style sheet and all your layout styles in another and attach both to the same document to make all the defined styles available to the page. Similarly, you create different style sheets for different purposes, such as one for printing the file and another for browser display.

Editing an external style sheet

You edit linked external style sheets the same way you edit internal style sheets: by using the CSS Styles panel, which lists all the styles available to a document, whether they're internal or external. You can use the Properties pane, which is located in the bottom portion of the CSS Styles panel, to edit the rules for each style, or you can double-click the name of any style in the CSS Styles panel to launch the CSS Rule Definition dialog box and edit the style there.

Any changes you make to a style in an external style sheet are automatically applied to all files to which the external style sheet is attached (as long as the style sheet exists in the same relative location as the file on the computer or Web server).

If you want to edit a remote CSS file, you should download the file to your hard drive before you open it in Dreamweaver. In Dreamweaver, you open .css files by double-clicking them or choosing File➪Open, both of which open the style sheet in code view. Code view is the only view available for CSS files because they're text files and have no layout components. When you view an external style sheet this way, you can still use the CSS panel to edit any defined styles, even if the style sheet isn't linked to an HTML page. Be sure to save it when you finish editing it!

If you prefer, you can also edit the code by hand directly in code view. Figure 5-18 shows an example of a style sheet opened directly in Dreamweaver. Notice that the CSS Styles panel displays all relevant style information and gives you access to the CSS editing tools.

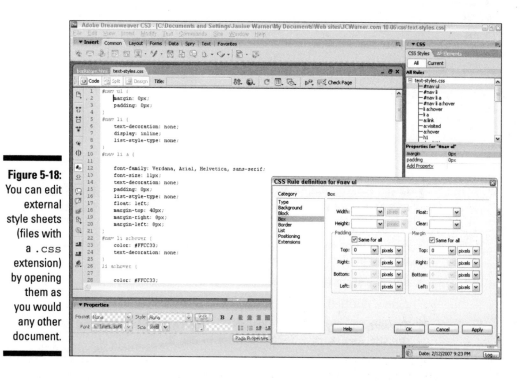

Figure 5-18: You can edit external style sheets (files with a .css extension) by opening them as you would any other document.

When you edit an external style sheet, you must upload it to your server before the style changes can be applied to pages on your live Web site.

Applying ready-made external style sheets

Adobe includes a bunch of sample style sheets for you to use to create new pages in your Web site. These come in the form of external styles sheets that have been created with some popular styles to help you get better acquainted with style sheets and give you a jump-start in designing with them. You can use these styles as is or modify them to suit your needs.

To access the sample style sheets provided by Adobe, follow these steps:

1. **Choose File⇨New.**

   The New Document dialog box opens, as shown in Figure 5-19.

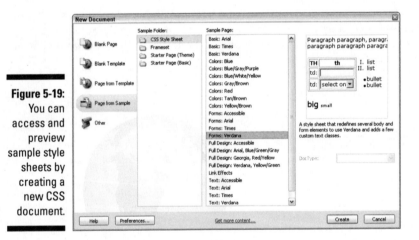

Figure 5-19: You can access and preview sample style sheets by creating a new CSS document.

2. **In the Sample Folder list, select CSS Style Sheet to display the list of CSS files, and then click to select any of the sample styles listed under Sample Page.**

   Notice that a preview of how the style appears is displayed on the right when you click any of the sample styles.

3. **Select a style you like and click Create.**

   A new, untitled style sheet opens in code view.

4. **To save the style sheet, choose File⇨Save (or Save As) and save it in the site directory where you plan to use it.**

If you want to customize your style sheet, you can also modify the rules before saving the file. When you do save a sample file, Dreamweaver saves a copy so that it doesn't overwrite the original sample file.

Appreciating the CSS Styles panel

The CSS Styles panel provides a great place to store, manage, organize, and edit CSS rules. To open the CSS styles panel, choose Window ➪CSS Styles or click the small arrow next to CSS at the top of the panel.

You can also use the CSS Styles panel, shown in Figure 5-20, to organize styles once style sheets are attached. For example, you can move styles from one style sheet to another by clicking to select the name of a style and dragging it over the name of the external style sheet you want to move it to in the CSS Styles panel. You can also use click and drag to change the order of styles within a style sheet and to move styles from an internal style sheet to an external style sheet.

You can also rename styles in the CSS Styles panel, but be aware that renaming a style does not change its corresponding reference in the HTML code of your Web pages. If you change a name in the CSS Styles panel, you must also change the corresponding name in the HTML code of the page or reapply the style with the new name. For example, if you create a style called .imagecaption and apply it to text in your Web page, and then later rename the style to .bigimagecaption in the CSS Styles panel, you need to reapply the style with its new name.

On the left side of the panel, you see the Show Category View, Show List View, and Show Only Set Properties icons (see Figure 5-20). These apply to the Properties panel in both Current and All modes. Here's how to use these:

- ✔ **Show Category View:** In the category view of the Properties view, Dreamweaver displays all the properties available to use for a rule organized by the category to which they belong. For example, all the font properties are grouped into a Font category.

- ✔ **Show List View:** In the list view, Dreamweaver displays all the properties available to use for a rule organized alphabetically.

- ✔ **Show Only Set Properties:** When you define a new rule, you set certain properties; but, of course, you can set many more. In this view, Dreamweaver displays only those properties you defined for this rule.

The second set of icons, on the bottom-right of the CSS Styles panel (see Figure 5-20) are useful no matter what mode the panel is in. From left to right, these icons represent Attach Style Sheet, New CSS Rule, Edit Style, and Delete

CSS Property. The easiest way to start a new style sheet is to create a new style and the style sheet at the same time. To do that, click the New CSS Rule icon (labeled in Figure 5-20).

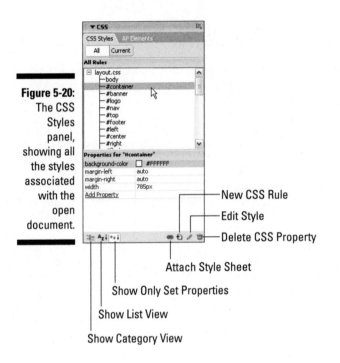

Figure 5-20:
The CSS Styles panel, showing all the styles associated with the open document.

New CSS Rule

Edit Style

Delete CSS Property

Attach Style Sheet

Show Only Set Properties

Show List View

Show Category View

The All mode of the CSS Styles panel

The CSS Styles panel has two modes, accessible by clicking the tabs at the top of the panel. The first tab displays All mode, which opens a list of all defined rules in a document or an attached style sheet or both, whether the styles are internal or contained in an external style sheet. When you are in All mode, you can select a style in the CSS Styles panel and its properties are displayed in the Properties pane in the bottom part of the CSS Styles panel. When a style is selected in All mode, you can add, edit, and delete existing style rules in the Properties pane. (see Figure 5-20).

If you don't see your styles listed in the CSS Styles panel when the All tab is selected, it's probably because you haven't opened the style sheet to see them. To view any defined styles in a style sheet, you need to click the plus sign (the triangle on the Mac) to open the style sheet. You'll find the arrow (or triangle) next to the `<style>` tag if you are using an internal style sheet or next to the style sheet name if you're using an external style sheet attached to the page. (If the CSS Styles panel is blank when you select the All tab at the top, it means no styles are associated with the page.)

Using CSS with templates

Templates, covered in Chapter 9, are a perfect complement to CSS because they enable you to recreate page designs easily and update them automatically when things change. You can use internal or external styles with templates and make automatic updates to any pages created from the template by changing the template design, the styles, or both. Although it may take a little longer to create a page using CSS and templates in the first place, the time you can save by creating new pages from the template and making updates across many pages at once more than makes up for the initial investment.

The Current mode of the CSS Styles panel

When you select the Current tab at the top of the CSS Styles panel, you can view the styles *currently* applied to any selected element on a page as you see in Figure 5-21. Current mode is useful for identifying how styles are applied to a particular element and for troubleshooting when styles conflict.

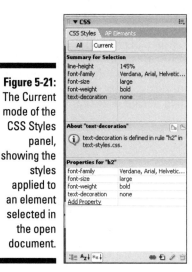

Figure 5-21: The Current mode of the CSS Styles panel, showing the styles applied to an element selected in the open document.

The Current mode has three sections: the Summary for Selection pane, the About pane, and Properties pane. In the Summary for Selection pane, you see the rules currently defined for the selected style. In the Rules pane, you see all the rules that are applied the currently selected element; this pane is exceptionally useful when you have created a complicated layout and are trying to understand how different styles may be affecting the same element. In the Properties pane, you can edit, add, or delete style rules just as you can in All mode.

Using Design Time Style Sheets

After you become savvy about using style sheets, you'll find that working with external style sheets affords the most power because you can link to them from multiple pages in your site rather than having to create a new internal style sheet for each page in your site. You have the added advantage that you can easily alter your styles in just one place if you need to make changes after styles are applied. Even better, you can create multiple external style sheets as part of the design process and use a Dreamweaver feature called design time style sheets to switch between them as you work on your document.

One benefit of the design time style sheets feature is that you can view how different external style sheets affect your page without having to link to them. This feature is a great way to quickly switch between style sheets in a document and explore various what-if scenarios with the style sheets you create before you apply them. You may begin to like this feature because you can play around with and explore the full power of CSS.

After you decide that you like a particular style sheet, you can apply it to your page as you do any other style sheet. (See the section, "Applying Styles in Dreamweaver," earlier in this chapter, for information on applying a style.)

Design time style sheets affect only the appearance of styles in Dreamweaver. Because they're not real links, they show up only at runtime when a Dreamweaver document is open. Design time style sheet info is also stored in a design note file. If you want to preserve your design time style sheet info, be sure that you don't delete the corresponding design note file.

To set up design time style sheets, follow these steps:

1. **Choose Text⇨CSS Styles⇨Design-Time.**

   The Design Time Style Sheets dialog box appears.

2. **To work with a specific style sheet, click the Add Item button (+) above the Show Only at Design Time field.**

   The Select File dialog box appears, and you can select a CSS file. Remember that CSS files usually end with a `.css` extension. You can also add multiple CSS files by clicking the Add button again.

3. **To hide a specific style sheet, click the Add Item button (+) above the Hide at Design Time field and select from the Select File dialog box the style you want to hide.**

4. **To delete a listed style sheet from either category, select the style sheet and click the Remove Item button (-) to delete it.**

Chapter 6

Creating CSS Layouts

. . . .

In This Chapter

▶ Creating page layouts with CSS

▶ Understanding the box model

▶ Comparing browser differences

▶ Creating CSS layouts with `<div>` tags

▶ Using Dreamweaver's AP Divs

▶ Learning more about CSS

. . . .

*I*f you want to create Web designs that can adapt to display well in a variety of browsers, screen sizes, and devices, and you want to ensure that your pages are accessible to everyone who may visit your site now and for years to come, CSS is your best option. In Chapter 5, you find an introduction to CSS and instructions for creating CSS styles for text formatting. In this chapter, you move on to more advanced uses of CSS by creating styles to position and align images, text, and other elements on a Web page.

Brace yourself. You're getting into some of the most complex Web design features Dreamweaver has to offer, but I think you'll find the power and precision of these options well worth the effort. Today, you can create Web page designs in many ways, but using CSS for formatting and layouts is clearly emerging as the best approach as browser support improves and accessibility becomes increasingly important.

Using CSS for Page Layout

The key to understanding the way CSS works when it comes to page layout is to think in terms of designing with a series of infinitely adjustable containers, referred to as the box model. Think of the *box model* this way: First you use HTML tags, such as the `<div>` tag or `<p>` (paragraph) tag to contain your content in a box. Then you use CSS to style each box, using attributes to control the position and alignment of each box, and specify such settings as margins, padding, and borders.

Comparing block and inline elements

As a general rule, HTML tags can be divided into block elements and inline elements. *Block elements*, such as the `<div>` tag, interrupt the flow of the page, creating a box or block around which other page elements align. In HTML, block elements include the paragraph (`<P>`) tag, which creates a line break before and after it is used and doesn't allow anything to appear alongside it. Heading tags, such as `<h1>`, `<h2>`, and `<h3>`, and list tags, such as `<ul>` and `<ol>`, are also block elements. In contrast, *inline elements* flow with text. For example, the `<strong>` and `<em>` tags are inline elements. You can place these elements one after another, and a new line break doesn't appear between each element. They simply flow with the text.

Although you can use any HTML element for page layout, the `<div>` tag is used most often to create page layouts with CSS. `<div>` stands for *div*ision. Think of the `<div>` tag as simply a container to hold other content or to make a division on the page, separating one section of content from another. Unlike other HTML tags, the `<div>` tag has no inherent formatting features. Unless CSS is applied to a `<div>` tag, it can seem invisible on a page. And yet it has a powerful purpose because any content surrounded by an opening and closing `<div>` tag becomes an object (or a box) that can be formatted with CSS. When you create a style that corresponds to a `<div>` tag ID, you can specify properties such as alignment, border, margin, height, and width to control how the `<div>` tag is displayed on the page. In the exercises that follow, you find step-by-step instructions for using `<div>` tags to contain content and CSS to create a layout.

Creating designs using the box model

Although you can create CSS layouts using many approaches, one of the most popular and effective is to create a series of block elements, such as `<div>` tags, assign each element an ID, and then create an ID style to control how the block element, or container, appears on the page.

In Figure 6-1, you see a diagram of a series of block elements with text describing the ID of the `<div>` tag and its corresponding style, which must use the same name. ID style names always begin with a # sign and must match the corresponding ID assigned to an element in the HTML code.

In Figure 6-2, you see how those same containers are arranged using CSS to control the width and positioning of the container `<div>` tag so that it's centered on the page and to position the story and sidebar `<div>` tags side by side. The CSS definitions are also used to specify the font and positioning of text within each `<div>` tag.

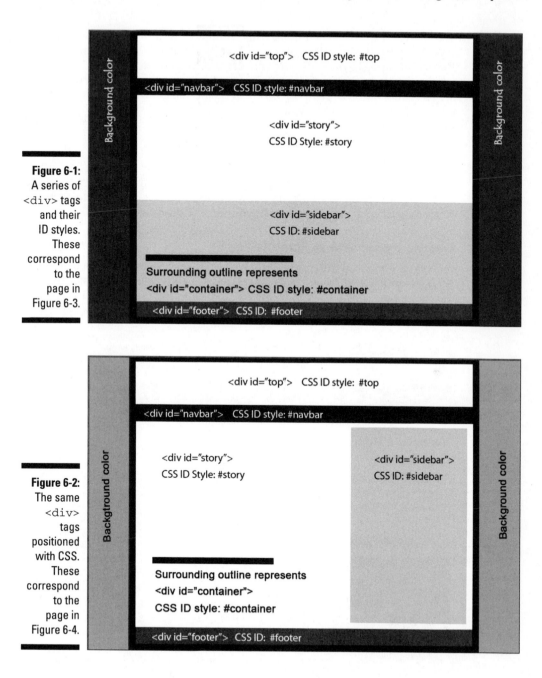

Figure 6-1:
A series of `<div>` tags and their ID styles. These correspond to the page in Figure 6-3.

Figure 6-2:
The same `<div>` tags positioned with CSS. These correspond to the page in Figure 6-4.

When you create a CSS layout like this, you begin by simply creating <div> tags that span the full width of the page and stack one on top of another. With the boxes in place, you can start adding content, such as text and images, into each box. With the content and boxes in place, you can then create the styles that position each of the boxes to create the design you want for the page. (Alternatively, you can create the CSS styles to position the boxes and then add content, but I find it easier to decide how to define the styles after I see the content in place.)

In the exercise that follows, you create a series of <div> tags with IDs and then insert text and images, as you see in Figure 6-3. In the second part of the exercise, you create ID styles that correspond to the IDs assigned to each <div> tag to create the page layout you see in Figure 6-4.

Viewing a page with no styles in Firefox

When you view an HTML page in the Web browser Firefox, you can use the No Style option to remove a style sheet and see the underlying structure of the Web page. This is a helpful way to understand how styles affect HTML documents and to test your own designs to ensure they are well organized.

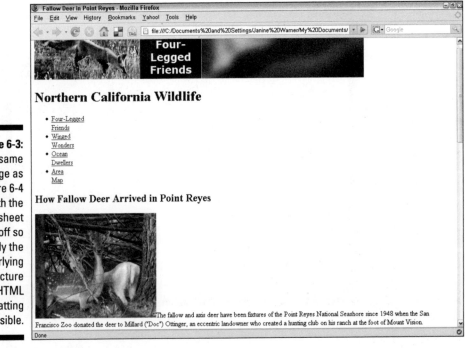

Figure 6-3:
The same page as Figure 6-4 but with the style sheet turned off so that only the underlying structure and HTML formatting are visible.

In Figure 6-3 you see the same page shown in Figure 6-4 but with the style sheet turned off. To turn off a style sheet using Firefox, choose View➪Page Style➪No Style. To reapply a style sheet to the page, choose View➪Page Style➪Basic Page Style. (Note that some Web pages are designed with multiple style sheets so you can choose among different styles using this feature.)

Creating semantic page designs

The page shown in Figures 6-3 and 6-4 was designed semantically, so that even if the styles are not visible or turned off, the content of the page is displayed in order of importance and with formatting that makes logical sense.

For example, with or without the style sheet turned on, the banner is the first thing at the top of the page. Below the banner is a list of links formatted using the <ul>, or unordered list, tag. The unordered list tag is an increasingly common convention for formatting *lists* of links because without CSS it is still clear that the list of links should be grouped together on the page. Using CSS, you can alter the display of the unordered list and link tags to cause links with this kind of formatting to be displayed in a different style, such as the horizontal display you see at the top in Figure 6-4. You find instructions for changing the display of an unordered list in the section, "Styling an Unordered List for Links," later in this chapter.

Figure 6-4: This page was designed using CSS to position the images and <div> tags to create the two-column layout and to wrap text around each image.

Comparing margins and padding

One of the more confusing aspects of the box model when it comes to design is the way margins and padding work. Essentially, padding adds space inside an element, and margins add space outside an element. In Figure 6-5, you see a `<div>` tag with a corresponding ID style that creates the border and places 25 pixels of padding inside the `<div>` tag border and 50 pixels of spacing outside the `<div>` tag border.

Think of padding as a way to add a cushion around the inside of a box so that your content doesn't bump into the sides of your box. Think of margins as a way to add space between boxes so that they don't bump into each other.

Here's the confusing part. If you specify a width for a `<div>` tag (or any other box element), as I have in the example in Figure 6-5, the width is affected by the padding. The ID style controlling the display of the `<div>` tag shown in Figure 6-5 is 350 pixels wide. But when you add padding to a container, the browser adds the padding to the overall width of the container, so the `<div>` tag is 400 pixels wide with the padding.

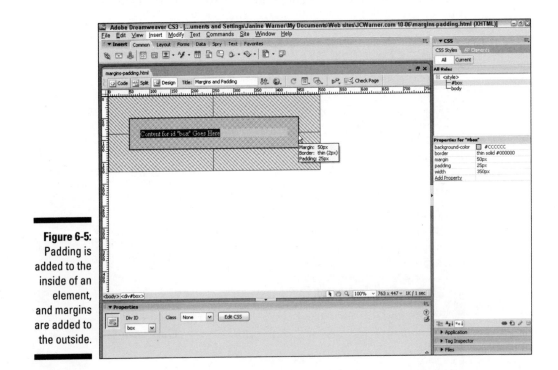

Figure 6-5:
Padding is added to the inside of an element, and margins are added to the outside.

The margins of the <div> tag style are set to 50 pixels, so the <div> tag is positioned 50 pixels from the top and left of the page and with 50 pixels of margin on the right and bottom. This prevents the display of any other element in that space.

The ID style for the <div> tag also includes border settings, which cause the dark border to surround the <div> tag. The thin border adds 2 pixels to the outline of the <div> tag and means the final width of the <div> tag is 404 pixels the 350 pixel width, plus 50 pixels of padding, plus 4 pixels of border. As you see in the exercise that follows, understanding how styles affect the width of elements is especially important when you want to place two containers side by side, such as the story and sidebar <div> tags used in the page design shown in Figure 6-4.

CSS options at a glance

As you create CSS page layouts, you'll be best served by using a combination of CSS selectors including class, tag, and ID selectors. Consider this sidebar a quick reference and handy reminder of how each of these selectors may be used in a Web page. (You find more detailed descriptions of these selectors in Chapter 5.)

Class selectors can be used to create completely new styles. Once you've created a class style, it can be applied to any element and used as many times as you like on the same Web page. For example, you could create a class style called .image-right and use it to align images to the right of other content by applying the style to the image tag like this:

```
<img src="deer.jpg" width="200"
        height="250" alt="Fallow deer"
        class="image-right" />
```

Tag selectors are used to redefine existing HTML tags. Once you create a style for an HTML tag, anytime that tag is used, the attributes in the style are applied. For example, you can redefine the <ul> and <li> tags to change the display of content formatted in an unordered List. You find instructions for doing just that in the section "Styling an Unordered List for Links," later in this chapter.

ID selectors are included in the category of Advanced selector options in Dreamweaver. You can use ID selectors to define elements that are used only once in a Web page. For example, if you create a copyright section at the bottom of a page, you might use an HTML <div> tag as the container for the copyright information and give the <div> tag an ID that corresponds to an ID style that controls the position and formatting of the copyright information. You can use the ID attribute with any tag, but it's commonly used with the <div> tag for positioning and formatting. A <div> tag with an ID style would look like this:

```
<div id="copyright">Copyright 2007</div>
```

Note that the margins of the page are set to 0 with a style that controls the `<body>` tag. Setting page margins to 0 means that any content on the page is aligned to the very top and left of the page instead of being offset by 10 pixels of space, which is the default in most Web browsers and in the Dreamweaver workspace area. You can set the page margins using the Page Properties dialog box by choosing Modify⇨Page Properties, and then entering 0 in each of the Margin fields in the Appearance category, as shown in Figure 6-6.

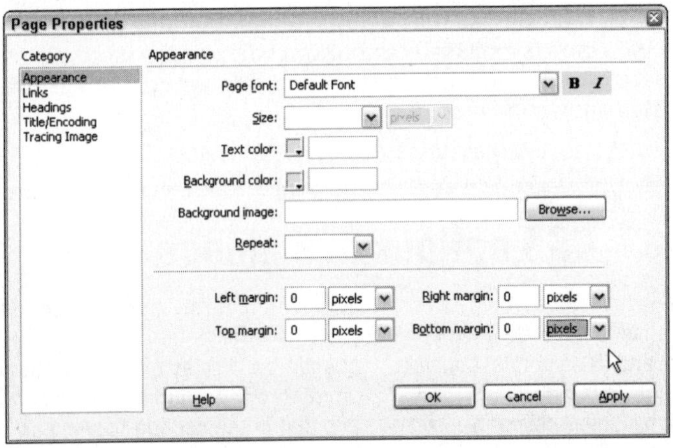

Figure 6-6:
Remove the automatic margins at the top and left of any Web page by setting the margin fields to 0.

Displaying CSS in different browsers

Neither Dreamweaver nor I can show you exactly how your Web pages will look to everyone who may ever view them on the Web because different browsers display Web pages differently, especially older browser versions that do not include standards-compliant support for CSS and many other features.

If you want a consistent appearance on every browser that might ever visit your pages, you have to move on to more advanced CSS training when you're finished with this book and explore the "hacks" that have been developed to get around browser differences. You'll find many books, Web sites, and training videos dedicated to advanced CSS training.

For a list of more advanced CSS training resources online and off, visit `www.DigitalFamily.com/dreamweaver`.

For the purposes of this book, I have designed pages that are consistent in their display on IE 6 and later, Firefox 1.5 and later, and Safari and Firefox on the Mac. I can't cover all the CSS hacks needed to design CSS layouts for every browser in use on the Web today, but the browsers that I targeted with these designs represent the majority of Web browsers. I leave it to you to decide whether to worry about visitors with older browsers and whether to explore more advanced CSS training when you're finished here.

Splitting the view

If you're creating a series of `<div>` tags to position content on a Web page, you may find it easier to keep track of the `<div>` tags if you use Dreamweaver's split view, which enables you to see the code view and design view simultaneously. To split the workspace area, choose View⇨Code and Design or click the Show Code and Design Views button, located just under the Insert bar at the top of the workspace.

As you see in the figure, if you select an image, text, or another element on a page in design view, it is automatically highlighted in code view, a great feature that makes it easier to find your place in the code when you are trying to troubleshoot what's happening behind the scenes.

I like to use split view to keep an eye on the code as I create page designs, especially when I'm inserting `<div>` tags, because it can be hard to keep track of how `<div>` tags are arranged and nested when you're using only design view.

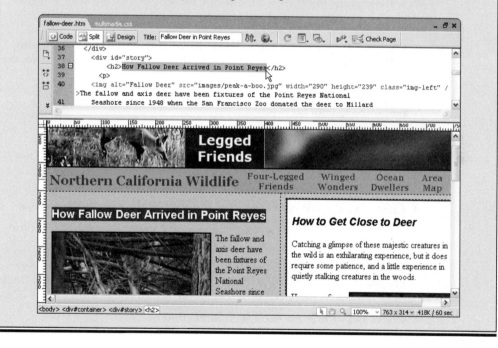

The following exercise walks you through the creation of a two-column CSS layout that displays well in all the latest browsers in use on the Web today.

Creating a CSS Layout

There are many approaches to creating layouts using CSS. You can create fluid layouts that expand and contract to fill the browser window no matter how wide or narrow, and you can create fixed layouts that remain a specified width no matter how wide the browser window. When you create fixed-width designs, such as the one in this exercise, it's good practice to center the design on the Web page so that it appears to float in the middle of the page no matter what the size of the browser window.

The following exercise walks you through the creation of the design shown in Figure 6-4 using a series of <div> tags created within a <div> tag called *container*. The corresponding container style defines the container with a fixed width of 780 pixels. As you see in Step 6, the trick to centering a <div> tag with a style is to set the left and right margins to Auto, which makes the browser display an equal margin on each side of the container and effectively center the <div> tag. This is an important trick because <div> tags and other block-level elements have no center option.

Follow these steps to create a fixed-width, two-column layout with a header and footer area using CSS and <div> tags:

1. **Choose File⇨New and then choose Blank Page from the left column, HTML from the Page Type options in the middle, and <none> from the Layout section.**

   Alternatively, you can use one of the predesigned CSS layouts listed under the Layout section.

2. **Save the page in the root folder of the Web site.**

   It's important to save all the pages of a Web site in the root folder. You find more about defining a Web site and specifying a root folder in Dreamweaver in Chapter 2.

3. **Choose Modify⇨Page Properties and specify the page-wide options.**

   For this example, I set the page margins to 0 and the Background color to a green color.

   Note that when you use the Page Properties dialog box, Dreamweaver creates the corresponding CSS styles for the <body> tag and saves them in an internal style sheet at the top of the HTML document.

4. **Insert <div> tags for each section of content.**

   This step can get a bit tricky, but the goal is simple — to insert a <div> tag for each collection of content that you want to appear on the page. To do so, click the Div button in the Common Insert bar at the top of the page and enter a name in the ID field for each <div> tag. When you click OK, the <div> tag is inserted onto the page and spans across the top of the workspace. The trick is to make sure that you create each <div> in order and that all section <div>s are placed inside the container <div>. I find it easier to ensure this if I have the design area set to Split so that I can see the code while I work, as you see in Figure 6-7.

In this example, I created one <div> tag with the ID container and then placed a series of other <div> tags inside that container. First I inserted a <div> tag and with ID top (for the banner graphic), and then I inserted a <div> tag with the ID navbar for the navigation links. After that, I inserted two more <div> tags, one with the ID story and the other with the ID sidebar, and finally I added a <div> tag with the ID footer.

Depending on the complexity of your design, you may want to further divide a page like this one by creating two main sections of the design, such as top and main. You then insert <div>s for the banner graphic and navigation elements inside the top <div> and the <div>s for the story and sidebar inside the main <div>. The more you divide a page's content, the better you can control the placement of elements as the design gets more complex.

5. **Add content to each <div> tag.**

   Although you can create the corresponding styles as you create the <div>s, I find it easier to get all my <div>s and content in place before I create the styles to position them. You can add content to <div>s as you would add content anywhere else on a page. For this example, I used copy and paste to insert text from a separate Word document and the Insert Image icon in the Common insert bar to add the images.

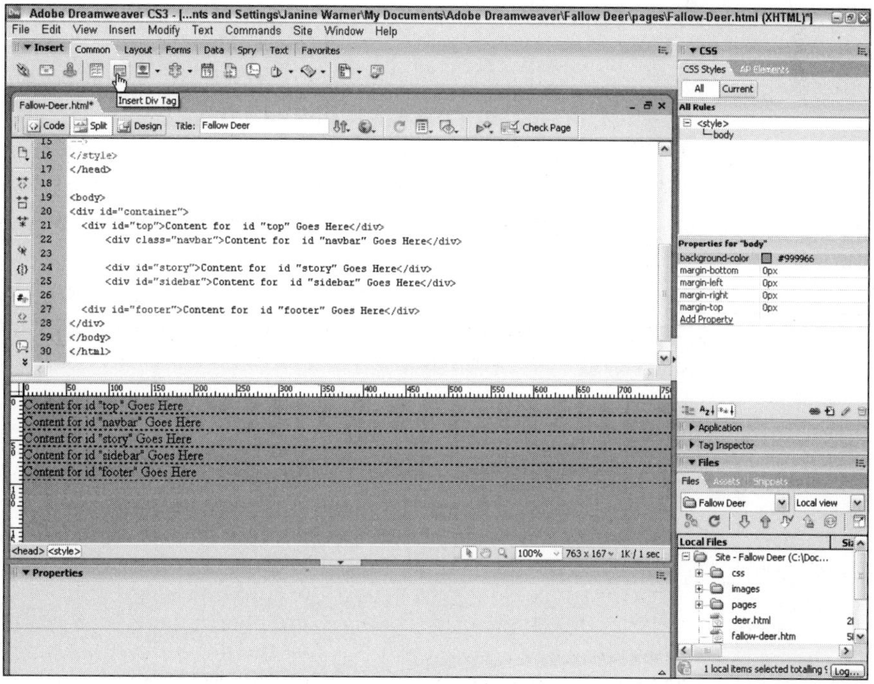

Figure 6-7:
As you insert <div> tags, using split view can help you see the order in which the tags are being added to the page.

6. Create a style for the container `<div>` tag.

To create a new style for the container `<div>`:

a. Choose Text⇨CSS Styles⇨New.

b. Select the Advanced option and enter a name (note, your style names must exactly match your `<div>` names).

Remember that when you create an ID style, the name must begin with a pound sign (#).

c. Specify whether the style should apply to This Document Only or be added to an external style sheet.

For this exercise, I chose This Document Only.

d. Click OK.

e. In the CSS Rule Definition dialog box, specify the formatting settings.

As you see in Figure 6-8, for the container `<div>` tag in this example, I set the width to 780 pixels. And here's the trick to centering a `<div>` tag like this: Set the left and right margins to auto. That way a browser will automatically add an equal amount of margin space to each side of the `<div>` tag, effectively centering it on the page. I also set the background to white to create a white box for the content.

When you create an ID style that matches the name of an ID assigned to a `<div><div>` tag, the style is immediately applied when you click the Apply button. (Make sure the ID and the style name are an exact match. If you add an extra space or mistype a character, this won't work.)

f. Click OK to close the CSS Rule Definition dialog box and save the style.

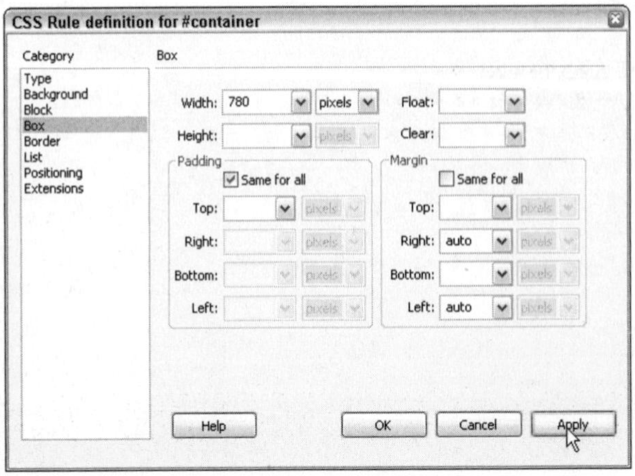

Figure 6-8:
Use the Box settings to define the width, margins, and other settings.

7. Calculate the width and positioning of the two columns in the design.

To ensure that your layout will work with two columns, you need to calculate how wide to define the styles for your story and sidebar `<div>`s. As you see in Figure 6-9, if the style #container is set to 780 pixels wide, and we want the #story style to make its corresponding `<div>` tag 410 pixels with 10 pixels of padding. That means a total width of 430 (10+10 =20 pixels in padding, plus 410). For the sidebar, which is further complicated by the border and margins to separate it from the sides of the container and the story, I set the width to 310 pixels, added 20 pixels of margin (10 on each side), then 16 pixels of padding (8 on each side), and finally 4 pixels of border (2 on each side) for a total width of 350 pixels. Because 350 and 430 equal 780, both `<div>`s fit within the container with room to appear side by side. (Yes, you can use a calculator).

If you don't specify a width for a `<div>` in a multicolumn design, the `<div>` automatically adjusts to fill the remaining space. Using this approach can save you math calculations and help with browser differences. For example, I could have set the width in the #story style to 410 pixels and not specified a width in the #sidebar style, and the page design would look the same in most browsers and be more adaptable to browser differences. Because browsers can display margin and padding settings differently, a column set with a fixed width within another column with a fixed width can overflow the boundaries of the container, causing one column to get bumped below the other. This is a simple example of one way you can design CSS to work more consistently across many browsers.

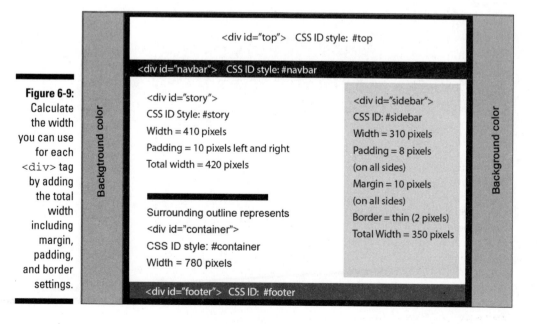

Figure 6-9:
Calculate the width you can use for each `<div>` tag by adding the total width including margin, padding, and border settings.

8. Create styles for the story and sidebar `<div>` tags.

With the calculations complete, you should be ready to define the styles for the two columns by creating ID styles for the story and sidebar. In addition to setting the width, padding, margins, and borders to the values in Step 7, I also used the Float option to align the `<div>`s to the left and right sides of the page as follows:

a. Choose Text⇨CSS Styles⇨New.

b. Select the Advanced option and enter a name.

In this case, I've named the first style #sidebar to match the name of the ID in the sidebar `<div>`.

c. Select the This Document Only option and then click OK.

d. Select the Box category and specify the formatting settings.

As you see in Figure 6-10, for the sidebar `<div>` in this example, I set the width to 310 pixels, the margins to 10, the padding to 8, and the Float to Right. In Figure 6-11 you can see that I also used the Border category to set the border to solid, thin, and a dark red color.

e. Create a second style for the story `<div>` by repeating Steps 8a through 8d.

Name the style #story and define the style with no border, a width of 410, padding 10, and Float set to left.

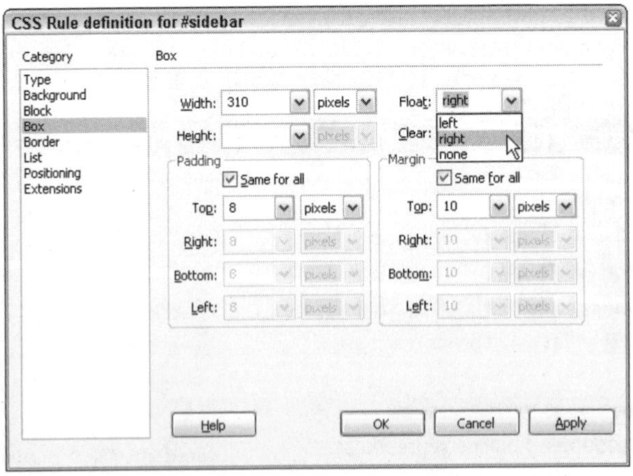

Figure 6-10:
Use the Box settings to define the width, margins, padding, and the float, which causes the element to align to the right or left of the page.

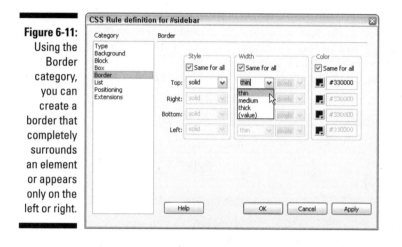

Figure 6-11:
Using the
Border
category,
you can
create a
border that
completely
surrounds
an element
or appears
only on the
left or right.

9. **Create a style for the footer using the Clear option to keep the footer positioned at the bottom of the page layout.**

If you are creating a two-column design like the one in this example, and you use the Float option to align the columns to the left and right, you run the risk that the footer `<div>` at the bottom of the design will be displayed beside one of the columns instead of below them. The reasons for this get complicated, but it has to do with how box elements change when you use the Float setting and take them out of the flow of the page. Because column heights can vary due to text size differences in different browsers and computer platforms, it's almost impossible to create two columns of text on a Web page that will always be displayed with the same height. As a result, it's good practice to use the Clear option to ensure that the footer remains at the bottom of the design no matter what. Using the Clear option also ensures that the container will surround all the content on the page when it is displayed in a browser. Follow these steps to create a style for the footer `<div>`:

   a. **Choose Text➪CSS Styles➪New.**

   b. **Select the Advanced option and enter a name.**

   I named the first style #footer to match the name of the ID in the footer `<div>`.

   c. **Select the This Document Only option.**

   d. **Click OK.**

   d. **Select the Box category and specify the formatting settings you see in Figure 6-12.**

Padding is set to 10 to create space around the text that will be added to the footer, and the Clear field is set to Both to force the footer to *clear* both columns above it to ensure that the footer appears at the very bottom of the page. I also set a background color for the footer to match the color of the navbar style.

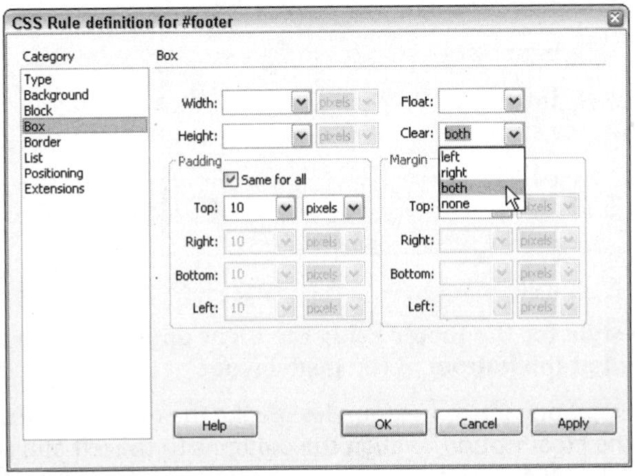

Figure 6-12: Use the Clear field to force an element to appear below any elements floated above it.

10. **Add a few more styles for the images and other elements in the design.**

To achieve the final design you see in Figure 6-4, I created styles to align the images to the right and left so the text would wrap around them, and I created a series of styles for the unordered list and link tags to create a navigation bar with a simple rollover effect using CSS. (You find instructions for creating these kinds of styles in the "Styling an Unordered List for Links" section later in this chapter.)

Creating Styles to Align Images

If you've ever been frustrated by the limitations of V space and H space (that's vertical and horizontal space for those unfamiliar with HTML), you're going to love what CSS can do for your images. In the days when H space and V space were the only options, you could add margins around images, but you had to add the same amount of space to both sides, which almost never looked good.

As you'll see in this exercise, using CSS to create styles for your images enables you to add margin space only where you want it. I routinely create two image styles for every site I work on, one that aligns an image to the right with a little margin space on the left and bottom, and another that aligns images to the left with a little margin space on the right and bottom. This enables me to position images with a margin that keeps them from bumping into text and other elements on the page, while still keeping their alignment flush with the side of the page or column.

To create images styles that use floats and margins, follow these steps:

1. **Open an existing page or create one.**

2. **Insert images into your page using Dreamweaver's standard insert image features.**

   You can choose Insert➪Image and then select the image you want to insert, or click the image icon in the Common Insert bar at the top of the screen to choose the image you want to insert.

3. **Create a new style to align images to the right by choosing Text➪CSS Styles➪New.**

   The New CSS Rule dialog box opens.

4. **Select the Class option.**

   Class styles are ideal for image styles like the one I'm creating in this example because they can be used as many times as you want on each page and can be applied to images as well as other elements.

5. **In the Name field, enter a name for your style.**

   I called the style *.image-right*. Note that all class styles must begin with a period. If you don't type one yourself, Dreamweaver will add a period to the beginning of the style name when you create a class style.

6. **Specify whether the style should apply only to this document or should be added to an external style sheet:**

   - To apply the style to only this document, select the This Document Only option and then click OK.

   - To add the style to an existing external style sheet, select Define In, select the style sheet from the drop-down list, and then click OK.

   - To add the style to a new external style sheet as you create a new style, select Define In and then click OK. Then in the Save Style Sheet File dialog box, enter a name for the external style sheet and click Save.

   The CSS Rule Definition dialog box opens.

   One of the advantages of saving an image style like this in an external style sheet is that you can attach the same external style sheet to any page in your Web site and use the same style throughout your site.

7. **Select the Box category.**

   The Box category options are displayed.

8. **Click the drop-down arrow next to Float and select Right, as shown in Figure 6-13.**

   This is what will cause an image to float to the right when the new CSS style is applied to an image.

9. **Deselect the Same for All option below Margin and set only the Left and Bottom Margins.**

   When I align an image to the right, I generally like to include 8 to 10 pixels of margin on the left to create a space between the image and the text that will wrap around the image when it is aligned right. I also like to include 8 to 10 pixels of margin on the bottom. You should enter a margin value that works best for your design.

10. **Click OK to save the new style.**

11. **Create a style to align images to the left.**

    Repeat Steps 3 through 10, naming the style *.image-left*. In the Box category, set the Float to left and enter a value for only the right and bottom margins.

To apply an image style to an image on a Web page, click to select the image and then select the image style in the Class field in the Property inspector, as shown in Figure 6-14.

When you apply a class style to an image, the effects of the style are displayed in the workspace. As you see in the example shown in Figure 6-14, applying the image-right style to the selected image caused the image to align to the right side of the page, made the text to wrap up beside it on the left, and created an 8-pixel margin between the image and the text.

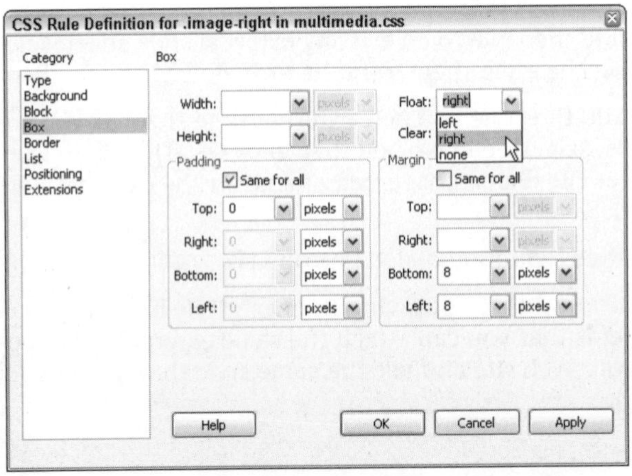

Figure 6-13: Use the Box category to set margins and floats for image styles.

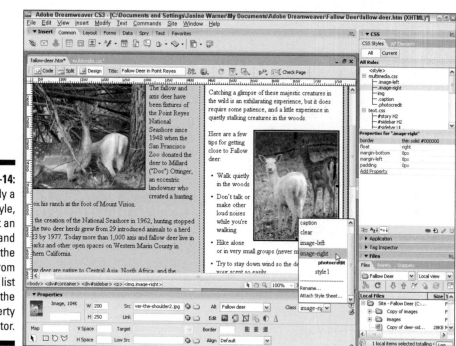

Figure 6-14:
To apply a
class style,
select an
image and
choose the
style from
the Class list
in the
Property
inspector.

If you want to add a border to your images, you can define the border as part of the same styles you use to align images left and right. In the example shown in Figure 6-14, the .image-right style includes a border set to solid, thin, and black.

Styling an Unordered List for Links

Here's a great CSS trick for turning a bulleted list into a navigation bar with a simple rollover effect. Using a bulleted list for navigation bars is a well-accepted convention for Web sites that meet current accessibility standards. A bulleted list is a logical choice for navigation elements because even if the style is removed, the links still stand out from the rest of the elements on the page and are clearly grouped together.

Thanks to CSS, you can gain the benefits of styling a list of links with the unordered list tag and still format your links with any style you choose so that you don't have to keep those boring bullets and can align your links horizontally or vertically. Using CSS instead of images to create a rollover effect helps your page load faster, too.

Creating contextual styles

When you redefine tags, such as the unordered list and link tags, the new style applies to all uses of that tag within a page unless you redefine the tags as contextual styles by including the name of their container as part of the style name.

For example, in the exercise in the "Styling an Unordered List for Links" section, instead of creating a new tag style with just the name of the `<ul>` tag, I could have created a new tag style called *#navbar ul* to redefine the `<ul>` tag only when it is contained within a `<div>` tag with an ID of navbar (see the figure).

When you create advanced styles like this, you use the name of the container followed by the tag name separated by a single space. In this example, I could have also created styles for the `<li>` and `<link>` tags in the same way, creating styles with names like #navbar li, #navbar a:link, and #navbar a:hover.

New CSS Rule	
Selector Type: ○ Class (can apply to any tag)	OK
○ Tag (redefines the look of a specific tag)	Cancel
⊙ Advanced (IDs, pseudo-class selectors)	
Selector: #navbar ul	
Define in: ⊙ text.css	
○ This document only	Help

To create a navigation bar using CSS to redefine the unordered list and link tags, follow these steps:

1. **Place your cursor in the HTML page where you want your navigation bar to appear and then click the Div button in the Common Insert bar at the top of the page to insert a `<div>` tag.**

2. **In the Insert Div dialog box, enter a name in the ID field.**

   You can name the ID for the `<div>` tag anything you like as long as you don't use spaces or special characters. In this example, I named the `<div>` tag *navbar*. (Note: ID styles are recommended for positioning `<div>` tag like this one for a navigation bar).

3. **Specify whether the style should apply only to this document or should be added to an external style sheet:**

   - To apply the style to only this document, select the This Document Only option and then click OK.

   - To add the style to an existing external style sheet, select Define In, select the style sheet from the drop-down list, and then click OK.

- To add the style to a new external style sheet as you create a new style, select Define In and then click OK. Then in the Save Style Sheet File dialog box, enter a name for the external style sheet and click Save.

The CSS Rule Definition dialog box opens.

4. **Select the Box category and specify a height for the navigation bar `<div>` tag.**

   I set the height to 20 pixels. You can also define a width. In this example, the width is already controlled by the style for the container `<div>` tag, so I left the width blank for the navbar `<div>` tag.

5. **Select the Background category and choose a background color for the navbar `<div>` tag.**

   If you don't specify a color, the color of the navbar `<div>` tag will be determined by the color of any `<div>` tag that contains it or by the specified page color. In this example, I've selected a golden color to set the navbar apart from the rest of the design.

6. **Select the Type category and specify the text options.**

   I set the font face to Geneva, the size to Small, and the text to a dark brown color.

7. **Click OK.**

   The `<div>` tag with the ID set to navbar automatically changes to reflect the settings in the corresponding #navbar ID style.

8. **Insert the text for each of the links into the navbar `<div>` area.**

   Make sure to separate each line of text with a Return (so that the text is formatted with a `<p>` tag in the code).

9. **To format the text as an unordered list, click and drag to select all the text in the navbar `<div>` and then click the Unordered List icon in the Property inspector.**

   If you have not redefined the unordered list tag already, the text will change to the default settings of an unordered list, removing the space between each line and adding bullets.

10. **Set links from each text section just as you would link any other text block or image.**

    You find detailed instructions for setting links in Chapter 2, but the simplest way is to first select the text and then click the Link icon in the Common Insert bar at the top of the screen. In the Hyperlink dialog box, enter the URL you want the text to link to or use the small folder icon to the right of the link field to locate the file you want to link to.

11. **Create a new style to redefine the unordered list tag by following these steps:**

    a. **Choose Text⇨CSS Styles⇨New.**

    b. **Under Selector Type, choose Tag.**

    c. **In the Tag field, enter ul or click the arrow and select ul from the drop-down list of HTML tags, as shown in Figure 6-15. Then click OK.**

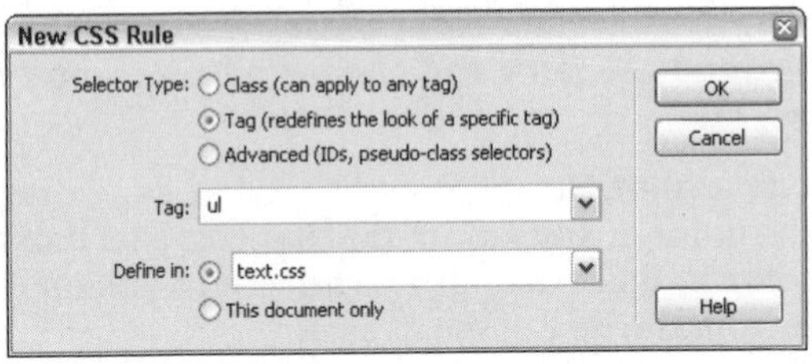

Figure 6-15:
You can
create a
style to
redefine any
existing
HTML tag.

New CSS Rule

Selector Type: ○ Class (can apply to any tag)
⊙ Tag (redefines the look of a specific tag)
○ Advanced (IDs, pseudo-class selectors)

Tag: ul

Define in: ⊙ text.css
○ This document only

OK   Cancel   Help

    d. **In the CSS Rule Definition dialog box, choose the Box category and set Margins and Padding to 0 with the Same for All box checked for both to remove the margins and padding included in the UL HTML tag.**

12. **Create a new style to redefine the list item tag by following these steps:**

    a. **Choose Text⇨CSS Styles⇨New.**

    b. **Under Selector Type, choose Tag.**

    c. **In the Tag field, enter li or select li in the drop-down list of HTML tags. Then click OK.**

    d. **In the CSS Rule Definition dialog box, select the Block category and set Display to inline (see Figure 6-16).**

    This changes the style of the li tag from vertical to horizontal.

    e. **Select the List category and set Type to none to remove the bullet.**

    f. **Select the Box category and set Margins left and right to 10 pixels.**

    This separates the list items from one another in the horizontal list. You can change the setting to any measurement to create the amount of space between links that best fits your design.

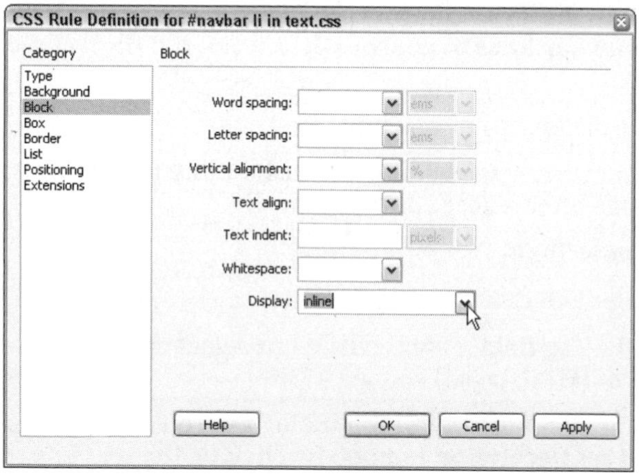

CSS Rule Definition for #navbar li in text.css

Category   Block

Type
Background
Block
Box
Border
List
Positioning
Extensions

Word spacing: ___ ems

Letter spacing: ___ ems

Vertical alignment: ___ %

Text align: ___

Text indent: ___ pixels

Whitespace: ___

Display: inline

Help   OK   Cancel   Apply

Figure 6-16: Setting Display to inline displays an unordered list as a horizontal list instead of a vertical list.

13. **Create a new style to redefine the link tag by following these steps:**

    a. **Choose Text➪CSS Styles➪New.**

    b. **Under Selector Type, choose Tag.**

    c. **In the Tag field, enter** a:link **or select a:link in the drop-down list of HTML tags. Then click OK.**

    d. **In the CSS Rule Definition dialog box, select the Type category and set Decoration to none by clicking the text box.**

    (This removes the underline from linked text.)

    e. **Still in the Type category, change the text color to the color you want your links to appear when they are first loaded on a page.**

    I set the text color to a dark brown.

14. **Create a new style to redefine the hover link tag so that the link color will change when a user rolls a cursor over the link:**

    a. **Choose Text➪CSS Styles➪New.**

    b. **Under Selector Type, choose Tag.**

    c. **In the Tag field, enter** a:hover **or select a:link in the drop-down list of HTML tags. Then click OK.**

    d. **In the CSS Rule Definition dialog box, select the Type category and set Decoration to none by clicking the text box.**

e. **Still in the Type category, change the text color to the color you want your links to appear when users roll their cursors over the link.**

I set the text color to a bright red color.

15. **Create a new style to redefine the visited link tag so that the link color will change after a user clicks a link:**

   a. **Choose Text⇨CSS Styles⇨New.**

   b. **Under Selector Type, choose Tag.**

   c. **In the Tag field, enter** a:visited **or select a:link in the drop-down list of HTML tags. Then click OK.**

   d. **In the CSS Rule Definition dialog box, choose the Type category and set Decoration to none by clicking the text box.**

   e. **Still in the Type category, change the text color to the color you want your links to appear when users roll their cursors over the link.**

   I set the text color to a light gray color.

16. **Preview the page in a browser to see the effect of the link styles.**

Working with AP Divs

AP Divs, which were called *layers* in Dreamweaver 8, permit precise positioning of elements on an HTML page. Think of an AP Div as a container for other elements, such as images, text, tables, and even other layers. You can put this container anywhere on an HTML page and even stack these containers on top of each other.

Using AP Divs, you can position text blocks and images exactly where you want them on a page by specifying the distance of the AP Div from the top and left sides of a page or from another <div> tag. Using AP Divs you can also layer, or stack, elements on top of each other. With AP Divs, a positioning option called the Z index adds this capability, which enables you to create separate layers with text, images, and other elements.

Because an AP Div is a container, you can manipulate everything in it as a unit. For example, you can move one AP Div so that it overlaps another. You can even make AP Divs invisible and use JavaScript or another scripting language to change visibility dynamically. Dreamweaver's Show Hide behavior can be used to create this level of interactivity. (Dreamweaver's behaviors are covered in Chapter 11.)

Creating AP Divs

To create an AP Div, follow these steps:

1. **Choose Insert⇨Layout Objects⇨AP Div.**

   A box representing an empty AP Div appears at the top of the page out-lined in blue. Alternatively, you can click the Draw AP Div button in the Layout Insert bar and then click and drag to create a new AP Div any-where in the work area (see Figure 6-17).

2. **Click anywhere along the outline of the AP Div to select it.**

   When you hold the mouse over the outline of the AP Div, the cursor turns to a four-pointed arrow (or a hand on the Macintosh). You also see eight tiny, square handles around the perimeter of the box.

3. **Click and drag any of the handles to resize the AP Div.**

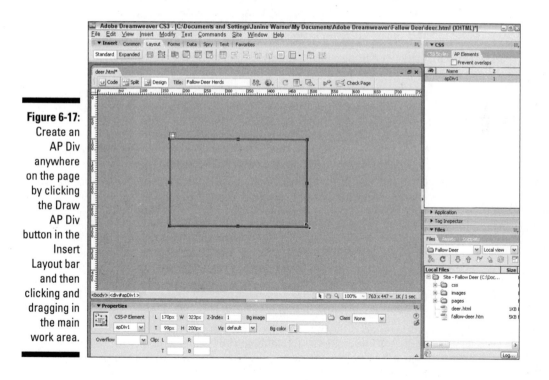

Figure 6-17:
Create an
AP Div
anywhere
on the page
by clicking
the Draw
AP Div
button in the
Insert
Layout bar
and then
clicking and
dragging in
the main
work area.

Adding elements, resizing, and repositioning layers

To make an AP Div useful, you have to put something inside it. You can place pretty much anything within an AP Div that you can place in a document. To add images or text to an AP Div, follow these steps:

1. **Click to insert your cursor inside the AP Div.**

   A blinking cursor appears inside the AP Div box.

2. **Choose Insert⇨Image.**

   The Select Image Source dialog box appears.

3. **Click the filename of the image you want to insert, and then click OK.**

   The Image Tag Accessibility Attributes dialog box opens.

4. **Fill in the Alternate text and Long description fields, and then click OK.**

   The image appears inside the AP Div.

5. **Select the image and use the Property inspector to make any formatting changes to it.**

   Formatting images inside AP Divs works the same as it does anywhere else on an HTML page. For example, you can use the Align Center icon to center the image within the AP Div.

6. **Click inside the AP Div again to insert your cursor and enter some text (see Figure 6-18).**

7. **Click the tab that appears in the upper-left area of the AP Div or anywhere along the border to select the AP Div.**

   You know that you have successfully selected an AP Div when you see the selection *handles,* the little black squares that appear at the corners and in the middle of each side.

8. **Click any handle and drag to resize the AP Div.**

   As a general rule, always size an AP Div so that its contents *just* fit within its boundaries. Positioning the AP on the page is then easier.

   Rather than dragging to resize, you can type exact measurements in the width (W) and height (H) fields in the Property inspector (as shown in Figure 16-19). The Property inspector displays these options only when the AP Div is selected.

Figure 6-18:
You can insert images, text, and other elements inside an AP Div, just as you'd insert an element anywhere else in a Web page.

AP Divs can be problematic when you're working with text because text size can change in Web pages when displayed on different computer platforms, and users can change the text size in their browsers. If you've created AP Divs that are sized to fit only around the text in the size it appears on your computer, the layout can change dramatically when the page is displayed on another computer. For example, if the text size is larger, the text can get cut off or overlap other elements on the page. The best way to avoid this problem is to leave the height unspecified so that the AP Div can adjust to fit the content and to make sure nothing is positioned under the AP Div in the layout that is likely to get hidden if the text overlaps the AP Div.

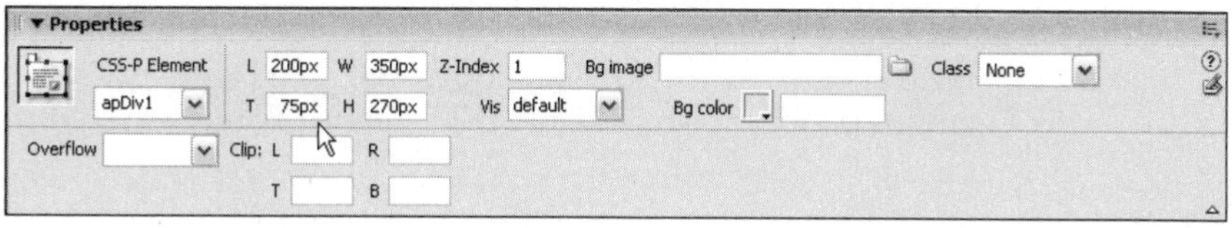

Figure 6-19:
Change the height and width of an AP Div in the Property inspector.

9. **To move an AP Div, click and drag the little tab (which appears in the upper-left area of the AP Div when it's selected).**

Because AP Divs use exact (or *absolute*) positioning, you can move them to any precise location on a page, and they will always appear in that exact position in relation to the left and top of a browser window.

The Property inspector displays the AP Div coordinates in relation to the left and top of a browser window when the AP Div is selected: L (for left), T (for top). As you see in Figure 6-19, the AP Div in this example is exactly 200 pixels from the left side of the browser window and 75 pixels from the top. In addition to using the click-and-drag method to move a layer, you can change a layer's position by entering a number in the position boxes: L (number of pixels from the left edge of the page) and T (number of pixels from the top of the page).

10. **Name your AP Div by typing a name in the AP Div ID text box in the upper-left corner of the Property inspector.**

When you create a new AP Div, Dreamweaver automatically names your AP Div for you, starting with apDiv1, apDiv2, and so on. I find it easier to keep track of AP Divs when I change the name to something more descriptive, especially if I'm working with lots of AP Divs on a page.

You must select the AP Div in the main work area first for its properties to appear in the Property inspector, where you can rename the AP Div and change the height, width, left, top, and other settings.

Stacking and changing visibility of AP Divs

A powerful feature of AP Divs is their maneuverability: You can stack them on top of each other and make them visible or invisible. To stack AP Divs, simply drag one AP Div on top of another. Unlike other elements in a Web page, AP Divs give you complete layout control by including the capability to overlap one another. And you can use AP Divs to position and layer any element on a page. For example, to overlap images, simply place each image in a separate AP Div and then move one AP Divs so that it overlaps the other. To let you control which AP Div is on top, Dreamweaver provides two ways of changing the stacking order using the Z index. You can change the Z index from the Property inspector or the AP Elements panel (see Figure 6-20). To open the AP Elements panel shown in Figure 6-20, choose Window➪AP Elements.

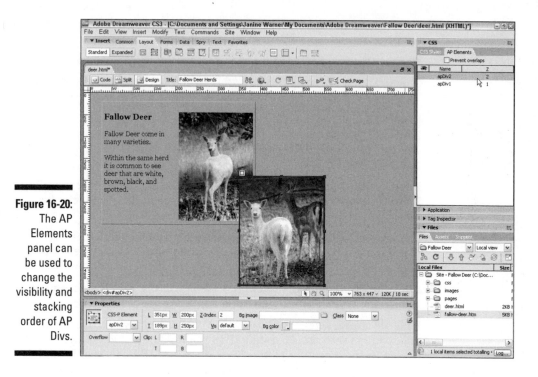

Figure 16-20:
The AP
Elements
panel can
be used to
change the
visibility and
stacking
order of AP
Divs.

To change the stacking order and visibility of AP Divs, follow these steps:

1. **Open a page that has two or more layers on it, such as the deer.html page shown in Figure 16-21.**

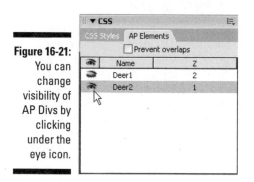

Figure 16-21:
You can
change
visibility of
AP Divs by
clicking
under the
eye icon.

2. **Select an AP Div by clicking anywhere on the border outline of the AP Div.**

3. **Choose Window⇨AP Elements to open the AP Elements panel.**

   The AP Elements panel lists any AP Divs that have been inserted into a Web page.

   If you're familiar with layers in Adobe Photoshop or Macromedia Fireworks, you may find some similarities here, such as the eye icon to control visibility and the capability to drag AP Divs around in the panel to change their order.

4. **Reorder the stacking of the AP Divs by changing their corresponding Z Index numbers in the Property inspector or in the AP Elements panel.**

   The lowest number is the bottommost layer. The highest number is the topmost layer. To change the stacking order, simply click to select the number under the Z index field and enter a higher or lower number.

5. **Click the eye icon to the left of any AP Div in the AP Elements panel to turn the layer visibility on or off.**

   If no eye appears, the visibility is set to the default, which usually means *on*, except in the case of nested AP Divs. (You find out about nested AP Divs in the next section.) If the eye is open, the AP Div is visible on the screen and in the browser. If the eye is closed, the layer is invisible.

   If you want to prevent any of your AP Divs from overlapping, select the Prevent Overlaps check box in the AP Elements panel.

Nesting AP Divs: One happy family

Another way to position AP Divs on a page is by nesting them. A *nested AP Div* is essentially an AP Div contained within another AP Div in a kind of parent-child relationship. The child AP Div uses the upper-left corner of the parent AP Div, rather than the upper-left corner of the browser window, as its orientation point for positioning. Even if the AP Divs are on different areas of the page, they still retain this parent-child relationship. When you move the parent AP Div around on the page, the nested AP Div moves along with it. You can also think of this scenario as an owner walking his or her dog on a leash — where the owner goes, the dog has to follow, even though the dog can still move independently of its owner within the confines of the length of the leash.

If you were to nest an AP Div inside another that is already nested inside a third AP Div, the newly nested AP Div would be both a parent and a child. The new AP Div would then use the upper-left corner of its parent as its orientation point. The first AP Div in the nested chain still retains control over all the child AP Divs, so they all move when the parent moves.

Nested AP Divs offer a great way to keep chunks of your layout working together as you move them around the page. Rather than trying to keep track of loads of different AP Divs and moving each one individually, you can group them into more easily manageable *family units*. Furthermore, you can make an entire family visible or invisible by clicking the eye icon of the parent AP Div in the AP Elements panel. If the child AP Div's visibility has been set to the default (no eye icon in the AP Elements panel), it inherits the visibility of its parent layer.

To create a nested AP Div, follow these steps:

1. **Choose Insert⇨Layout Objects⇨AP Div or click the AP Div icon in the Layout Insert bar and click and drag to create the AP Div anywhere on the page.**

   A box representing the AP Div appears at the top of the page, and Dreamweaver automatically gives it a name such as apDiv1.

2. **Place the cursor inside the first AP Div, and choose Insert⇨Layout Objects⇨AP Div to create a second AP Div inside the first.**

3. **Position the second AP Div anywhere on the page by dragging the small tab in the upper-left corner of the AP Div box or by clicking and dragging anywhere on the AP Div's border.**

   Visually, nested AP Divs don't need to reside inside their parent AP Divs; they can be placed anywhere on the page or stacked on top of each other.

4. **Choose Window⇨AP Elements to open the AP Elements panel.**

   In the AP Elements panel, you can see how AP Divs are nested because the name of the nested AP Div is shown underneath and slightly indented from its parent, as you see in Figure 6-22.

You can nest an existing AP Div inside another by holding down the Control key (Option key on the Mac), clicking to select an AP Div, and dragging it over the name of another existing AP Div in the AP Elements panel.

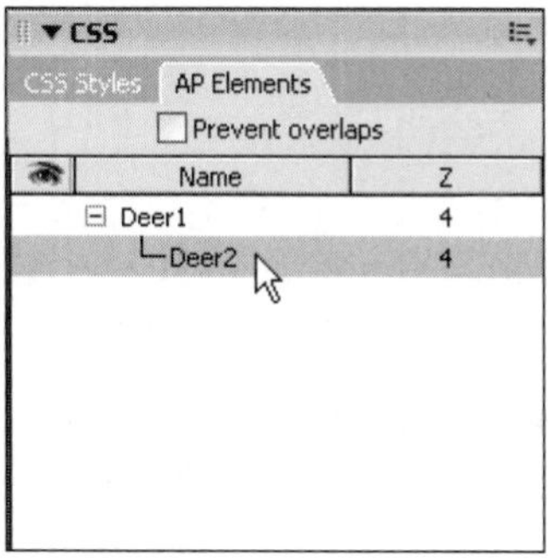

Figure 6-22:
You can manage nesting options in the AP Elements panel.

Setting AP Div options

Like other HTML elements, AP Divs have many attributes you can set. Dreamweaver makes these options available in the Property inspector whenever you select an AP Div.

This list describes the AP Div options and what they control:

- ✔ **AP Div ID:** You can type your own descriptive name in this drop-down list in the upper-left corner of the Property inspector. If you don't name an AP Div, Dreamweaver names it for you. When you name AP Divs, don't use special characters, such as spaces, hyphens, slashes, or periods.

- ✔ **L (Left):** This value specifies the distance of the AP Div from the left side of the page or parent AP Divs. Dreamweaver automatically enters a pixel value when you create or move an AP Div using drag and drop. You can also enter a numeric value in pixels or percents (positive or negative) to control the positioning.

- ✔ **T (Top):** This value specifies the distance of an AP Div from the top of the page or parent layer. Dreamweaver automatically enters a pixel value when you create or move an AP Div using drag and drop. You can also enter a numeric value in pixels or percentages (positive or negative) to control the positioning.

- ✔ **W (Width):** Dreamweaver automatically specifies the width when you create an AP Div on a page. You can also enter a numeric value to specify the width. You can change the px (pixels) default measurement to any of the following: pc (picas), pt (points), in (inches), mm (millimeters), cm (centimeters), or % (percentage of the page or parent layer's width). Don't put any spaces between the number and the measurement abbreviation.

- ✔ **H (Height):** Dreamweaver automatically specifies the height when you create an AP Div on a page. You can also enter a numeric value to specify the height. You can change the default measurement of px (pixels) to any of the following: pc (picas), pt (points), in (inches), mm (millimeters), cm (centimeters), or % (percentage of the page or parent's height). Don't put any spaces between the number and the measurement abbreviation.

- ✔ **Z-Index:** This option determines the position of an AP Div in relation to other AP Divs when they are stacked. Higher-numbered AP Divs appear on top of lower-numbered AP Divs, and values can be positive or negative.

- ✔ **Vis:** This visibility setting controls whether an AP Div is visible or invisible. You can modify this setting with a scripting language, such as JavaScript, to dynamically change the display of AP Divs.

You can choose from these visibility options:

- **Default:** The default option in most browsers is the same visibility property as the parent's value. If there is no parent AP Div, the default state is visible.

- **Inherit:** This option always uses the visibility property of the AP Div's parent.

- **Visible:** This option always displays the AP Div, regardless of the parent's value.

- **Hidden:** This option always makes the AP Div invisible, regardless of the parent's value. Even when it's hidden, all the content in an AP Div downloads when the page is viewed in the browser, but is not displayed. You can dynamically control visibility by using the JavaScript behaviors covered in Chapter 10.

✔ **Bg Image:** With this option, you can select a background image for the AP Div in the same way you would select a background image for a Web page. Click the folder icon to select an image or enter the name and path in the text box.

✔ **Bg Color:** Use this option to set a background color for an AP Div. Clicking the color square opens the color palette. If you want the background to be transparent, leave Bg Color blank.

✔ **Overflow:** These options determine how the contents of an AP Div display if they exceed the size of the AP Div.

You can choose from these Overflow options:

- **Visible:** If the AP Div has too much content, this option lets the content spill out over the edges of the AP Div — though this effect may not perform as expected in certain browsers. Making sure that content won't escape the confines of an AP Div is usually the best. Be sure to preview the results in the browser to make sure you get the effect you want.

- **Hidden:** Clips off the edges of content that doesn't fit within the specified size of an AP Div. Be careful with this option; it doesn't provide scroll bars.

- **Scroll:** Adds scroll bars to the sides of an AP Div regardless of whether its content exceeds the AP Div's size.

- **Auto:** Displays scroll bars only if the AP Div's content doesn't fit within the AP Div's boundaries.

✔ **Clip:** This option controls which sections of the content of an AP Div are cropped if the AP Div isn't large enough to display all its content. You should specify the distance from the L (Left), T (Top), R (Right), and B (Bottom). You have to specify clips in pixels or choose the Auto value.

Using Dreamweaver's CSS Layouts

In addition to all the tools, panels, and dialog boxes you can use to create your own CSS layouts and styles in Dreamweaver, you'll find many pre-designed CSS layouts and styles included in the program.

To create a new page using one of Dreamweaver's CSS layouts, choose File➪New, choose Blank Page on the left, choose HTML from the Page Type options, and then choose any of the CSS layouts listed under Layout on the right. In Figure 6-23, I'm selecting a predesigned CSS layout that creates a two-column page layout with a header and a footer using a fixed width.

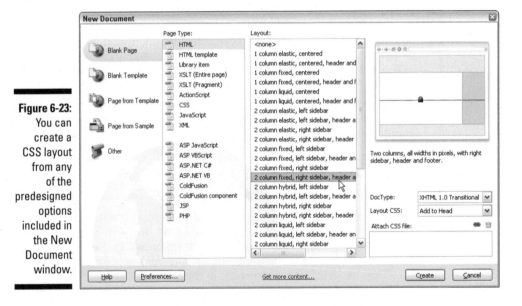

Figure 6-23:
You can create a CSS layout from any of the predesigned options included in the New Document window.

Once you've created a page with a CSS layout, you can change the layout by changing the various styles included with the page. For example, to change the width of the sidebar in the CSS layout shown in Figure 6-24, you would first select the style for the sidebar in the CSS panel and then use the CSS Properties below the CSS panel to edit the style. Alternatively, you could double-click the style name in the CSS panel and open the CSS Definition dialog box to make any changes there.

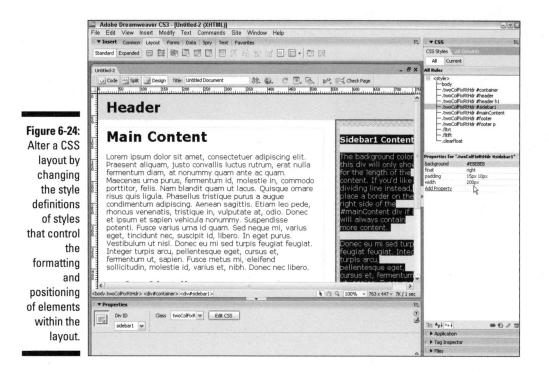

Figure 6-24:
Alter a CSS layout by changing the style definitions of styles that control the formatting and positioning of elements within the layout.

To use any of the collections of CSS styles included in Dreamweaver, choose File➪New. In the New Document window, choose the Page from Sample option on the left, choose CSS Style Sample from the Sample Folder, and then choose from any of the Sample Pages listed on the right. When you click the name of a Sample Page, a preview of the CSS styles is displayed on the far right.

Want to discover more about CSS? You'll find many advanced CSS resources on the Web. Visit www.DigitalFamily.com/dreamweaver for a list of great places online to find more tips, tricks, hacks, and other reassurances as you work to master CSS.

Chapter 7

Coming to the HTML Table

*I*n the early days of Web design, HTML tables offered one of the only options for creating complex page layouts. By splitting and merging table cells and using them as containers for text and images, Web developers were able to create intricate page designs despite the limits of HTML. Most of us were frustrated by this solution.

Using tables to create designs was far from ideal, and we often had to resort to special tricks, such as using a clear GIF to control spacing (see the sidebar on the clear Gif trick later in this chapter). But at least with tables you could position text, images, and other elements, anywhere you wanted on a page. For example, you could use a table to align two columns of text side by side with a headline across the top like the format you might see in a newspaper or magazine. And because you could make the borders of a table invisible, you could use tables to create these kinds of designs without the table itself being visible on the page.

Today CSS is quickly changing the way Web pages are created. Although tables are still an ideal way to present tabular data on the Internet (for example, just about any content you could display in a spreadsheet can be formatted easily and effectively with a table), they are no longer the recommended solution for creating page layouts like those you'd find in a magazine or newspaper. Instead, a growing number of designers are using CSS to create page designs because these pages download faster, are easier to update, and are more flexible and accessible than tables ever were. Chapters 5 and 6 are dedicated to CSS and the latest developments in Web design.

Choosing between tables and CSS

More and more pages on the Web are designed with CSS, and you can expect to see that trend continue. As Internet users upgrade their browsers and newer browsers support CSS better and better, the advantages of CSS are quickly outweighing the limitations. CSS offers much better design control than tables, especially in Dreamweaver, where you can simply click and drag to place them wherever you want on a page. You can put any element in a layer, including images, text, and multimedia files. You can even stack layers on top of each other, and you get down-to-the-pixel design control, which is far better than what you get with tables.

This chapter is designed to help you appreciate how to create and edit tables in Dreamweaver. Even though tables are no longer *recommended* for most Web page layouts, you still find them used on many Web sites; so I've included instructions for working with tables for page layouts, as well as formatting and sorting tabular data with tables in Dreamweaver.

I also show you how to create HTML tables for everything from columnar data to complex page designs. Tables are a bit complicated to create and not as precise as you might like them to be, but Dreamweaver has a number of tools that make creating tables easier.

Creating HTML Tables

Tables are made up of three basic elements: rows, columns, and cells. If you've ever worked with a spreadsheet program, you're probably familiar with tables. Tables in HTML differ from spreadsheet tables mainly in that they're used for more complex alignment of data, which requires lots of merging and splitting of cells. Back in the days when you had to design Web pages in raw HTML code by hand, even simple tables were difficult to create. The code behind an HTML table is a complex series of `<tr>` and `<td>` tags that indicate table rows and table data cells. Figuring out how to type those tags so that they created a series of little boxes on a Web page was never an intuitive process. If you wanted to merge or split cells to create rows or columns with varying numbers of cells, you faced a truly complex challenge.

Thank the cybergods that you have Dreamweaver to make this process easy. Using Dreamweaver, you can easily create tables and modify both the appearance and the structure of a table by simply clicking and dragging its edges. You can add any type of content to a cell, such as images, text, and multimedia files — even nested tables. Using the Property inspector, you can merge and split cells, add color to the background or borders, and change the vertical and horizontal alignment of elements within a cell.

You can create tables in Standard or Expanded mode in Dreamweaver. Expanded mode, shown in Figure 7-1, makes it easier to select inside and around tables by adding space around table borders. However, the display of a table changes in Expanded mode — it literally expands table cells. The added space makes it easier to edit content within tables, but it also changes the display. Because Standard mode (shown in Figure 7-2) is more consistent with how tables will appear in a browser, you should generally do most of your table editing, especially resizing and moving tables, in Standard mode. You can switch between these two modes by clicking the Standard and Expanded mode buttons in the Layout menu bar at the top of the work area shown in Figures 7-1 and 7-2.

Expanded mode

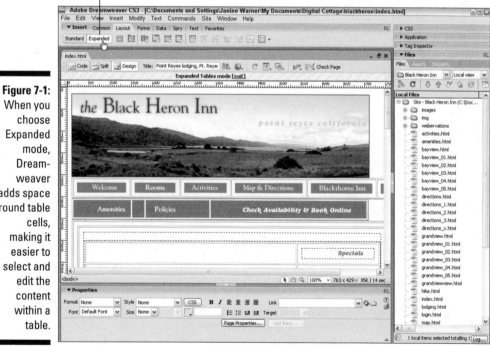

Figure 7-1:
When you choose Expanded mode, Dream-weaver adds space around table cells, making it easier to select and edit the content within a table.

Standard mode

Figure 7-2:
In Standard
mode,
Dream-
weaver's
table display
is more
consistent
with how
the layout
will look
in a Web
browser
such as
Firefox or
Internet
Explorer.

Creating Tables in Standard Mode

Although Expanded mode is useful for selecting and editing the contents of a table, Standard mode is best for creating tables. You can insert a table by choosing Insert➪Table or by clicking on the Table icon in the Common or Layout Insert bar.

When you insert a new table, the Table dialog box, shown in Figure 7-3, makes it easy to specify many table settings at once. Don't worry about getting them all perfect, you can always change these options later (a list of common Table settings and their descriptions is included later in this section).

Don't skip the Accessibility options at the bottom of the Table dialog box. They are important for anyone who uses a browser that "reads" Web pages, such as those used by people with limited vision. If you enter a table caption, it will be displayed within the table. (You can specify with the Align Caption option where the caption will appear.) The Table Summary does not appear on the page and is used only to describe the table for visitors who can not see the table contents and layout.

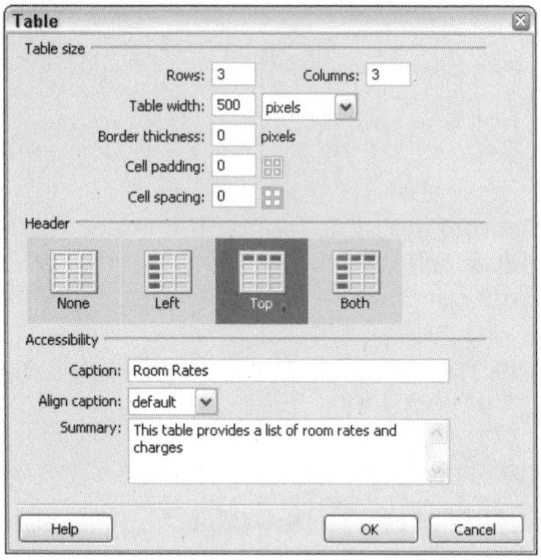

Figure 7-3:
When you
insert a
table into a
Web page,
you can
specify
many table
settings in
this dialog
box.

You can edit all the table options, except the Accessibility options, in the Property inspector. When you select a table or cell, the attributes appear in the Property inspector at the bottom of the work area. Click the border of any table to select the entire table, and the Property inspector displays the table options shown in Figure 7-4. To view all the options, click the expander arrow in the lower-right corner of the Property inspector. (Cell properties are described in the next section.)

How wide should you make a table?

Designers often wonder how wide to make a table when they are using tables to control page layout. My advice is that if you are designing your pages for an 800 x 600 screen resolution (still a popular resolution among Internet users), a safe bet is to make your table no more than 780 pixels wide and center it in the middle of the page. That leaves a little room on each side to prevent the appearance of sideways scrollbars and causes the table to "float" in the middle of the page if users have a larger monitor.

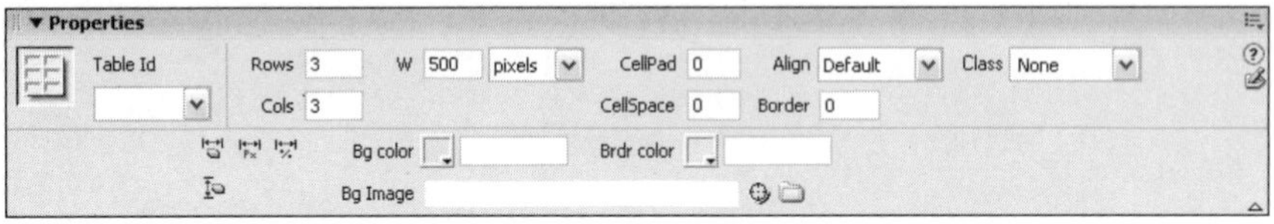

Figure 7-4:
The
Property
inspector
when a
table is
selected.

If you're having trouble selecting the table (sometimes selecting the entire table and not just an individual cell is tricky), simply place your cursor anywhere inside the table and choose Modify⇨Table⇨Select Table.

The Property inspector gives you access to the following table options for customizing the appearance of your table:

- ✔ **Table Id:** Provides a text area where you can enter a name or table.

- ✔ **Rows:** Displays the number of rows in the table. You can alter the size of the table by changing the number. Be careful, though: If you enter a smaller number, Dreamweaver deletes the bottom rows — contents and all.

- ✔ **Cols:** Displays the number of columns in the table. You can alter the size of the table by changing the number. Again, if you enter a smaller number, Dreamweaver deletes the columns on the right side of the table — contents and all.

- ✔ **W (Width):** Displays the width of the table. You can alter the width by changing the number. You can specify the width as a percentage or a value in pixels. Values expressed as a percentage increase or decrease the table's size relative to the size of the user's browser window or any enclosing container, such as another table or a `<div>` tag.

- ✔ **H (Height):** Displays the height of the table. You can alter the height by changing the number. You can specify the height as a percentage or a value in pixels. Values expressed as percentages increase or decrease the table's size relative to the size of the user's browser window. This table attribute is no longer supported in XHTML 1.0. Although many browsers still recognize this setting, it may not be supported in future browser versions, and it is generally recommended that you leave the height setting unspecified so that the table adjusts to automatically fit the contents.

Table dimensions expressed as a percentage enable you to create a table that changes in size as the browser window is resized. For example, if you want a table to always take up 75 percent of the browser window, no matter how big the user's monitor or display area, set the size as a percentage. If you want a table to always be the same size — that is, to remain the same size regardless of the browser window size — choose pixels rather than percentages for your table dimensions.

If a table is inserted inside another container, such as a `<div>` tag or a table with a fixed width, it will not change size based on the browser window but will be sized based on the container.

✔ **CellPad:** Specifies the space between the contents of a cell and its border.

✔ **CellSpace:** Specifies the space between table cells.

✔ **Align:** Controls the alignment of the table. Options are Default, Left, Right, and Center. As a general rule, the Default setting aligns the table from the left side of the browser window or other container.

✔ **Border:** Controls the size of the border around the table. The larger the number, the thicker the border. If you want the border to be invisible, set it to 0.

✔ **Class:** Provides easy access to style sheet options. (See Chapters 5 and 6 for more on CSS.)

✔ **Clear and Convert:** The icons in the lower-left area of the Property inspector (click the expander arrow in the lower-right corner to view them) provide these formatting options:

- **Clear Row Heights** and **Clear Column Widths** enable you to remove all height and width values at one time.

- **Convert Table Heights to Pixels** and **Convert Table Heights to Percents,** and **Convert Table Widths to Pixels** and **Convert Table Widths to Percents** enable you to automatically change Height and Width settings from percentages to pixels. Pixels specify a fixed width; a percent setting means the browser automatically adjusts the specified percentage of the browser display area.

✔ **Bg Color:** Controls the background color. Click the color square next to this label to open the color palette. Click to select a color from the box or click the color wheel at the top-right corner to choose any color. Also note that when you click the color square, the cursor changes to an eye-dropper, enabling you to pick up a color by clicking anywhere on the page. You can apply this option to a single cell by placing your cursor in a particular cell before specifying the color or to the entire table by selecting the table.

✔ **Bg Image:** Enables you to select a background image. Specify the filename or click the folder icon to locate the image. You can apply this option to a single cell or to the entire table.

✔ **Brdr Color:** Controls the border color of the entire table. Click the color square next to this label and select a color from the box that appears, or use the color wheel at the top-right corner to choose any color. Also note that when you click the color square, the cursor changes to an eyedropper, enabling you to pick up a color by clicking anywhere on the page.

Make sure the table fits the contents

Be aware that table cells automatically adjust to accommodate whatever you insert into them. For example, if you create a cell that is 100 pixels wide and then insert a 300-pixel-wide image, the table cell adjusts to fit the image. This can cause problems if the overall size of the table is not set large enough to accommodate all the objects within the table cells. As you build your tables, be aware of the size of the images and multimedia files you are inserting into cells or you may have unpredictable results. For example, if you set a table to a total width of 400 pixels and then insert 600 pixels worth of images, the table may not appear the same in all browsers.

You can also apply formatting options and change the attributes of any element, such as text, an image, or a multimedia file, that you have placed within a table cell. To do so, click to select the element and then use the options in the Property inspector to make any desired changes, just as you would if the element were not in a table cell.

Merging and splitting table cells

Sometimes, the easiest way to modify the number of cells in a table is to *merge* cells (combine two or more cells into one) or *split* cells (split one cell into two or more rows or columns). Using this technique, you can vary the space in table sections and customize their structures. For example, you may want a long cell space across the top of your table for a banner and then multiple cells below it so that you can control the spacing between columns of text or images. The following two sets of steps show you how to merge and split cells in a table.

You can merge and split cells only in Standard mode.

To merge cells, create a new HTML page or open an existing HTML file and follow these steps (see Chapter 2 for more information on creating files):

1. **Choose Insert⇨Table and create a table with four rows and four columns, a 75 percent width, and a border of 1. Skip header and accessibility. Click OK and the table appears on the page.**

2. **Highlight two or more adjacent cells by clicking and dragging the mouse from the first cell to the last.**

   You can merge only cells that are adjacent to one another and in the same row or column.

3. **Click the Merge Selected Cells icon, in the lower-left region of the Property inspector, to merge the selected cells into a single cell.**

   The cells are merged into a single cell by using the Colspan or Rowspan attributes. These HTML attributes make a single cell merge with adjacent cells by spanning extra rows or columns in the table.

To split a cell, follow these steps:

1. **Click to place the cursor inside the cell you want to split.**

2. **Click the Split Selected Cell icon, in the lower-left region of the Property inspector.**

   The Split Cell dialog box appears.

3. **Select Rows or Columns in the dialog box, depending on how you want to divide the cell.**

   You can split a cell into however many new rows or columns you want.

4. **Type the number of rows or columns you want to create.**

   The selected cell is split into the number of rows or columns you entered.

Controlling cell options

In addition to changing table options, you can control options for individual cells within a table. When you select a cell, which you do by clicking the cursor anywhere inside the cell area, the Property inspector changes to display the individual properties for that cell (see Figure 7-5). The Property inspector is where you find the controls to merge and split cells, as well as to change the alignment of the contents of a particular cell.

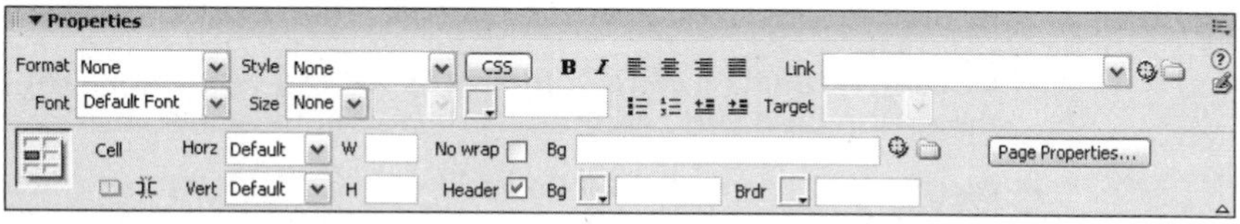

Figure 7-5:
The Property inspector when a table cell is selected.

You can also change multiple cells at the same time. For example, suppose that you want to have some (but not all) cells in your table take on a certain color background and style of text. You can apply the same properties to multiple cells by selecting more than one cell at a time. To select adjacent cells, press the Shift key while clicking to select cells. To select multiple cells that are not adjacent, press the Ctrl key (the ⌘ key on the Mac) and click each cell you want to select. Any properties you change in the Property inspector apply to all selected cells.

 If you're having trouble selecting an individual cell because it contains an image, click the image and then use either the ← or → key on your keyboard to move the cursor and deselect the image, which activates the Property inspector and displays the options for that cell.

When one or more cells are selected (they have to be adjacent for this to work), the top half of the Property inspector controls the formatting of text and URLs within the table cells. The lower half of the Property inspector provides these table cell attribute options (refer to Figure 7-5):

✔ **Merge Cells icon:** Merges two or more cells. To merge cells, you must first select two or more cells by clicking and dragging or by pressing either the Shift or Ctrl key while selecting multiple cells.

✔ **Split Cell icon:** Splits one cell into two. When you select this option, a dialog box lets you specify whether you want to split the row (you split the cell horizontally) or the column (you split the cell vertically). You can then specify the number of columns or rows, which controls how many times the cell divides. Note that you can apply the Split Cell option to only one cell at a time.

✔ **Horz:** Controls the horizontal alignment of the cell contents.

✔ **Vert:** Controls the vertical alignment of the cell contents.

✔ **W:** Controls the width of the cell.

✔ **H:** Controls the height of the cell.

✔ **No Wrap:** Prevents word wrapping within the cell. The cell widens to accommodate all text as you type or paste it into a cell. (Normally, the excess text just moves down to the next line and increases the height of the cell.)

✔ **Header:** Formats a cell's contents by using a header tag, which displays the text in bold and centered by default in most Web browsers.

✔ **Bg (Image):** The Bg field followed by a text field with a browse icon enables you to browse to select a background image or to enter the name and path of a background image by typing it.

✔ **Bg (Color):** The Bg field below it features a color well you can click in to select a background color from the color palette and a text field where you can enter a hexadecimal color code. If you use the color palette, the hexadecimal code is automatically entered into the Bg color field.

✔ **Brdr (Color):** Allows you to change the border color of the cell.

Formatting multiple columns in a table

When you're working with lots of cells in a table, you may want to format multiple cells in the same way. Dreamweaver makes that task easy, whether you want to align numbers, make the headings bold, or change the color scheme. But before you start planning how to line up all your numbers perfectly, be aware that you don't have as much control in HTML as you have in a program such as Excel, where you can align numbers to the decimal point. You can, however, align the content of columns to the left, right, or center. Thus, if you use the same number of digits after the decimal point in all your numbers, you can get them to line up. For example, if one price is $12.99 and another is $14, express the latter as $14.00; then, when you right align, the numbers line up properly. (If your columns are still not lining up the way you want them to, consider using a monospace font such as Courier, which lines up better.)

The steps in this section explain how to create a table in Standard mode and align all the data cells to the right so that the numbers or other content align consistently. You can use these exercises also to align the contents of table cells to the left or center and to apply other formatting options, such as bold or italic. In these steps, I insert the data into the table after I create the table in Dreamweaver.

If you want to import data from a table you have created in a program such as Word or Excel, see the section, "Importing Table Data from Other Programs," later in this chapter. If you're working with a table that already has data in it and just want to format or align the cells, go directly to Step 7.

If you're starting from scratch, create a new, blank HTML page and follow these steps from the beginning:

1. **Make sure that you're in Standard mode. (Choose View⇨Table Mode⇨ Standard Mode.)**

2. **Click to place the cursor where you want to create a table.**

   In both Standard and Expanded modes, tables are automatically created in the top-left area of the page, unless you insert them after other content.

3. **Click the Table icon on the Common or Layout Insert bar.**

   Alternatively, you can choose Insert⇨Table. The Insert Table dialog box appears.

4. **In the appropriate boxes, type the number of columns and rows you want to include in your table.**

   Remember you can always add or remove cells later using the Property inspector.

5. **Specify the width, border, cell padding, and cell spacing. Then click OK.**

   The table automatically appears on the page.

6. **Click to place the cursor in a cell and then type the data you want in that cell. Repeat for each cell.**

   Alternatively, you can use Edit⇨Paste Special to insert columnar data from another program such as Excel.

7. **Select the column or row for which you want to change the alignment.**

   Place the cursor in the first cell in the column or row you want to align; then click and drag your mouse to highlight the other columns or rows that you want to change.

8. **Right-click (Windows) or Ctrl+click (Mac) in any cell in the highlighted column or row.**

   A pop-up menu appears, as shown in Figure 7-6. Alternatively, you can use the Property inspector to change selected items.

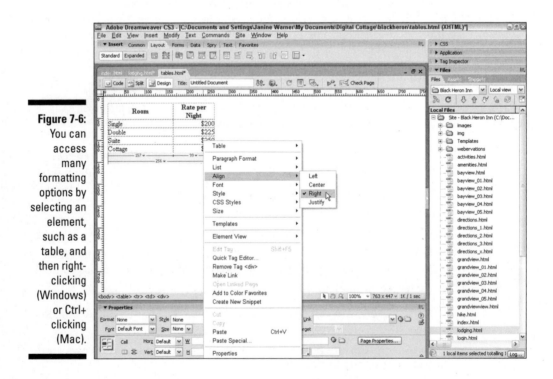

Figure 7-6:
You can access many formatting options by selecting an element, such as a table, and then right-clicking (Windows) or Ctrl+ clicking (Mac).

9. **From the pop-up menu, choose Align and then choose Left, Center, Right, or Justify from the submenu.**

   This option enables you to change the alignment of all highlighted cells in the column or row at one time. If you're working with financial data, choose Align⇨Right, which produces the best alignment for numbers. You can also apply other formatting options, such as bold or italic, to selected cells and their contents by choosing the option from the pop-up menu or from the Property inspector.

If you want to format one cell in a column or row differently from the others, click to place the cursor in just that cell and then click one of the formatting options in the Property inspector. You can also choose to align multiple cells that aren't *contiguous* (they don't touch each other) by pressing and holding the Ctrl key (⌘ on the Mac) in Windows while you click the cells you want to select. Any options you change on the pop-up menu or in the Table Property inspector apply to all selected cells.

Sorting Table Data

When you're working with lots of columnar data, you want to be able to sort that data just as you do in a spreadsheet program such as Excel. In Dreamweaver, you can sort data even after it's formatted in HTML (something you couldn't easily do before). You still don't have as many options as you do in Excel. For example, you can't sort different rows individually, but you can sort an entire table based on a specified row.

To use the Sort Table Data feature, create a new, blank HTML page, add a table with several rows and columns, and add some content. (I explain how in the preceding section.) You may also open an existing page with a table of columnar data. Then, follow these steps:

1. **Select the table you want to sort.**

   Place the cursor in any cell of the table you want to sort.

2. **Make sure that you're in Standard mode. (Choose View⇨Table Mode⇨Standard Mode.)**

3. **Choose Commands⇨Sort Table.**

   The Sort Table dialog box appears, as shown in Figure 7-7.

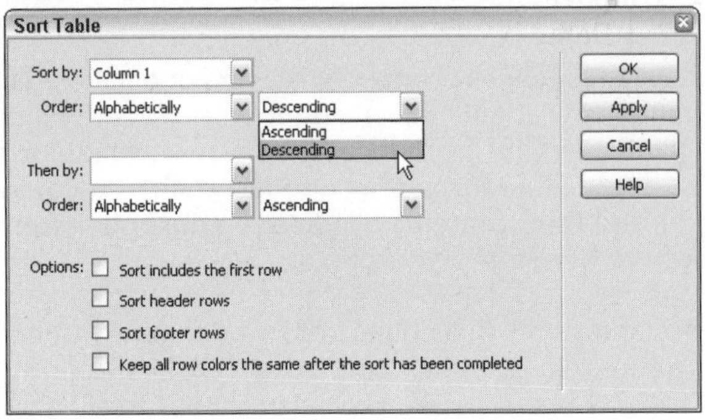

Figure 7-7:
You can
sort cell
contents
alphabeti-
cally or
numerically,
even after
they're
formatted in
HTML.

4. **Specify which column you want to sort by. Then choose Alphabetically or Numerically, and Ascending or Descending.**

   You can set up one or two sorts to happen simultaneously and opt whether to include the first row and whether to keep the TR (Table Row) attributes with a sorted row by selecting Keep All Row Colors the Same.

5. **Click OK.**

   The selected cells are sorted, just as they are in a program such as Microsoft Excel. (Pretty cool, huh?)

Importing Table Data from Other Programs

Manually converting financial data or other spreadsheet information can be tedious. Fortunately, Dreamweaver includes a special feature that enables you to insert table data created in other applications such as Microsoft Word or Excel. To use this feature, the table data must be saved from the other program in a *delimited* format, which means that the columns of data are separated by tabs, commas, colons, semicolons, or another type of delimiter. Most spreadsheet and database applications, as well as Microsoft Word, enable you to save data in a delimited format, such as CSV (which stands for Comma Separated Values) because that's the file extension they're given. Consult the documentation for the application you're using to find out how. After the data is saved in a delimited format, you can import it into Dreamweaver.

To import table data into Dreamweaver after it has been saved in a delimited format (such as CSV) or in its native application (such as Access or Excel), create a new, blank HTML page or open an existing file and follow these steps to import the data:

1. **Choose File⇨Import⇨Tabular Data or choose Insert⇨Table Objects⇨ Import Tabular Data.**

   The Import Tabular Data dialog box appears (see Figure 7-8).

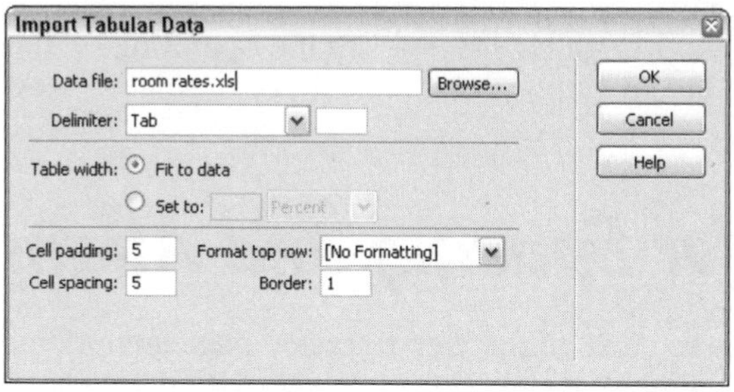

Figure 7-8:
You can import tabular data into Dream-weaver from other programs such as Excel.

2. **In the Data File text box, type the name of the file you want to import or use the Browse button to locate the file.**

3. **In the Delimiter drop-down list, select the delimiter format you used when you saved your file in the native application.**

   The delimiter options are Tab, Comma, Semicolon, Colon, and Other. You should have made this choice when you exported the data from the original program in which you created it, such as Excel or Access. If you don't remember what you chose, you can always go back to the original program and export the data again. You must select the correct option for your data to import correctly.

4. **Select the table width.**

   If you choose Fit to Data, Dreamweaver automatically creates the table to fit the data being imported. If you choose Set, you must specify a per-cent or pixel size.

5. **Specify the cell padding and cell spacing only if you want extra space around the data in the table to be created.**

6. **Choose an option from the Format Top Row option only if you want to format the data in the top row of the table.**

   Your options are Bold, Italic, or Bold Italic.

7. **Specify the border size.**

   The default is 1, which puts a small border around the table. Choose 0 if you don't want the border to be visible. Choose a larger number if you want a thicker border.

8. **Click OK to automatically create a table with the imported data.**

Dreamweaver also enables you to export data from a table into a delimited format. This capability is useful if you want to export data from a Web page so that you can import it into another program, such as Word or Excel, or into a database program, such as FileMaker or Access. To export data from Dreamweaver, place the cursor anywhere in the table and choose File⇨Export⇨ Table. In the Export Table dialog box, choose from the options on the Delimiter drop-down list (you can choose Tab, Space, Comma, Semicolon, or Colon). From the Line Breaks drop-down list, specify the operating system (you can choose Windows, Mac, or Unix).

Using Tables for Spacing and Alignment

Tables have long been used on the Web to create page layouts that require more than basic alignment of elements on a page. Using tables, you could get around many of the limitations of basic HTML and accomplish some otherwise impossible design feats, such as evenly spacing bullets, creating columns side-by-side on a page, and spanning headlines or images across multiple columns. Today, CSS offers a much better option for these kinds of designs, but many people are still using tables and you may inherit a design that uses them, so I've included this exercise to help you appreciate how to use tables to format complex content, such as the elements of the form that are displayed in a table in the bottom of the upcoming Figure 7-10.

Using tables to design forms

Creating text boxes and drop-down lists for HTML forms is easy in Dreamweaver, but if you want all the fields to line up, you may want to use tables or CSS to help with the formatting. You find instructions for formatting forms, text, and other elements with CSS in Chapters 5 and 6. In Chapter 12, you find step-by-step instructions for creating a variety of forms; for now, I assume that you have already created a form and want to align the text boxes evenly using a table. I've use a simple form with just a few questions as an example, but you can use this technique to align any form elements.

I've left this exercise in this revision of the book for two reasons: Tables offer a simple way to control the alignment and positioning of form elements, and what you discover in this exercise will help you with the formatting of any table design. That said, CSS provides a much better option for formatting forms like the one featured in this example and is the recommended option if you want your Web site to comply with contemporary Web standards.

The transparent, or clear, GIF trick

One of the ways Web designers have created complex layouts within the limitations of HTML tables is to use a technique commonly known as the transparent, or clear, GIF trick. Essentially, you create an invisible image (a GIF with a transparent background and nothing else), and then you insert that invisible GIF into your page and use the image height and width settings in Dreamweaver to control the image's size. The effect is the creation of empty space on a page that can be precisely controlled by the height and width attributes.

In the old days, this was one of the only ways you could precisely control margins and other spacing within a table and between elements on a Web page. Today, CSS offers far superior ways to control spacing and add margins and padding.

Among the challenges with the clear GIF trick is how hard it can be to manage them within the design area because they are invisible. When you select a transparent GIF, you can see the outline of the image while it's selected, but as

soon as you deselect the image, it becomes invisible in Dreamweaver (unless you add a border in the image properties). You can always reselect an image by clicking the area until the cursor highlights it. Just be aware that selecting it, especially if it's very small, can be tricky because it's not visible.

Because CSS offers better ways to control spacing (using margin and padding settings, for example), I no longer recommend that you use the clear GIF trick. However, if you are editing a Web page layout that someone else created using HTML tables, you may discover lots of little invisible GIFs. I offer this brief explanation only because I wanted to make sure you know about this trick so you're not baffled by why anyone would place invisible graphics all over a Web page.

If you inherit a Web site that used this design method, I strongly recommend that you redesign the pages using `<div>` tags and CSS (covered in Chapter 6) instead of tables with clear GIFs.

To use a table to align form elements, such as text boxes, on your page, follow these steps:

1. **Open a page containing an HTML form (or create an HTML form).**

   See Chapter 12 to find out how to create HTML forms.

2. **Click to place the cursor where you want to start formatting your form.**

3. **Choose Insert⇨Table.**

   The Insert Table dialog box appears.

4. **Type the number of columns and rows you want in your table.**

   I set the table to three rows and two columns.

5. **Set the width to whatever is most appropriate for your design and then click OK.**

   Remember, up to 760 pixels is a good width if you are designing for an 800-by-600 screen resolution, which many designers consider the best size to reach the most users.

6. **Enter 0 for the border.**

   When you set the border to 0, the edges of your table change from solid lines to dotted lines so that you can still see where the borders are while you're working in Dreamweaver. When you view the page in a browser, as shown in Figure 7-9, the border of the table is invisible.

7. **Click OK.**

   The table automatically appears on the page.

8. **You need to copy the data from your form into the table. Using the Cut and Paste commands from the Edit menu, cut the text preceding the form's first text field and paste it into the cell in the upper-left corner of the table.**

   Alternatively, you can select the text and then click and drag it into each table cell.

   In my example in Figure 7-10, I cut the words *What's your favorite song?* and pasted them into the first table cell.

9. **Select the first text field (the empty box where users type their responses) and cut and paste (or click and drag) the field into the desired cell of the table.**

10. **Repeat Steps 8 and 9 until you have moved all form elements into table cells.**

11. **Click the vertical column divider line between the first and second columns and drag it to the left or right to create the alignment you want for your form.**

Vertical alignment solves common problem

If you're having trouble getting the contents of adjacent cells to line up with each other, setting Vertical alignment to Top may solve your problem. A common frustration when you're building tables is that you have two or more rows side by side with text in one and images in the other and you want the top of the image and the top of the text to line up. Often they don't because they are different lengths, and the table is trying to adjust the contents to best use the space within their respective cells. The solution is simple: Select all the cells you want to align, and in the Property inspector, change Vertical alignment to Top. Seemingly like magic, all the content jumps right to the top of the cells and lines up perfectly. This is such a common problem, I routinely set the Vertical alignment of table cells to Top.

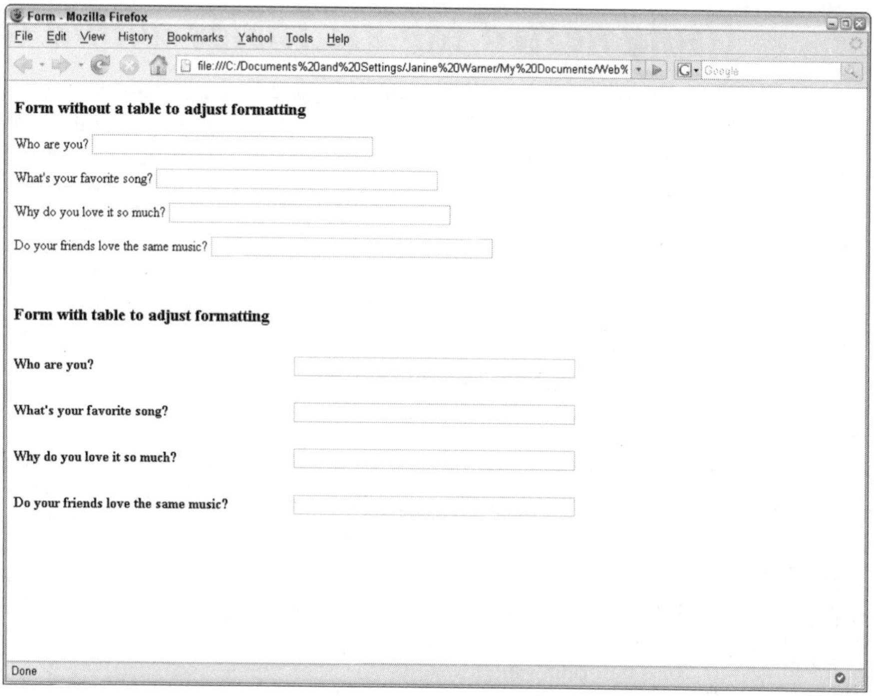

Figure 7-9:
When the form fields in the table are displayed in the browser, they line up evenly; with the border set to 0 you can't even tell it's there.

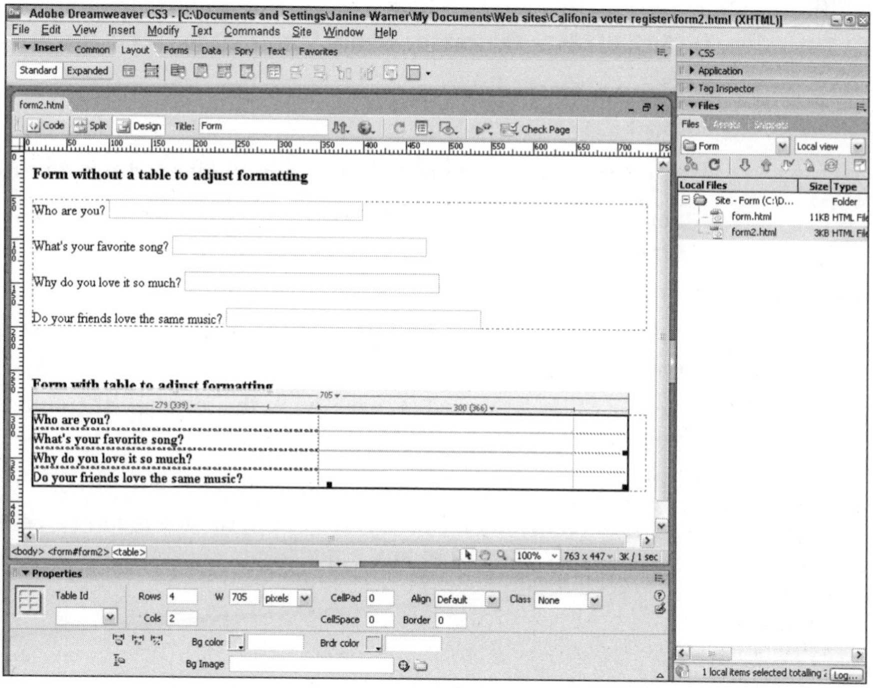

Figure 7-10:
You can use a table to better align form data and elements.

Using nested tables: Tables within tables

Placing tables within tables, called *nested tables*, can help you create extremely complex designs. You create nested tables by inserting a table within a cell of another table. In the days when you had to write your own code, this task was daunting. Dreamweaver now makes nesting tables easy, enabling you to create complex designs without ever looking at the HTML code.

The best Web designs communicate the information to your audience in the most elegant and understandable way and are easy to download. To make sure that your designs don't get too messy, remember these guidelines:

✔ A table within a table within a table is nested three levels deep. Anything more than that gets hairy.

✔ Pages that use nested tables take longer to download because browsers have to interpret each table individually before rendering the page. For some designs, the slightly longer download time is worth it, but in most cases you're better off adding or merging cells in one table, as I explain in the section "Merging and splitting table cells," earlier in this chapter. One situation that makes a nested table worth the added download time is when you want to place a table of financial or other data in the midst of a complex page design.

To place a table inside another table, follow these steps:

1. **Click to place the cursor where you want to create the first table.**

2. **Choose Insert⇨Table.**

   The Insert Table dialog box appears.

3. **Type the number of columns and rows you need for your design.**

4. **Set the Width option to whatever is appropriate for your design, and then click OK.**

   The table is automatically sized to the width you set.

5. **Click to place the cursor in the cell in which you want to place the second table.**

6. **Repeat Steps 2 through 4, specifying the number of columns and rows you want and the width of the table.**

   The new table appears inside the cell of the first table.

7. **Type the information that you want in the nested table cells as you would enter content in any other table.**

Chapter 8

Framing Your Pages

*N*o one wants to be "framed," whether that means being falsely accused of something you didn't do or trapped in the HTML frameset of a Web site with no escape. Appreciating not only the best way to create frames but also the best way to use them to enhance site navigation is important if you don't want to leave your visitors feeling stuck in your pages.

Many experienced Web designers say you should never use frames. I take a more open approach — I don't *recommend* frames, but I think you should decide for yourself. Besides, I can think of a few instances when frames come in quite handy, such as when you want to bring in content from another Web site and still maintain your own navigation and logo. Of course, you should do this only with permission from the other site (see the sidebar later in this chapter, "Resist using frames when you link to other people's Web sites").

To help you make the most of this HTML design feature, this chapter covers how to build HTML framesets in Dreamweaver and also discusses when frames are most useful and when you should avoid them. Frames add a wide range of design possibilities, but they can also create confusing navigation systems and can be frustrating to viewers. As you go through this chapter, consider not only how to create frames but also whether they are really the best solution for your Web site project.

Appreciating HTML Frames

Frames add innovative navigation control because they enable you to display multiple HTML pages in one browser window and control the content of each framed area individually. Web developers commonly use frames to create a design with two or more sections within one browser window. Each section consists of a different HTML page, and you can place links in one section that, when selected, display information in another page in a different section within the same browser window.

Web pages that use frames are split into separate sections — or individual *frames*. All the frames together make up a *frameset*. Behind the scenes, each frame of the frameset is a separate HTML file, which makes a page with frames a little complicated to create, even with Dreamweaver. If you choose to create your frame files in a text editor, you have to juggle multiple pages, working on one frame at a time, and you can see what you create only when you preview your work in a browser. The visual editor in Dreamweaver makes creating frames a lot easier because you can view all the HTML files that make up the frameset at the same time and can edit them while they appear in the way in which they will appear in a browser.

As a navigational feature, frames enable you to keep some information constant while changing other information in the same browser window. For example, you can keep a list of links visible in one frame and display the information each link brings up in another frame, as the site shown in Figure 8-1 does.

Figure 8-1: Frames keep thumbnail photos and links visible on the left and keep the headline at the top, while changing the main part of the page to display different photos.

You can create as many frames as you want within a browser window. Unfortunately, some people overuse them and create designs that are so complex and broken up that they're neither aesthetically appealing nor easily navigable. Putting too many frames on one page can also make a site hard to read because the individual windows are too small. This has led many Web surfers to passionately hate frames. And some sites that rushed to implement frames when they were first introduced have since either abandoned frames or minimized their use.

Here's a list of guidelines when using frames:

- **Don't use frames just for the sake of using frames.** If you have a compelling reason to use frames, create an elegant and easy-to-follow frameset. But don't do it just because Dreamweaver makes creating them relatively easy.

- **Limit the use of frames and keep files small.** Remember that each frame you create represents another HTML file. Thus, a frameset with three frames requires a browser to fetch and display four Web pages, and that may dramatically increase download time.

- **Turn off frame borders.** Browsers that support frames also support the capability to turn off the border that divides frames in a frameset. If you turn the borders off, your pages look cleaner. Frame borders, shown in Figure 8-1, are thick and an ugly gray, and they can break up a nice design. You can change the color in the Property inspector, but I still recommend that you use them only when you feel that they're absolutely necessary. I show you how to turn off frame borders in the "Changing Frame Properties" section toward the end of this chapter.

- **Don't use frames when you can use CSS or tables instead.** Tables are easier to create than frames and provide a more elegant solution to your design needs because they're less intrusive. I include lots of information on creating tables in Chapter 7, and you find coverage of CSS — an increasingly popular design option — in Chapters 5 and 6.

- **Don't place frames within frames.** The windows get too darned small to be useful for much of anything, and the screen looks horribly complicated. You can also run into problems when your framed site links to another site displayed in your frameset. The "Resist using frames when you link to other people's Web sites" sidebar provides many more reasons to limit using frames inside of frames.

- **Put in alternate `<noframes>` content.** The number of users surfing the Web with browsers that don't support frames becomes smaller every day. Still, showing them *something* other than a blank page is a good idea. I usually put in a line that says, "This site uses frames and requires a frames-capable browser to view." `<noframes>` content can also be read by search engines, which may otherwise fail to catalog the content within framed pages.

Understanding How Frames Work

Frames are a bit complicated, but Dreamweaver helps make the whole process of creating them somewhat easier. When you create a Web page with frames in Dreamweaver, you need to remember that each frame area is a separate HTML file, and Dreamweaver saves each frame area as a separate page. You also want to keep track of which file displays in which of the frames so that you can aim links properly.

Figure 8-2 shows a simple frameset example with three frames, each containing a different HTML page and different text (*Page 1, Page 2,* and *Page 3*) so that I can clearly refer to them in the following numbered steps.

In addition to the files that appear in each frame, you need to create a separate HTML file to generate the frameset. This page doesn't have a <body> tag, but it describes the frames and tells the browser how and where to display them. This gets a little complicated, but don't worry: Dreamweaver creates the frameset HTML file for you. I just want to give you a general understanding of all the files that you're creating so that the following steps make more sense.

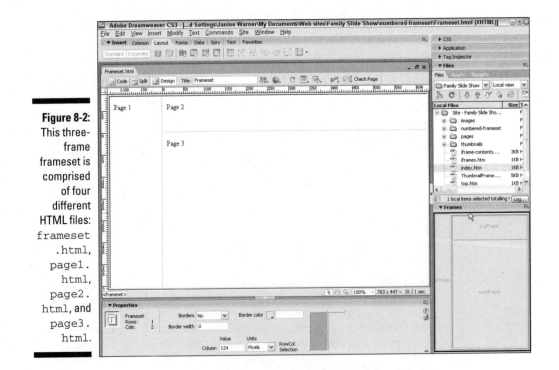

Figure 8-2:
This three-frame frameset is comprised of four different HTML files: `frameset .html`, `page1. html`, `page2. html`, and `page3. html`.

To help you understand how this works, look at the example in Figure 8-2. In this document, you see three frames, each displaying a different HTML page. The fourth HTML file that makes up the frame page *contains* the other frames but doesn't show up in the browser. This file is the frameset file, and it describes where and how each frame is displayed. For example, whether they are on the left or the right side of the page, the top or bottom, and how large they are. The frameset file also contains other information, such as the name of each frame, which is used to specify which frame a link opens into, or *targets*. You find out more about linking frames in the "Setting Targets and Links in Frames" section, later in this chapter.

Creating a frame in Dreamweaver

When you create a frame page in Dreamweaver, realizing that the file you are starting with is the *frameset* file is important — the file doesn't show up in the browser but merely instructs the browser how to display the rest of the frames and which pages to use as content for each frame. When you edit the *content* of any of the frames in the frameset, you are editing not the frameset file but the files that populate the framed regions within the frameset.

If you're not using a program like Dreamweaver, you have to edit the files separately, but Dreamweaver makes designing with frames easier by letting you edit the content of each frame in the *context* of the frameset as it looks in a browser. If you can grasp this concept, you've come a long way toward understanding how frames work and how to use Dreamweaver to create and edit them. If it hasn't sunk in yet, read on and it will.

Creating a frame by using the Split Frame command

You can create frames in two ways in Dreamweaver. The first method for creating frames is to split a single HTML file into two sections, which then become individual frames. When you do that, Dreamweaver automatically generates an untitled page with the `<frameset>` tag and then additional untitled pages appear in each of the frames within the frameset. Suddenly, you're managing several pages, not just one. This concept is important to understand because you have to save and name each of these pages as a separate file, even though Dreamweaver makes you think you're working on only one page that's broken into sections.

Always save your HTML files first before inserting anything into them. However, the opposite is true when you work with frame files in Dreamweaver. Wait until after you create all the frames in your frameset and *then* save them one at a time; otherwise, tracking your files is too complicated and confusing. I explain more in the "Saving files in a frameset" section, later in this chapter.

To create a simple frameset in Dreamweaver, such as the one shown in Figure 8-2, follow these steps:

1. **Choose File⇨New.**

   The New Document dialog box opens, as shown in Figure 8-3.

2. **From the icons on the left, select Page from Sample.**

3. **In the Sample Folder list, select Frameset.**

   The predefined framesets are displayed in a list under the Sample Page category.

4. **In the Sample Page list, select a Frameset design.**

   When you click to select the name of a predefined frameset, a preview is displayed in the far right of the dialog box, as shown in Figure 8-3.

5. **Click the Create button.**

   The frameset is created automatically and opens in Dreamweaver's workspace. If you have Accessibility alerts turned on in Dreamweaver's Preferences, you will be prompted with an alert and an Accessibility dialog box, where you can enter Accessibility attributes for the frameset.

6. **Click and drag any of the bars dividing the frames to adjust the size of the frame area.**

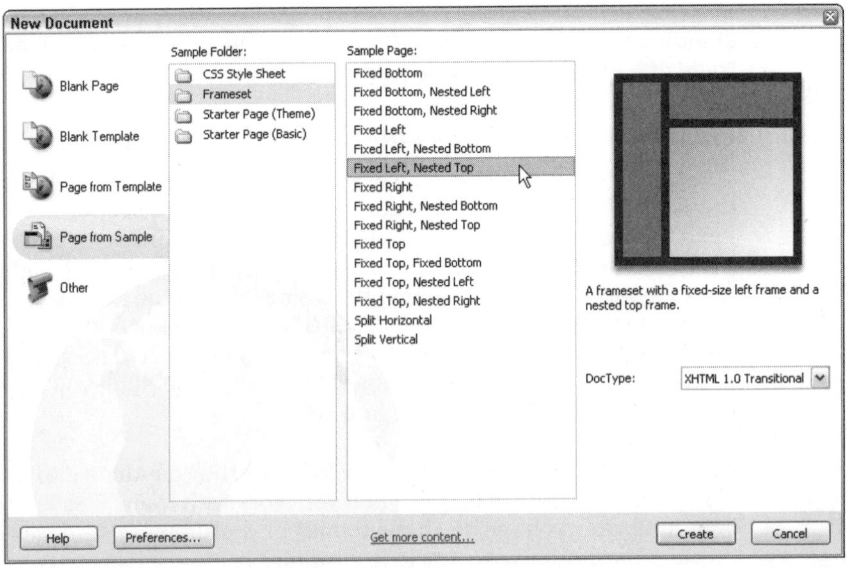

Figure 8-3: A long list of predefined framesets among the Sample pages makes creating new frames easier.

7. **To edit each section of the frameset, click inside the frame that you want to work on and edit it as you would any other HTML page.**

Remember, always save your files before setting links or inserting images and other files.

You can type text, insert images, create tables, and add any other features just as you do for any other page.

For instructions on saving all the files in a frameset, continue with the instructions in the section "Saving files in a frameset," later in this chapter.

Creating a frame by using the Frames icon on the Layout Insert bar

Another way to create frames is with the Frames icon, which displays several predefined framesets in a drop-down list, as shown in Figure 8-4. The Layout Insert bar (available by clicking the Layout tab from the Insert bar at the top of the work area) includes the Frames icon.

To create a framed page using the Frames icon on the Layout Insert bar, follow these steps:

1. **Choose File⇨New⇨Blank Page.**

2. **In the Page Type list, select HTML. Then in the Layout list, select <none>.**

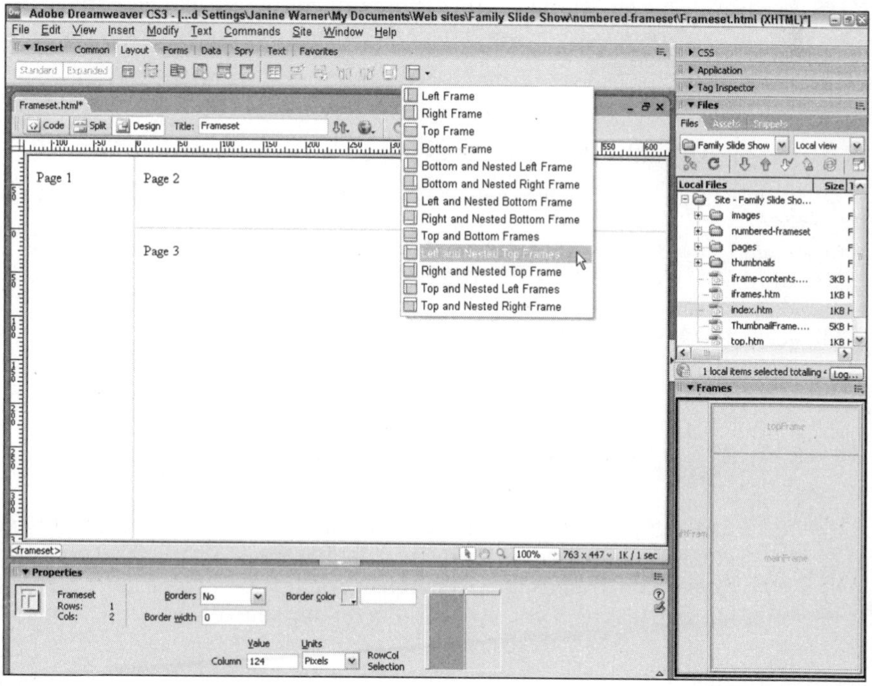

Figure 8-4:
Click the Frames icon and select from predefined framesets.

Viewing frame borders

If you don't see the borders of your frames displayed in Dreamweaver's workspace, as you see in Figures 8-1, 8-2, and 8-4, you may need to change the View settings in Dreamweaver. To make frame borders visible, click to place your cursor in one of the frames within your frameset and choose View➪Visual Aids➪Frame Borders. Your frame borders should automatically appear in the workspace. To hide frame borders in Dreamweaver's workspace, choose View➪Visual Aids➪Frame Borders again. Note that this does not turn off the display of frame borders in a browser. If you don't want your borders to be seen by visitors to your site, you need to turn off frame borders, as described in the "Changing Frame Borders" section later in this chapter.

3. **Click the Create button to create a new blank page.**

   A blank HTML page is created and opened in the main Dreamweaver workspace.

4. **From the Layout Insert bar, click the Frames icon. In the drop-down list, select the design that most closely approximates the type of frameset you want to build (refer to Figure 8-4).**

   The selected frameset is created automatically and opens in the Dreamweaver workspace, replacing the blank HTML page created in Step 3.

   Don't worry if it isn't exactly the design you want; you can alter it later.

5. **Modify the frameset as needed.**

   You can resize the frames by clicking and dragging the borders.

   You can also split frames by choosing Modify➪Frameset and then choosing to split the frame left, right, up, or down.

To save your files, continue with the instructions in the next section, "Saving files in a frameset."

Saving files in a frameset

As I mention earlier, you shouldn't save your frameset file until *after* you add all your frames; otherwise, keeping track of your files gets complicated. Remember, frames in HTML consist of at least two or more HTML files, even if it appears as if you are working on only one file.

When you are ready to save, Dreamweaver gives you two save options for saving all the files. You can either save everything all at once or save each frame and frameset individually. The example in the preceding section, "Creating a frame in Dreamweaver," is comprised of four separate HTML files, and each needs to be named and saved to your hard drive.

To save all the files in the frames document you create, follow these steps:

1. **Choose File⇨Save All.**

   The Save As dialog box appears, asking you to name the file and designate a folder to save it in. This is the first of several Save As dialog boxes you see (how many depends on how many frames your document contains).

2. **Enter a name for the file.**

   Dreamweaver suggests a name, but you can choose your own. The first file you save represents the *frameset* file (the file that holds all the other frames in place). You can tell this by looking at the Dreamweaver Document window behind the Save As dialog box: The entire document has a thick dotted highlight around it, representing the frameset.

3. **Browse your hard drive to locate the desired folder for the HTML files and then click the Save button.**

   The first frameset file is saved, and a new Save As dialog box appears for the next one. For each frameset file, you need a distinct name. I like names such as `frame1.html` and `frame2.html`, or `leftframe.html`, `rightframe.html`. It doesn't matter too much, but such names can help you distinguish the frame files later. After you save all the frames, the Save As dialog box disappears.

Carefully name the files that you save in a way that helps you keep them in order and identify which area they represent. Notice that as you are prompted to save each file, Dreamweaver indicates the frame area by highlighting it with a dark border on-screen behind the dialog box.

After you save and name your documents the first time, choosing Save All saves all files in your frameset without prompting you separately for each frame. Choosing Save All is a good way to make sure that all the pages in your frameset are saved whenever you edit a frames-based document.

Sometimes, you may not want to save all the files at once. To save an individual frame displayed in a frameset without saving all the other frames, place your cursor in any of the frames and choose File⇨Save Frame just as you save any other individual page. Dreamweaver saves only the file for the frame in which your cursor is located.

Resist using frames when linking to other Web sites

I understand that most people don't want to lose viewers to another site when they create a link, but that's the nature of the Web. If your site is designed well, you shouldn't have to worry about losing people. Instead, you should show them around your informative site and then politely guide them to other resources they may find of interest — and let them go. If you link to another site and target that link within your frames, you keep users captive and usually leave them annoyed with you for taking up valuable browser space and making it harder to navigate to the site they've followed your link to visit. By displaying content from other sites within one or more of the frames in your site, you risk doing yourself far more harm than good.

If you insist on using frames when you link to another site, do so discreetly by placing a small, narrow frame across the bottom of the screen or the left side — not a wide band across the top, and certainly not more than one frame that still contains information from your site. Not only is this rude and ugly, but some people have been sued by sites who charged that using frames when they linked misled visitors into thinking the content belonged to them when it didn't.

Another reason not to use frames when you link to someone else's site is that other sites use frames, too. If you link a site that uses frames into a site that uses frames, you quickly create a mess of frames within frames that makes navigation confusing at best. Not everyone knows you can get out of frames by right-clicking a link in Windows or clicking and holding a link on a Mac and choosing Open Frame in Separate Window. Now that you know this trick, at least you can get out of a framed situation if you ever find yourself trapped in one.

To save only the page that defines the frameset, make sure the entire frameset is selected (you can do this by clicking in the upper-left corner of the workspace), and then choose File⇨Save Frameset. If you have not selected the entire frameset, the Save Frameset option doesn't appear on the File menu. *Remember:* This page doesn't appear in any of the frames; it simply defines the entire display area, specifying which of the other pages appear in each frame as well as the position and size of the frames.

As you continue to work on your frame page, remember that whenever you make a change in one of the content frames, you edit content in a *different* file from the one you started with (the frameset file). You may get confused as to which file you need to save when working in this manner. Don't worry — this is what confuses a lot of people about using frames in Dreamweaver. When you edit the content in one of the frames, make sure that your cursor is still in that frame when you choose File⇨Save Frame so that you save the page that corresponds to the frame you are working on. To be safe, you can always choose File⇨Save All Frames to save all changes to all files in the frameset, including the frameset file itself. The Save All command is also useful when you make changes to several of the frames and want to save all the changes with just one command.

Setting Targets and Links in Frames

One of the best features of frames is that you can change the contents of each frame separately within the Web browser. This feature opens a wide range of design possibilities that improves navigation for your site. One common way to use a frameset is to create a frame that displays a list of links to various pages of your site and then opens those links into another frame on the same page. This technique makes it possible to keep a list of links constantly visible and makes navigation a lot simpler and more intuitive.

Setting links from a file in one frame so that the pages they link to open in another frame is like linking from one page to another, and that's essentially what you're doing. What makes linking within a frameset distinctive is that, in addition to indicating which page you want to open with the link, you have to specify which frame section it _targets_ (opens into).

But before you can set those links, you need to do a few things: First, you need to create some other pages that you can link to (if you haven't done so already). Create new pages as you would create any other page in Dreamweaver, using any of the template or sample page options, and then save each of the pages individually. If your pages already exist, you're more than halfway there; it's just a matter of linking to those pages.

The other thing you have to do before you can set links is to name each frame so that you can specify where the linked file loads. If you don't, the page just replaces the frameset altogether when someone clicks the link, and this defeats the purpose of using frames in the first place.

Naming frames

Naming a _frame_ is different from naming the _file_ that the frame represents. You find out how to name the files in the previous section, "Saving files in a frameset." The _frame name_ is like a nickname that allows you to distinguish your frames from one another on a page and refer to them individually — this becomes important when you set links and want to target a link to open in a particular area of the frameset. The filename is the name of the HTML file for the frame. The frame name is the nickname you refer to when you want to set links.

You can see the names of your frames in the Frames panel, shown in Figure 8-5. If you're happy with the names that Dreamweaver automatically assigned to your frames, you can skip the following steps.

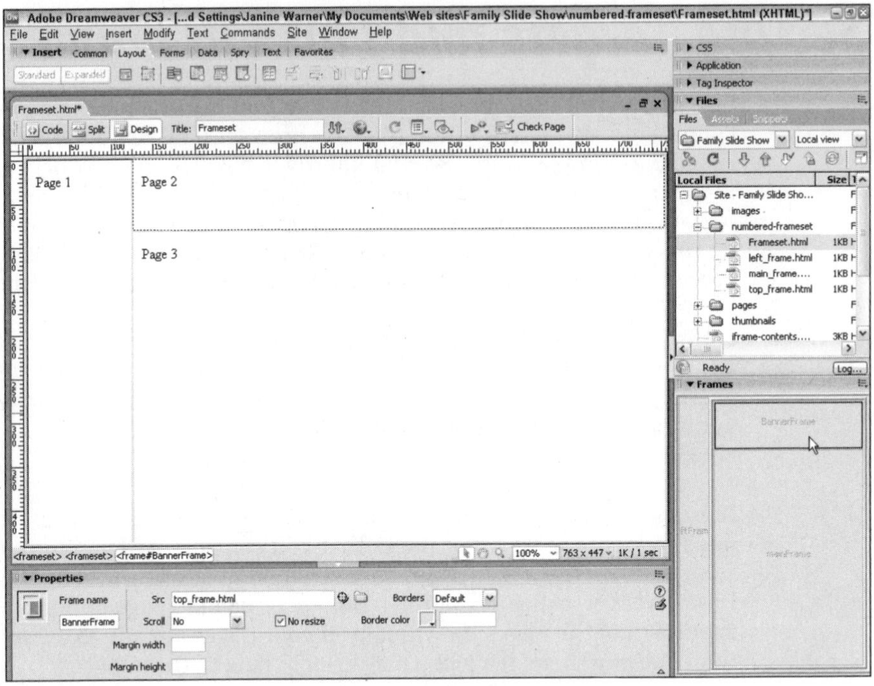

Figure 8-5:
The Frames panel provides access to frame properties, such as frame names.

If you want to change the names of the frames in your frameset or assign your own name as you create a new frame, follow these steps:

1. **Open an existing frameset or create a new one.**

   See the "Creating a frame in Dreamweaver" section, earlier in this chapter, if you don't know how to create a frameset.

2. **Choose Window➪Frames.**

   The Frames panel opens to the right of the work area (refer to Figure 8-5). The Frames panel is a miniature representation of the frames on your page that enables you to select different frames by clicking the corresponding frame area within the panel.

3. **Click to place your cursor in the area of the Frames panel that corresponds to the frame you want to name.**

   In Figure 8-5, I selected the top frame. You can click to select any of the frames in the panel. The Property inspector displays the properties for that particular frame. You can make any changes to the frame's properties by altering the properties in the Property inspector after selecting the frame. You can also select the entire frameset by clicking the border around all the frames in the Frames panel. The Frames panel allows you to select only one frame or frameset at a time.

4. **In the Frame Name text box on the left side of the Property inspector, type a name for the frame.**

   Dreamweaver assigns names automatically when you save the files in a frameset. In the example shown in Figure 8-5, Dreamweaver assigned the names `topFrame`, `mainFrame`, and `leftFrame`. You can leave these names as is or change them to anything else in the Property inspector (just don't use spaces or special characters in the names).

   In the example, I changed `topFrame` to `bannerFrame`. You should name your frames in a way that makes sense to you and helps you remember what they are so you can better target them.

5. **Choose File⇨Save Frameset to save the frameset page.**

   The frameset is the file you don't see in the display area that describes the other frames and contains information such as frame names.

   Remember, you can save any individual frame by placing your cursor in the frame and choosing File⇨Save, or you can save all the files in your frameset (including the frameset page) by choosing File⇨Save All Frames. Refer to the "Saving files in a frameset" section, earlier in this chapter, for more information on saving frames.

Now that you identified or changed the names of your frames, you're ready to start setting links that target frames. Don't close these files yet — you want to use them to follow the steps in the next section to set links.

I like to save my work on a regular basis so that I never lose more than a few minutes of work if my system crashes or the power goes out. Be aware, however, that when you work with frames, you need to save all your pages to save your work.

Setting links to a target frame

Setting links in a frameset requires some preliminary work. If you jumped to this section without creating a frameset or naming your frames, you may want to refer to the sections earlier in this chapter. If you already have a frameset, have named the frames, and just want to find out how to set links, this section is where you want to be.

Setting links in a frameset is like setting any other links between pages, except you need to specify the *target frame,* meaning the frame where the linked page will appear when a user clicks the link. For example, if you want a link in the left frame to control what's in the main frame, you need to specify the main frame as the target in the link. If you don't specify a target, the link opens in the same frame the link is in. Because the most common reason to use frames is to keep navigation links in one frame and open their corresponding pages in another, you probably want to target a frame when you set a link.

If this seems confusing, don't fret. After you try the following steps, it should become clear how targets work in framesets:

1. **Open an existing frame set or create a new frameset.**

   In Figure 8-6, you see that I am using the My Summer Family Slide Show Web site, which I created to use as an example in this chapter.

2. **Highlight the text or click to select the image you want to serve as the link.**

   In my example, I selected the second thumbnail image in the left column. Note that the process of targeting a link works the same whether you are creating a link with text or an image.

3. **In the Property inspector, enter any URL in the Link text box or use the Browse button to select the page you want to link to.**

   In my example, I used the Browse button to set a link to the file named Yeah.html (this page includes a larger version of the thumbnail picture I've selected).

4. **In the Target drop-down list in the Property inspector, choose the name of the frame that you want the link to open into.**

   In my example, I selected the frame named *main* as the target. You should choose the name that corresponds to the frame where you want your linked page to open. Notice that Dreamweaver conveniently lists all the frames you named in your document in the Target drop-down list, which I have open in Figure 8-6.

   The result is shown in Figure 8-7. When the frameset appears in a browser and a user clicks the second thumbnail of the two little girls clapping their hands in the left frame, the page named Yeah.html with a larger version of that photo appears in the main frame area.

You can't test your links until you preview your work in a browser, and you have to save all your framed pages to ensure that your preview will work properly. To save all the pages in a frameset, choose File➪Save All.

Comparing target options

You have many options when you target links in a frameset. As shown in the preceding section, "Setting links to a target frame," you can specify that a linked page open in another frame within your frameset. But in addition, you can set linked pages to open in the same frame as the page with the link, to open a completely new page with no frames, and even to open a second browser window and display the page without affecting the original framed design. Table 8-1 provides a list of target options and what they mean. You can find all these options in the Target drop-down list in the Property inspector.

Figure 8-6:
Use the
Target field
in the
Property
inspector to
specify
where a
linked page
will appear
within a
frameset.

Figure 8-7:
The
selected link
opens the
page and
targets the
main frame
area.

The Target drop-down list in the Property inspector is activated only when you select a linked image or section of text — there must be a link in the Link field of the Property inspector before you can set a target.

Table 8-1	Understanding Frame Target Options
Target Name	**What It Does**
_blank	Opens the linked document into a fresh new browser window.
_parent	Opens the linked document into the parent file of the page that has the link. (The *parent* is the file, frame, or frameset that contains the frame with the link.)
_self	Opens the linked document in the same frame as the original link, replacing the current content of the frame. This is the default option and usually does not need to be specified.
_top	Opens the linked document into the outermost frameset, replacing the entire contents of the browser window.

Changing Frame Properties

As you get more sophisticated in using frames, you may want to further refine your frames by changing properties, which enables you to turn off frame borders, change the frame or border colors, limit scrolling, and so on. To access these options in Dreamweaver, choose Window➪Frames, click inside the Frames panel in the area that corresponds to the frame that you want to change, and then use the Property inspector to access the options I describe in the following four sections. Figure 8-8 shows the Property inspector as it appears when you select a frameset in the Frames panel.

Changing frame borders

I think the best thing you can do with a frame border is to turn it off. You can turn the borders off for your site by choosing No from the Borders drop-down list in the Property inspector for either the frameset or any of the individual frames in the frameset. Your other options include Yes, which forces the borders to be visible, and Default, which usually means Yes. In the case of individual frames, however, the Default option inherits the settings for the parent frameset.

Figure 8-8:
The
selected
frames or
framesets
and their
properties
are visible
in the
Property
inspector.

You can make global border settings by using the Property inspector and applying the settings to the frameset. To select the frameset so that its properties are visible in the inspector, click the border that encloses the frameset in the Frames panel. Figure 8-8 shows a frameset selected in the Frames panel and its corresponding properties displayed in the Property inspector.

If you choose to keep your borders visible, you may want to customize the color by clicking the Border Color square in the Property inspector and then choosing a color from the color palette.

If you select a specific border, the Property inspector also enables you to specify the border width. Simply enter a value in pixels in the Border Width text field to change the width of the selected border.

Frame border colors are not well-supported by all browsers and may not display as you intend. Most designers simply turn off frame borders, but if you do keep them make sure your design still looks okay if the borders are thick and grey, which is the default. Many browsers, including recent ones, don't display a different border color.

Changing frame sizes

The easiest way to change the size of a frame is to select the border and drag it until the frame is the size you want. When you select the border, the Property inspector displays the size of the frame, enabling you to change the size in pixels or as a percentage of the display area by entering a number in the Row or Column text boxes. If you specify 0 width for your frame borders, you may not see them on the page in order to drag and resize them. If this is the case, you can view the borders by choosing View➪Visual Aids➪Frame Borders, and Dreamweaver indicates the borders with a thin gray line that you can easily select.

Changing scrolling and resizing options

Scrolling options control whether a viewer can scroll up and down or left and right in a frame area. As shown in Figure 8-9, the scrolling options for frames are Yes, No, Auto, and Default. As a general rule, I recommend leaving the Scroll option set to Auto because a visitor's browser can then turn on scrolling if necessary. That is, if the viewer's display area is too small to see all the content of the frame, the frame becomes scrollable. If the content fits within the visible boundaries, the scroll arrows don't appear.

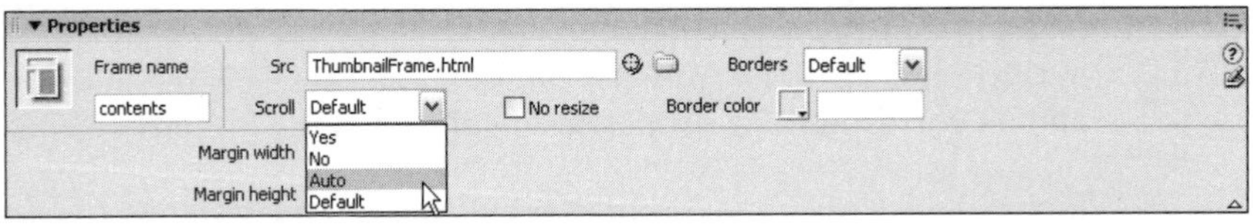

Figure 8-9:
The Scroll options list in the Property inspector.

If you set this option to Yes, the scroll arrows are visible whether they're needed or not. If you set it to No, they won't be visible, even if that means your viewer can't see all the content of the frame — a sometimes dangerous proposition because there's no easy way to scroll. Default leaves it up to the browser. In most browsers, the Default option results in the same display as the Auto option, but Default yields unpredictable results. As a general rule, using Auto is best.

Also note the No Resize option in Figure 8-9. If you select this option, a visitor to your site can't change the size of the frames. If you leave this option unchecked, your user can select the border and drag it to make the frame area smaller or larger, just as you can when you develop your frames in Dreamweaver. Generally, I like to give viewers control, but I sometimes select the No Resize option if I want to ensure that my viewers don't alter the design.

Setting margin height and width

The Margin Width and Margin Height options enable you to specify the amount of margin space around a frame. Normally in a browser window, a small margin is visible between the edge of the window and any content, such as images or text. That's why you can't normally place an image on your page flush against the edge of the browser. With frames, though, you can actually control the size of the margin or even eliminate the margin.

I generally recommend that you set the margin to at least two pixels and make the margin larger if you want to create more space around your content. If you want to get rid of the margin, set it to 0 and any images or text in the frame appear flush against the edge of the frame or the browser window if the frame touches the edge of the browser. If the frame touches another frame, you can use this technique to create the impression of seamless images across frames.

Chapter 9

Coordinating Your Design Work

· ·

In This Chapter

▶ Creating a template to speed development

▶ Making global changes with templates

▶ Saving elements in the Dreamweaver Library for easy access

▶ Using predesigned templates

▶ Designing a Web page with the Dreamweaver Tracing Image feature

· ·

Strive for consistency in all your designs — except when you're trying to be unpredictable. A little surprise here and there can keep your Web site lively. But, generally, most Web sites work best and are easiest to navigate when they follow a consistent design theme. Case in point: Most readers take for granted that books don't change their designs from page to page, and newspapers don't change headline fonts and logos every day. Books and newspapers want to make life easier for their readers, and consistency is one of the primary tools for making sure readers find publications familiar. That doesn't mean you should limit modern Web design to what's possible in print, but it does means we can all learn a thing or two from hundreds of years of print design.

Dreamweaver offers several features to help you develop and maintain a consistent look and feel across your site. In this chapter, you discover three of my favorite Dreamweaver features — templates, Library items, and the Tracing Image feature. Find out how they combine to make your design work faster and easier to manage, and you'll be well on your way to simplifying your work even before you start. At the end of this chapter, you also find instructions for using Dreamweaver's predesigned templates, starter pages, and style sheets.

Templating Your Type

Many Web design programs boast about their HTML templates. Often what they really mean is that the program includes some ready-made page designs. Dreamweaver takes this concept a few leaps further by providing template design features that enable you to create a predesigned page and specify which sections can and can't be altered. This is a valuable feature if you work with a team of people with varying skill levels or if you have to create dozens of pages with the same basic layout. For example, if you're building a site for a real-estate company and want to let the employees update the sales listings without messing up the page design, a template with locked regions can be an ideal way to allow sales staff to add new information without accidentally breaking anything.

Templates are best used when you're creating a number of pages that share the same characteristics, such as the same background color, column design, or image arrangement. For example, if you're creating a Web site for a bed-and-breakfast inn, you might create a template for all the pages where you want to show off the rooms in the Inn. In that case, you might create a room template design with a spot for a photo, descriptive text, and forward and back arrows so that visitors can easily move through the pages for all the rooms. As you create each new page, you would start with the template, changing only the photo, descriptive text, and links.

The most powerful aspect of Dreamweaver's template feature is the capability to make global changes to every page created from a template.

Creating Templates

Creating a template is as easy as creating any other file in Dreamweaver. You can start by creating an HTML page as you would any other page (or modifying an existing page as you would edit any other page). The main difference is that when you save the file, you save it as a template and the file is stored in a special Templates folder, which Dreamweaver automatically creates in the main folder for your Web site. Templates must be kept in this common folder for the automated features in Dreamweaver to work properly.

The template features work only if you define your Web site in Dreamweaver. If you haven't gone through the setup process to define your site yet, refer to Chapter 2.

Creating editable and uneditable regions

Perhaps the most difficult concept to grasp when it comes to templates is how editable and uneditable regions work and why they're important. Here's the short answer (we'll get into the details later in this chapter).

When you create a template design, every aspect of the design is automatically locked, or uneditable, until you designate it as an *editable region* — that's what Dreamweaver calls areas of a template that can be changed in any page created from the template. The steps for making a region editable are relatively simple (you find detailed instructions in the exercises that follow). When you create a new page from a template, *only* the editable regions can be altered. If you want to make global changes using a template, only the uneditable areas can be used to make changes across multiple pages.

For example, suppose you create a design for an online magazine with the logo and navigation bar at the top of the page and the copyright and navigation links at the bottom of the page set up as uneditable. Then you create a design area where a story and photo will be added to the middle of each page created from the template; you designate that area as an editable region. As you create new pages from the template, you can replace the photo and story on each page because they are in an editable area, but you would not be able to change the logo, navigation links, or copyright. As a result, you can create many pages that are the same, except each features a different story and photo in the area designated as the editable region.

Now imagine that one day you decide to change the logo for your company. It must be changed on all the pages made from the template. No problem. You simply open the template file you created in the first place and edit the logo there. Those changes are automatically applied to all the pages created from that template because the logo is in an uneditable region. That saves a ton of time because you don't have to replace the logo on each page. You could make the same kinds of global changes to the copyright at the bottom of the page because it's also in a locked, or uneditable, region and can be changed only on the template.

Any changes you might make to the story or photo area in the template are not applied to any of the pages created from the template because you've created that section as an editable region. This is important because you wouldn't want to make a global change and overwrite all the individual stories and photos you've inserted into each of your pages. If this is still confusing, it may help you to see this in action in the lessons that follow.

It comes down to this: Locked areas of a template (areas you don't designate as editable) can be changed only in the template itself, but those changes can then be applied automatically to all the pages created from that template. Areas of a template designated as editable can be changed in any page created from the template, but those areas cannot be automatically updated by changing the template.

You can create both *editable regions* and *editable attributes* in a Dreamweaver template. Editable attributes relate only to specific elements in a template. For example, you may want to make the attributes of an image editable to allow the alignment to be changed from left to right, even if the image itself is not editable.

Why the head section is editable by default

In a new template, all elements are locked by default except for the document head section, which is indicated by the `<head>` `</head>` tags. These tags enable you to change the title in any page created from a template or to insert JavaScript if you use behaviors on the page. For the template to be of much use for building new pages, you must make areas in the body of the page editable as well. Remember that you can always go back to the template later to alter the design, make more areas editable, or lock areas so they can't be changed.

Creating a new template

To create a template that you can use to create new pages, follow these steps:

1. **Choose File⇨New.**

   The New Document window opens.

2. **In the list on the left, click the Blank Template icon, shown in Figure 9-1.**

3. **In the Template Type list, choose HTML Template.**

   You can also choose from a variety of other template options, including templates for ASP (Active Server Pages), ColdFusion, JSP, and PHP. These file types are used when creating dynamic Web sites. You find an introduction to creating dynamic Web sites in Chapters 13, 14, and 15. In this example, I am creating a new HTML page template.

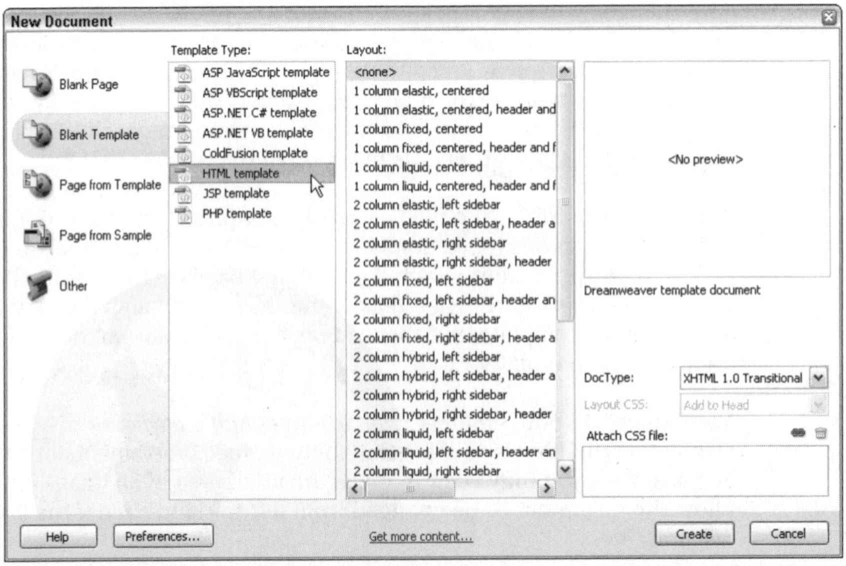

Figure 9-1:
The Templates panel displays a list of all available templates in the selected site and provides access to template editing functions.

4. In the Layout area, choose <none> to create a blank page.

Alternatively, you can choose from the many CSS layout options. These CSS layout options are covered in Chapter 6.

5. Click the Create button.

A new blank template is created and opens in the main work area, and the New Document dialog box closes.

6. Choose File⇨Save.

If you have not disabled it, a dialog box should appear stating that the template doesn't have any editable regions and asking whether you really want to save it.

7. Click OK to save the page as is for now.

The Save As Template window appears

8. Give the template a name and a description, as shown in Figure 9-2.

The description field is optional. Note that the Save As Template dialog box includes a list of any templates that are already associated with the site. It also includes a Site field at the top with a drop-down list that includes all the sites you've defined in Dreamweaver. This makes it possible to save a template into any site you've defined as you created it.

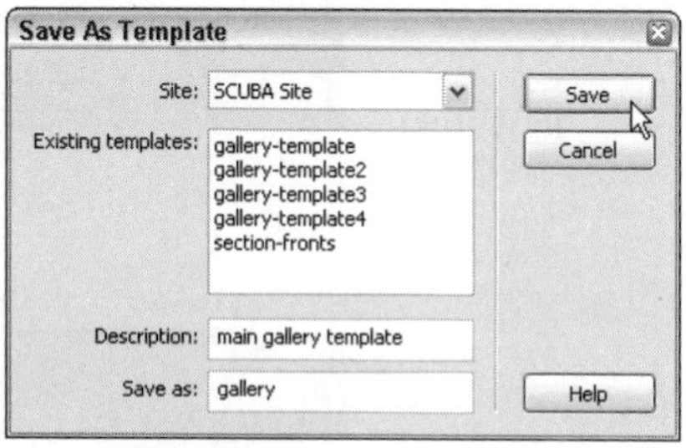

Figure 9-2: The Save as Template window displays existing templates.

Save As Template

Site: SCUBA Site

Existing templates: gallery-template
gallery-template2
gallery-template3
gallery-template4
section-fronts

Description: main gallery template

Save as: gallery

Save

Cancel

Help

9. Click Save and the template is automatically saved with a `.dwt` extensions.

When you save the file, Dreamweaver automatically adds the `.dwt` extension, designating the file as a Dreamweaver template. You can now edit this page as you edit any other HTML page, inserting images, text, tables, and so on.

10. Choose Modify⇨Page Properties and specify the page-wide settings.

Use the Page Properties dialog box to specify background, text, and link colors, as well as other options that apply to the entire page (Page Properties options are covered in Chapter 2).

When you set page properties, Dreamweaver creates the corresponding CSS styles in the template file and displays them in the CSS panel. You find more information about CSS editing options in Chapters 5 and 6.

11. **To create an editable region:**

    a. **Select any content area, image, or text.**

    b. **Right-click (Windows) or Control+click (Mac), and choose Templates⇨New Editable Region (as shown in Figure 9-3).**

       The New Editable Region dialog box opens.

    c. **Give the new region a name. I recommend something that identifies the type of content it is, such as *headline* or *main-photo*.**

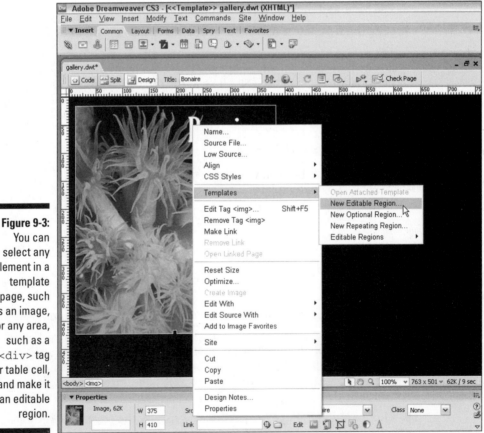

Figure 9-3:
You can select any element in a template page, such as an image, or any area, such as a `<div>` tag or table cell, and make it an editable region.

The region you define as editable becomes an area that can be changed in any page created from the template. You can have multiple editable regions in one template, such as a photo that is an editable region and a photo caption that is a separate editable region. Each editable region must have a different name, and editable region names cannot use spaces or special characters (underscores and hyphens are okay).

d. Click OK.

The editable region is enclosed in a highlighted area with a tab at the top left, identified by the name you gave the region.

12. **When you finish designing the page, choose File⇨Save to save your template.**

When you save a new template page or you save an existing page as a template, Dreamweaver automatically adds the .dwt extension and saves the file into a folder called Templates. If you don't already have a Templates folder in your local root folder, Dreamweaver creates one for you. (If Dreamweaver does not automatically create a Template file, make sure you create a new folder named Templates and save all your template files inside it.) For templates to be listed in the New Document window, they must be saved in a folder called Templates.

If you save a template in Dreamweaver before you specify any editable regions, you will be prompted with a warning because templates aren't useful without editable regions. You do not have to create editable regions before you save a template, but you will not be able to make any changes in any pages created from a template until you create one or more editable regions. You can always go back and add editable regions later, so it's not a problem if you want to save your work before you create editable regions.

Saving any page as a template

Sometimes you get partway through creating a page before you realize that you're likely to want more pages like it and you should create a template so you don't have to re-create the same page design over and over. Similarly, you may be working on a page that someone else created that you want to turn into a template. No matter where the original page comes from, creating a template from an existing page is just as easy as creating a new template from scratch.

To save a page as a template, follow these steps:

1. **Open the page that you want to turn into a template.**

Choose File⇨Open and browse to find your file. Or open the site in the Files panel and double-click the file to open it.

2. **Choose File⇨Save As Template, as shown in Figure 9-4.**

   The Save As Template dialog box appears (refer to Figure 9-2).

3. **In the Site drop-down list, select a site.**

   The menu lists all the sites you have defined in Dreamweaver. By default, the site you have defined and opened in the Files panel is selected when the dialog box opens. If you're working on a new site or haven't yet defined your site, read Chapter 2 for information on defining the site.

   You can use the Save As Template option to save a page as a template into any defined site, which makes it easy to save a page design from one site as a template for another site.

4. **In the Save As text box, type a name for the template.**

5. **Click the Save button.**

   Notice that the file now has the `.dwt` extension, indicating that it's a template. You can now make changes to this template the same way you edit any other template.

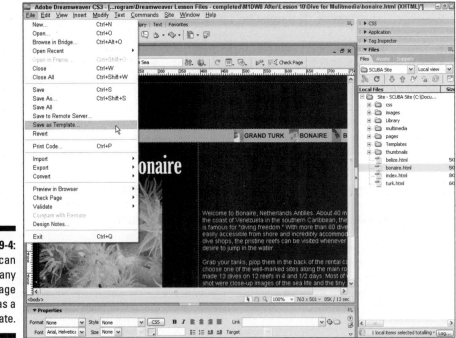

Figure 9-4:
You can save any HTML page as a template.

6. **Update links in the template.**

   When you save a new template page or you save an existing page as a template, Dreamweaver automatically adds the .dwt extension and saves the file into a folder called Templates. (If Dreamweaver does not automatically do this, make sure you create a new folder named Templates and save all your template files inside the Templates folder in your root site folder.) Because your original file was probably not saved in the Templates folder, any links to other pages or images must be updated when the file is saved. Click OK and Dreamweaver corrects any links in the file as it saves the file in the Templates folder.

7. **Make any changes that you want and then choose File⇨Save.**

   You edit a template just as you edit any other page in Dreamweaver.

8. **To create an editable region:**

   a. **Select any content area, image, or text.**

   b. **Right-click (Windows) or Control+click (Mac), and choose Templates⇨New Editable Region (as shown in Figure 9-3).**

   The New Editable Region dialog box opens.

   c. **Give the new region a name.**

   The region you define as editable becomes an area that can be changed in any page created from the template. You can create multiple editable regions in any template.

   d. **Click OK.**

   The editable region is enclosed in a highlighted area with a tab at the top left, identified by the name you gave the region.

9. **When you finish designing the page, choose File⇨Save to save your completed template.**

Making attributes editable

To create editable attributes in a template, follow these steps:

1. **In any Dreamweaver template, select an item that you want to have an editable attribute.**

   In the example shown in Figure 9-5, I selected a section of text and am in the process of making text attributes editable.

2. **Choose Modify⇨Templates⇨Make Attribute Editable.**

   The Editable Tag Attributes dialog box appears, shown in Figure 9-6.

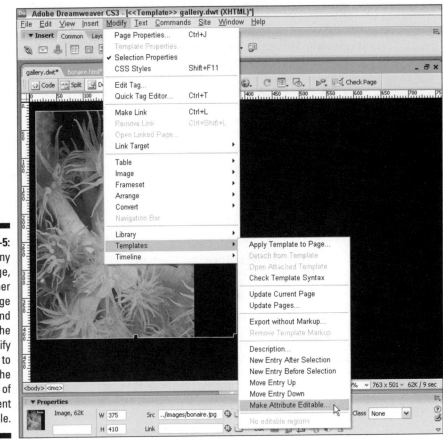

Figure 9-5:
Select any
text, image,
or other
page
element and
use the
Modify
menu to
make the
attributes of
that element
editable.

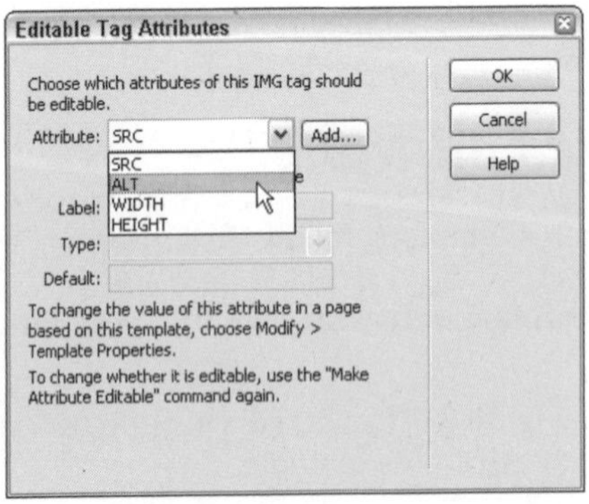

Figure 9-6:
Identify
which
attributes
you want to
be editable.

3. **From the Attribute drop-down list, choose the attribute you want to be editable.**

   If the attribute doesn't exist yet, click the Add button.

4. **Select the Make Attribute Editable option, and fill in the Label, Type, and Default options.**

   The attribute options vary depending on whether you select an image, text, or another element on the page. With these options, you can control whether an image can be changed and what specific attributes of the image tag may be altered when the template is used.

5. **Click OK.**

Creating a new page from a template

After you create your a template, you'll want to put it to use. You can use one template to create or modify all the pages in your Web site or create different templates for different sections. For example, in a site such as the SCUBA site shown in these examples, you might create one template for each of the sections that feature photos from a different country, or use one template for all the photo galleries and another for the main pages in each section. Once you've created a template or a collection of templates, using a template to create a new page is similar to creating any other HTML page.

To use a template to create a page, follow these steps:

1. **Choose File⇨New.**

   The New Document window opens.

2. **In the list on the left, click the Page from Template option, as shown in Figure 9-7.**

3. **In the Site list in the middle of the page, choose the name of the site that contains a template you want to use.**

   The templates in the selected site appear in Template for Site section just to the right of the Site list in the New Document window (see Figure 9-7).

4. **In the Template for Site list, select the template you want to use.**

   Notice that when you click the name of a template, a preview of the selected template appears on the far right of the New Document window. In the example shown in Figure 9-7, I selected the template called gallery-template4 from the SCUBA site.

5. **Click the Create button.**

   A new page is created from the template and appears in the main work area.

6. **Edit any of the regions of the page that are editable using Dreamweaver's regular editing features and save the file as you would save any other HTML page.**

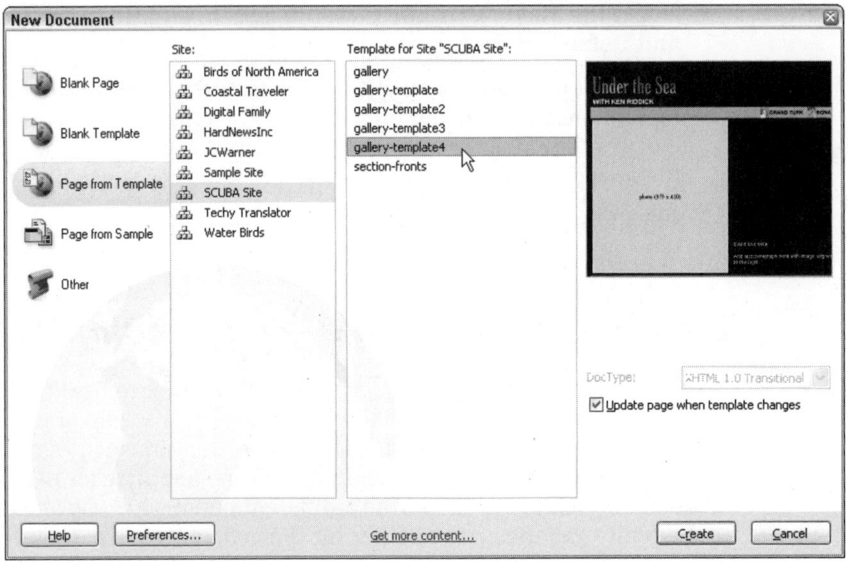

Figure 9-7:
From the
New
Document
window, you
can preview
and select
any template
saved in any
defined Web
site to
create a
new page.

New Document

Blank Page	Site:	Template for Site "SCUBA Site":
Blank Template	Birds of North America	gallery
Page from Template	Coastal Traveler	gallery-template
Page from Sample	Digital Family	gallery-template2
Other	HardNewsInc	gallery-template3
	JCWarner	gallery-template4
	Sample Site	section-fronts
	SCUBA Site	
	Techy Translator	
	Water Birds	

Under the Sea
WITH KEN RIDDICK

DocType: XHTML 1.0 Transitional
☑ Update page when template changes

Help   Preferences...   Get more content...   Create   Cancel

Making Global Changes with Templates

One of the greatest advantages of using templates is that you can automatically apply changes to all the pages created with a template by altering the original template. For example, if I created a series of pages using the gallery template shown in the preceding example, I could make changes to those pages by editing any of the uneditable regions in the template.

When you create new pages from a template, you can change only the editable regions in each of the files created from the template. When you edit a template, only the regions that are not defined as editable can be used to make global changes to all the pages created from the template.

To update files in a site that were created from a template, follow these steps:

1. **Open the template file.**

   Note that template files are distinguishable by the .dwt extension and are saved into the Template directory unless you have saved them to another location on your Web site.

2. **Use Dreamweaver's editing features to make any changes you want to the template.**

   Remember that only changes to uneditable regions will be automatically updated.

3. **Choose File➪Save.**

The Update Template Files dialog box appears, as shown in Figure 9-8.

4. **Click the Update button to modify all pages listed in the Update Template Files dialog box. Click the Don't Update button to leave these pages unchanged.**

   If you click Update, Dreamweaver automatically changes all the pages listed in the Update Template Files dialog box to reflect any changes made to uneditable regions of the template.

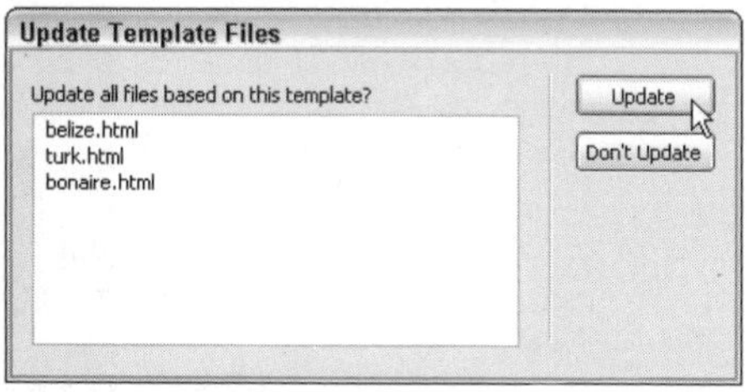

Figure 9-8:
You can update all files created from a template.

Update Template Files

Update all files based on this template?

belize.html
turk.html
bonaire.html

Update
Don't Update

Identifying a template

If you're not sure what template was used to create a page, you can open the template while you have the page open, make changes to the template, and update all pages created with it by following these steps:

1. **Open a document that uses the template that you want to change.**

2. **Choose Modify➪Templates➪Open Attached Template, as shown in Figure 9-9.**

   The template opens.

3. **Use Dreamweaver's regular editing functions to modify the template as you would edit any page or template.**

4. **Choose File➪Save.**

   The Update Template Files dialog box appears (refer to Figure 9-8).

5. **Click the Update button to modify all the pages listed in the Update Template Files dialog box. Click the Don't Update button to leave these pages unchanged.**

   If you chose Update, Dreamweaver automatically changes all the pages listed in the Update Template Files dialog box.

You can also apply changes to all the pages created from a template using the Update Pages option. To do so, you have to first open the template, and then make and save your changes without applying those changes to pages created with the template. Then anytime later, you can choose Modify➪ Templates➪Update Pages to apply the update.

Figure 9-9:
You can
open an
attached
template
from within
any page
created
from a
template.

Attaching and detaching templates

You can apply a template to an existing page by attaching it, and you can remove a template from a page by detaching it. When you apply a template to an existing document, the content in the template is added to the content already in the document. If a template is already applied to the page, Dreamweaver attempts to match editable areas that have the same name in both templates and to insert the contents from the editable regions of the page into the editable regions in the new template. This happens automatically if all region names are the same.

Remove or detach a template from a page if you want to ensure that changes to the original template don't affect the page created with the template. Detaching a template also unlocks all regions of a page, making it completely editable.

You can apply a template to an existing page by using any one of the following techniques:

- ✔ Choose Modify➪Templates➪Apply Template to Page and then double-click the name of a template to apply it to the page.
- ✔ Drag the template from the Template panel into the Document window.

If the editable regions don't match, Dreamweaver asks you to match inconsistent region names in a dialog box. After the region conflicts are resolved, click OK.

You can detach a template, or remove the template association from a file, by choosing Modify➪Templates➪Detach from Template. This action makes the file fully editable again, but any future changes you make to the template will not be reflected on the detached page.

Reusing Elements with the Library Feature

The Library feature is not a common feature in other Web design programs, so the concept may be new to you even if you've been developing Web sites for a while. The Library is handy when you have a single element you want to reuse on many pages, such as a copyright statement you want to appear at the bottom of each page or even something as complex as a row of navigation links.

A *Library item* is a snippet of code that can contain almost anything, including image references and links. After you save a section of code in the Library, you can insert it into any page with drag-and-drop ease. And if you ever need to change a Library item (by adding or changing a link, for example), you simply edit the stored Library item and Dreamweaver automatically updates the contents of the Library item on any or all pages where it appears throughout the site.

Like templates, Library items are a great way to share the work of your best designers with less experienced ones. For example, one designer can create a logo and another the navigation elements, and then these can be placed in the Library and made available to the entire team. You have more flexibility with Library items than templates because they are elements you can place anywhere on any page, even multiple times. Libraries are not shared among sites the way templates are, but you can copy and paste the same Library element from one site into another.

Library items cannot contain their own style sheets because the code for styles can appear only as part of the head area of an HTML file. You can, however, attach an external style sheet to a Library item to see how the styles will affect the display of the Library item, but the same styles must be available on each page where the Library item is used for the styles to be applied. (For more on style sheets, see Chapters 5 and 6.)

Creating and using Library items

The following sections show you the steps for creating a Library item, adding one to a page, and editing and updating a Library item across multiple pages. For these steps to work properly, you must do them in sequential order. Before creating or using Library items, you must first define a site and open it in the Files panel. (See Chapter 2 for instructions on defining a site in Dreamweaver.)

Creating a Library item within an existing page works well because you can see how the item looks before you add it to the Library. You can edit an item after it's in the Library, but it may not look just as it will on a Web page. For example, Library items don't include <body> tags when they are saved in the Library, so link colors are displayed as default blue when viewed in the Library, even if the link colors have been changed to, say, purple in the <body> tag of the page.

Creating a Library item

To create a Library item that you can use on multiple pages on your site, follow these steps:

1. **Open any existing file that has images, text, or other elements on the page that you want to save as a Library item.**

   Alternatively, you can create a new page and insert only the element you want to save to the Library.

2. **From this page, select an element or collection of elements that you want to save as a Library item, such as the row of images used for your site navigation.**

3. **Choose Modify⇨Library⇨Add Object to Library.**

   The Assets tab of the Files panel opens and displays the Library. Your new Library item appears as *Untitled*.

4. **Name the element as you would name any file in Explorer on a PC or the Finder on a Mac.**

   When you name a Library item, you automatically save it to the Library. You can then easily apply the item to any new or existing page in your site. The Library section of the Assets panel lists all Library items, as shown in Figure 9-10.

Figure 9-10:
The Assets
panel
displays all
Library
items, and
you can use
drag and
drop to save
and insert
Library
items to and
from pages.

Adding a Library item to a page

You can easily add elements from the Library to your pages by simply dragging them from the Assets panel to the page. When you add a Library item to a page, the content is inserted into the document and a relationship is established between the content on the page and the item in the Library. This is important because it enables you to edit the Library item later and apply the changes to all pages where the item appears, but it also means that you cannot edit the item on the page where it is inserted. You must edit Library items from within the Library, as you see in the following section.

To add a Library item to a page, follow these steps:

1. **Create a new document in Dreamweaver or open any existing file.**

2. **From the Files panel, click the Assets tab, and then click the Library icon.**

   The Library opens in the Assets panel (refer to Figure 9-10).

3. **Drag an item from the Library to the Document window.**

   Alternatively, you can select an item in the Library and click the Insert button. The item automatically appears on the page. After you insert a Library item on a page, you can use any of Dreamweaver's formatting features to position it on the page.

Highlighting Library items

Library items are highlighted to distinguish them from other elements on a page. You can customize the highlight color for Library items and show or hide the highlight color in the Preferences dialog box. To change or hide Library highlighting, follow these steps:

1. **Choose Edit⇨Preferences (Windows) or Dreamweaver⇨ Preferences (Mac).**

   The Preferences dialog box appears.

2. **In the Category section on the left, select Highlighting.**

3. **Click the color box to select a color for Library items. Check the Show box to display the Library highlight color on your pages.**

   Leave the box blank if you don't want to display the highlight color.

4. **Click OK to close the Preferences dialog box.**

Making global changes with Library items

One of the biggest timesaving advantages of the Dreamweaver Library feature is that you can make changes to Library items and automatically apply those changes to any or all pages where the Library item appears. To edit a Library item, follow these steps:

1. **From the Files panel, click the Assets tab and then click the Library icon.**

   The Library opens in the Assets panel (refer to Figure 9-10).

2. **Double-click any item listed in the Library to open it.**

   Dreamweaver opens a new window where you can edit the Library item.

   Because the Library item is just a snippet of code, it won't have a <body> tag in which to specify background, link, or text colors. Don't worry about this — the Library item acquires the right settings from the tags on the page where you insert it.

3. **Change the Library item as you would edit any element in Dreamweaver.**

   For example, you can change a link, edit the wording of text, change the font or size, and even add images, text, and other elements.

4. **Choose File⇨Save to save changes to the original item.**

   The Update Library Items dialog box opens, displaying a list of all pages where the Library item appears.

5. **To apply the changes you made to the Library item on all listed pages, click the Update button. If you don't want to apply the changes to all the pages where the Library item appears, click the Don't Update button.**

    If you clicked the Update button, the Update Pages dialog box appears and shows the progress of the updating. You can stop the update from this dialog box, if necessary.

If you want to create a new Library item based on an existing one without altering the original, follow Steps 1 through 3, and in place of Step 4, choose File⇨Save As and give the item a new name.

Editing one instance of a Library item

If you want to alter a Library item on a specific page where you have inserted it, or if you want to make changes to just a few pages, you can override the automated Library feature by detaching it, or breaking the link between the original item in the Library and the item inserted into the page.

After you break a connection, you can no longer update that page's Library item automatically.

To make a Library item editable, follow these steps:

1. **Open any file that contains a Library item and select the Library item.**

    The Property inspector displays the Library item options shown in Figure 9-11.

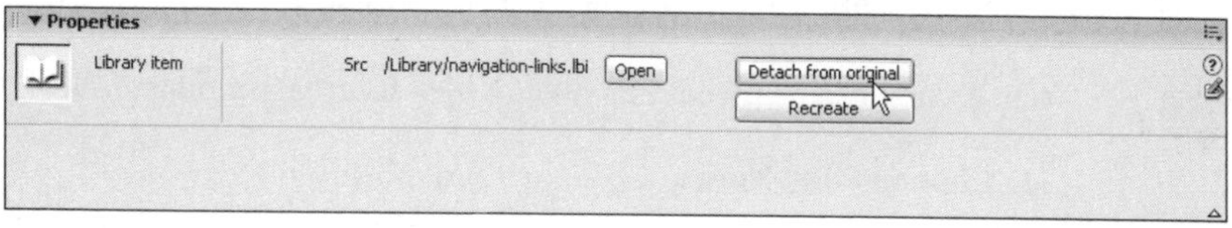

Figure 9-11:
You can detach a Library item in the Property inspector.

▼ Properties						
	Library item	Src /Library/navigation-links.lbi [Open]	[Detach from original] [Recreate]			

2. **Click the Detach from Original button.**

    A warning message appears, letting you know that if you proceed with detaching the Library item from the original, you can no longer update this occurrence of it when the original is edited.

3. **Click OK to detach the Library item.**

Creating Predesigned Pages with Dreamweaver's Design Files

Dreamweaver has a collection of predesigned pages you can use to create Web sites with Cascading Style Sheets, frames, and other complex page designs. Adobe calls these *samples and starter pages*. Essentially, these are predesigned pages you can customize with your own content. Using a sample to create a new page is similar to creating any other page in Dreamweaver with the advantage that much of the work is already done for you.

You can combine the power of Dreamweaver's samples with Dreamweaver's template features by creating a new page with a sample layout or design and then saving it as a template file using the steps in the "Saving any page as a template" section, earlier in this chapter.

Among Dreamweaver's sample and design files, you can find the following:

- ✔ **CSS Style Sheet:** These files use Cascading Style Sheets to control layout and design.

- ✔ **Framesets:** These page designs are specific to HTML frames, which enable you to display multiple pages on the screen at once. Chapter 7 has instructions for working with frames and frame templates.

- ✔ **Starter Pages (Theme):** These page designs include basic layouts, written content, and color schemes.

- ✔ **Starter Pages (Basic):** These page designs include basic layouts and written content.

- ✔ **CSS Layouts:** These layouts are not included with the samples but are available when you select Blank template from the New Document dialog box. (Using Dreamweaver's CSS layouts is covered in Chapter 6.)

To use one of Dreamweaver's design files to create a page, follow these steps:

1. **Choose File➪New.**

   Alternatively, you can choose any of the options in the Create from Samples section on the Dreamweaver Start page.

2. **In the list on the left, select Page from Sample.**

3. **In the Sample Folder list, select one of the four collections: CSS Style Sheet, Frameset, Starter Page (Theme), or Starter Page (Basic).**

   A preview of the sample is displayed in the far right of the New Document dialog box. In Figure 9-12, I selected the Starter Page (Theme) option, and the sample pages in that collection are displayed.

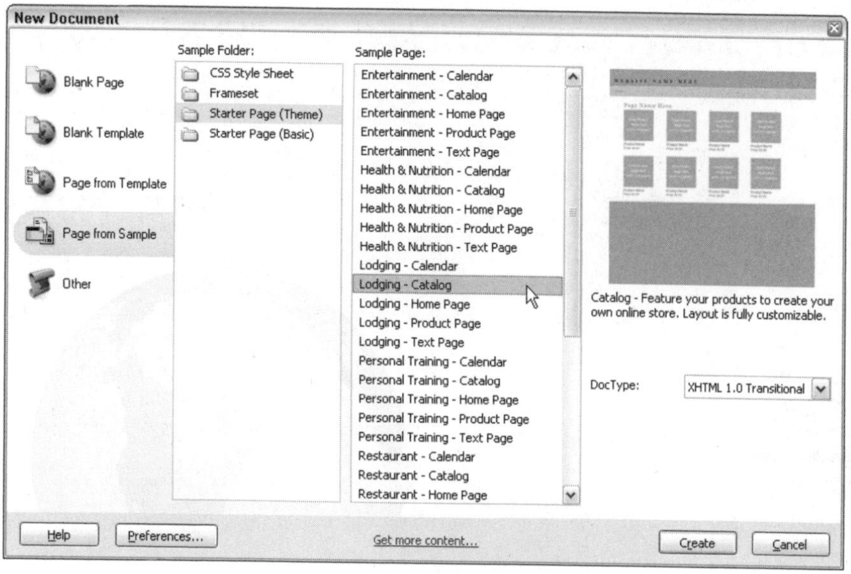

Figure 9-12:
You can
preview
each of
Dream-
weaver's
sample files.

4. **In the Sample Page list, select the design you want to use to create a new page.**

5. **With the sample file selected, click Create to create a new page.**

   A new page is created from the design file and opens in the main work area.

6. **Choose File⇨Save to save the page before you make any changes.**

   Make sure you save the new page within the local root folder of the Web site where you want to use the page.

7. **Click to select any text area, image, link, or other element on the page and replace it with your own images or text to customize the design.**

   In the example shown in Figure 9-13, I've selected the text *insert website name* and can now replace it with any text I'd like to use as the name of my site; the new text will retain the font, color, and other formatting.

8. **Continue to edit the page, replacing images and filler text (Dreamweaver often uses Latin as filler text), setting links, and making any other alterations or additions to the page.**

9. **When you are finished, choose File⇨Save to save your changes.**

You can save the files as a template and use any of the sample files with Dreamweaver's template features, described earlier in this chapter.

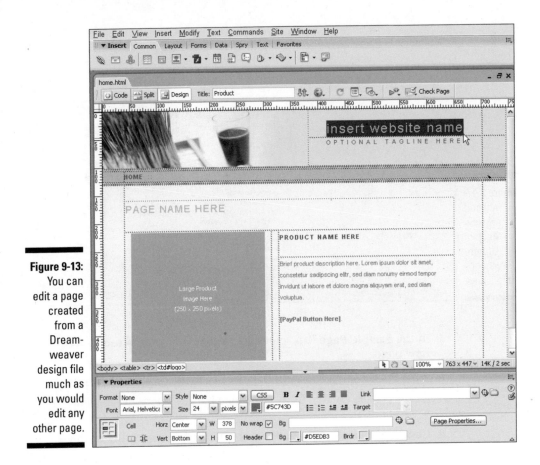

Figure 9-13:
You can edit a page created from a Dream-weaver design file much as you would edit any other page.

Using a Tracing Image to Guide Your Layout

The Tracing Image feature is especially popular among designers. The concept dates back to the earliest days of design. The Tracing Image feature enables you to use graphics as guides for your page designs, much as you might copy a cartoon through thin transparent paper.

The Tracing Image feature is ideal for people who like to first create a design in a program such as Photoshop or Fireworks and then model their Web page after it. By using the Tracing Image feature, you can insert any Web-ready image into the background of any Dreamweaver page. Then you can position `<div>` tags or create tables on top of the tracing image, making it easier to re-create your design in Dreamweaver. You can use JPG, GIF, or PNG images as tracing images, and you can create them in any graphics application that supports these formats.

Although the tracing image appears in the background of a page, it doesn't take the place of a background image and will not appear in a browser.

To add a tracing image to your page, follow these steps:

1. **Create a new page or open an existing page in Dreamweaver.**

2. **Choose Modify⇨Page Properties.**

   The Page Properties dialog box opens.

3. **In the Category list, select Tracing Image.**

   The Tracing Image options appear on the right, as shown in Figure 9-14.

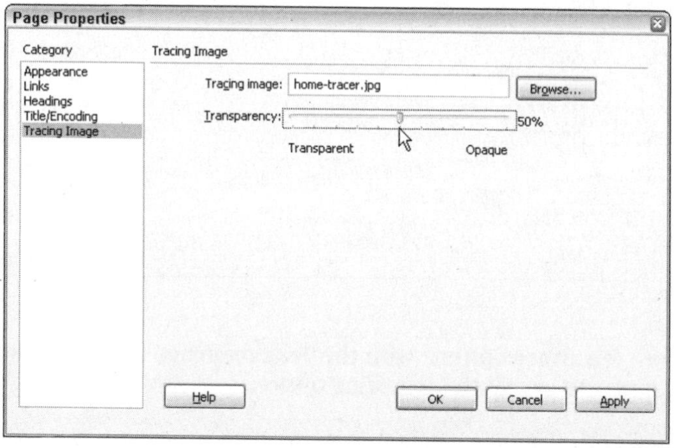

Figure 9-14:
The Page
Properties
dialog box
lets you set
a tracing
image to
use when
laying out
your HTML
page.

4. **Click the Browse button to locate the image you want to use as a tracing image.**

   The Select Image Source dialog box appears.

5. **Click the image you want to trace from, and then click OK.**

6. **Set the opacity for the tracing image with the Transparency slider.**

   Lowering the transparency level causes the tracing image to appear faded, which makes distinguishing between the tracing image and content on the page easy. You can set the transparency level to suit your preferences, but somewhere around 50 percent works well with most images.

7. **Click OK.**

   The tracing image appears in the Document window (see Figure 9-15).

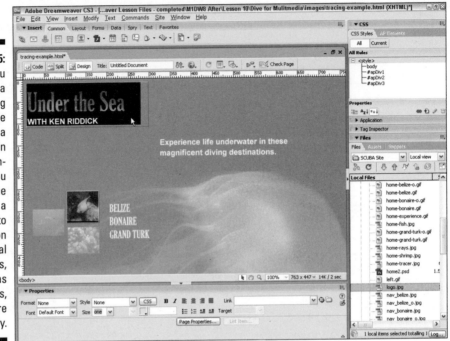

Figure 9-15:
When you
place a
tracing
image
behind a
page in
Dream-
weaver, you
can use the
image as a
guide to
position
individual
elements,
such as
images,
more
precisely.

You have a few other options with the Tracing Image feature. Choose View⇨ Tracing Image to reveal the following options:

- **Show:** Hides the tracing image if you want to check your work without it being visible but don't want to remove it.

- **Align with Selection:** Enables you to automatically line up the tracing image with a selected element on a page.

- **Adjust Position:** Enables you to use the arrow keys or enter X, Y coordinates to control the position of the tracing image behind the page.

- **Reset Position:** Resets the tracing image to 0, 0 on the X, Y coordinates.

- **Load**: Enables you to add or replace a tracing image.

Part III

Making It Cool with Multimedia and JavaScript

The 5th Wave   By Rich Tennant

Well, there's your Web page, Crypto. Designed like you asked. But personally, I think it has too many spinning spirals and blinking lights. It makes...hard reading. Make...tired... look...at...lose...all... con...cen...tra...tion...

Perfect!

CRYPTO THE HYPNOTIST

In this part . . .

Dreamweaver's behaviors make it possible to use JavaScript to create interactive features, such as rollover images and pop-up windows. The multimedia options help your Web pages sing, dance, and delight. In Chapter 10, you find an introduction to the Behaviors panel and step-by-step instructions for creating rollovers, image swaps, and more. In Chapter 11, you find out how to add multimedia files, such as sound, video, and Flash animations, to your Web pages. And in Chapter 12, you discover that Dreamweaver has all the tools you need to create forms for your Web site.

Chapter 10

Adding Interactivity with Behaviors

*W*ant to add cool effects like rollovers and pop-up windows? Dreamweaver's behaviors make it easier than ever to create these kinds of interactive features using a scripting language called JavaScript.

Behaviors are ready-to-use scripts that can be customized to create a variety of features. You can apply behaviors to almost any element on an HTML page and even to the entire page itself. For example, you can use the Swap Image feature to create an interactive slide show or the Open Browser Window option to play a video in a small separate browser window.

When you set up a behavior, you can choose from a number of *triggers,* or *events,* such as OnMouseOver or OnClick. Consider this slightly corny example: If you tickle someone and make the person laugh you used an event to trigger an action. Dreamweaver would call the tickling the *event* and the laughter the *action.* The combination is a Dreamweaver *behavior.*

You may already be familiar with the *rollover* behavior, when one image is switched for another. In a rollover, putting your mouse over an image is the *event.* The *action* is the switching of the original image for another image of the same size. Rollovers are common in navigation. You can create rollovers with simple effects that use two images, but by using the Swap Image behavior, you can create much more complex effects, such as causing any or all images on a page to change when any other element is triggered.

Writing JavaScript is more complex than writing HTML code, but not as difficult as writing in a programming language such as C # or Java. (No, Java and JavaScript are not the same.) Dreamweaver takes most of the challenge out of JavaScript by giving you a graphic interface that doesn't require you to write the complicated code behind the scenes.

To fully appreciate what Dreamweaver can do for you, you may want to switch to code view after setting up a behavior just to see the complex code required when you use JavaScript. If you don't like what you see, don't worry: Go back to design view and you can continue to let Dreamweaver take care of the code for you. (I just want you to see how lucky you are that Dreamweaver includes these features.)

Dreamweaver includes about 20 behaviors, and you can download and install more. (You find instructions in the "Installing New Extensions for Behaviors" section, at the end of this chapter.) In this chapter, I introduce you to the Behaviors panel and show you how to use some of Dreamweaver's most popular options, such as rollovers, shown in Figure 10-1.

Figure 10-1:
When a cursor is rolled over one of the links on this page, a second image is displayed with the long red gradient you see under the cursor. Although the second image looks longer, the two images are exactly the same size.

Creating a Rollover Image

Rollover images, as the name implies, are designed to react when someone rolls a cursor over an image. The effect can be as dramatic as a picture of a dog being replaced by a picture of a lion, or as subtle as the color of a word changing as one image replaces another. Either way, Dreamweaver includes a special dialog box for rollovers that makes creating a simple rollover effect one of the easiest behaviors to apply.

You can create more complex image effects, using the Swap Image option from the Behaviors panel, which makes it possible to change multiple images at the same time, as you'll see in the following section.

To create a rollover image using Dreamweaver's Insert Image Rollover dialog box, follow these steps:

1. **Click to place your cursor on the page where you want the rollover to appear.**

   Rollover effects require at least two images: one for the initial state and one for the rollover state. You can use two different images or two similar ones, but they both should have the same dimensions. Otherwise, you get some strange scaling effects because both images must be displayed in exactly the same space on the page.

2. **Choose Insert⇨Image Objects⇨Rollover Image.**

   The Insert Rollover Image dialog box appears, as shown in Figure 10-2.

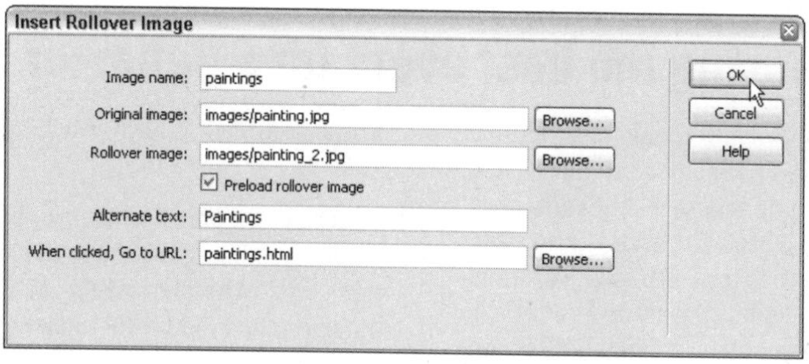

Figure 10-2:
Specify the original and rollover images.

Image name:	paintings	
Original image:	images/painting.jpg	Browse...
Rollover image:	images/painting_2.jpg	Browse...
	☑ Preload rollover image	
Alternate text:	Paintings	
When clicked, Go to URL:	paintings.html	Browse...

(Insert Rollover Image dialog box with OK, Cancel, Help buttons)

3. **In the Image Name box, name your image.**

   Before you can apply a behavior to an element, such as an image, the element must have a name so that the behavior script can reference it. You can name elements anything you like as long as you don't use spaces or special characters.

4. **In the Original Image box, specify the first image you want visible. Use the Browse button to locate and select the image.**

   If the images are not already in your site's root folder, Dreamweaver will copy them into your site when you create the rollover. (If you have not already defined your site in Dreamweaver, refer to Chapter 2 for more on this important preliminary step.)

5. **In the Rollover Image box, enter the image you want to become visible when visitors move their cursors over the first image.**

   Again, you can use the Browse button to locate and select the image.

6. **Select the Preload Rollover Image check box to load all rollover images into the browser's cache when the page first loads.**

   If you don't choose to do this step, your visitors may experience a delay because the second image will not be downloaded until a mouse is rolled over the original image.

7. **In the When Clicked, Go to URL box, enter any Web address or browse to locate another page in your site that you want to link to.**

   If you don't specify a URL, Dreamweaver automatically inserts the # sign as a placeholder.

8. **Click OK.**

   The images are automatically set up as a rollover.

9. **Click the globe icon at the top of the workspace to preview your work in a browser where you can test how the rollover works.**

Choosing the best event for a behavior

Events, in interactive Web-speak, are things a user does to trigger a behavior or an action in a Web page. Clicking an image is an event, as is loading a page into a browser, or pressing a key on the keyboard. Different browser versions support different events (the more recent the browser, the more events are available). Some events are available only for certain kinds of objects or behaviors. If an event cannot be used with a selected element or behavior, it will appear dimmed. This list describes the most common events:

✔ **onAbort:** Triggered when the user stops the browser from completely loading an image (for example, when a user clicks the browser's Stop button while an image is loading).

✔ **onBlur:** Triggered when the specified element stops being the focus of user interaction. For example, when a user clicks outside a text field after clicking in the text field, the browser generates an onBlur event for the text field. onBlur is the opposite of onFocus.

✔ **onChange:** Triggered when the user changes a value on the page, such as choosing an option from a pop-up menu, or when the user changes the value of a text field and then clicks elsewhere on the page.

✔ **onClick:** Triggered when the user clicks an element, such as a link, a button, or an image.

✔ **onDblClick:** Triggered when the user double-clicks the specified element.

✔ **onError:** Triggered when a browser error occurs while a page or an image is loading. This event can be caused, for example, when an image or a URL can't be found on the server.

✔ **onFocus:** Triggered when the specified element becomes the focus of user interaction. For example, clicking in or tabbing to a text field of a form generates an onFocus event.

✔ **onKeyDown:** Triggered as soon as the user presses any key on the keyboard. (The user doesn't have to release the key for this event to be generated.)

✔ **onKeyPress:** Triggered when the user presses and releases any key on the keyboard. This event is like a combination of the onKeyDown and onKeyUp events.

✔ **onKeyUp:** Triggered when the user releases a key on the keyboard after pressing it.

✔ **onLoad:** Triggered when an image or the entire page finishes loading.

✔ **onMouseDown:** Triggered when the user presses the mouse button. (The user doesn't have to release the mouse button to generate this event.)

✔ **onMouseMove:** Triggered when the user moves the mouse while pointing to the specified element and the pointer doesn't move away from the element (stays within its boundaries).

✔ **onMouseOut:** Triggered when the pointer moves off the specified element (usually a link).

✔ **onMouseOver:** Triggered when the mouse pointer moves over the specified element. Opposite of onMouseOut.

✔ **onMouseUp:** Triggered when a mouse button that has been pressed is released.

✔ **onMove:** Triggered when a window or frame is moved.

✔ **onReset:** Triggered when a form is reset to its default values, usually by clicking the Reset button.

✔ **onResize:** Triggered when the user resizes the browser window or a frame.

✔ **onScroll:** Triggered when the user scrolls up or down in the browser.

✔ **onSelect:** Triggered when the user selects text in a text field by highlighting it with the cursor.

✔ **onSubmit:** Triggered when the user submits a form, usually by clicking the Submit button.

✔ **onUnload:** Triggered when the user leaves the page, either by clicking to another page or by closing the browser window.

Creating Swaps with Multiple Images

Before we start creating this design using Dreamweaver's Swap Image behavior, let's first take a look at the finished page so you can see what we'll be doing before we get into the details. Notice in Figure 10-3 that a collection of thumbnail images is on the left side of the page and a larger version of one of those images is on the right side of the page.

Figure 10-3:
When you
use the
Swap Image
behavior,
you can
replace any
or all
images
on a page.

Then notice in Figure 10-4 that when the page is displayed in a browser, you can see the swap image effect as I'm rolling my cursor over one of the thumbnail images on the left to change the large image displayed on the right. Using the Swap Image behavior, you can replace any or all images on a page.

Follow these steps to use the Swap Image behavior:

1. **Create a page design with all the images you want displayed initially.**

   In Figure 10-3, the initial page design includes all thumbnail images positioned on the left, and the first of the big images in the area on the right.

   You can use the Swap Image behavior to change images on any Web page no matter how the layout is created. In the design featured in this lesson, I used a CSS layout creating a separate div for each row of thumbnails on the left and another div for the bigger image on the right. These divs are positioned with CSS. (You find instructions for creating CSS layouts in Chapter 6.) You could use an HTML table or Dreamweaver's Absolute divs to create a similar layout. These instructions for using the Swap Image behavior work the same no matter how you create the layout.

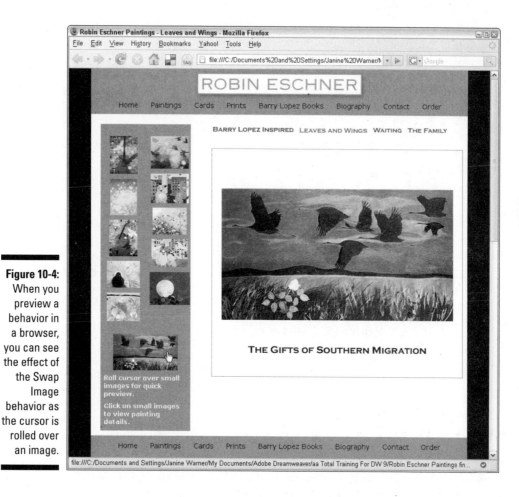

Figure 10-4:
When you preview a behavior in a browser, you can see the effect of the Swap Image behavior as the cursor is rolled over an image.

2. **Name your images in the Property inspector.**

   To target your images with JavaScript, which is how behaviors work, you first need to give each image a unique name. In this example, I've named each thumbnail image based on the title of the painting, which I've also used in the image filenames. Using the same or similar names for your images and the image filenames helps make it easier to match them up when you create the behavior. I named the larger image on the right `bigpainting`, as you see in Figure 10-5. Because this is the first image loaded on the page, I will be replacing it each time I set up a Swap Image for one of the thumbnails. Naming it something simple, such as `bigimage` or `bigpainting`, makes it easy to keep track of which image I'm replacing each time.

   Although Dreamweaver automatically assigns a name to each image on the page, I find it easier to keep track when I set up the Swap Image behavior if I use names that have meaning and describe the images.

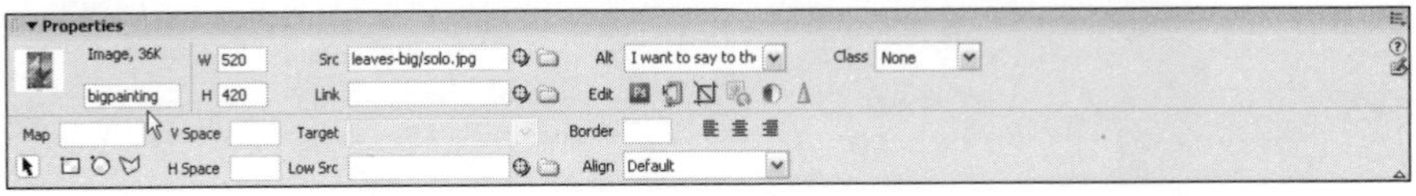

Figure 10-5:
In the top
left of the
Property
inspector,
enter a
name for
each image.

3. **Choose Window⇨Behaviors.**

   The Behaviors panel opens on the right side of the work area (or the left if you've set Dreamweaver's display to Coder). You can drag the Behavior panel elsewhere on the page, and you can expand it by dragging its bottom or side. You may also want to close some of the other panels to make room.

4. **Specify the target browser for behaviors.**

   In the Behaviors panel, click the small arrow just under the plus sign and select Show Events For (second from the last at the bottom of the drop-down list). Then select a target browser. In the example shown in Figure 10-6, I've chosen IE 6. When you specify a target browser, you limit the behaviors to only those that will work in the selected browser and later versions. Behaviors that are not supported by that browser version are dimmed and unavailable. *Note:* Behaviors may also be dimmed if they are not available for a selected element.

5. **Select an image and choose the Image Swap behavior.**

   First click to select the image in the page that will serve as the trigger for the action. In this example, I'm using the thumbnail images as triggers, so I select them one at a time. With the trigger image selected in the workspace, click the Add Behavior arrow in the Behaviors panel (the small arrow under the plus sign) to open the drop-down list of actions and then select the action you want to apply. In the example, I selected the Swap Image action, which opens the Swap Image dialog box.

6. **Specify the images to swap.**

   In the Swap Image dialog box, select the image that will be replaced. In Figure 10-7, I'm selecting the bigpainting image. Then use the Browse button to select the image that will replace bigpainting. I selected the gifts thumbnail, at the bottom of the left side of the page, and the bigger version of the same image called gifts. Now when a user rolls a cursor over the thumbnail of the gifts image, the bigpainting on the right will be replaced with the bigger version of the gifts image.

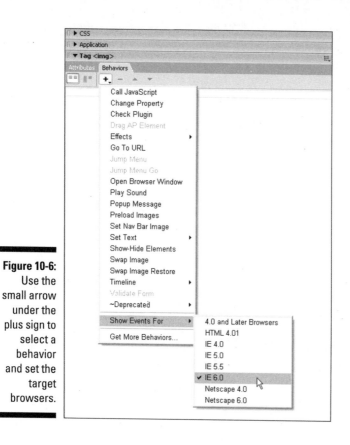

Figure 10-6:
Use the small arrow under the plus sign to select a behavior and set the target browsers.

At the bottom of the Swap Image dialog box, select Preload Images to instruct the browser to load all images into the cache when the page is loaded. If you don't select this option, there may be a delay when the image swap is used. The Restore Images OnMouseOut option means that when an event is completed (such as the mouse is moved off the triggering thumbnail), the original image is replaced. By default, Dreamweaver preselects this option for the Swap Image behavior, but in the example shown here, I chose to deselect it because I found that replacing the original image each time was distracting when I rolled the cursor over the thumbnails.

7. After you've specified all the settings for the behavior, click OK.

The new behavior appears in the Behaviors panel.

8. Specify an event for the behavior.

After the action is applied, you can go back and specify the event that will trigger the action (shown in Figure 10-8). By default, Dreamweaver applies the `OnMouseOver` event when you use the Swap Image action, but you can change that to any available event, such as OnClick, which requires that the user click the image to trigger the Swap Image action. I'll leave it set to OnMouseOver. For more information about events and what each one accomplishes, see the "Choosing the best event for a behavior" section, later in this chapter.

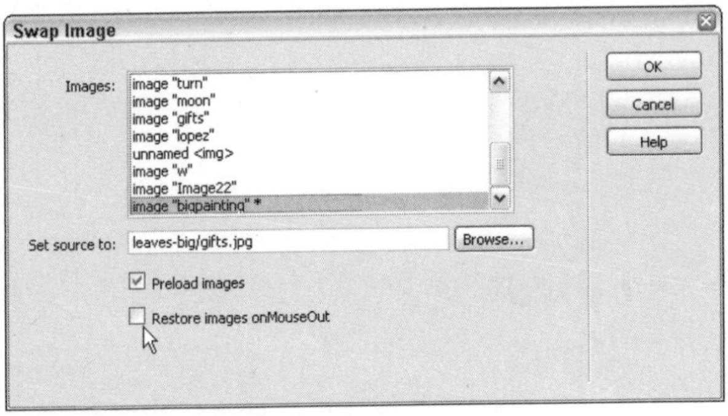

Figure 10-7:
Use the Browse button to select the image you want to swap.

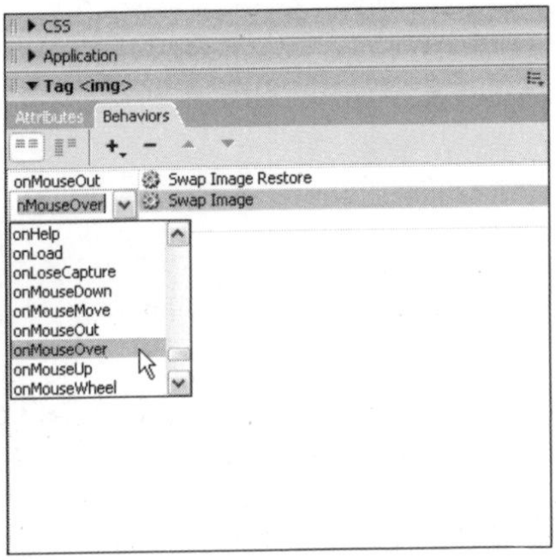

Figure 10-8:
When you set up a behavior, you can specify any available action to trigger an event.

You can display or hide events by clicking the Show All Events icon in the top left of the Behaviors panel. Note that if you are using Windows, you will also see a collection of events that begin with an <A> and are for elements that are linked.

9. **Apply additional behaviors.**

To apply the Swap Image behavior to other images on a page, repeat Steps 5 through 7, clicking to select the image you want to serve as a trigger and then specifying the corresponding image that should be swapped. In this example, I selected each of the thumbnails in turn and set up a Swap Image behavior that replaced the image named bigpainting with the corresponding larger version of the image in the thumbnail.

Although the paintings shown in this example are different sizes, I created versions of them in Photoshop with the same canvas size, using a larger or smaller white background to keep the overall image size consistent. I also included the name of the painting in the image so that it would change as the image changed.

10. **Test your work in a browser.**

You won't be able to see the effects of behaviors like this one until you preview your page in a browser such as Firefox or Internet Explorer. (If you want to see this example in action, visit www.RobinEschner.com.)

Using the Open Browser Window Behavior

You can use behaviors in Dreamweaver to create many interactive features, such as opening a new browser window when someone clicks a link. As you can see in Figure 10-9, this is a great way to make supplemental information available without losing the original page a visitor was viewing. The Open New Browser Window behavior enables you to specify the size of the new window and to display it over the existing window.

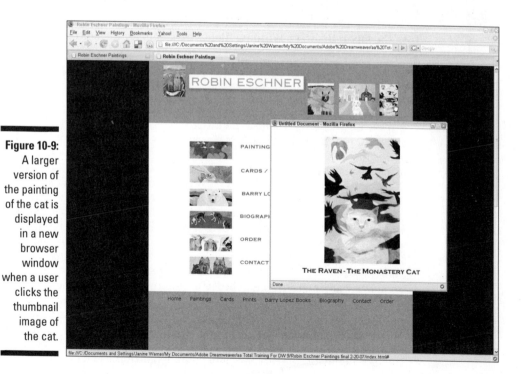

Figure 10-9:
A larger version of the painting of the cat is displayed in a new browser window when a user clicks the thumbnail image of the cat.

To add the Open Browser Window behavior to a selected image (or any other element) on a page, follow these steps:

1. **Create the page that will open in the new browser window.**

   For this example, I create a new blank HTML page and inserted a larger version of the image that corresponds to the thumbnail I will be using as a trigger. The goal is that when a user clicks the trigger image, a browser window will open that is sized exactly to fit the larger image but much smaller than the full browser window.

2. **Select the image, text, or other element you want to serve as the trigger for the action.**

   You can select any image, text, or layer on a page and apply a behavior to it the same way.

3. **Choose Window⇨Behaviors to open the Behaviors panel.**

4. **Click the plus sign (+) and choose the behavior you want from the drop-down list.**

   In this example, I selected the Open Browser Window behavior.

   If a behavior appears dimmed, it can't be associated with the selected element. For example, the Drag Layer behavior can be applied only to a layer, so it appears dimmed if you've selected an image or text.

5. **In the Open Browser Window dialog box, specify the settings.**

   You can set a number of options that control how the new browser window appears. (For example, you can restrict the size of the new browser window, like the one shown in Figure 10-9.)

   In Figure 10-10, you see the Open Browser Window dialog box. Use the Browse button to the right of the URL to Display box to select the page you want to open in the new browser window. (You can also enter a URL in this box to open a page in another Web site.) Set the window width and height to specify the size of the new browser window that will open. In this example, I set the width to the exact size of the image and made the height 20 pixels larger to provide a little breathing room under the painting name. Select the options Navigation Toolbar, Location Toolbar, Status Bar, Menu Bar, Scrollbars as Needed, or Resize Handles if you want the new browser window to include any of these features. I selected Scrollbars As Needed in case my visitor's browser window is smaller than the size I specified for the photo, but I left all the others deselected because I want a clean, simple browser window without any menus or other features. Finally, you can name the new window, which is important if you want to target that same window to load other pages into it.

6. **After you've specified all the settings for the behavior, click OK.**

   The new behavior appears in the Behaviors panel.

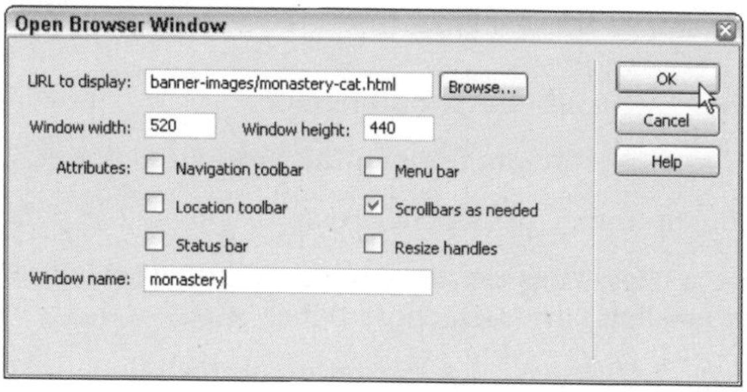

Open Browser Window

Figure 10-10:
Specify
settings for
the display
of the
window.

7. **To change the event that triggers your behavior, select the current event from the left side of the Behaviors panel.**

   In the Events drop-down list, select any available event to serve as the trigger for the behavior. For more information about events and what each one accomplishes, see the "Choosing the best event for a behavior" section, later in this chapter.

8. **To test the action, choose File➪Preview in Browser.**

   Click the image to test whether a new browser window opens as shown in Figure 10-9).

If you're using behaviors, avoid using slashes anywhere in the name or numbers at the beginning of a filename (you can use numbers anywhere else in the name).

Attaching multiple behaviors

You can attach multiple behaviors to the same element on a page (as long as they don't conflict, of course). For example, you can attach one action that is triggered when users click an image and another when they move their cursors over the image. You can also trigger the same action by using multiple events. For example, you can play the same sound when a user triggers any number of events.

To attach additional behaviors to an element, click the plus sign in the Behaviors panel and select another option from the pop-up menu. Repeat this process as many times as you want.

Editing a behavior

You can always go back and edit a behavior after you create it. You can choose a different event to trigger the behavior, choose a different action, or remove behaviors. You can also change behavior options after a behavior is applied.

To edit a behavior, follow these steps:

1. **Select an object with a behavior attached.**

2. **Choose Window⇨Behaviors to open the Behaviors panel.**

   Here are some options you can choose in the Behaviors panel:

   - **Change a triggering event:** Choose a different event in the Events drop-down list in the Behaviors panel.

   - **Remove a behavior:** Click the action in the Behaviors panel to select it and then click the minus sign at the top of the pane. The behavior disappears.

   - **Change parameters for an action:** Double-click the gear icon next to the action and change the parameters in the dialog box that opens.

   - **Change the order of actions when multiple actions are set:** Select an action and then click the Move Event Value Up or Move Event Value Down buttons to move the action to a different position in the list of actions.

Installing New Extensions for Behaviors

Even with all the cool features in Dreamweaver, there will almost certainly come a day when you will want to do things that Dreamweaver can't do with the features that shipped with the program. Fortunately, the programmers who created Dreamweaver made it possible for other programmers to add features using the Extension Manager. The result? You can add new functionality by adding extensions from a variety of third-party sources.

You can find extensions that do everything from adding Flash buttons to fly-out menus to full-featured shopping cart systems. Keep in mind that not all extensions are well supported. They're not all free, either. Some cost hundreds of dollars, but most are in the $20 to $50 range. When you visit the Dreamweaver Exchange site, you'll find reviews and rankings to help you sort through the best options.

In this last exercise in this chapter, I walk you through the steps to find, download, and install a free extension that adds Flash buttons to Dreamweaver. Although how extensions work once they are installed can differ dramatically, the basic process of adding them to Dreamweaver is nearly the same.

1. **Visit the Dreamweaver Exchange Site.**

   You can get to the Dreamweaver Exchange site by clicking the link in the bottom right of the Dreamweaver launch screen, or you can get there by visiting www.adobe.com/exchange and following the link to the Dreamweaver section.

   Note: If you launch Dreamweaver and find a link to download an update for Dreamweaver instead of the link to the Exchange site, by all means download and install the update first. After you're finished, the update link will be replaced by the link to the Exchange site.

2. **Sort through the many available extensions.**

   You'll find a wide range of extensions on the Dreamweaver Exchange site. You can search through extensions by category, keyword, and ranking options. I found the Flash buttons featured in this tutorial at the top of the Most Downloaded list in the right column of the main page.

   Also note that many of the extensions featured on the Exchange site include links back to their creators' sites where you'll often find even more extensions.

3. **Select an extension and review its features.**

   When you click a link to an extension on the Exchange site, you'll find more information about the extension, including system requirements and the version of Dreamweaver that the extension was designed for. In general, you can use extensions designed for earlier versions of Dreamweaver in more recent versions. In this example, I'm adding to Dreamweaver 8 Flash buttons designed for Dreamweaver 4. Be aware, however, that extensions designed for later versions of Dreamweaver usually won't work in earlier versions of the program.

   Before you leave the extension's page, I highly recommend that you take the time to read the special instructions in the middle of the page. In the case of this Flash button extension, these instructions explain that the extension includes 13 button designs and that the source files for the Flash buttons will also be installed at the root of the Dreamweaver folder in a directory named Flash Button Source (a handy tip if you ever want to be able to edit the Flash buttons yourself using Adobe Flash).

   Some extensions include even more important instructions, such as where you'll find the new feature in the Dreamweaver interface after it's installed or warnings that some of the functionality of an extension will work only when previewed on a live Web server (this is true for the random image extension, for example).

4. **To download an extension, click the Download button near the top of the page and save the extension to your hard drive.**

5. **Install the new extension after it's downloaded by choosing Help⇨ Manage Extensions to open the installation dialog box.**

   Most extensions require that you close Dreamweaver before installation, and most install with the click of a button. In the case of the Flash buttons, all I had to do was click the downloaded file; Dreamweaver's Extensions Manager launched automatically to install the buttons.

6. **In the Extension Manager dialog box, choose File⇨Install Extension and then browse your drive to select the extension file you downloaded.**

   After the installation is complete, Dreamweaver displays instructions for using the extension. These are usually the same as the instructions included in the middle of the page on the Exchange site.

   Pay special attention to the part of the instruction that tells you where you'll find your newly installed extensions. Extensions may be added to menus, dialog boxes, and other parts of Dreamweaver depending on their functionality and how the programmer set them up, and it can be hard to find them if you don't know where to look.

   In this case, the final line of the instructions (which I've highlighted in the figure), informs me that my new Flash buttons have been added to the Flash Button Object dialog box.

7. **Put your new extensions to work by launching Dreamweaver and finding the new menu option, button, or other interface feature that controls your new extension.**

   In the example of the new Flash buttons, all I had to do was open an existing page or create a new page in Dreamweaver and then open the Flash button dialog box (choose Insert⇨Media⇨Flash button) to see my new Flash buttons.

   Adobe is constantly updating the Exchange site at www.Adobe.com/ exchange. Visit it regularly to find new extensions you can download and install to enhance Dreamweaver's feature set.

Chapter 11

Showing Off with Multimedia

Get your Web pages singing and dancing with multimedia. Audio, video, and animation are exploding on the Web and transforming static pages into rich multimedia experiences. You can use Dreamweaver to link to multimedia files, or you can insert audio, video, and other files so that they play within your pages. You can even control when and how they play for your users.

Not all Web sites warrant multimedia; if your goal is to provide information in the fastest way possible to the broadest audience, text is still generally the best option. But if you want to provide a richer experience for your users, to *show* rather than just *tell*, or to entertain as well as inform, adding sound, video, and animation can help you share more information more vividly and even make you look more professional.

The most complicated aspect of multimedia on the Web is choosing the best format for your audience, which is why you'll find a primer on audio and video formats in this chapter. You can't create or edit multimedia files in Dreamweaver; but after your files are optimized and ready for the Internet, Dreamweaver makes it relatively easy to add them to your Web pages.

As you discover in this chapter, inserting video, audio, and Flash files is similar to adding image files to Web pages, but with many more options such as controlling how and when they play.

Understanding Multimedia Players

When you add sound, video, or any other kind of multimedia to a Web site, you should know that your visitors may need a special player (sometimes with an associated plug-in) to play or view your files.

Players are small programs that work alone or with a Web browser to add support for functions, such as playing sound, video, and animation files. Some of the best-known multimedia players are the Flash Player, Windows Media Player, Real Networks RealPlayer, and Apple QuickTime.

The challenge is that not everyone on the Web uses the same player, and viewers must have the correct player to view your multimedia files. As a result, many Web developers offer audio and video in two or three formats so users can choose the one that best fits the players they already have. Some developers also include the same multimedia files in different file sizes so that visitors with slower connection speeds don't have to wait as long. Optimizing multimedia for the Web works much as it does with images: the smaller the file size, the lower the quality but the faster the file will download. Many Web developers also include information about how visitors can download and install the best player if they need it to view the files.

You can use Dreamweaver to insert or link to any type of multimedia file, but it's up to you to choose the format that's best for your audience. Although dozens of plug-ins are available for Web pages, only a few, such as Flash, Windows Media, and Quicktime, have become common on the Web today.

In general, I recommend that you avoid the more obscure players unless you are offering specialized content that users have a good reason to download such as a three-dimensional game that requires a special program to run.

Describing multimedia files on your site

Because multimedia files require special players, it's a good idea to include a description any time you add video, audio, or other multimedia files to your Web site. A good practice is to include an explanation of the type of file you're using, the file size, how long it will play, and what kind of player is required to view it.

For example, you might want to include a warning such as this one for a video file:

To play this video file, click the play button above. This video clip of my dog playing the piano is 30 seconds long. If you're using a modem connection, the video may take a minute or two to download before it begins to play (but it's worth it). If the video does not play within a minute or two, you may need to download the XXX player to view it.

(Tip: You should insert the name of the player your multimedia file requires in place of the XXX in that sentence.)

Working with Adobe Flash

Flash has clearly emerged as the favorite technology for creating animations and a wide variety of interactive features on the Web. You can even integrate sound and video into Flash, making it a common choice for combining formats. And with the new Flash video file, you can create all your video using Flash, a great choice because Flash is such a popular player.

One thing that makes Flash animations so flexible and so fast on the Internet is that Flash uses *vector graphics* instead of *bitmaps*. That means the graphics in Flash are based on mathematical descriptions (vectors) instead of dots (bitmaps), and those vector equations take up far less space than bitmapped images. Vector graphics can also be scaled up or down in size without affecting the image quality or the size of the downloaded file. This capability to scale makes Flash ideally suited for the many different monitor sizes used by Web viewers as well as for the tiny displays on cell phones and other handheld devices. You can even project Flash graphics on a wall or movie screen without losing quality, although any photographs or video files integrated into a Flash file may lose quality or look distorted at higher or lower resolutions.

Flash files use the file extension `.swf`, and you can insert them into any Web page. Flash video uses `.flv` (covered in detail in the video section later in this chapter). In addition to the capability to insert Flash files and Flash videos (created in Adobe Flash), you can create Flash buttons and text within Dreamweaver. If want to know how to create full-featured Flash files, check out *Adobe Flash CS3 For Dummies,* by Ellen Finkelstein and Gurdy Leete (published by Wiley Publishing, Inc.).

On the downside, Flash may not print as you would hope and may cause accessibility problems. In addition, text included in Flash files may not be read by search engines (although including alternative text can help with these limitations). And if those aren't enough reasons, sites created entirely in Flash are harder to link to, especially if you want to link to a section within the site and not just to the front page of the site.

Adding Flash buttons and text with Dreamweaver

You can create and edit simple Flash files, such as Flash buttons and text, from within Dreamweaver. Although you can't create full-featured Flash animations with Dreamweaver, these built-in Flash features enable you to create graphical text objects and cool, interactive Flash buttons. Dreamweaver even includes a library of Flash objects to get you started.

Even better, because Dreamweaver is extensible, you can download new Flash button styles from the Adobe Exchange Web site by clicking the Get More Styles button in the Insert Flash Button dialog box. (You must have a live Internet connection to use this feature.)

In Chapter 10 you find instructions for downloading Flash buttons as well as other extensions from the Adobe Exchange site at www.adobe.com/exchange.

Using scripts to make Flash function better

When you insert Flash or other multimedia files with Dreamweaver CS3, the program creates a JavaScript that helps the file play automatically. The file is named AC_RunActiveContent.js and is stored in a folder called Scripts, which Dreamweaver automatically creates inside your root site folder. The first time Dreamweaver creates this file, a dialog box alerts you that you need to upload the script for your multimedia file to work properly. Make sure you include this script when you publish your site on your Web server.

If you don't include the script, your multimedia file may not play properly, or your visitor may be required to click the play button twice before the file begins to play. The reason for this is a long, complicated saga about standards and rights to technologies that I won't bore you with (especially since it may change in the future anyway). The good news is that Adobe has stayed on top of these multimedia challenges; as long as you include this script and make sure to update Dreamweaver with any future updates offered by Adobe, your multimedia should play well on the Web.

Creating Flash text with Dreamweaver

With the Flash text object, you can create and insert a Flash (.swf) text file into your document. Like other Flash files, Flash text files are created with vectors, so they load faster than most image files and automatically resize to adjust the available display area. Another advantage of Flash text is that you can use any fonts you want and can create rollover effects without the need to create separate images.

To insert a Flash text object, follow these steps:

1. **Open any existing page in Dreamweaver, or create and save a new document.**

   Always save a new document before inserting a Flash text object.

2. **Select Common from the Insert bar, if it isn't already selected.**

3. **From the Media drop-down list on the Common Insert bar, choose Flash Text, as shown in Figure 11-1.**

Or you can choose Insert➪Media➪Flash Text. The Insert Flash Text dialog box appears, as shown in Figure 11-2.

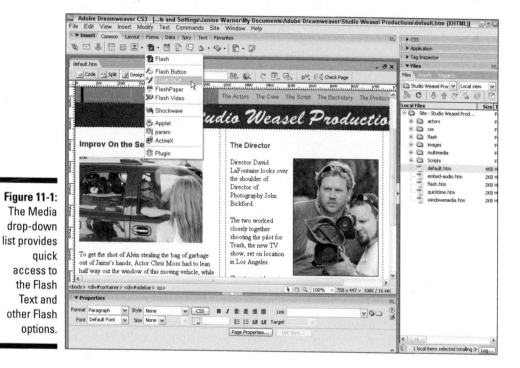

Figure 11-1: The Media drop-down list provides quick access to the Flash Text and other Flash options.

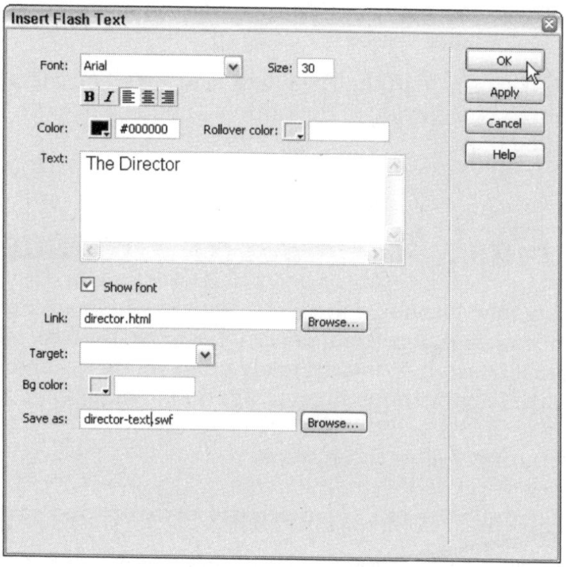

Figure 11-2: You can create and edit interactive Flash text within Dreamweaver.

4. **Select the options, including font, style, size, color, alignment, and background color:**

   - **Font and Size:** Select any font you have available on your hard drive and specify the size in which you want it to display. The size of the font determines the size of the box around the Flash text. To see the text previewed in your font of choice, check the Show Font box. Use the formatting options below the Font box to specify the alignment of the text and if it should display in bold or italic.

   - **Color:** Use this option to specify the color of the text.

   - **Rollover Color:** This is the color the text changes to when the user rolls the mouse over the text.

   - **Link, Target:** In the Link box, specify the page or file that opens when the viewer clicks the link. In the Target box, specify where the linked page opens.

   - **Bg Color (background color):** If you make this option the same as the background color of the Web page on which you're placing the text, the text appears to float on the page. If you specify a different color, a box appears around the text filled with this color. If you don't specify a color, the background is white, not transparent.

   - **Save As:** Because you're creating a Flash file when you use this option, you need to name the new file. Always save the file with the `.swf` extension. Click the Browse button to specify where you want to save the Flash file on your hard drive.

5. **Click OK.**

   You can also click the Apply button to preview the Flash text in your Dreamweaver document before clicking OK.

   The dialog box closes, and the Flash text is inserted on the page. To edit the text again or change any of the options, double-click the Flash text to open the dialog box.

Creating Flash buttons with Dreamweaver

Even more exciting than Flash text are *Flash buttons,* which are predesigned graphics that you can customize and use as interactive buttons on your Web sites. Like Flash text, Flash buttons are made up of vector graphics, so you can scale and resize them without any degradation in quality.

To insert a Flash button, follow these steps:

1. **Open any existing page in Dreamweaver, or create and save a new document.**

   You must save the document before inserting a Flash button.

2. **Select Common from the Insert bar, if it isn't already selected.**

3. **From the Media drop-down list on the Common Insert bar, choose Flash Button (refer to Figure 11-1).**

   Or choose Insert⇨Media⇨Flash Button. The Insert Flash Button dialog box appears, as shown in Figure 11-3.

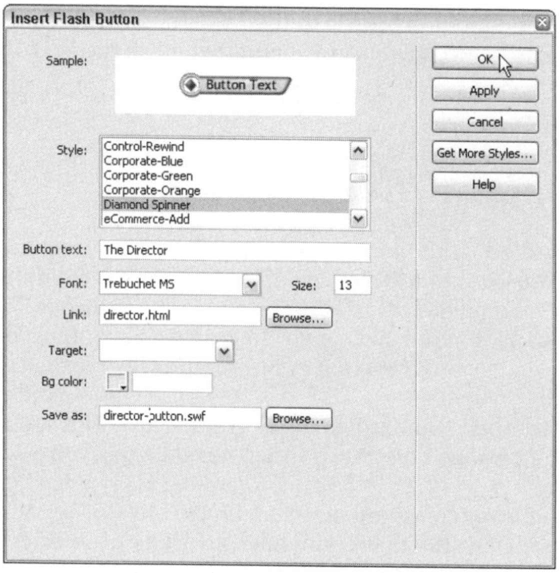

Figure 11-3: You can create and edit interactive Flash button graphics within Dreamweaver.

4. **In the Style field, scroll to select the type of button you want to use.**

   The selected button appears in the Sample field at the top.

5. **Customize your button by entering the text you want to appear on the button, selecting a font, and so on.**

   In the Button Text field, type the text you want to use or leave it blank if you don't want any text on the button. Select the other text options, including font, style, size, color, and alignment.

6. **If you want the button to serve as a link, select the link, target, and background colors in the appropriate fields.**

   Because you are creating a Flash file when you use this option, you need to name the new file. Always save the file with the `.swf` extension. Use the Browse button to specify where you want to save the Flash file on your hard drive.

 7. **Click OK to insert the button.**

You can also click the Apply button to preview the button in your Dreamweaver document before clicking OK.

The dialog box closes, and the button is inserted on the page. To edit the button again or change any of the options, double-click the button to open the dialog box.

To view the rollover effect in your Flash text, you have to preview the page in a browser or click to select the Flash file and then click the Play button in the Property inspector.

Inserting Flash files

Flash files, often called Flash *movies* even when they don't include video, are relatively easy to insert into a Web page using Dreamweaver. In this section, I assume you have a completed Flash file (an animation or other Flash movie), and you want to add it to your Web page. To create a Flash file, you need Adobe Flash or a similar program that supports the Flash format.

Because Flash is an open standard, you can create Flash files with a variety of programs, including Adobe Illustrator, which has an Export to SWF option.

You insert a Flash file much as you insert an image file. But because Flash can do so much more than a still image, you have a variety of settings and options for controlling how your Flash file plays.

Before you start, make sure to save the Flash file you want to insert in the main folder for your Web site. I recommend creating a multimedia folder in your main Web site folder for audio and other multimedia files, just as most designers create an image folder for image files.

To add a Flash file to a Web site, open an existing page or create a new document and save the file. Then follow these steps:

 1. **Click to insert the cursor where you want the Flash file to appear on your Web page.**

 2. **Select Common from the Insert bar, if it isn't already selected.**

 3. **From the Media drop-down list on the Common Insert bar, choose Flash (refer to Figure 11-1).**

You can also choose Insert⇔Media⇔Flash. The Select File dialog box appears.

4. **Browse your drive to locate the Flash file that you want to insert in your page. Click to select the file.**

5. **If you have accessibility options turned on, you will be prompted to add alternative text to describe the Flash file. Enter a description of the file and click OK.**

    The dialog box closes, and the Flash file is inserted into your document.

Dreamweaver displays Flash as a gray box with the dimensions of the Flash file. To display the Flash file, click to select it and then click the green Play button on the right side of the Property inspector. (In the upcoming Figure 11-4, you see the Stop button because I've already clicked the Play button and it has changed to the Stop button as the file began playing.) If you have the Flash player installed on your computer, the Flash file will also play when you preview the page in a browser.

Setting options for Flash

Like most HTML tags, the tags that link Flash and other multimedia files to Web pages have *attributes* that define how a file is displayed within a browser, controlling such actions as whether an animation plays automatically when a page is loaded or whether a visitor must click a link for the animation to begin. Dreamweaver automatically sets some of these options, such as the height and width of the Flash file, and you may want to specify others.

If you don't see all the options in the Property inspector, click the expander arrow in the lower-right corner to display the more advanced options.

You can set any of these Flash options in the Property inspector, as shown in Figure 11-4:

 ✔ **Name field:** Use the text field in the upper-left corner of the Property inspector, just to the right of the F icon, to assign a name to the file. If you leave this field blank, Dreamweaver doesn't enter a name automatically. The name is important because it can be used to refer to the file in JavaScript.

 ✔ **W (Width):** Use this option to specify the width of the file. The file is measured in pixels.

 ✔ **H (Height):** Use this option to specify the height of the file. The file is measured in pixels.

 ✔ **File:** Dreamweaver automatically fills in this field when you insert a Flash file with the filename and path. You risk breaking the link to your flash file if you alter this field.

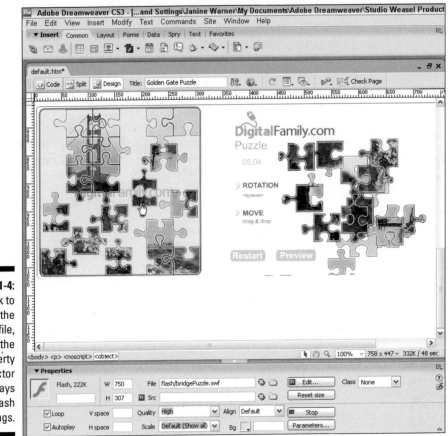

Figure 11-4:
Click to select the Flash file, and the Property inspector displays these Flash settings.

✔ **Src (Source):** This text field enables you to identify the source file you used to create the `.swf` file inserted into a page. After this option is set, clicking the Edit button automatically opens the source file in Flash and provides a Done button to integrate changes back into Dreamweaver. Because the programs are integrated, any changes you make in Flash automatically reflect in Dreamweaver when you use this option.

✔ **Edit:** Click this button to open a Flash file with the Adobe Flash program so you can edit it. Note that you can edit only the source Flash file. After saving the Flash file for Web use with the `.swf` extension, you can't edit it again.

✔ **Reset Size:** You can change the display size of a Flash file by clicking a corner and dragging it. Clicking this button reverts the Flash file to its original size. You can resize Flash files, unlike images, video, and many other file types, without affecting image quality because they are vector based. To keep the file proportionate, hold down the Shift key as you drag to resize the file.

- **Class:** Use the drop-down list to apply any style sheets defined for the document.

- **Loop:** Selecting this box causes the Flash file to repeat (or *loop*). If you don't select this box, the Flash movie stops after it reaches the last frame.

- **Autoplay:** Selecting this box causes the Flash movie to play as soon as it downloads to the viewer's computer. If you don't select this box, whatever option you've set within the Flash file itself (such as onMouseOver or onMouseDown) is required to start the movie. You can also apply a behavior elsewhere in the document to start play (Chapter 9 covers Dreamweaver behaviors).

- **V Space (Vertical Space):** If you want blank space above or below the file, enter the number of pixels.

- **H Space (Horizontal Space):** If you want blank space on either side of the file, enter the number of pixels.

- **Quality:** This option enables you to prioritize the anti-aliasing options of your images versus the speed of playback. *Anti-aliasing,* which makes your files appear smoother, can slow down the rendering of each frame because the computer must first smooth the edges. The Quality parameter enables you to regulate how much the process is slowed by letting you set priorities based on the importance of appearance versus playback speed. You can choose from these Quality options:

    - **Low:** Anti-aliasing is never used. Playback speed has priority over appearance.

    - **High:** Anti-aliasing is always used. Appearance has priority over playback speed.

    - **Auto High:** With this option, playback is set to begin with anti-aliasing turned on. However, if the frame rate supported by the user's computer drops too low, anti-aliasing automatically turns off to improve playback speed. This option emphasizes playback speed and appearance equally at first but sacrifices appearance for the sake of playback speed, if necessary.

    - **Auto Low:** Playback begins with anti-aliasing turned off. If the Flash player detects that the processor can handle it, anti-aliasing is turned on. Use this option to emphasize speed at first but improve appearance whenever possible.

- **Scale:** Specify this option only if you change the file's original Height and Width size settings. The Scale parameter enables you to define how the Flash movie appears within those settings. The following options in the Scale drop-down list enable you to set preferences for how a scaled Flash movie appears within the window:

    - **Default (Show All):** This option enables the entire movie to appear in the specified area. The width and height proportions of the original movie are maintained and no distortion occurs, but borders may appear on two sides of the movie to fill the space.

Finding Flash resources online

One of the best places to learn more about creating Flash files is on the Internet, where a wide range of Web sites offer everything from pre-designed Flash files you can easily customize to great ideas for getting the most out of this award-winning technology. You may find these Web sites useful if you want to learn more about Flash.

✔ **Adobe** (www.adobe.com): You find loads of tips and tricks for creating and using Flash files (as well as many inspiring examples of Flash in action).

✔ **Swish** (www.swishzone.com): If you're looking for an alternative to Adobe Flash, Swish is a great little program that's more reasonably priced.

✔ **Flash Kit** (www.flashkit.com): You find a wide range of resources for Flash developers.

✔ **Flash Arcade** (www.flasharcade.com): This site has some of the best interactive games created in Flash.

- **No Border:** This option enables you to scale a Flash movie to fill a specified area. No borders appear and the original aspect ratio is maintained, but some cropping may occur.

- **Exact Fit:** The Flash movie is the exact width and height that are set, but the original aspect ratio may not be maintained and the movie may look squished.

✔ **Align:** This option controls the alignment of the file on the page. This setting works the same for plug-in files as for images.

✔ **Bg:** This option sets a background color that fills the area of the file. This color appears if the specified height and width are larger than the file and during periods when the movie isn't playing, either because it's loading or has finished playing.

✔ **Play button:** Click the green Play button to play a Flash file in Dreamweaver. Note that when the Play button is activated, the button changes to Stop, as shown in Figure 11-4.

✔ **Parameters:** This button provides access to a dialog box where you can enter parameters specific to your Flash files.

Working with Video and Audio on the Web

As bandwidth has grown on the Web, the use of video files has grown more dramatically than almost any other multimedia file type. From YouTube to

Revver and Odeo to small personal Web sites, millions of video files are being added to the Web every day.

Adding a video file to a Web page with Dreamweaver is relatively easy, especially if you use the Flash video format described in the "Adding Flash Audio and Video Files" section later in this chapter. If you use another video format, such as Windows Media Video or Quicktime, you find instructions for adding both audio and video files to your pages in the following section, "Adding Audio and Video Files to Web Pages." You can specify video and audio settings, such as autoplay, by changing setting parameters, an option that is a little more complicated in Dreamweaver and covered in the "Setting Options for Audio and Video Files," later in this chapter.

The first challenge to working with multimedia is choosing the right format and optimizing your video so it downloads quickly and still looks good. Optimizing video is beyond the scope of this book, but I have included some general information about video formats to help you make more informed decisions about the type of video files to add to your pages.

Unfortunately, no single video format works for everyone on the Web (although Flash video is gaining popularity fast). Most new computers come with preinstalled video and audio players that play the most common file formats. If you use a Windows computer, you probably have Windows Media Player on your computer. If you use a Mac, you have QuickTime. Both video players can handle multiple video formats, so anyone with a relatively new computer can likely view video in common formats.

Many people surf the Web in their offices, in libraries, and in other locations where unexpected sound can be jarring, disruptive, or worse. Always give people a warning before you play video or audio and always give users a way to turn it off quickly when necessary.

Streaming media plays faster

To *stream* multimedia means to play a file while it's downloading from the server. This is a valuable trick on the Web because video and audio files can take a long time to download. Here's how streaming works. When you click a link to a video file, your computer begins to download it from the server. If you're using a player that supports streaming, the video or audio file begins to play as soon as enough of the file downloads successfully to ensure an uninterrupted experience. If you don't use streaming, the entire file must download before playing. Although it can take the same amount of time to download the entire file, streaming can greatly reduce the time your visitors need to wait before they can start viewing a video online.

Comparing popular video formats

You can convert video from one file format to another relatively easily using most video-editing programs. For example, you can open a video in AVI format in a program such as Adobe Premier Elements (a good video editor for beginners) and then choose File➪Export to convert it to any of a dozen formatting and compression options. For example, you could convert an AVI file to the Windows Media format with the compression setting for a 56K modem or into the QuickTime format with the compression setting for a cable modem. Editing video can get complicated, and optimizing video for the best quality with the fastest download time is both an art and a science, but the most basic process of converting a video file isn't difficult after you understand the conversion options.

The following sections provide a brief description of the most common digital video formats, their file extensions, and a Web address where you can find out more about each option.

Flash Video

You can create Flash videos with Adobe Flash, the newest video format on the Web and arguably the one growing fastest in popularity. Because the Flash player is so popular on the Web, many developers consider Flash one of the best options available today.

- ✔ File extension: `.flv`
- ✔ Web site: `www.adobe.com`

Windows Media Video

Defined by Microsoft and popular on the PC, this video format supports streaming and plays with Windows Media Player as well as many other popular players.

- ✔ File extension: `.wmv`, `.asx`
- ✔ Web site: `www.microsoft.com/windows/windowsmedia`

RealVideo

RealNetworks designed the RealVideo file format to play in RealPlayer (available for Mac and PC). RealMedia provides optimization well suited to low-speed and high-speed connections but requires special software on your Web server for streaming.

- ✔ File extension: `.rm`, `.rv`
- ✔ Web site: `www.real.com`

QuickTime

The QuickTime player is built into the Macintosh operating system and is used by most Mac programs that include video or animation. QuickTime is a great format for video on the Web and supports streaming, but it's used primarily by those who favor Macs (although QuickTime files can be viewed on Windows computers as well).

- ✔ File extension: `.qt`, `.mov`
- ✔ Web site: `www.quicktime.com`

AVI

Created by Microsoft, AVI (Audio Video Interleave) is one the most common video formats on Windows computers and can play on most common video players. AVI is fine if you're viewing video on a CD or on your hard drive, where the file doesn't have to download, but you can't optimize AVI files well for use on the Internet. If your files are in AVI, you should convert them to one of the other formats before adding them to your Web site. Otherwise, you force your visitors to download unnecessarily large video files.

- ✔ File extension: `.avi`
- ✔ Web site: No one site about AVI exists, but you can find information if you search for *AVI* at `www.microsoft.com`

Comparing popular audio formats

Audio works much like video on the Web. You can link to a sound file or embed the file into your page; either way, your visitors need to have the right player to listen to the file. You find instructions for adding both audio and video files to your pages in the following section, "Adding Audio and Video Files to Web Pages."

The following sections provide a brief description of the most common digital audio formats, their file extensions, and a Web address where you can find out more about each option:

MP3

One of the most successful audio compression formats, MP3 supports streaming audio. Most music you can download from the Internet is in MP3 format, and it is clearly the first choice of many Web developers. MP3 files can be played by most popular multimedia players on the Web.

- ✔ File extension: `.mp3`
- ✔ Web site: `www.mp3.com`

Windows Audio

Microsoft's Windows Audio format supports streaming and can be played with Windows Media Player as well as many other popular players. It also offers digital rights management functionality.

- ✔ File extension: `.wma`
- ✔ Web site: `www.microsoft.com/windows/windowsmedia`

RealAudio

RealNetworks, designed RealAudio, is a streaming file format that plays in RealPlayer (available for Mac and PC). RealAudio is especially popular among radio stations and entertainment sites.

- ✔ File extension: `.ra`
- ✔ Web site: `www.real.com`

WAV

The WAV file format is popular in digital media because it offers the highest sound quality possible. But audio files in this format are often too big for use on the Web, averaging 10MB for a minute of audio. (In comparison, an MP3 file that is five times longer can be less than one-third the size.) Although WAV files are commonly used on the Internet because of their nearly universal compatibility, I recommend that you convert WAV files (especially for long audio clips) to one of the other audio formats.

- ✔ File extension: .wav
- ✔ Web site: No official Web site exists for WAV files, but you can find some documentation at `www.microsoft.com` if you search for *WAV*.

Adding Audio and Video Files to Web Pages

Like other multimedia files, you can link to an audio or a video file or you can insert it into a page. Linking to a multimedia file is as easy as linking to any other file, as you see in the instructions that follow. Inserting an audio or a video file is a little more complicated, but it lets a visitor play the file without leaving the Web page. Inserting audio and video files is covered in this section. If you are using Flash video or audio, refer to the "Adding Flash audio and video files" section, earlier in this chapter.

Linking to audio and video files

Many people like to have multimedia files, such as video, pop up in a new browser window. To do this, create an HTML file and embed your multimedia file in it. Then use the Open Browser Window behavior in Dreamweaver to create a pop-up window that displays your multimedia page. For more on how to work with Dreamweaver behaviors, see Chapter 10.

To use Dreamweaver to link to a video file, an audio file, or another multimedia file, follow these steps:

1. **Click to select the text, image, or other element you want to use to create a link.**

   This works just like creating a link to another page (see Figure 11-5).

   If you're linking to a video file, a good trick is to take a single still image from the video and insert that into your Web page. Then create a link from that image to the video file.

2. **In the Property inspector, click the Browse button just to the right of the link field.**

   The Browse button looks like a small file folder.

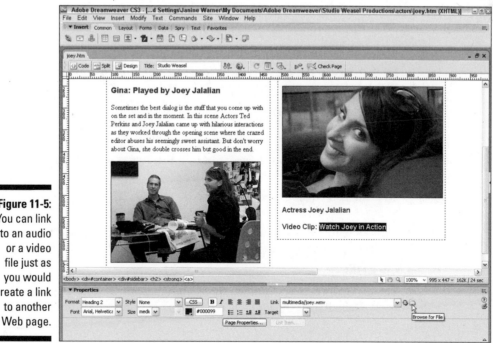

Figure 11-5: You can link to an audio or a video file just as you would create a link to another Web page.

3. **Browse your hard drive to find the video or audio file you want to link to.**

   As with any other file you link to, make sure you've saved your audio or video files into your main Web site folder.

4. **Click to select the file you want to link to and then click OK.**

   The dialog box closes, and the link is automatically created.

5. **Click the Preview button (at the top of the work area) to open the page in a browser, where you can test the link to your multimedia file.**

   Dreamweaver launches your specified Web browser and displays the page. If you have the necessary player, the file downloads, your player launches, and then your file automatically plays.

Inserting audio and video files

When you insert an audio or a video file into a Web page, you can set the file to play automatically when the page loads (as long as your visitor has the necessary player), or you can require that your visitors click the Play button first. Either way, when you insert an audio or a video file into a page, the file will play within the page instead of requiring that the video or audio player be opened separately.

To use Dreamweaver to embed an audio or a video file into a Web page, follow these steps:

1. **Click to insert the cursor where you want the file to appear on your Web page.**

   If you're inserting a sound file, the play, pause, and stop controls appear wherever you insert the file. If you're inserting a video file, the first frame of the video should appear where you insert the file.

2. **Select Common from the Insert bar. In the Media drop-down list, choose Plugin (refer to Figure 11-1).**

   You can also choose Insert⇨Media⇨Plugin. The Select File dialog box appears.

3. **Browse your drive to locate the sound or video file you want inserted in your page and then click to select it.**

4. **Click OK.**

   The dialog box closes, and the file is automatically inserted into the page. A small icon (resembling a puzzle piece) represents the file.

When you add audio or video, Dreamweaver does not automatically determine the file size, so you'll need to add that information in the Property inspector after you insert the file. After you've set the correct file size, the plug-in icon will change to reflect the specified size.

5. **Click the icon to display the file options in the Property inspector and specify your desired settings.**

   You find a description of each of these options in the next section, "Setting options for audio and video files."

 6. **Click the Preview button (at the top of the work area) to open the page in a browser.**

   Dreamweaver does not include a play button for audio and video files (unless they are in the Flash format). If you have the necessary player on your computer, and you have the file set to autoplay (the default setting), your file plays automatically when the page loads into the browser. To change video and audio settings, such as autoplay, see the "Setting multimedia parameters" section later in this chapter.

Setting options for audio and video files

When you select an inserted multimedia file, such as a sound or video file, by choosing Insert➪Plugin, the Property inspector displays the options for the file, as shown in Figure 11-6. The following describes those options:

✔ **Name field:** Use the text field in the upper-left corner of the Property inspector, just to the right of the plug-in icon, if you want to assign a name to the file. If you leave this field blank, Dreamweaver doesn't enter a name automatically. The name is important because it can be used to refer to the file in JavaScript.

Unlike image files or Flash files, Dreamweaver cannot automatically detect the height and width of an audio file or a video file, so it's important to set these options in the Property inspector. To determine the height and width of a video file, you may need to open it in a video-editing program. For audio files, you should set the height and width based on the size required for the player you are using.

✔ **W (Width) and H (Height):** Specify the measurement of the file in pixels. For most plug-ins, the height and width tags are required, but Dreamweaver doesn't automatically insert them. Instead, you need to note the size of the file in the program used to create it, or take a best guess and preview your file in a browser to ensure it displays properly. If you're adding a sound file, the height and width specify the size of the control buttons.

- ✔ **Class:** This option enables you to apply Class styles to multimedia files.

- ✔ **Src (Source):** This option specifies the name and path to the file. You can type a filename or click the folder icon to browse for the file. This field is filled in automatically when you embed the file.

- ✔ **Align:** This option enables you to specify how the element aligns on the page. Alignment works just as it does for images.

- ✔ **Play button:** Click the green Play button to preview the media file. The media plug-in must be installed in Dreamweaver (in the Configuration/Plugins folder) for it to be previewed in Dreamweaver.

- ✔ **Class:** Use the drop-down list to apply any style sheets defined for the document.

- ✔ **Plg URL:** This option enables you to provide a URL where viewers can download the plug-in if they don't already have it.

- ✔ **V Space (Vertical Space):** If you want blank space above and below the plug-in, enter the number of pixels here.

- ✔ **H Space (Horizontal Space):** If you want blank space on either side of the plug-in, enter the number of pixels or use a percentage to specify a portion of the browser window's width.

- ✔ **Border:** This option specifies the width of the border around the file when it is displayed.

- ✔ **Parameters:** Click this button to access a dialog box in which you can enter additional parameters specific to the type of multimedia file you inserted. For more information, see the following section.

Setting multimedia parameters

You can use parameters to control a wide range of multimedia options, such as whether a video file or an audio file starts playing as soon as a page is loaded. Setting parameters is not intuitive, and I don't think Dreamweaver does the best job of helping with these settings; but with some research on the options for the file type you are using and a little care in using the parameters dialog box in Dreamweaver, you can have a lot more control over your multimedia files.

In fairness to the programmers who created Dreamweaver, it would be hard to include all the parameters for all the possible multimedia file types in use on the Web today. However, I think they could have included the common ones. Because they don't, I offer you this brief primer on using the parameters setting and a few common options for a few common file types. You also find Web addresses where you can find more complete lists of parameters for a few of the most popular audio and video formats.

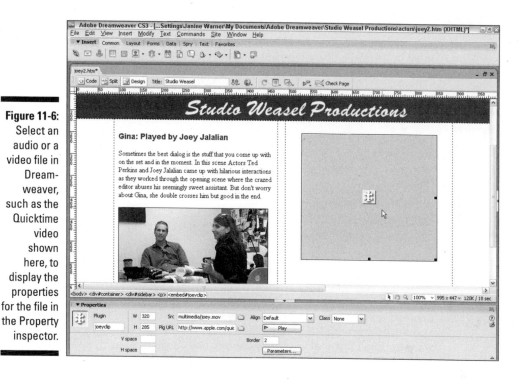

Figure 11-6:
Select an audio or a video file in Dreamweaver, such as the Quicktime video shown here, to display the properties for the file in the Property inspector.

Two of the most common and valuable parameters are Autoplay and Autostart (depending on the file type). Be default, when you add video or audio to an HTML file, most browsers will play the file as soon as the page loads (except Firefox, which likes to give users more control). If you want to prevent your multimedia files from playing automatically in Internet Explorer and other browsers, you can set the Autoplay or Autostart parameter to false. Think of true and false as on and off when it comes to parameters.

In Figure 11-7 you see the Parameter dialog box with settings for a Windows Media Video file. To access the Parameters dialog box, click to select the multimedia file in the Web page and then click the Parameters button in the Property inspector. Use the plus sign (+) at the top of the dialog box to add a parameter; use the minus sign (–) to delete a selected parameter. On the left side of the dialog box, you enter the name of the parameter, such as Autostart; on the right side you enter the value you want, such as false, which I've entered in this example to prevent the Windows Video file from playing automatically.

Loop is a common parameter. This enables you to control whether a video file or an audio file will loop or continue to play over and over. Another common parameter is showControls. This option makes it possible to hide the video or audio controls for a file. Be careful about combining options like these. For example, if you set AutoPlay to false and showControls to false, your visitor will never be able to play your file. By default, the controls for most multimedia files are visible unless you set the showControls parameter to false.

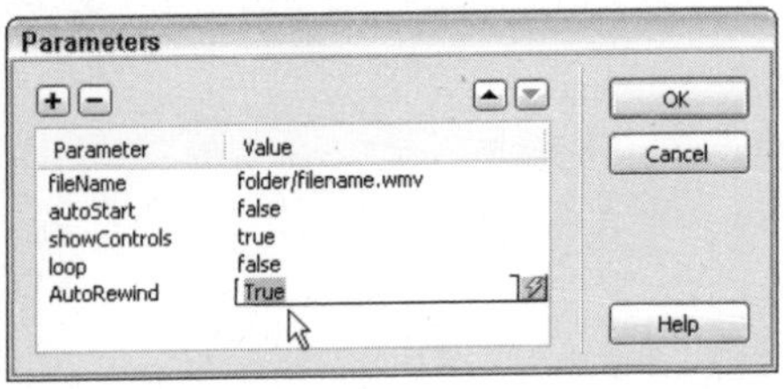

Figure 11-7:
You can
further
specify how
audio and
video files
should play.

Parameters		
+ −	▲ ▼	OK
		Cancel
Parameter	Value	
fileName	folder/filename.wmv	
autoStart	false	
showControls	true	
loop	false	
AutoRewind	True	
		Help

You'll find more attributes for the Windows Media format at www.Microsoft. com when you search for WMV attributes. For Quicktime attributes, visit www. Apple.com and search for Quicktime attributes or go directly to www.apple. com/quicktime/tutorials/embed2.html. You'll find lots of great info about working with Real Media files, including all the settings you could want for RealPlayer, at www.realnetworks.com/resources/samples/ embedded.html.

Adding Flash audio and video files

Flash video is fast becoming the video format of choice among many designers. Video on the Web has been problematic for a long time because there are so many different formats, and you can never guarantee that everyone in your audience will be able to view your videos in any one format.

But while the video players have been fighting it out, Flash has stepped in to provide an option that is increasingly well supported because so many people have the Flash player and it's such a small and easy download for those who don't have it.

Because Adobe owns both Flash and Dreamweaver, you find much better support for Flash files in Dreamweaver. An insert dialog box makes it easy to set parameters for Flash. The Insert Flash dialog box is displayed in Figure 11-8. Dreamweaver can even detect the size of Flash video files automatically. You can also use Flash to create and insert audio files, displaying only the player (called a skin in Flash), as you see in the example in Figure 11-9.

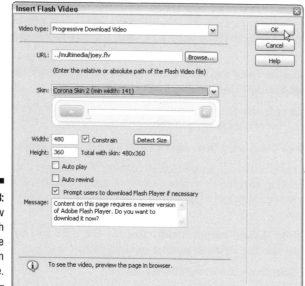

Figure 11-8:
Specify how
your Flash
file will be
displayed in
a Web page.

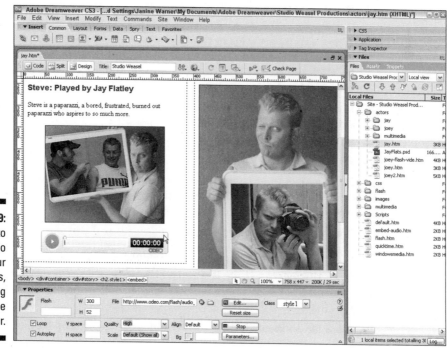

Figure 11-9:
Use Flash to
add audio
files to your
Web pages,
displaying
only the
player.

Follow these steps to insert a Flash video file into a Web page.

1. **Click to insert the cursor where you want the file to appear on your Web page.**

2. **Select Common from the Insert bar, and from the Media drop-down list, choose Media⇨Flash Video (refer to Figure 11-1).**

   You can also choose Insert⇨Media⇨Flash video. The Insert Flash Video dialog box appears, as shown in Figure 11-8.

3. **At the top of the dialog box, specify streaming or progressive.**

   You must have a special server for streaming video. Check with your Internet hosting service or system administrator to find out whether your Web server supports streaming Flash files. If not, choose progressive.

4. **The URL field should automatically display the path to your Flash file, but you can use the Browse button to change it.**

5. **Choose a Skin from the drop-down list.**

   Dreamweaver calls the controls for a Flash file a *skin*. As you can see in Figure 11-8, a preview of the selected skin is displayed in the dialog box so you can better decide which one is best for your Flash file and your design. You can also create custom skins in Adobe Flash.

6. **When you insert a Flash file into a Web page, Dreamweaver should automatically set the height and width, but if these fields are not filled in, click the Detect Size button to insert the height and width of the inserted Flash file.**

7. **If you want the Flash video to play as soon as the page is loaded, select the Auto Play option.**

8. **If you want the video to rewind after play is complete, select the Auto Rewind option.**

9. **If you select the Prompt Users to Download Player If Necessary option, anyone who visits your site who does not have the player installed already will be prompted to retrieve it.**

   You can edit the message in the Message box if you want to change it to something like: "Join the modern world — get the latest Flash player already!" (Okay, maybe you shouldn't say that, but you may want to tailor the message to better reflect the style of your site.) Any message you enter in the Message box will appear only if the browser detects that the visitor doesn't have the right player

10. **Click OK to insert the Flash file and close the dialog box.**

    The Flash file appears on the page, represented by a gray box that is the height and width of the file. To view the Flash video, click to select it and then click the Play button in the Property inspector.

When you insert a Flash video file and include a skin for the player, Dreamweaver creates a Flash file with the .swf extension and saves it in your root site folder. This Flash file contains the player controls and must be uploaded to your Web site when you publish the page with the Flash file for the player controls to work.

You can change the skin by double-clicking the inserted Flash file to open the Flash dialog box. Each time you choose a skin, Dreamweaver creates a new .swf file. You can delete any skins that aren't being used and you can move any or all .swf files into a subdirectory using the Files panel; Dreamweaver adjusts the corresponding references in your code to keep the skin associated with the video file.

If you want to find out more about other Flash parameters, visit www.Adobe. com and search for *setting Flash parameters.*

Working with Java

Java is a programming language, similar to Basic, C, or C++, that you can use to create programs that run on a computer. What makes Java special is that it can run on any computer system and can display within a browser.

If you create a program in another programming language, you usually have to create one version for the Macintosh, another for the PC, and a third for Unix. But Java, created by Sun Microsystems, is platform-independent, so developers can use it to create almost any kind of program — even complex programs such as sophisticated games or even a word processing program — that works on any type of computer without the user having to customize the code for each platform.

Another advantage of Java is that the program (often called an *applet*) can run within a Web browser, allowing the program to interact with different elements of the page or with other pages on the Web. This capability has made Java popular on the Internet because it provides a way to add sophisticated capabilities to Web pages irrespective of the operating system the Web browser is running on. You can embed Java applets in Web pages, you can use Java to generate entire Web pages, or you can run Java applications separately after they download.

Inserting Java applets

To insert a Java applet in your Web page, follow these steps:

1. **Click to insert the cursor where you want the applet to appear on your Web page.**

JavaScript is not Java

JavaScript, a scripting language; Java is a programming language. Despite the similarity in their names, the two have little in common. Although JavaScript is much more complex than HTML, it is much simpler than Java and has far fewer capabilities. Unlike Java, JavaScript can be written directly into HTML code to create interactive features, such as rollover effects. Dreamweaver uses JavaScript to create most of the features included in the Behaviors panel (covered in Chapter 10).

You can use Java to create more complex programming than you can create with JavaScript.

Java programs, or applets, are usually small, self-contained programs that can run on any operating system. If you search the Web for Java applets, you're likely to find cool little clocks and converters and other programs that you can download and add to your Web pages. You can use Java to create programs that work on both the Mac and PC, an advantage over other programming languages that makes Java especially well-suited to the multiplatform world of Web design.

2. **Select Common from the Insert bar, if it isn't already selected. In the Media drop-down list on the Common Insert bar, choose Applet (refer to Figure 11-1).**

   Alternatively, you can choose Insert⇨Media⇨Applet. The Select File dialog box appears.

3. **Use the Browse button to locate the Java applet file you want to insert on the page.**

4. **Click to highlight the filename, and then click OK to close the dialog box.**

   Dreamweaver doesn't display applets in the Dreamweaver work area. Instead, you see an icon that represents the applet. To view the applet on your Web page (the only way to see the applet in action), preview the page in a browser that supports applets, such as Navigator 4.0 and later or Internet Explorer 4.0 and later.

5. **Click the Applet icon to open the Property inspector.**

   You can set many options in the Property inspector. If you want to know more about these options, read on.

Setting Java parameters and other options

Like other file formats that require plug-ins or advanced browser support, the display of Java applets can be controlled by specifying a number of options. If you click to select a Java applet in Dreamweaver, the Property inspector displays the following options:

- **Applet name:** Use this field in the upper-left corner if you want to type a name for your applet. Dreamweaver doesn't apply a name if you leave this field blank. This name identifies the applet for scripting.

- **W (Width):** This option specifies the width of the applet. You can set the measurement in pixels or as a percentage of the browser window's width.

- **H (Height):** This option specifies the height of the applet. You can set the measurement in pixels or as a percentage of the browser window's height.

- **Code:** Dreamweaver automatically enters the code when you insert the file. Code specifies the content file of the applet. You can type your own filename or click the folder icon to choose a file.

- **Base:** Automatically entered when you insert the file, Base identifies the folder that contains the applet.

- **Align:** This option determines how the object aligns on the page. Alignment works just as it does for images.

- **Alt:** This option enables you to specify an alternative file, such as an image, that appears if the viewer's browser doesn't support Java. That way, the user doesn't see a broken file icon. If you type text in this field, the viewer sees this text; Dreamweaver writes it into the code by using the Alt attribute of the `<applet>` tag. If you use the folder icon to select an image, the viewer sees an image; Dreamweaver automatically inserts an `<img>` tag within the `<applet>` and `</applet>` tags of the applet.

- **V Space (Vertical Space):** If you want blank space above or below the applet, enter the number of pixels here.

- **H Space (Horizontal Space):** If you want blank space on either side of the applet, enter the number of pixels here.

- **Parameters:** Click this button to access a dialog box in which you can enter additional parameters for the applet.

- **Class:** Use this drop-down list to access style sheets created with CSS.

You can find lots more information in *Java For Dummies,* 4th Edition, by Barry Burd (published by Wiley Publishing, Inc.).

Use PDFs When They're Warranted

Adobe's Portable Document Format (PDF) has become increasingly popular on the Internet, and with good reason. Now that Acrobat Reader is widely distributed and even built into more recent browser versions, you can assume that most of your audience can read files in PDF.

Unfortunately, like many popular technologies, PDF has become overused and, dare I say, a shortcut for people who don't want to take the time to design their pages in HTML. That said, PDF is a great option for files that you want to make easy to download in their entirety to be saved on a hard drive, as well as documents that you want printed exactly as they are designed.

To add a PDF file to your Web site, simply copy the file into your main root folder and link to it as you would link to any other Web page on your site.

Chapter 12

Forms Follow Function

*F*orms follow function, to paraphrase the old saying. On the Web, many of the most advanced and interactive features you can add to a Web page require forms to collect information from users — information that can then be used in a variety of ways. Forms are commonly used to create guest books, contact forms, search engine entry fields, chat rooms, and discussion areas.

When you design a form, Dreamweaver makes it relatively easy to create check boxes, radio buttons, text boxes, and other common form elements. You'll also find options in Dreamweaver for specifying text box sizes, character limits, and other features. After you've built your form, you may want to consider formatting options, such as CSS, to make it look good.

But if you want your form to actually do something, you'll have to pair it with a program on your Web server. One of the most confusing aspects of working with HTML forms is that they don't do much until you've connected them to a script. Most forms are processed by Common Gateway Interface (CGI) scripts or some other program. These scripts can be written in different programming languages, including C, C#, Java, and Perl. CGI scripts are far more complex than simple HTML files, and even experienced Web designers often purchase third-party solutions or hire experienced programmers to develop CGI scripts for them, especially for complex features such as discussion boards or shopping carts.

Fortunately for those of us who don't have a computer science degree or a huge budget for programmers, many free and low-priced scripts are available on the Web. Search the Internet for *CGI scripts* and you'll find an impressive collection of ready-to-use programs, many of them free. Be aware, however, that when you download a program, you could be creating a security risk for your server (so look for trustworthy scripts with good reviews and support).

You also have to know how to configure and install any script you download on your Web server, which may require special access. How you install a script on your server depends on how your server is set up. Unfortunately, in this book I can't show you everything there is to know about working with all the different kinds of scripts available on the Web on all the different kinds of servers, but I will try to give you an idea of what's involved in working with CGI scripts and what you'll need to do in Dreamweaver to make sure your HTML form will work with a script.

The first part of this chapter includes instructions for creating the common elements in an HTML form, from radio buttons to text boxes. In the last part of the chapter, I include instructions for configuring a form to work with a common CGI that you can use to send the contents of a form to any specified e-mail address. The steps and features covered in the final exercise will also help you with other kinds of CGI scripts.

You also need to create forms when you build dynamic Web sites using Dreamweaver's ColdFusion, ASP.NET, or PHP features. If you're creating a dynamic or database-driven site, you'll need to use the features specific to those technologies, which are covered in Chapters 13, 14, and 15. In this chapter, you find out how to create the HTML forms in Dreamweaver.

Creating HTML Forms

The basic elements of HTML forms — radio buttons, check boxes, and text areas, for example — are easy to create with Dreamweaver, as you see demonstrated in this main section. Remember that your form won't do anything unless it is configured to work a script. Although Dreamweaver doesn't provide any scripts, it does make linking your HTML forms to a script or database relatively easy.

The following steps walk you through creating an HTML form. Start with an open page — either a new page or an existing page to which you want to add a form:

1. **Choose Insert⇨Form⇨Form or click the Form icon on the Forms Insert bar.**

   The Forms Insert bar displays all the common form elements. An empty `<form>` tag is inserted in your document and is displayed as a rectangle outlined by a red dotted line like the one shown in the Document area in Figure 12-1. This dotted line defines the boundaries of a form in the HTML code.

Form   Forms Insert bar

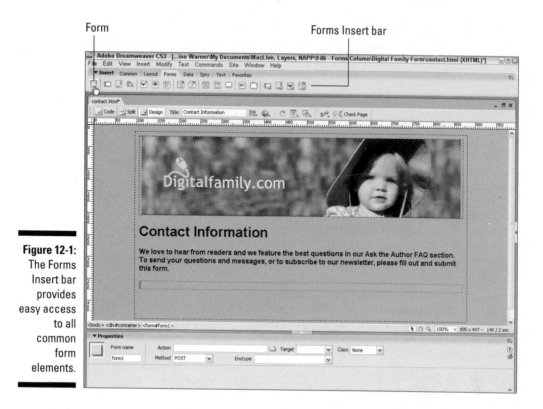

Figure 12-1:
The Forms Insert bar provides easy access to all common form elements.

You can control the display of invisible elements, such as `<form>` tags. Choose Edit⇨Preferences (Windows) or Dreamweaver⇨Preferences (Mac). Then, in the Invisible category, select or deselect the Form Delimiter box.

2. **Click the red outline to select the `<form>` tag and display the `<form>` tag options in the Property inspector (shown in the bottom of Figure 12-1).**

3. **In the Form Name text box, type a name.**

   You can choose any name for this field as long as you don't use spaces, special characters, or punctuation.

Most of the fields displayed in the Property inspector when the `<form>` tag options are displayed should be set based on the CGI script or other program that will be used to collect and process the data from the form. You find instructions for filling in these fields in the "Configuring your form to work with a script" section, at the end of this chapter.

Making forms accessible

You can make your forms much easier to use and more accessible to all your visitors by using the label tag and other Accessibility attributes with form items. Dreamweaver makes this easy by including an Input Tag Accessibility Attributes dialog box, shown in the figure. For this dialog to appear when you insert a form item, such as a radio button or check box, you must have accessibility features turned on in Dreamweaver's Preference settings. To turn on these features, choose Edit➪Preferences (Dreamweaver➪ Preferences on a Mac); in the Preferences dialog box, click the Accessibility category and select the Forms option.

With the accessibility options turned on, when you insert a form item such as a radio button or text box, the Input Tag Accessibility Attributes dialog box opens automatically. Use this dialog box to specify the following options:

- **ID:** Use the ID field to assign a name to a form element. You can leave this field blank, and Dreamweaver won't enter a name automatically. The name is important because it can be used to refer to the file in JavaScript. The ID is also used if you choose Attach Label Tag Using For option under the Style options.

- **Label:** Enter a name that corresponds to the radio button or check box. This is the name that will be read by a screen reader.

- **Style:** Check one of these three options to specify how the label should be included with the radio button or text box in the HTML code. The Attach Label Tag Using For option is recommended as the best option for accessibility. If you choose this option, most browsers will associate a focus rectangle to the check box or radio button. This enables a user to select the check box and radio button by clicking anywhere in the text associated with it, instead of having to click precisely inside the check box or radio button.

- **Position:** Check the corresponding box to specify whether the label should appear before or after each form item.

- **Access Key:** This attribute enables you to create a keyboard shortcut for each of your form items. You can enter any letter in this field, and your users will be able to select the form item by holding down the Alt key (Windows) or the Control key (Macintosh) and typing the letter you specify. For example, if you enter Q as the Access Key, visitors to your site who use a Windows computer could press Alt+Q to select the form item.

- **Tab Index:** By default, you can use the tab key to move from one form field to another when you view a form on the Web. Using the Tab Index, you can specify the order in which the tab key will progress from one form item to another. This is especially helpful if you have links and other form items on a page, and you want the user to be able to tab through them in a specific order. To control the order, assign a number to each form.

Creating radio buttons and check boxes

Radio buttons and check boxes make filling in a form easy for viewers of your site. Rather than make users type a word, such as *yes* or *no,* you can provide radio buttons and check boxes so that users can simply click boxes or buttons.

What's the difference between radio buttons and check boxes? *Radio buttons* enable users to select only one option from a group. Thus, radio buttons are good for either/or options or situations in which you want users to make only one selection. *Check boxes,* on the other hand, enable users to make multiple choices, so they're good for "choose all that apply" situations or for situations that require approval, such as: "Check this box if. . ."

Creating radio buttons

To create radio buttons on a form, follow these steps:

1. **Click to place your cursor inside the boundary of the `<form>` tag where you want to add a radio button.**

   If you haven't yet inserted the `<form>` tag, follow the steps in the section "Creating HTML Forms," earlier in this chapter.

2. **Click the Radio Button icon on the Forms Insert bar.**

   You can also choose Insert⇨Form⇨Radio Button. Either way, a radio button appears inside the form's red boundary line.

   If you have Accessibility options turned on in Preferences, the Input Tag Accessibility Attributes dialog box opens. (See the sidebar "Making forms accessible," to find out more about these options.)

3. **Repeat Step 2 until you have the number of radio buttons you want.**

4. **Select one of the radio buttons on the form to reveal the radio button's properties in the Property inspector, as shown in Figure 12-2.**

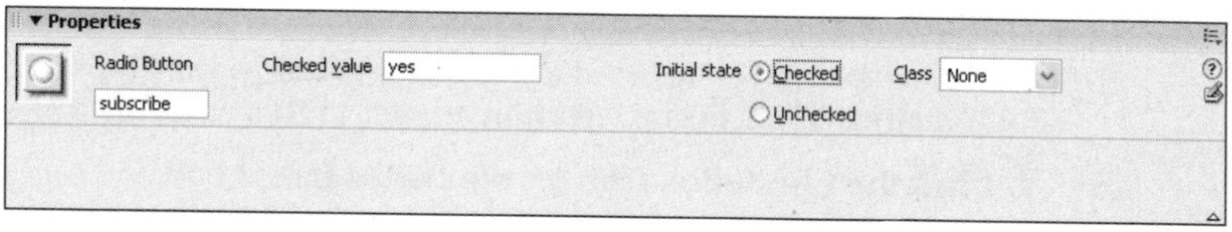

Figure 12-2: Radio button properties.

5. **In the Radio Button text box on the far left of the Property inspector, type a name.**

   All radio buttons in a group should have the same name so that the browser associates them with one another and prevents users from being able to select more than one. If you want users to be able to choose more than one item from a list, use check boxes as described in the following section.

6. **In the Checked Value text box, type a name.**

Each radio button in a group should have a different Checked Value name so that it can be distinguished from the others. Naming radio buttons for the thing they represent is often a good practice, for example, *yes* when the choice is yes and *no* when it's no. If you're asking users about their favorite ice cream flavors, you might use as values the flavor each button represents. This name is usually included in the data you get back when the form is processed and returned to you (it can be returned in an e-mail message or sent directly to a database). How the data is returned depends on the CGI script or other programming used to process the form. If you're looking at the data later, interpreting it is easier if the name is something that makes sense to you.

7. **For the Initial State option, select Checked or Unchecked.**

These two options determine whether the radio button on your form appears already selected when the Web page loads. Select Checked if you want to preselect a choice. You should set only one radio button option to be preselected and remember that the user can always override this setting by selecting another radio button.

8. **Select the other radio buttons one by one in the main design area and repeat Steps 5 through 7 to specify the properties in the Property inspector for each one.**

If your form is complete, jump ahead to the "Finishing your form with Submit and Reset buttons" section, later in this chapter.

Creating check boxes

To create check boxes, follow these steps:

1. **Click to place your cursor inside the boundary of the `<form>` tag where you want to add a check box.**

If you haven't yet inserted a `<form>` tag, follow the steps in the "Creating HTML Forms" section, earlier in this chapter.

2. **Click the Check Box icon on the Forms Insert bar.**

You can also choose Insert⇨Form⇨Check Box.

If you have Accessibility options turned on in Preferences, the Input Tag Accessibility Attributes dialog box opens. (See the sidebar "Making forms accessible," to find out more about these options.)

3. **Repeat Step 2 to place as many check boxes as you want.**

4. **Select one of the check boxes on your form to reveal the check box properties in the Property inspector, as shown in Figure 12-3.**

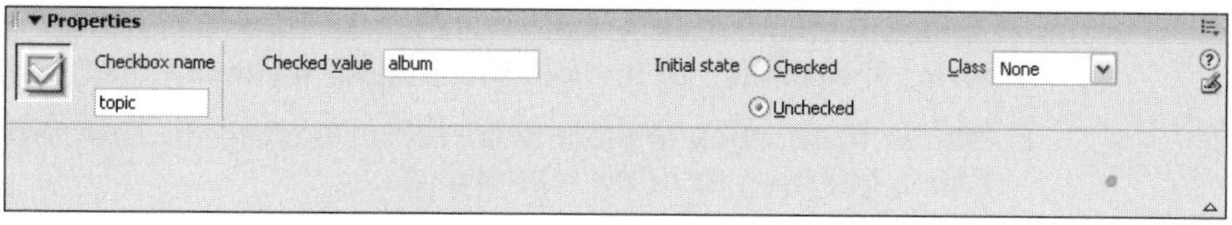

Figure 12-3:
Check box
properties.

5. **In the Checkbox Name text box, type a name.**

You should use a distinct name for each check box because users can select more than one check box, and you want to ensure that the information submitted is properly associated with each individual check box.

6. **In the Checked Value text box, type a name.**

Each check box in a group should have a different Checked Value name so that the CGI script can distinguish it. Naming them for the things they represent is a good practice. As with radio buttons, the Checked Value is usually included in the data you get back when the form is processed and returned to you. If you're looking at the data later, interpreting it is easier if the name is something that makes sense to you.

7. **For the Initial State option, select Checked or Unchecked.**

This option determines whether the check box appears already selected when the Web page loads. Select Checked if you want to preselect a choice. A user can always override this preselection by clicking the text box again to deselect it.

8. **Select the other check boxes one by one and repeat Steps 5 through 7 to set the properties in the Property inspector for each one.**

If your form is complete, jump ahead to the "Finishing your form with Submit and Reset buttons" section, later in this chapter.

Adding text fields and text areas

When you want users to enter text, such as a name, an e-mail address, or a comment, you need to use a text field. To insert text fields, follow these steps:

1. **Click to place your cursor inside the `<form>` tag where you want to add a text field.**

If you haven't yet inserted a `<form>` tag, follow the steps in the "Creating HTML Forms" section, earlier in this chapter.

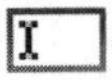

2. Click the Text Field icon on the Forms Insert bar.

You can also choose Insert⇨Form⇨Text Field. A text field box appears.

If you have Accessibility options turned on in Preferences, the Input Tag Accessibility Attributes dialog box opens. (See the sidebar "Making forms accessible," to find out more about these options.)

3. On the form, click to place your cursor next to the first text field and type a question or other text prompt.

For example, you may want to type *Email Address:* next to a text box where you want a user to enter an e-mail address.

4. Select the text field on your form to reveal the Text Field properties in the Property inspector, as shown in Figure 12-4.

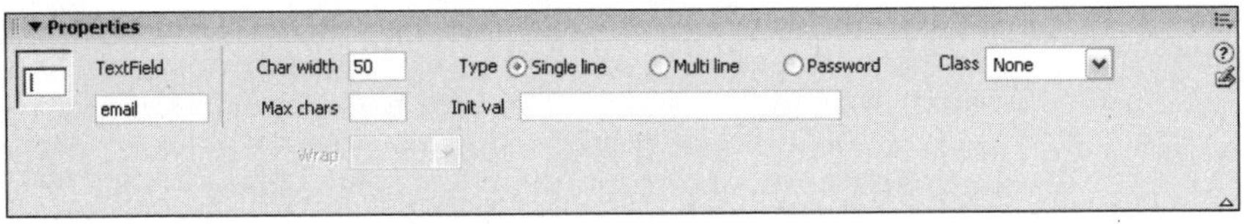

Figure 12-4:
Use the Text
Field option
to create
form fields
in which
users can
enter one or
more lines
of text.

5. In the TextField text box, type a name.

Each text area on a form should have a different text field name so that the CGI script can distinguish it. Naming text areas for the things they represent is usually best, but don't use any spaces or special characters. In Figure 12-4, you can see that I named the Email Address option *email.* Many scripts return this name next to the contents of the text field a visitor enters at your Web site. If you're looking at the data later, you can more easily interpret it if the name corresponds to the choice.

6. In the Char Width box, type the number of characters you want to be visible in the field.

This setting determines the width of the text field that appears on the page. In the example shown here, I've set the character width to 50 to create a text box that is more than wide enough for most e-mail addresses. How wide you make your text boxes should depend on the amount of information you expect users to enter and the constraints of your design.

7. **In the Max Chars box, type the maximum number of characters you want to allow.**

   If you leave this field blank, users can type as many characters as they choose, even if they exceed the physical length of the text box specified in the Char Width field. I usually limit the number of characters only if I want to maintain consistency in the data. For example, I like to limit the State field to a two-character abbreviation.

   You can set the Char Width field to be longer or shorter than the Max Chars field. If users type more characters than can appear in the text field, the text scrolls so that users can still see all the text they enter, even if it can't be displayed in the text field all at once.

8. **Next to Type, select one of the following options:**

   - **Single Line** creates a one-line text box such as the kind I created for the Name and Address fields shown in Figure 12-4.

   - **Multi Line** gives users space to enter text. (Note that if you select Multi Line, you also need to specify the number of lines you want the text area to cover by typing a number in the Num Lines field, which appears as an option when you choose Multi Line.)

   - **Password** is used if you're asking users to enter data that they might not want to display on-screen. This type of field causes entered data to appear as asterisks and disables copying from the field.

9. **Use the Class drop-down list to apply any Class CSS styles that may be defined in the site.**

   You can create Class styles for many purposes, including formatting form elements. You learn more about creating and applying Class styles in Chapters 5 and 6.

10. **In the Init Val text box, type any text you want displayed when the form loads.**

    For example, you can include the words `Add comments here` on the form in the text field under Comments. Users can delete the Init Val text or leave it and add more text in the same text field.

11. **If you are creating a multiline text area, specify the Wrap options.**

    The Wrap field controls how the users' data is displayed if it exceeds the length of the text field. Selecting Off or Default prevents the users' text from wrapping to the next line. (Note this option is available only for multiline text boxes.)

12. **Select the other text areas one by one and repeat Steps 5 through 9 to set the properties in the Property inspector for each one.**

If your form is complete, jump ahead to the "Finishing your form with Submit and Reset buttons" section, later in this chapter.

Forms display differently in different browsers

Firefox, Netscape, Safari, and Microsoft Internet Explorer don't display text fields in forms equally. The differences vary depending on the version of the browser, but the general result is that a text field appears with different dimensions in one browser than in another. Slight differences also exist with color, scroll bars, and shape in the case of check boxes. Forms are also displayed differently on Macintosh and PC computers. Unfortunately, this problem has no perfect solution, but as long as your forms look okay in the browsers you consider most important, it should not be a problem that they display slightly differently in other browsers. For best results, test your pages on a variety of browsers and on both Macs and PCs, and be especially careful that form fields and other elements are not cut off.

Creating drop-down lists

When you want to give users a multiple-choice option but don't want to take up lots of space on the page, drop-down lists are an ideal solution. To create a drop-down list using Dreamweaver, follow these steps:

1. **Click to place your cursor inside the `<form>` tag where you want to add a drop-down list.**

   If you haven't yet created a `<form>` tag, follow the steps in the "Creating HTML Forms" section, earlier in this chapter.

2. **Click the List/Menu icon on the Forms Insert bar.**

   You can also choose Insert⇨Form⇨List/Menu. A drop-down list appears.

   If you have Accessibility options turned on in Preferences, the Input Tag Accessibility Attributes dialog box opens. (See sidebar "Making forms accessible," to find out more about these options.)

3. **Click to place your cursor next to the List field and enter a question or other text prompt.**

   I typed *What state do you live in?*

4. **Select the field that represents the list on your page to reveal the List/Menu properties in the Property inspector, as shown at the bottom of Figure 12-5.**

5. **In the List/Menu text box, type a name.**

   Each list or menu on a form should have a different name so that you can differentiate the lists when the form data is returned.

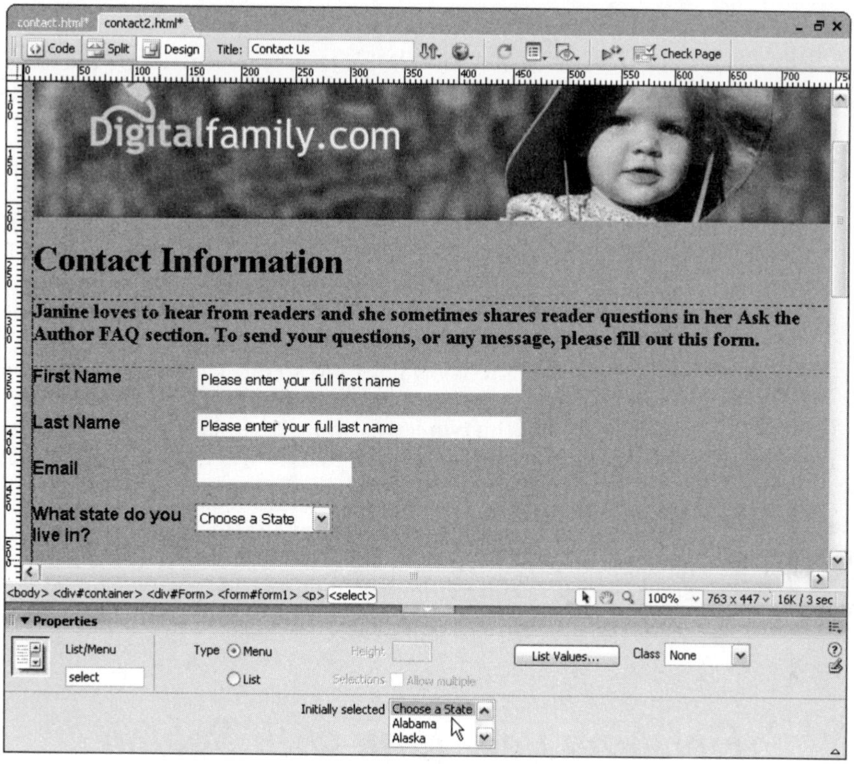

Figure 12-5:
The List/
Menu
option
enables you
to create a
drop-down
list of
options that
doesn't take
up lots of
room on
your page.

6. **Next to Type, select the Menu or List option.**

   This step determines whether the form element is a drop-down menu or a scrollable list. If you choose List, you can specify the height and control how many items are shown at a time. You can also specify whether a user can select more than one item. If you choose Menu, these options aren't available.

7. **Click the List Values button, in the upper-right of the Property inspector.**

   The List Values dialog box appears, as shown in Figure 12-6.

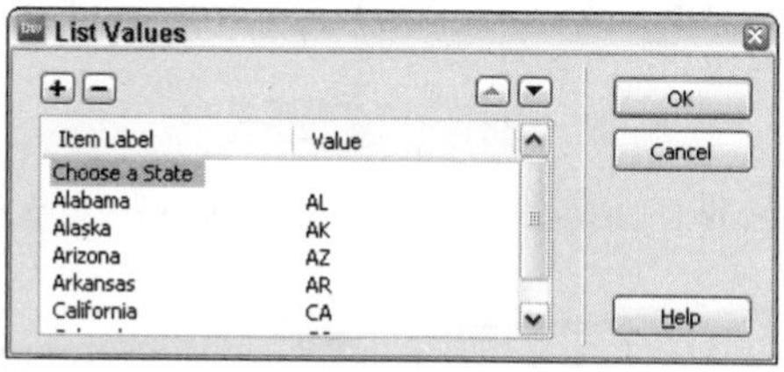

Figure 12-6:
Create the
options
in the List
form field.

8. **Enter the choices you want to make available.**

Click the plus sign (+) to add an item label; then type the label text you want in the text box that appears in the dialog box. Item labels appear on the menu or list on the Web page in the order in which you enter them. Use the minus sign (–) to delete a selected option.

Press the Tab key to move the cursor to the Value side of the dialog box, where you can enter a value. Values are optional, but if present, they are sent to the server instead of the label text. This provides a way of including information that you don't want to display on the drop-down menu. For example, if you enter **Alabama** as a label on the left, you can enter the abbreviation **AL** as a value on the right. If you enter **Alaska** as a label, you can **AK** as a value, and so on. That way, you visitors can select from a list that displays the full name of each state, but your script can collect only the two-letter abbreviations. If you don't enter a value, the label is used as the submitted data when the form is processed.

The first label entered in the List Values dialog box is the only one that's displayed on the page until a user clicks the drop-down arrow. Thus, it's good practice to include an instruction in this space, such as Choose a State, shown in the example in Figures 12-5 and 12-6.

8. **Click OK to close the dialog box.**

Finishing your form with Submit and Reset buttons

For your users to be able to send their completed forms to you, you need to create a Submit button, which, when clicked, tells the user's browser to send the form to the CGI script or other program that processes the form. You may also want to add a Reset button, which enables users to erase any information they have entered if they want to start over.

Many developers don't use the Reset button because they find that it can be confusing to visitors (and annoying if it means they accidentally erase all the information they just entered). Because visitors can always leave a page before clicking the Submit button if they choose not to complete a form, the simplest way to avoid this problem is to avoid using a Reset button.

To create a Submit, Reset, or other button in Dreamweaver, follow these steps:

1. **Click to place your cursor inside the `<form>` tag where you want to add a button.**

If you haven't yet inserted the `<form>` tag (which appears as a red dotted line around your form), follow the steps in the first exercise in the "Creating HTML Forms" section before continuing with this exercise.

You might also want to enter at least one text field or other field option. There's not much point in having a Submit button if you don't provide any fields where a user can enter data to be submitted.

 2. Click the Button icon on the Forms Insert bar.

You can also choose Insert⇨Form⇨Button. A Submit button appears, and the Property inspector changes to reveal the form button properties shown in Figure 12-7. You can change the button to a Reset button or other kind of button by altering the attributes in the Property inspector, as shown in the remaining steps.

TIP

When you insert a button or other form item, the Property inspector automatically changes to display the attributes for that item. If you de-select the button by clicking somewhere else on the page, you need to click and select the button again to view the button attributes in the Property inspector.

Figure 12-7:
Submit and
Reset
buttons
enable
users to
submit
information
or clear
forms,
respectively.

 4. Next to Action, click the Submit Form or Reset Form option.

The Submit Form option invokes an action, such as sending user information to an e-mail address. The Reset Form option returns the page to the way it was when the page loaded. There is also a None option, which creates a button that doesn't do anything unless it is used with one of Dreamweaver's JavaScript behaviors.

 5. In the Value text box, type the text you want to display on the button.

You can type any text you want for the label, such as Search, Go, Clear, or Delete.

REMEMBER

Clicking a Submit button in a form won't do much unless you've configured the form to work with a CGI script or other program to collect or process user-entered data.

Using jump menus

Many designers use jump menus as navigational elements because they can provide a list of links in a drop-down list without taking up lots of room on a Web page. You can also use a jump menu to launch an application or start an animation sequence.

To create a jump menu, follow these steps:

1. **Click to place your cursor inside the `<form>` tag where you want to add a button.**

   If you haven't yet inserted the `<form>` tag (which appears as a red dotted line around your form), follow the steps in the first exercise in the "Creating HTML Forms" section before continuing with this exercise.

2. **Click the Jump Menu icon on the Forms Insert bar.**

   You can also choose Insert➪Form➪Jump Menu. The Insert Jump Menu dialog box opens.

3. **In the Text field, under Menu Items, type the name you want to display in the drop-down list.**

   Click the plus sign (+) to add more items. As you type items in the Text field, they appear in the Menu Items list, as shown in Figure 12-8.

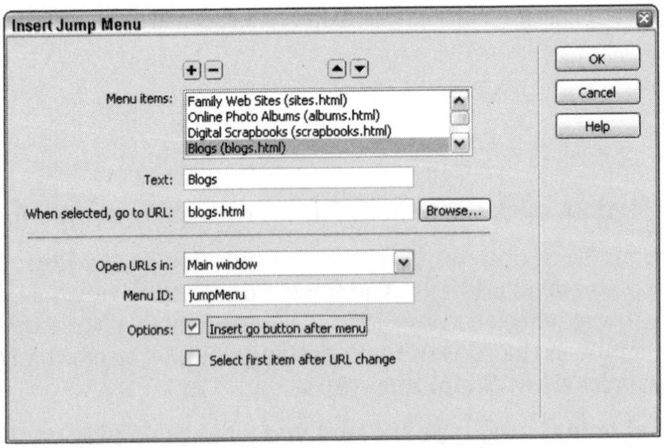

Figure 12-8: When you create a jump list, items you type in the Text field appear in the Menu Items list.

4. **Click the Browse button to locate the page you want to link to or type the URL for the page in the When Selected, Go to URL field.**

   You can link to a local file or enter any URL to link to a page on another Web site, and you can use the Browse button to specify the URL you want to link to.

Making your forms look good

The best way to get your form fields to line up nicely is to use CSS. By creating styles that control the spacing and padding of form elements, you can make all of your fields, buttons, and other elements line up neatly. You can also use an HTML table to align fields. If you use a table to align a form, consider putting all your text in one row of cells and all your text fields in an adjacent row. You may also want to place all your radio buttons in the cells on the left and the text that the buttons correspond to in the cells on the right. (Chapters 5 and 6 cover CSS; Chapter 7 shows you how to create and edit HTML tables .)

---

5. **If you're using frames, use the Open URLs In field to specify a target.**

   If you're not using frames, the default is Main Window. Then, when the user selects an option, the new page replaces the page he or she is viewing.

6. **If you want to enter a unique identifier for this menu, use the Menu Name field.**

   This option can be useful if you have multiple jump menus on a page. You can use any name you want, but you can't use spaces, special characters, or punctuation.

7. **If you want to force users to click a button to activate the selection, select the Insert Go Button After Menu option.**

   If you don't add a Go button, the linked page loads as soon as the user makes a selection. The Go button works like a Submit button for the jump menu options.

Understanding How CGI Scripts Work

Common Gateway Interface (CGI) scripts are programs written in a programming language such as Perl, Java, C++, ASP, or PHP. They work in tandem with your Web server to process the data submitted by a user. Think of CGI scripts as the engine behind an HTML form and many other automated features on a Web site. These scripts are much more complex to create than HTML pages, and these languages take much longer to figure out than HTML. CGI scripts reside and run on the server and are usually triggered by an action a user takes, such as clicking the Submit button on an HTML form.

A common scenario with a script may go like this:

1. A user loads a page, such as a guest book, fills out the HTML form, and clicks the Submit button.

2. The browser gathers all the data from the form and sends it to the Web server in a standard format.

3. The Web server takes the incoming data and hands it off to the CGI script, which unpacks the data and does something with it, such as places the data in an e-mail message and sends the message to a specified e-mail address or adds the data to a database.

4. The CGI script sends instructions or a block of HTML back to the browser through the Web server to report on the outcome of the script, such as a Thank You page.

Configuring your form to work with a script

After you've created a form using the features covered in the previous sections of this chapter, it's time to configure the form to work with a CGI script or program. To help you understand how this process works, I'll use a common script called `formmail.pl` in the following exercise. This clever little script is designed to collect data entered into an HTML form and send it to a specified email address. You can find out more about `formmail.pl` at `www.scriptarchive.com` (a great place to find lots of free CGI scripts).

Every script is different, and the details of how you install and configure each script depend on the program and how your server is set up.

If your service provider doesn't offer a form mail script, you can download and configure the script yourself if you have the right access on your server and knowledge of how your server is configured. Ask your service provider for more information. If it doesn't provide the interactive scripts you want, you may want to consider moving your site to a hosting service that does provide CGI scripts you can use.

The following exercise shows you how to use Dreamweaver with the `form-mail.pl` script. It should give you a good introduction to how you would set up any form to work with any script, but be aware that you may have to alter some of the steps to work with the program you are using:

1. **Select the `<form>` tag that surrounds your form by clicking anywhere on the red dotted line that represents the boundary of the `<form>` tag or by clicking the `<form>` tag in the tag selector at the bottom of the work area, as shown in Figure 12-9.**

   With the `<form>` tag selected, the Property inspector changes to feature the form tag options. *Note:* All HTML forms must be enclosed by the `<form>` tag. If your script doesn't have a `<form>` tag, you'll need to add one around the entire contents of your form by following the steps in the first exercise in this chapter.

Here's a tip for selecting the `<form>` tag in Dreamweaver. Place your cursor anywhere in the body of your form, and then use the tag selector at the bottom of the work area to select the `<form>` tag. Make sure you've selected the `<form>` tag and not just one of the form elements, such as the text box I created in this form for comments.

2. **In the Property inspector, give your form a name.**

   Dreamweaver automatically gives each form you create a distinct name (form1, form2, and so on), but I prefer to change the name to something that has more meaning, such as *contact* for this contact form. You can name your form whatever you like, but don't use spaces or special characters.

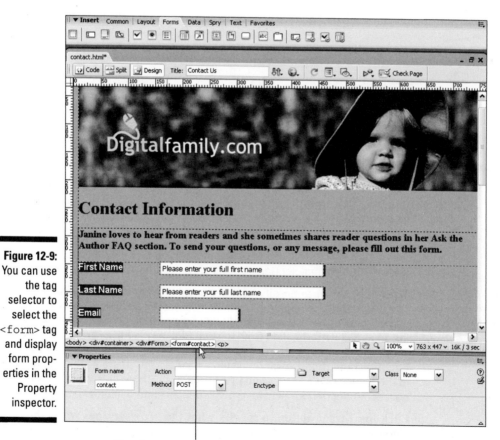

Figure 12-9: You can use the tag selector to select the `<form>` tag and display form properties in the Property inspector.

The `<form>` tag in the Tag selector

3. Specify the Action for the form.

For the `formmail.pl` script used in this example (as well as many other scripts you might use), the action is simply the path to the script's location on your server. In Figure 12-10, you can see that I've entered the address `/cgi-bin/formmail.pl`. The address you enter depends on your service provider, but it is a common convention to call the folder where CGI scripts are stored `cgi-bin`. The last part of the address (`formmail.pl`) is the name of the script. In this case, it's a Perl script, indicated by the `.pl` extension.

You can only use the Browse button (the yellow folder icon in the Property inspector) to automatically enter an address in the Action field if you are working on a live server and Dreamweaver has identified the location of your script, or if you have the script on your local system in the same directory structure that exists on your server. In most cases, however, it's simplest just to ask your service provider or programmer for the address and type it in the Action field.

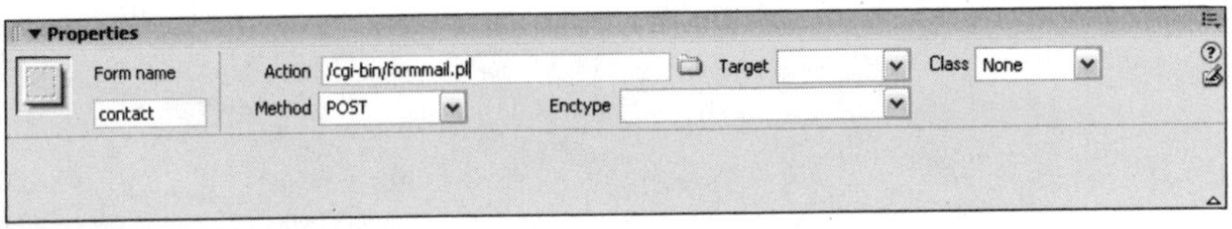

Figure 12-10:
In the
Action field,
enter the
path to the
script.

4. In the Method field, use the pull-down arrow to select Get, Post, or Default.

Again, what you choose depends on your script, but Dreamweaver's default is Post. And if you're using a script such as `formmail`, which is featured in the final sections of this chapter, the best option is Post.

The Get option is generally used for nondestructive, "safe" form transactions that may be repeated, such as a search engine. The Post option is generally used for transactions that should occur only once, such as sending an e-mail with the data from a form, registering for a service, or unsubscribing to a newsletter. Post can also handle larger chunks of data than Get. Also note that transactions using the Get option are generally stored in the log files on a server and in a browser's history files, so this option is not recommended for sensitive data such as financial information.

5. Click the Target option to specify what the browser does when the submit action is completed.

If you choose _top, the results page opens in a new browser window. If you leave this field blank, the browser window is simply replaced with the results page. A results page is usually a simple HTML page with a message such as *Thanks for playing,* delivered when the Submit button is clicked.

6. **Use the Enctype field to specify how the data is formatted when it is returned (see Figure 12-11).**

   For example, if you're using a form mail script, the Enctype field will determine how the text appears in your e-mail when the contents of the form are sent to you. By default, enctype is set to `application/x-www-form-urlencoded`.

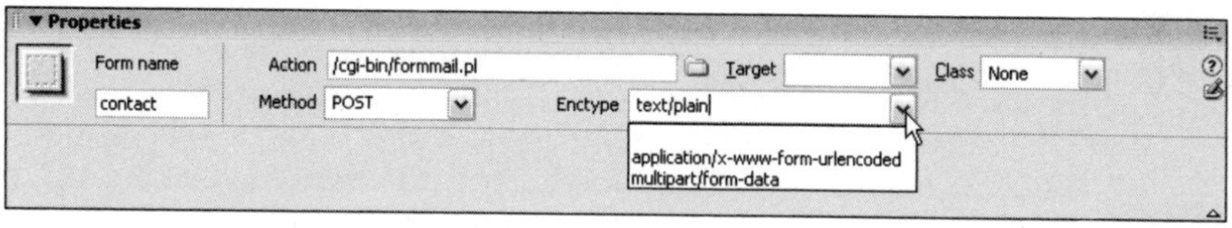

Figure 12-11:
Enter an
encode
type.

7. **Use the class field at the far right of the Property inspector to apply a CSS style to the form.**

   In this example, I applied CSS to some of the elements in the form, such as the text, but not to the entire form.

That takes care of all the options in the Property inspector. You'll still need to insert a hidden form field into this form to make it work with the `formmail.pl` script, as you see in the next exercise.

Using hidden fields

Many scripts, including the `formmail.pl` script, require the use of hidden fields. To insert and use a hidden field, follow these steps:

1. **Click to place your cursor inside the `<form>` tag.**

   If you haven't yet inserted the `<form>` tag (which appears as a red dotted line around your form), follow the steps in the first exercise in the "Creating HTML Forms" section before continuing with this exercise.

   Even though the hidden field won't appear in the form area, you need to make sure that it is inside the `<form>` tag before you add a hidden field. Placing your cursor at the top or bottom of the form area before inserting a hidden field is a good option because it makes the hidden field easier to find in the HTML code.

   Once the hidden field is inserted into the `<form>` tag, the Property inspector will change to feature the hidden field options.

2. **In the Property inspector, enter a name.**

   If you're using `formmai.pl`, you'd enter *recipient* as the name and the e-mail address where you want the form data sent as the value. You can even enter more than one e-mail address, separated by commas. So, for example, I could enter "*janine@jcwarner.com, janine@digitalfamily.com* in the value field, and the data from the form would be e-mailed to both of these e-mail addresses when a user clicks the Submit button. See Figure 12-12.

Figure 12-12:
The Hidden
Field
properties.

▼ Properties

HiddenField

recipient   Value janine@jcwarner.com, janine@digitalfa

3. **Click to place your cursor inside the `<form>` tag and then click on the Hidden Field icon in the Forms Insert Bar to add another hidden field to create a subject line.**

4. **In the Property inspector, enter the name *subject*. In the value field, include a subject line you want inserted into the e-mail message automatically when a user submits the form.**

   In this example, I entered *Contact Information from DigitalFamily.com* as the value.

   You can add many other hidden fields to a form, depending on the script you are using and how much you want to customize the results.

And that's it. Assuming all fields are filled in correctly and the `formmail.pl` (or a similar) script is properly installed and configured on your server, you should receive via e-mail any data a user enters into your form and submits.

There are so many reasons to create forms on the Web, but e-mailing the contents of a contact form is one of the most common. I hope this little exercise has helped to give you an idea of what you need to do to make your HTML forms interact with a CGI script on your server.

Remember, most service providers offer a collection of scripts you can use for common tasks such as discussion boards and guest books. All you should have to do is create the HTML part of the form and then specify the form fields to interact with your script.

Part IV
Working with Dynamic Content

The 5th Wave — By Rich Tennant

@RICHTENNANT

"Evidently he died of natural causes following a marathon session animating everything on his personal Web site. And no, Morganstern — the irony isn't lost on me."

In this part . . .

The most sophisticated and technically complicated Web sites are created using databases to dynamically generate Web pages — ideal for content-heavy Web sites. Although creating a Web site with these advanced features is far more complex than using methods you find in earlier parts of this book, the rewards can be worth the trouble. In Chapters 13, 14, and 15, you discover the benefits of creating a dynamic site, find out how to work with a database on the Web, and follow step-by-step instructions to build a simple, database-driven site.

Chapter 13

Building a Dynamic Web Site: Getting Started

*T*he most sophisticated Web sites on the Internet, such as Amazon.com or CNN.com, were created using complex programming and databases. Combining a database that records information about users with the capability to generate pages automatically is what enables Amazon to greet you by name when you return to its site, track your orders, and even make recommendations based on your previous purchases.

Static Web sites, which you can build using the instructions in Chapter 11, work well for many Web sites (including my own at www.JCWarner.com). But for anyone creating a really large, content-heavy site, such as a magazine or newspaper Web site or large e-commerce sites where you need to track inventory and want users to be able to search through products, dynamic Web sites are a better choice.

Before you even start down this path, let me warn you of two things. First, creating a database-driven Web site is far, far more complex than creating the kinds of Web sites described in the earlier chapters of this book. And second, the most sophisticated sites on the Web, such as Amazon and CNN, use highly customized systems that require teams of very experienced programmers to create (and are far beyond what you can do with Dreamweaver's dynamic site features).

That said, Dreamweaver does include basic database development features that you can use to create dynamic Web sites. In this chapter and the two that follow, you find an introduction to these features and instructions for creating a basic, database-driven site.

A description of the more advanced Dreamweaver database features is beyond the scope of this Dummies book. If you want to use Dreamweaver's most advanced database features, you find more information in *Dreamweaver CS3 Bible*, written by Joseph Lowery (published by Wiley).

This chapter begins by introducing you to what a dynamic Web site and a database are and the many ways in which, through a dynamic Web site, you can display and edit information contained in a database. You also discover what you need to have in place to create a dynamic Web site. In Chapters 14 and 15, you find step-by-step directions for creating various dynamic features on a real-world Web site.

Understanding the Dynamic Web Site

A *dynamic* Web site is usually connected to a *database,* which delivers different data to each Web site visitor based on his or her requests. Many dynamic Web sites also have Web pages that permit an administrator or a site visitor to make changes to the information that is displayed through a series of simple steps without ever leaving the Web browser. A good example of a dynamic Web site is a search engine. You type what you want to find into a search field and, when you submit your request, you get instant results with information that is relevant (ideally, anyway!) to your search request.

If you want to add just a simple search engine to a Web site, see Chapter 17 for tips about using Google's free search engine features on any Web site.

A dynamic Web site has many advantages besides the capability to create a site-wide search. Suppose that you have a Web site where you sell 657 kinds of candy. On a *static* Web site, you would have to create 657 pages, one for each candy product. With a dynamic Web site, you create just *one* page that contains special code that runs on a server to describe where to display the product name, image, description, and any other pertinent information on the page. Other techniques, like Asynchronous JavaScript and XML (Ajax), move some of the work of displaying and formatting the information to the Web browser itself. Either way, you enter all your product information into a database or XML files (if it's not in there already), and the special code in the page communicates with the data source, collecting each product's information and creating a page on-the-fly for each product as visitors request that product.

Not only can this kind of system save lots of time (because you don't have to create all those individual pages), dynamic Web sites also enable you to make changes and updates with less effort. And you can even display the same product information in multiple page designs, in different combinations, and even on different sites with much less effort.

These sites are usually set up so that the Web site can be administered through a Web browser, allowing staff with little or no technical skills to easily add or remove products and make changes to existing products. They simply enter or edit information in a form using a Web browser and click Submit to update those changes to the site or even change the database if that's how the system is set up. Once updated, that new information appears instantly the next time a product page is loaded for a visitor.

Usually, you would limit the capability to make these changes to a few people on your staff. You don't necessarily want your customers making price changes or altering product descriptions, but you may want your sales staff to be able to easily make changes, even when they're out in the field. You can control this situation by setting up different levels of password access to your site. That way, customers can search for certain information, and staff members with special access and the right passwords can search for even more information and make changes to it. The system you use to do both these tasks is essentially the same, but you set up different levels of access to make it all work this way.

Beware, however, that before a nontechnical staff person can easily make changes and updates to a dynamic site, someone who is technically savvy has to do a significant amount of setup work to create the dynamic system. Again, this kind of Web site system makes sense only if you're creating a very large, complex, and data-rich Web site. A programmer could spend much more time setting up even a simple database site than it takes to create quite a few static Web pages, but once a site gets to about 100 pages or more, the initial setup time is probably worthwhile.

Talking the Talk: Key Concepts

If you're sure that you want to create a dynamic Web site and that the basic database features in Dreamweaver are up to the task for you, then read on. You can do some cool things with a database-driven site, even if you're not creating the next Amazon. Before jumping into your first dynamic Web site, however, the following pages are designed to help you become familiar with a few key concepts that play an integral role in dynamic Web site development.

A *database* is a collection of information compiled in one or more *tables*. Each table has multiple *fields* (also called *columns*) and individual *records* in rows. What? Okay, picture a mail-order catalog, such as Pottery Barn. (Indulge me — it's my favorite.)

The catalog itself is the *database*. It contains a collection of information about various products. Each product is a *record* in the database. In this case, all particular products have an item number, a price, and a color — and each of those is a *field*. A *record* in a database consists of one complete set of all fields in a table. Taking it a step further, within the catalog, the various products are organized in categories often because they have something in common (furniture, rugs, bedding). Each category is a *table* — a grouping of various records from a database that have something in common.

This type of table isn't the same kind discussed in Chapter 7, where you find out how HTML tables are used to format information, much as you would use a spreadsheet program, such as Excel. Database tables aren't used for formatting; they're for grouping and organizing content.

Modern browsers let you change the Web page after it has already loaded from the server. Using JavaScript and Dynamic HTML (DHTML), the Web page can be changed in the browser without ever reloading the page from the Web server using Asynchronous JavaScript and XML (Ajax). Ajax is not a technology in and of itself. It describes some combination of JavaScript, DHTML, and XML used to display content or interact with someone browsing the Web without having to load entire pages from a Web server each time a user clicks a link. This capability makes a Web site seem faster and more interactive.

Databases on the Web work in much the same way. Suppose that you go to www.poweryoga.com to get more information about power yoga. Starting on the home page, you can hover your mouse over the About Yoga menu item and click Library of Articles in the menu. On the next page you can choose from a number of articles to find out more about Yoga (see Figure 13-1).

The Library of Articles page is dynamically generated by the server using a list of stories pulled from a database. Clicking a story link takes you to a page that shows you the entire article from the database in your browser.

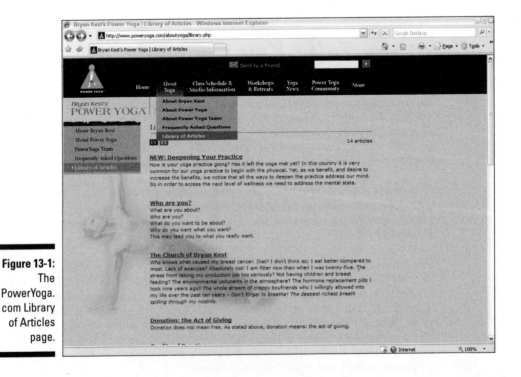

Figure 13-1: The PowerYoga.com Library of Articles page.

Database applications

Various applications are made specifically for creating and managing data, including Microsoft Access, Filemaker Pro, SQL Server, MySQL, FoxPro, and Oracle. Novices most commonly use Access to create small databases (MDB files). Access is also commonly used to communicate visually with bigger databases, such as Microsoft SQL Server.

I created the examples in this book in Microsoft Access 2000 running with the Windows XP Professional operating system. If you want to dig deeper into the world of databases, consider purchasing *Database Development For Dummies* and *SQL For Dummies*, 6th Edition, both written by Allen G. Taylor; *Access 2003 For Dummies,* by John Kaufeld; *Oracle8i For Dummies,* 2nd Edition, by Carol McCullough-Dieter; *SQL Bible,* by Alex Kriegel and Boris M. Trukhnov (all published by Wiley).

Now that you have the database basics covered, you need to provide a way for the Web site and the database to communicate. In the next section, I show you how to set up a Web server and an application server step-by-step so that you can get started.

While working with Web sites that are *static* (the content is entered by hand and isn't permanently altered by or customized for the person viewing the site), you may be used to previewing pages directly from your local hard drive. It's not that simple when the content is dynamic because Dreamweaver adds some special code that the server needs to process before the content is published to the viewer. Having a Web server is crucial when you're working with a dynamic Web site because you need to test your work along the way to make sure that you get the results you're shooting for.

A *Web server* is both a piece of computer hardware on which a Web site is stored and the software on that system that provides the server functionality. In this case, the Web server I'm referring to is the software installed on a system, not an actual computer chip in a large beige case.

Dynamic Content Technologies Supported by Dreamweaver

Dreamweaver supports these five server technologies (described in detail in the following sections):

> ✔ Active Server Pages (ASP)
> ✔ ASP.NET

- ✔ JavaServer Pages (JSP)
- ✔ ColdFusion
- ✔ PHP (which stands for PHP: Hypertext Preprocessor — a recursive acronym, for you wordsmiths)

The examples in this book use ASP in Microsoft Windows. In essence, all five work toward the same outcome: dynamic content on a Web page or Web site. They all provide the capability to generate HTML dynamically. Using server-side code, they can display information from a database and create HTML based on whether certain criteria are met or specified by a particular user. I selected ASP and Microsoft Windows for this book because ASP is one of the most common and relatively easy-to-use server software options. However, to recommend one technology over the other really wouldn't be fair because they all offer similar functionality with slight variations in speed and efficiency.

Dreamweaver CS3 now includes support for Ajax for client side interactive content using Adobe's new toolset, the Spry framework for Ajax.

To find out more about these technologies, check out these other titles, all published by Wiley Publishing, Inc.: *Active Server Pages For Dummies,* by Bill Hatfield; *ASP.NET For Dummies,* by Bill Hatfield; *JavaServer Pages For Dummies,* by MacCormac Rinehart; *ColdFusion MX For Dummies,* by John Paul Ashenfelter; *PHP 5 For Dummies,* by Janet Valade; *Ajax for Dummies* by Steve Holzner.

The following sections provide more detail on each of these scripting languages.

ASP

ASP is a server technology that is built into Windows 2003 Server, Windows 2000, Windows XP Professional, and Windows Vista at no additional cost and can be easily installed into Windows 98 and NT. Used with Microsoft IIS or Personal Web Server, ASP isn't a stand-alone programming language because much of the code you write for ASP pages is in VB Script or JScript (Microsoft's version of JavaScript). You can check out www.4guysfromrolla.com to find out more about ASP in what more closely resembles plain English.

ASP.NET

ASP.NET is Microsoft's replacement for ASP. It's not a revision of ASP 3.0; in fact, it's a complete redesign of the language. This installment of ASP isn't what 3.0 was to 2.0 — Microsoft has done more than add new tags. The language is more similar to traditional programming languages, such as C++, where code is compiled. This arrangement suggests that applications written in ASP.NET can run faster than anything now available because Web servers work more efficiently with less coding overhead. However, ASP.NET isn't as verbose as

ASP 3.0, so it's much harder for novice programmers to read. ASP.NET is a Microsoft technology, and you can find more information at `http://msdn.microsoft.com/asp.net/`. You can also find more about ASP.NET from `http://aspnet.4guysfromrolla.com/`.

JavaServerPages (JSP)

JSP is from Sun Microsystems. Because its dynamic code is based on Java, you can run the pages from non-Microsoft Web servers. You can use JSP on Allaire JRun Server and IBM WebSphere. Using JSP, you can create and keep the dynamic code separated from the HTML pages (by using JavaBeans), or you can embed the JSP code into the page. Unless you're a hard-core programmer, however, this language isn't for you. JSP is horribly complex.

ColdFusion MX

ColdFusion, owned by Adobe, uses its own server and scripting language. ColdFusion is probably the easiest language to figure out, and it offers built-in XML processing and custom tags that also allow you to separate dynamic code from HTML, which makes it similar to JSP. Also like JSP, it's ultimately based on Java.

PHP

PHP was native to Unix-based servers. However, you can now download Windows binaries from `www.php.net` to run Apache (a server software typically used with PHP) from any version of Windows as well as IIS on NT, 2000, XP Professional, and 2003 Server. You can even configure PHP to run on Personal Web Server (although doing so is tricky). The PHP scripting language is based on C, Perl, and Java. You can get more functionality with PHP right out of the box than you can with ASP. For example, virtually every ASP add-on that's on sale at `www.serverobjects.com` comes built-in or is available for free from `www.php.net`.

Spry

The Adobe Spry framework for Ajax is a client side JavaScript library that enables Web designers to deliver a richer user experience to their customers. Dreamweaver supplies various Spry widgets and effects to include in Web pages. Spry effects are a way to boost the look and feel of a Web site. Spry widgets are ready-to-use, common Web page components that can be customized using CSS. With Dreamweaver you can add XML-driven lists and tables, accordions (interactive collapsible panels), tabbed sections, and HTML form element validation. You can see some cool examples of Spry at `http://labs.adobe.com/technologies/spry/demos/index.html`. In Chapter 15, you find instructions for using Spry validation widgets to make sure a user enters correct information into a Web form.

Serving Dynamic Web Pages

To set up a Web server, you need server software. A *Web server,* sometimes called an HTTP server, responds to requests from a Web browser by serving up Web pages based on those requests. You also need to set up an *application server,* which helps the Web server process specially marked Web pages. When the browser requests one of these pages, the Web server hands the page off to the application server, which processes it before sending it to the browser.

For the examples in this book, I chose ASP, mostly because it's much easier to set up than any of the other technologies. Once you see how the basics work using ASP, you can graduate to other options, such as PHP or ASP.NET. So consider the lessons in this chapter and the next two as an introduction to dynamic site design. I didn't want to throw you into the deep end (at least, not yet).

And here's a warning. Even using ASP, which is a relatively simple option, these next few lessons (and the two chapters that follow) get a lot more technical than the previous chapters in this book. We'll start by setting up a Web server on your local computer so you can test your dynamic site on your own hard drive as you develop your site.

Setting up a local Web server

To use ASP, the server choices are Microsoft IIS or Personal Web Server (PWS). Either one works as both a Web server and an application server. PWS runs with Windows XP, Windows NT, and Windows Vista; and you can install either from your Windows CD. If you have Windows 2000 Server, NT 4, XP Professional, or Vista Professional, IIS is part of the package. If you can't find your CD, you can always download IIS or PWS for free from the Microsoft Web site.

If you're running Windows XP or Vista Professional, IIS is already in your system, and all you have to do is make sure it's started.

If you're running Windows XP or Vista Professional and IIS isn't enabled, you can install it by choosing Control Panel⇨Add/Remove Programs⇨Add/Remove Windows Components. When the Windows Components screen appears, scroll down the list and make sure that a check mark appears next to the Internet Information Server option.

IIS doesn't work on Windows XP Home Edition. You must upgrade to Windows XP Professional to use it.

To download and install Microsoft Personal Web Server, go to www. microsoft.com/downloads/ and search for *option pack*. Click the Windows NT 4.0 Option Pack option.

Giving permission

Windows NT-based operating systems (Windows NT and XP Professional) have security features that limit how computer accounts can access the computer. If you are using one of these operating systems, your hard drives are probably using Microsoft's security-conscious NTFS (New Technology File System) format. For the database examples in the following chapters to work, the IIS user needs permission to read and write to your database. To set the permissions correctly, I assume the following:

- ✔ You are using Windows XP Professional.
- ✔ You already installed IIS.
- ✔ Your have an existing Microsoft Access database file in the following folder C:\inetpub\wwwroot\dreamweaver_database\.
- ✔ Your C: drive's file system is NTFS.
- ✔ Simple file sharing is disabled on your computer.
- ✔ Your computer's name is Computer.

Follow these steps to give IIS permission to use your database:

1. **Choose Start➪Programs➪My Computer.**

   My Computer opens with a list of your hard drives.

2. **Double-click the C: drive, double-click Inetpub, and then double-click wwwroot.**

   The Intetpub folder is created when IIS is installed, and wwwroot is the default Web site's root folder.

3. **Double-click Dreamweaver, and then click _database once to select the folder.**

4. **Choose File➪Properties.**

   The _database Properties dialog box appears.

5. **Click the Security tab and then click the Add button.**

   The Select Users or Groups dialog box appears, as shown in Figure 13-2.

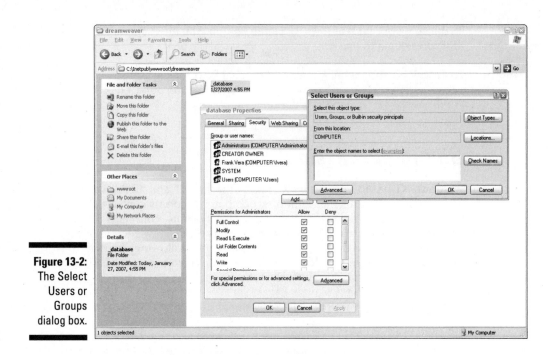

Figure 13-2:
The Select
Users or
Groups
dialog box.

6. **In the Enter the Object Names to Select field, type COMPUTER\ IUSR_COMPUTER and then Click OK.**

   When IIS is installed, it creates a user using the template IUSR_COMPUTER NAME. I am assuming your computer is named COMPUTER in this example. If your computer uses a different name, use that here.

7. **In the Group or User Names list, click to select Internet Guest Account (COMPUTER\IUSR_COMPUTER). In the Permissions for Internet Guest Account list box below it, make sure that Modify is selected in the Allow column.**

   This gives the Internet Guest Account permission to modify the folder, as shown in Figure 13-3.

8. **Click the Advanced button.**

   The Advanced Security Settings for the _datatabase dialog box appear, as shown in Figure 13-4.

9. **At the bottom of the dialog box, select the Replace Permission Entries on All Child Objects . . . option and then click OK.**

   This setting makes sure that all files in the _database folder are modifiable by the Internet Guest Account

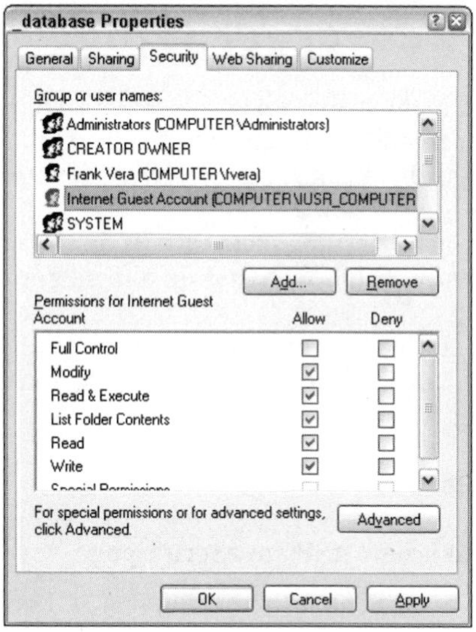

Figure 13-3:
The
_database
Properties
dialog box.

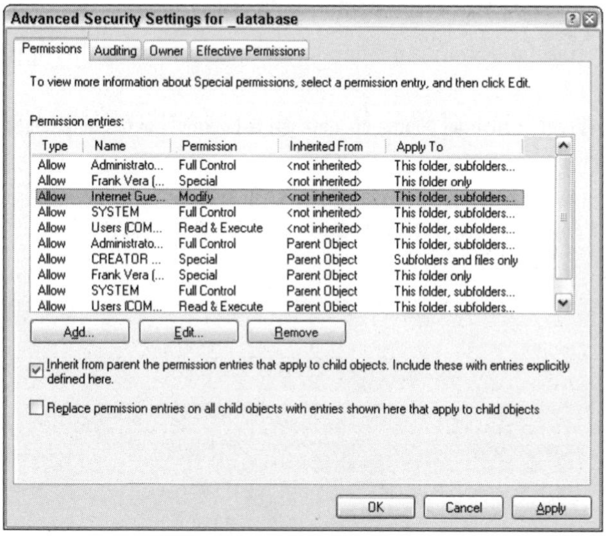

Figure 13-4:
The
Advanced
Security
Settings for
_database
dialog box.

10. **When the Security dialog box appears, click Yes.**

    This dialog box warns you that the permissions you set will replace the existing permissions on all files in the _database folder. This warning is expected.

11. **Click OK to close the _database Properties dialog box.**

Setting up Dreamweaver for Windows

Creating the data connection in Dreamweaver takes a few quick steps. You start by setting up your site's local information and remote site information. If you're not comfortable with this process, check out Chapter 2 to get reacquainted.

In this example, I assume that you're running IIS (or PWS) on the same machine as Dreamweaver, so I show you how to set up a local connection.

To check whether IIS or PWS is enabled, open a Web browser and type **http:// localhost** in the address bar. If IIS or PWS are set up properly, you see a page confirming that your Web server is up and running.

To get started, follow these steps:

1. **Choose File⇨New to create a new ASP JavaScript page.**

   The New Document dialog box opens, as shown in Figure 13-5.

2. **Choose the Blank Page icon from the left.**

3. **In the Page Type list, click ASP JavaScript.**

   You must have a document open to do anything with the Application panel.

4. **Under Layout, choose None to create a blank page, and then click Create.**

   You can also choose from any of the CSS layouts included in the Layout list if you want to start your page with one of these designs.

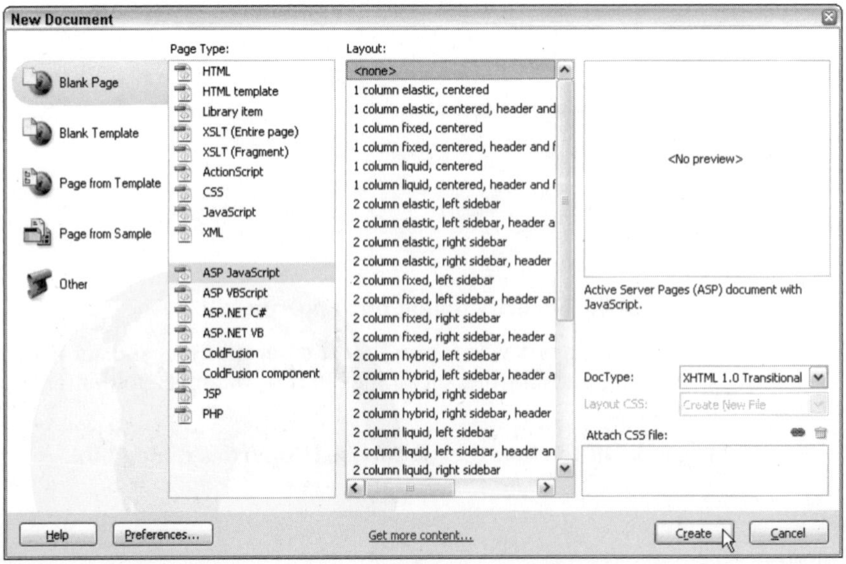

Figure 13-5:
The New Document dialog box.

5. **Choose Window⇨Databases to open the Database panel.**

   It the Application panel is already open in the workspace, you can click the small arrow next to the panel to expand it and then click the Databases tab.

6. **Click the plus sign (+) and select Custom Connection String from the list, as shown in Figure 13-6.**

   You see the Custom Connection String dialog box.

7. **Enter the name for the new connection.**

   For example, type **myContacts**.

8. **Type the connection string (see Figure 13-7).**

   For this example, I assume that you have the Microsoft Access driver installed on your computer and an MS Access database at c:\Inetpub\wwwroot\dreamweaver\database\contacts.mdb with the appropriate permissions. Type the following into the box exactly as you see it here (make sure to include the space between Data and Source): `"Provider=Microsoft.Jet.OLEDB.4.0;Data Source=c:\Inetpub\wwwroot\dreamweaver\database\contacts.mdb;"`

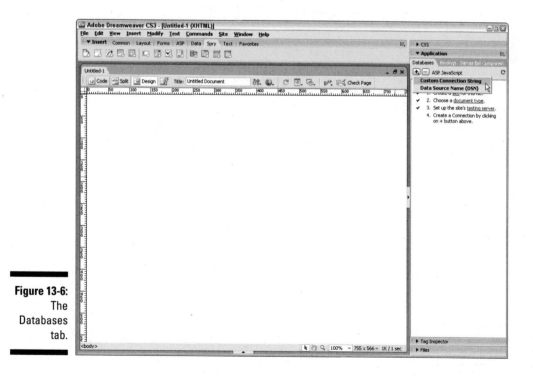

Figure 13-6:
The
Databases
tab.

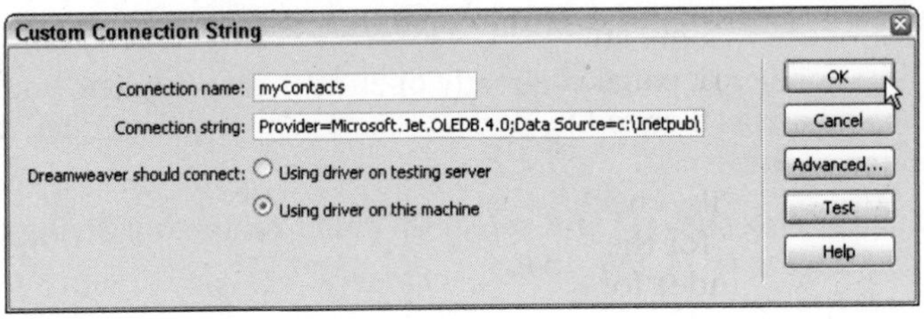

Figure 13-7:
The Custom
Connection
String dialog
box.

8. **Click the Test button.**

A pop-up message appears, letting you know that the connection was made successfully, and your database is now listed on the Databases tab (see Figure 13-8).

In the Files panel, you also see on your local drive a Connections folder, which contains an ASP file with the connection information for this database. Dreamweaver automatically references this file on any page you create that uses this database connection, saving you from having to insert it every time.

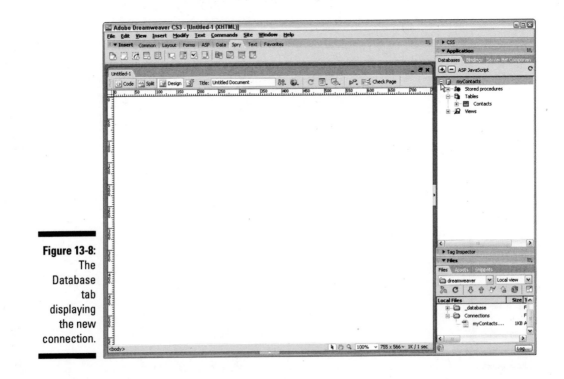

Figure 13-8:
The
Database
tab
displaying
the new
connection.

The ASP files in the Connections folder store necessary information that makes your page work correctly with the database. Upload this folder when you upload your site files to the application server.

If your connection fails, check your Custom Connection String again, and check the URL prefix for the application server. You can also check the Dreamweaver Help Index for other troubleshooting tips.

Now you're ready to build a dynamic Web site. In Chapters 14 and 15, I get into more details so that you can start putting these great Dreamweaver features to use on your site right away.

Setting up Dreamweaver for Mac users

Setting up a data connection on a Mac is a little more complicated because you can't run one of Dreamweaver's support Web servers or application servers locally unless you're running OSX; you must connect to a remote server. Ideally, you can connect your Mac to an NT server with permission to browse the Mac. After you're networked, you make the data connection. Dreamweaver includes information in its help files that specifically covers this process for Mac users.

OSX users can alternatively download Apache's HTTP server from `http://httpd.apache.org/`. However, anyone using OS9 and earlier is out of luck.

Chapter 14

Bringing Data into the Mix

· ·

In This Chapter

▶ Taking a look at the panels

▶ Covering the recordset basics

▶ Getting dynamic with your data

· ·

*I*f you've never used the dynamic development capabilities of Dreamweaver, you'll want to get familiar with the windows and inspectors covered at the beginning of this chapter before you start creating your first project. In the rest of this chapter, you find out how these elements work together to create a Web site full of dynamic features.

For the purposes of illustration, all the figures and steps in this chapter are based on an example site with a contact management system that features information for various people — names, addresses, and pictures. If your site features another type of data, such as product descriptions or articles, don't worry — you can apply the info in this chapter to your own data to create any kind of dynamic Web site.

Make sure your application server is running and, because this chapter assumes that you're using Internet Information Server or Peer Web Services for Windows, make sure that you save all the pages as ASP pages (`filename.asp`) so that the server parses the code correctly. For a quick reminder on how to set up the application server, refer to Chapter 13.

Exploring the Panels

In Dreamweaver, the most fundamental elements of creating a dynamic Web site are in the Application panel, which includes the Databases, Bindings, Components, and Server Behaviors panels. In this section, I introduce you to these panels, which help you create your dynamic site.

The Databases panel

The Databases panel lets you look at the databases on your application server. In the Databases panel, you can view your entire database structure within Dreamweaver — tables, fields, views, and stored procedures — without needing to use separate database software.

You can find the Databases panel by choosing Window⇨Databases.

You can create a custom connection string by clicking the plus sign (+) in the Databases panel (shown in Figure 14-1). If this is all new to you, you find instructions for creating a connection with a custom connection string using the Databases panel in Chapter 13.

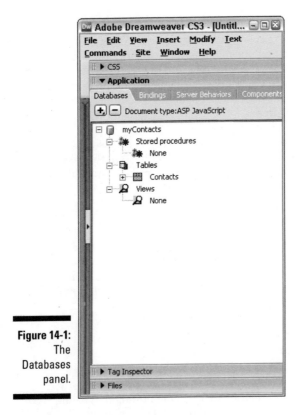

Figure 14-1:
The
Databases
panel.

The Bindings panel

The Bindings panel enables you to add and remove dynamic content data sources from your document. The number and kinds of available data sources can vary depending on whether you use ASP, JSP, or any other server technology. (Chapter 13 offers a refresher on servers.) A *data source* is where you get information to use on your dynamic Web page. An example of a data source is a recordset from a database, which you explore further in the next few sections of this chapter. A *recordset* is used to hold a collection of data from a database. Once you've created a recordset, the data can be displayed on a Web page.

If you don't see the Bindings panel, you can open it by choosing Window⇨ Bindings.

With the Bindings panel, you can access data sources in several ways. You can find out what data source objects you have available by clicking the plus sign (+) in the Bindings panel to display the Add Bindings pop-up menu (see Figure 14-2).

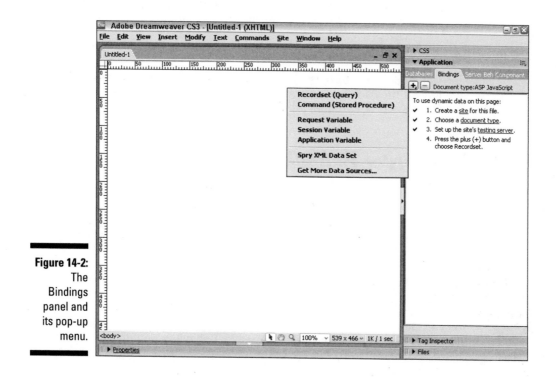

Figure 14-2:
The Bindings panel and its pop-up menu.

The Add Bindings pop-up menu has the following options:

- ✔ **Recordset (Query):** A recordset stores data from your database for use on a page or set of pages. I explain recordsets in more detail in this chapter.

- ✔ **Command (Stored Procedure):** *Commands,* or *stored procedures,* are reusable database items that contain SQL code and are commonly used to modify a database (insert, update, or delete records).

- ✔ **Request Variable:** Commonly used wherever a search is involved, a *request variable* carries information from one page to another. When you use a form to submit data to another page, a request variable is created.

- ✔ **Session Variable:** *Session variables* store and display information for the duration of a user's *session* (or visit). A different session is created on the server for each user and is kept in use either for a set period of time or until a specific action on the site terminates the session (such as a logging out).

- ✔ **Application Variable:** *Application variables* store and display information that must be present for all users and is constant throughout the lifetime of an application. These types of variables are commonly used for page counters or date and time counters. Application variables are available only for ASP and ColdFusion pages, not for PHP and JSP.

- ✔ **Spry XML Data Set:** *XML data sets* link existing XML files to display with any of the various Spry widgets.

- ✔ **Get More Data Sources:** Use this option to open Dreamweaver Exchange in your browser. You can use Exchange to download extensions for Dreamweaver. For more information about extensions, see Chapter 15.

The Server Behaviors panel

Server behaviors are server-side scripts that perform some type of action. Through the Server Behaviors panel, you can add server-side scripts, such as user authentication and record navigation, to your pages. You can read more about this later in this chapter and in Chapter 15. Server behaviors available to you vary depending on the server technology you use.

You can get to the Server Behaviors panel by choosing Window➪Server Behaviors.

You can view the available server behaviors by clicking the plus sign (+) in the Server Behaviors panel to get the Server Behaviors pop-up menu (see Figure 14-3).

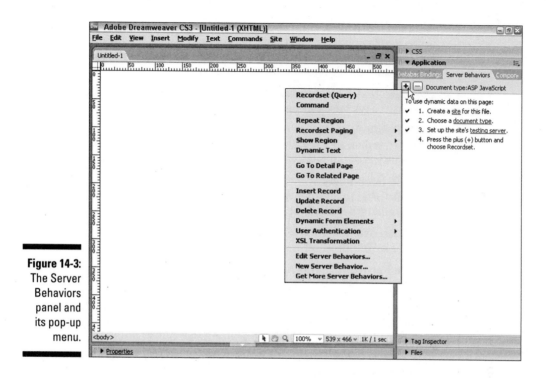

Figure 14-3:
The Server
Behaviors
panel and
its pop-up
menu.

The Server Behaviors pop-up menu has the following options:

- **Recordset (Query):** A *recordset* stores data from your database for use on a page or set of pages. I explain recordsets in more detail later in this chapter.

- **Command:** *Commands* are reusable database items that contain SQL code and are commonly used to modify a database (insert, update, or delete records).

- **Repeat Region:** This server object displays multiple records on a page. Repeat region is most commonly used on HTML tables or HTML table rows. You can find out more about this behavior later in this chapter.

- **Recordset Paging:** If you have to display a large number of records and want them to appear a page at a time, this set of behaviors allows you to navigate from page to page or from record to record.

- **Show Region:** With this set of server behaviors, you can show or hide record navigation based on the records displayed. For instance, if you have Next and Previous links on the bottom of every page and your user is on the first page or first record of the recordset, you can set a behavior to display only the Next link. The same is true if the user is on the last page or record — you can set the behavior to hide the Next link and display only the Previous link.

✔ **Dynamic Text:** This option enables you to display information from your recordset anywhere on the page.

✔ **Go to Detail Page:** Using this behavior, you can link each record in your repeated region to a detail page for that particular record. The behavior also tells the detail page which record's information to display.

✔ **Go to Related Page:** You can use this behavior to link a particular dynamic page to another page that contains related information, passing the parameters of the first page to the related page.

✔ **Insert Record:** Use this behavior on a page to add new records to a database via a Web browser.

✔ **Update Record:** Use this behavior on a page to update existing records in a database via a Web browser.

✔ **Delete Record:** Use this behavior on a page to permanently delete a record from a database via a Web browser.

✔ **Dynamic Form Elements:** This set of server behaviors turns text fields, list or menu fields, radio buttons, or check boxes into dynamic form elements, which you can set to retrieve and display particular information from a recordset.

✔ **User Authentication:** The User Authentication set of behaviors allows you to log in a user, log out a user, check a username against the information in your database, and restrict access to a page.

✔ **XSL Transformation:** Extensible Stylesheet Language Transformation (XSLT) is a language that displays XML data on a Web page after transforming it into HTML.

✔ **Edit Server Behaviors:** Use this option to customize or remove existing server behaviors. Unless you are very comfortable with coding or SQL, I advise you to not mess with this option. (If you're curious about SQL, see *SQL For Dummies*, 6th Edition, by Allen G. Taylor, published by Wiley Publishing, Inc.)

✔ **New Server Behavior:** Use this option to create new server behaviors and add them to the list of existing behaviors. Again, this option is for more advanced users who are comfortable with coding.

✔ **Get More Server Behaviors:** Use this option to open Dreamweaver Exchange in your browser. You can use Exchange to download extensions for Dreamweaver. For more information about extensions, see Chapter 15.

The Components panel

Components are reusable bits of code that you can create and insert directly into your pages. To open the Components panel, choose Window➪Components. In Dreamweaver, you can create components for JSP, Cold Fusion, and ASP.NET pages to use (or *consume*) Web services, display information, or for any other use that you can imagine.

Creating a Recordset

A *recordset* holds data from your database for use on a page or set of pages. A *query* gathers information from a database to be used on a page, selecting only the records matching the fields and conditions of the particular query. The queries for a recordset are built with SQL (Structured Query Language), but you don't need to know SQL to get the job done. Dreamweaver writes it all for you.

With your recordset in place, you can display information from your database in various ways.

Before you can create a recordset, you must first connect to a database. Chapter 13 includes instructions for creating a custom connection string, which you must do before you can create a recordset.

To define a recordset in Dreamweaver:

1. **Open the ASP page that will use the recordset.**

2. **In the Bindings panel, click the plus sign and select Recordset (Query).**

   You see the Recordset dialog box.

3. **In the Name box, enter a name for your recordset.**

   Usually, adding the letters *rs* to the beginning of the name is recommended to distinguish it as a recordset in your code, but it isn't necessary. I used *rsContacts,* as shown in Figure 14-4.

4. **In the Connection drop-down list, select your connection.**

   This list includes any data connections defined from the Databases panel. Chapter 13 explains how to create a connection.

5. **In the Table drop-down list, choose a database table where the data for your recordset will be collected.**

   You can select all the columns or only specific columns of data to be displayed.

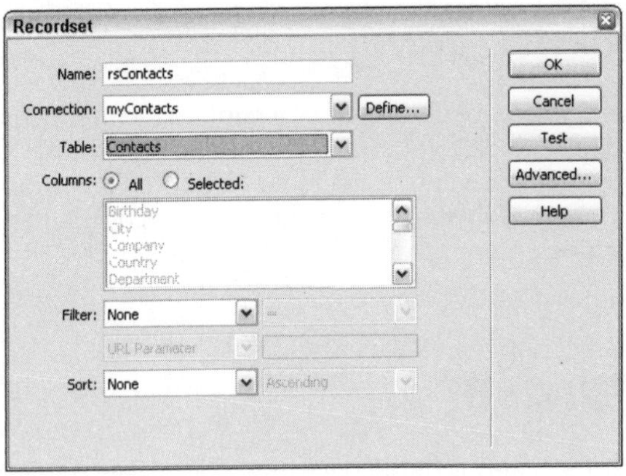

Figure 14-4:
The
Recordset
dialog box.

6. **If you want the available information to show only records that meet specific criteria, select a filter in the Filter area.**

7. **If you want to change the sort order of the displayed records, use the Sort drop-down list to specify the field by which you want the records sorted (Name, Phone Number, and so on) and then specify Ascending or Descending.**

If you want to tweak the results further and you feel comfortable working with SQL, you can click the Advanced button to edit the SQL statement directly.

8. **To test the connection to the database, click the Test button.**

You can find the Databases panel by choosing Window⇨Databases. To create more complicated recordsets, click the Advanced button and you can create SQL statements directly.

If the test is successful, you see a window with the data in the recordset (similar to Figure 14-5).

9. **Click OK to close the Test screen.**

10. **Click OK to complete the Recordset dialog box.**

The Bindings panel appears the recordset. You can expand it by clicking the plus sign next to the recordset, as shown in Figure 14-6.

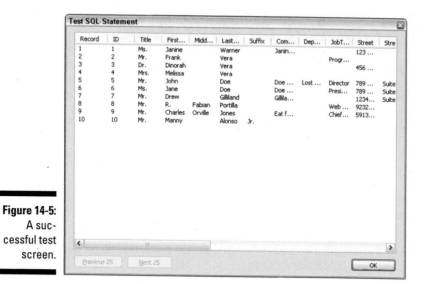

Figure 14-5:
A successful test screen.

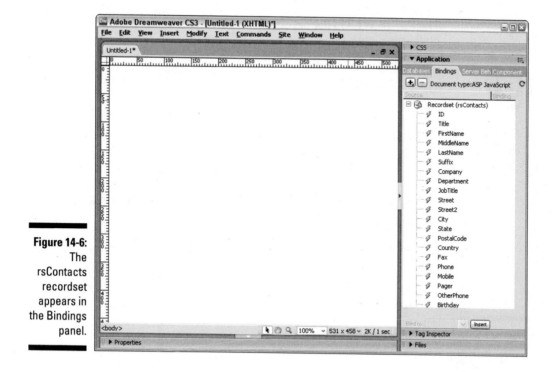

Figure 14-6:
The rsContacts recordset appears in the Bindings panel.

Using a Recordset on Your Page

After you create a recordset, you can place the information on your page as you want. For this section, I made a basic list of all the contacts in the database, with a name, an e-mail address, a phone number, and a Web site URL. I already built a page with a table showing the appropriate number of cells for all the dynamic text that I'm inserting (see Figure 14-7).

After you set up the document the way you want it, you can drag and drop each data source to its appropriate spot on the page by following these steps:

1. **From the Bindings panel, select your first data source and drag it onto your page, dropping it where you want it to go.**

   The name of the dynamic text appears inside curly brackets. You can now format this piece of text any way you want, treating it like normal HTML text (see Figure 14-8).

2. **Test the result by clicking the LiveData button.**

   The first record of your database appears in place of the dynamic text code (see Figure 14-9).

To display more than just the first record in a Web page, you need to define and repeat a region, which you find out how to do in the next sections.

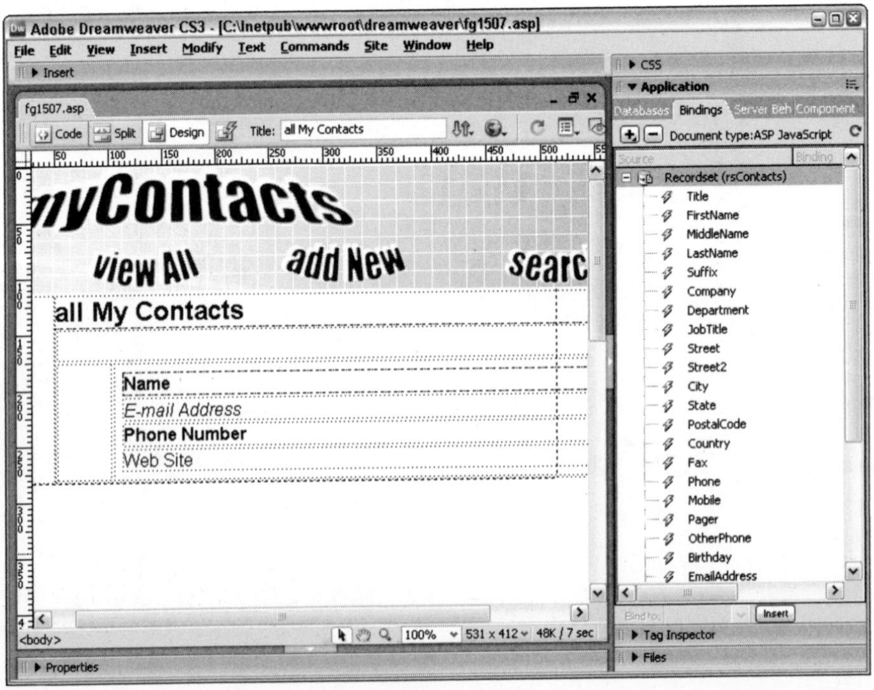

Figure 14-7: I created a page showing where each piece of information goes.

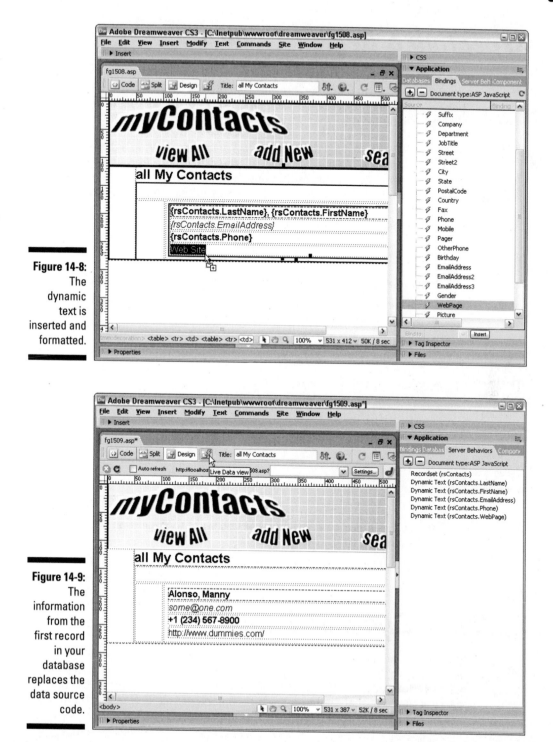

Figure 14-8:
The dynamic text is inserted and formatted.

Figure 14-9:
The information from the first record in your database replaces the data source code.

Repeating a Region

You probably want to display more than one record at a time on a page that's supposed to list all your contacts. You can do this by applying a server behavior to your region. *Server behaviors* are code blocks that let you add dynamic capabilities to your Web site.

A *region* is any area of a page that displays information from a database on your page. After you define your region, you can apply a Repeat Region server behavior, which causes that area to be written to the page over and over, displaying every record, or as many as you tell it to, in the database defined by your recordset until all records appear. Repeat Region is most commonly used on HTML tables or table rows.

To add a Repeat Region server behavior to your page:

1. **Select the area on your page that you want to define as a region.**

2. **Click the Server Behaviors panel, click the plus sign (+), and select Repeat Region from the menu that appears.**

   The Repeat Region dialog box appears (see Figure 14-10).

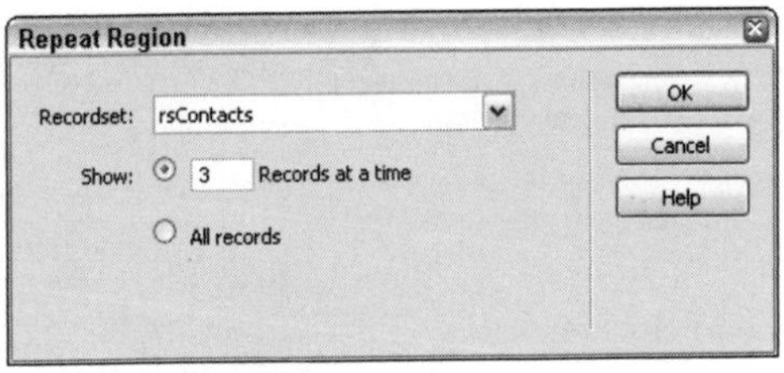

Figure 14-10:
Define a region in the Repeat Region dialog box.

Repeat Region	
Recordset: rsContacts	OK
	Cancel
Show: ● 3 Records at a time	Help
○ All records	

3. **Select the number of records that you want to appear on the page and then click OK.**

4. **Click the LiveData button to see the results (see Figure 14-11).**

Adding a Dynamic Image

Whenever you have a dynamic Web site, whether it is a catalog Web site or a news archive, images are usually involved. You can bind an image to a record-set in various easy ways so that your images change depending on the other parts of the page that are bound to the same recordset. Before you bind the image, though, you need to take a few preliminary steps:

1. **Make sure that you have a field for each record in your database that lists the actual path of the image for that record.**

   For example, if your images reside in a folder called *images,* one level above your dynamic page, you enter the following in the image field in your database: **images/*imagename.gif***, remembering to replace the *imagename.gif* part with the actual filename for each image.

2. **Upload your image folder to the server.**

   This step is necessary if you want to preview the page with images in LiveData view.

3. **Place a placeholder image in the spot where you want an image to appear for all the records.**

   You can use any of the images in your image folder as a placeholder, or choose Insert➪Image Object➪Image Placeholder to use the built-in image placeholder.

You can find out more about inserting images in Chapter 2.

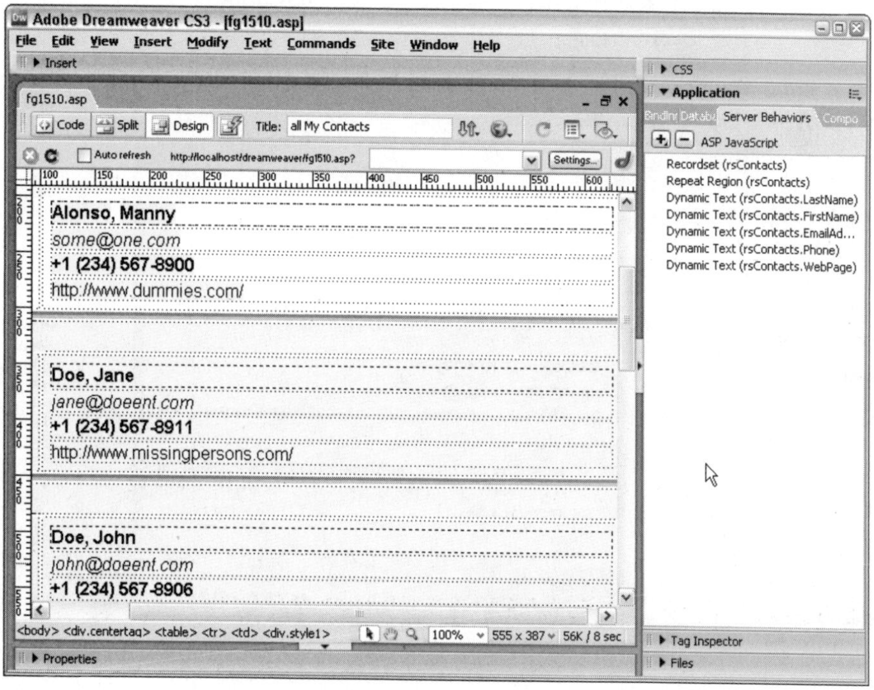

Figure 14-11:
With Repeat Region, you can show more than one record at a time.

Binding the Image

After you insert the placeholder image, you can bind images in two easy ways — with the Bindings panel or the Property inspector.

Follow these steps to bind images using the Bindings panel:

1. **Select your placeholder image in the open document.**

2. **Click the plus sign (+) to expand your recordset. (If you're using a Mac, click the triangle.)**

3. **Select the field in your recordset that contains the name of the image file.**

4. **Click the Bind button at the bottom of the Bindings panel (see Figure 14-12).**

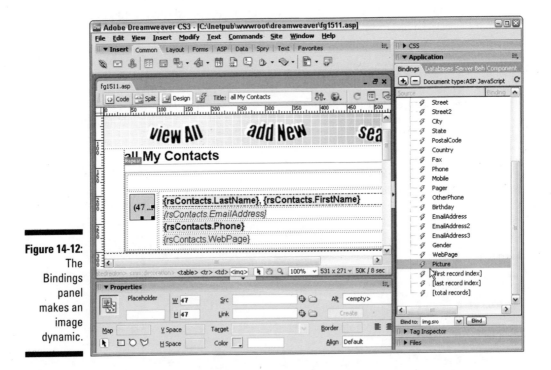

Figure 14-12: The Bindings panel makes an image dynamic.

Follow these steps to bind images using the Property inspector:

1. **Click your placeholder image in the open document to select it.**

2. **In the Property inspector, click the Browse button next to the Src box.**

3. **In the Select File Name From section (at the top), select the Data Sources option.**

   The Select Image Source dialog box appears (see Figure 14-13).

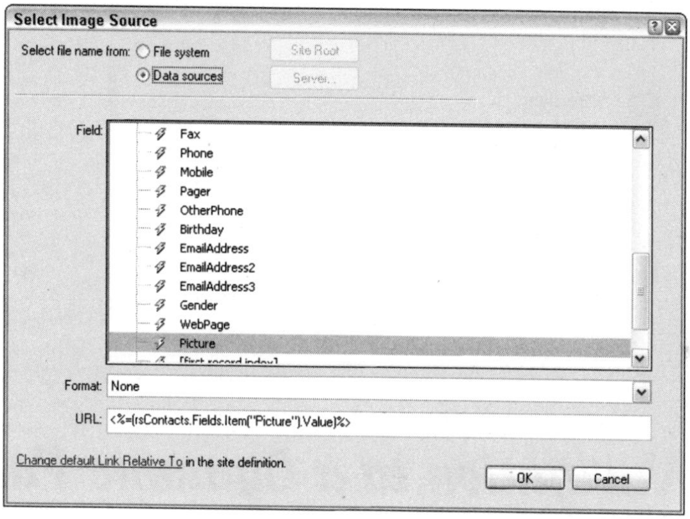

Figure 14-13: The Select Image Source dialog box.

4. **Select the field that contains your image information.**

5. **Click OK.**

   The image changes to a tree with a lightning bolt along its side.

After performing either of these two methods to bind your images to the page, click the LiveData button to check out the results (see Figure 14-14).

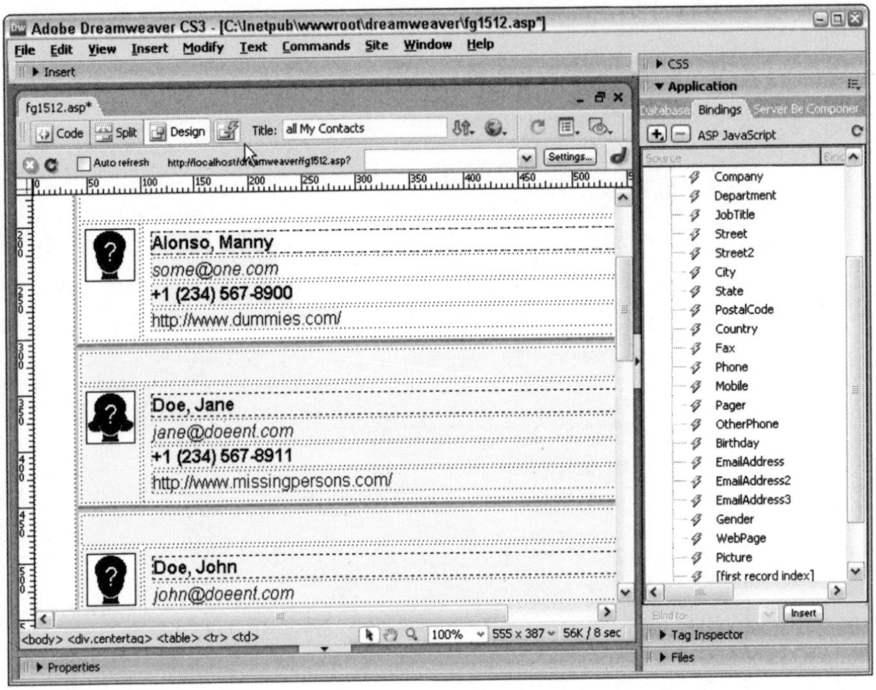

Figure 14-14:
Test your images to find out whether they're bound correctly. (Note that I used placeholder images in this example.)

Adding Navigation to a Dynamic Page

If your database contains many records, you may opt to show only a small number of records per page so that you don't overwhelm the user. The Dreamweaver Server Behaviors panel allows you to add navigation to your pages so that you can move forward or backward through records.

Define your Repeat Region, which I explain how to do earlier in this chapter, and make sure that you do not select a value large enough to show all records. You can add button images or text links at the bottom of the page to indicate some kind of navigation, such as Previous Page and Next Page links. With the buttons in place, you can activate them by using the Server Behaviors panel.

For example, to add the navigation movements for the Next and Previous buttons:

1. Select the Previous Page button you added in the Document window.

For these steps I am assuming you already inserted images or text into a table at the bottom of the page with the captions First, Previous, Next, and Last.

REMEMBER

2. **Open the Server Behaviors panel.**

   You can open the Server Behaviors panel by choosing Window⇨Server Behaviors on the main menu.

3. **Click the plus sign (+) and then select Recordset Paging from the menu.**

4. **From the submenu, choose the appropriate navigation movement (Move to Next Record or Move to Previous Record), as shown in Figure 14-15.**

   The Move to Record dialog box appears and, in most cases, you can just click OK because the defaults are correct.

5. **Follow Steps 1 through 4 for the Next button.**

6. **Choose File⇨Preview in Browser and select the browser you set up as your default preview browser.**

   You can now page through your records.

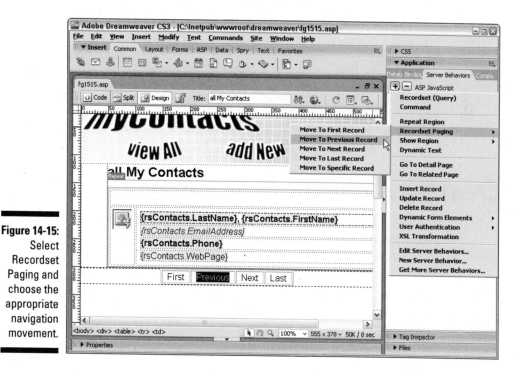

Figure 14-15: Select Recordset Paging and choose the appropriate navigation movement.

That's a pretty nifty trick. But did you notice that on the first page, the Previous Page button or link still appears, even though there is no previous page? Not to worry — a server behavior tells the navigation button when to show up:

1. **Click the Previous Page button in the Document window to select it.**

2. **Click the plus sign (+) in the Server Behaviors panel and then select Show Region from the menu.**

3. **If you are working with the Previous Page button, select Show Region If Not First Record. If you are working with the Next Page button, select Show Region If Not Last Record. See Figure 14-16.**

   The Show Region dialog box appears. Usually the selected recordset is correct, so just click OK.

4. **Preview in your browser by clicking the Preview in Browser button on the Document toolbar.**

   Notice that now when you're on the first page of records, the Previous Page button does not appear, and when you're on the last page, the Next Page button does not appear.

Now that you know how to add navigation to your recordsets, you can get fancy and add buttons to go to the first or last record. So if you have, say, 100 pages of records, you can jump from page 1 to page 100 without having to click Previous Page or Next Page through countless other pages of records. The server behaviors for those two are Move to Record⇨Move to First Record and Move to Record⇨Move to Last Record. It's useful stuff to know.

Creating a Master-Detail Page Set

A common way to display information on a Web site is to show a list of records, such as a list of contacts, with a link to each individual record for more detailed information.

A master page displays a list of records and a link for each record. When a user clicks a particular link, a detail page appears with more information about that record. There are two types of master pages. The first type is a list of records determined by you. Users can't alter the list of records on this page; they can only click to view more information about those records displayed. The second type is a dynamically created master page. A good example of this type of master page is a search results page that appears when a user performs a search for specific records.

A detail page is the page that appears when a user clicks a particular link from a master page. This page can either display more information about a record (such as an online catalog), or it can be set up for administrative purposes, such as updating or deleting a record.

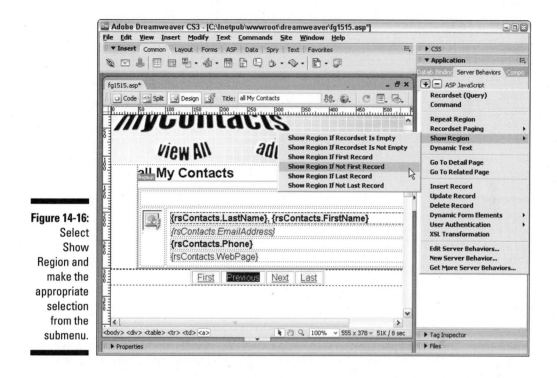

Figure 14-16:
Select
Show
Region and
make the
appropriate
selection
from the
submenu.

Creating a master-detail page requires just a few clicks of the mouse. Using the functions described earlier in this chapter, create a page that you will use to list all your contacts, and name it something like *contacts.asp*. This is your master page. Next, create the page you use as the detail page in the same way and call it something like *contactdetails.asp*. Now you're ready to create the master-detail page set:

1. **Open the contacts.asp page you created to be the master page and choose Insert➪Data Objects➪Master Detail Page Set.**

    The Insert Master-Detail Page Set dialog box opens (see Figure 14-17). The top part of the dialog box is where you define the properties of the master page. The bottom part is where you define the detail page.

2. **In the Recordset drop-down list, select the recordset that you use for your master page.**

3. **Next to Master Page Fields, use the plus sign (+) and minus sign (–), respectively, to add fields to or remove fields from the master page.**

4. **Select the field from which you want to provide a link to the detail page for each record.**

    For example, if you list a bunch of contacts, you can use the contact's name as the link to the detail.

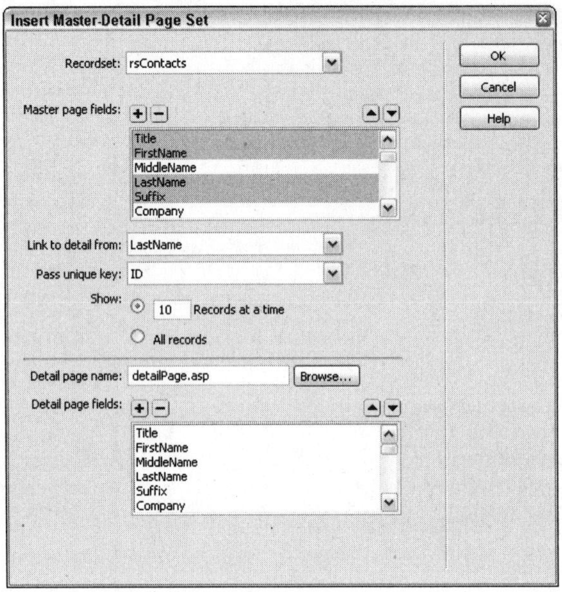

Figure 14-17:
The Insert
Master-
Detail Page
Set dialog
box.

5. **In the Pass Unique Key drop-down list, usually the default is correct; if it is not, select the unique identifier that you want to pass on to the detail page.**

6. **Select the number of records you want to show at one time on the master page.**

Showing only a partial listing is okay because you can add navigation to view more records.

7. **In the Detail Page Name box, type the filename for the detail page or click the Browse button to search for the file.**

8. **Just as with the Master Page section, use the plus and minus signs to add or remove fields that you want or don't want to appear on the detail page.**

9. **Click OK.**

Dreamweaver automatically adds all the necessary recordset information and SQL code for you to begin using your master-detail page set. Everything from navigation to record status is in there.

After you create the master and detail pages, you may want to rearrange and format the fields. (Dreamweaver just plops the stuff onto the pages, creating a generic look.) For example, you can change the column labels to text that has more meaning and is friendlier to your visitors. You can also format the font, color, and size, add padding to the table cells, and change the order of the columns.

Chapter 15

Using Forms to Manage Your Dynamic Web Site

*D*ynamic Web sites let you do a lot more than provide content and product listings to your Web site visitors. You can use Dreamweaver to create various types of forms that serve many useful purposes. Some examples include a login page so that users can register to use your Web site, a search page so that users can search your Web site for specific information, a shopping cart system for e-commerce, or a data-entry form to safely allow nontechnical data-entry personnel to easily edit the content of a Web site.

Establishing User Authentication

One of the good things about a dynamic Web site is that you can retain a lot of control over it, from who can view it and how much a user can view, to who can edit it and how much that person can edit. You can also assign different users different levels of access depending on criteria that you determine. For example, you may have an online employee directory that all employees can use to look up departmental information, titles, and phone extensions. However, if that directory also contains every employee's home phone number and home address, you wouldn't want the entire company to have access to everyone's personal information, right? The Dreamweaver User Authentication Server Behavior enables you to create different levels of access that restrict the kind of information a user can see, so you can make things such as personal information something only certain people may access.

Creating a login page

In the first exercise for this chapter, you create a user login form that checks information against a database. I use a sample database of employees that contains the following fields:

- ✔ Employee number
- ✔ Password
- ✔ Last name
- ✔ First name
- ✔ Department
- ✔ Title
- ✔ Access level

If you want to use a prebuilt database, I have provided a sample database called `employees.mdb` on my Web site at `www.digitalfamily.com/dwd`. I created it using Microsoft Access 2000.

Once you have the database you want to use on your computer, create a page that contains a form with the following fields: a Username text box, a Password text box, and a Submit button. Refer to Chapter 11 for more details on how to create a form. Next, create a database connection and a recordset that contains your employee number, last name, first name, password, department, title, and access level. Check out Chapters 13 and 14 if you need a quick review on this stuff.

Now that you have everything in place, you're ready to add user authentication to your form. These steps walk you through the setup for user authentication on a company's employee directory. I use the employee number as the username.

1. **Select the form and click the plus sign (+) in the Server Behaviors panel.**

   Selecting a form in Dreamweaver can be a bit tricky sometimes. A quick way to select the entire form is to click anywhere inside the form and then select the word *form* from the status bar at the bottom of the Dreamweaver window. This selects the entire form.

2. **From the menu, choose User Authentication⇨Log In User, as shown in Figure 15-1.**

   The Log In User dialog box appears.

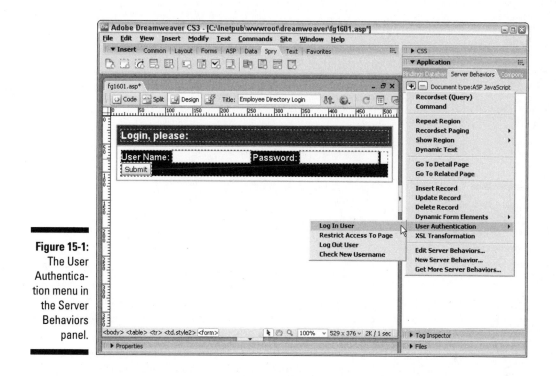

Figure 15-1:
The User
Authentica-
tion menu in
the Server
Behaviors
panel.

3. In the Get Input from Form field, enter the form name.

Naming forms is good practice, especially if you have a page with multi-ple forms. Naming your forms makes each one easier to identify within the code.

4. In the Username Field and Password Field boxes, enter the names of the appropriate text boxes from your form.

In my example, the username field is called *user,* and the password field is called *pass.* See Figure 15-2.

5. In the Validate Using Connection and Table drop-down lists, make the appropriate selections.

Select the connection and table that correspond to your user database. For example, if you're using the sample `employees.mdb` table, you'd use the Employees connection and the employees table.

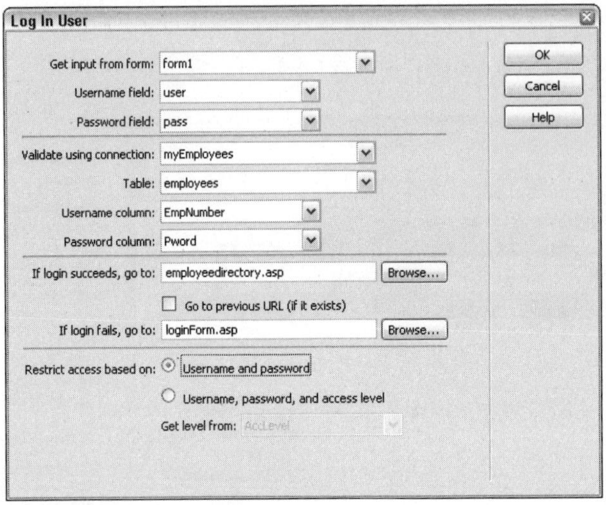

Log In User

Get input from form:	form1
Username field:	user
Password field:	pass
Validate using connection:	myEmployees
Table:	employees
Username column:	EmpNumber
Password column:	Pword
If login succeeds, go to:	employeedirectory.asp [Browse...]
	☐ Go to previous URL (if it exists)
If login fails, go to:	loginForm.asp [Browse...]
Restrict access based on:	⦿ Username and password
	○ Username, password, and access level
Get level from:	AccLevel

[OK] [Cancel] [Help]

Figure 15-2:
The Log
In User
dialog box.

6. **In the Username Column and Password Column drop-down lists, select the fields in your database that verify the username and password provided by the user at login.**

   Because I use the employee number as the username, I selected that field as my Username Column, but if you have a specific username field in your database, select that one instead.

   Dreamweaver expects the username field to be a text field and includes a radio button that adds some encryption to a text field if it is used as a password. If you decide to use a field such as an employee number, make sure that it is defined as a text field in the database.

7. **Enter the name of the page where users are redirected if the login succeeds.**

   If you want to use this as a generic page for logins, check the Go to Previous URL box as well. That way, after a user tries to access a restricted page and is sent to this login page, that user is returned to the restricted page after entering the correct username and password. Find out more about restricted pages in the following section, "Restricting access to pages."

   In my example, the page is employeeDirectory.asp, which is the actual employee directory listing.

8. **Enter the name of the page where users are redirected if the login fails.**

   You can direct them to the same login page, or you can create a secondary login page that looks like the first one but contains an error message saying something like That username and/or password is incorrect. Please try again.

9. **Select the Restrict Access Based on Username and Password option.**

   If you want to further control access for users with a certain access level (say, Manager or Employee), you can define that in this area as well. The effect is that only the users in the database whose access level matches what you specify are taken to the login success page. The rest are redirected to the login failed page.

10. **Click OK.**

You can now preview this page in your browser and test the form by entering a username and password from your database.

Restricting access to pages

When you have a page you want to restrict (such as a user detail page) and a login page, you are ready to go. In the following steps, I assume that the name of the page that you want to restrict access to is *directory.asp*, the name of your login page is *user_auth.asp*, and the Go to Previous URL option is defined for the login page. (See the previous section, "Creating a login page," for more information.)

To restrict access to a Web page, follow these steps:

1. **Open `employeeDirectory.asp` or whichever page you want to restrict.**

2. **In the Server Behaviors panel, click the plus sign and choose User Authentication⇨Restrict Access to Page.**

   The Restrict Access to Page dialog box opens (see Figure 15-3).

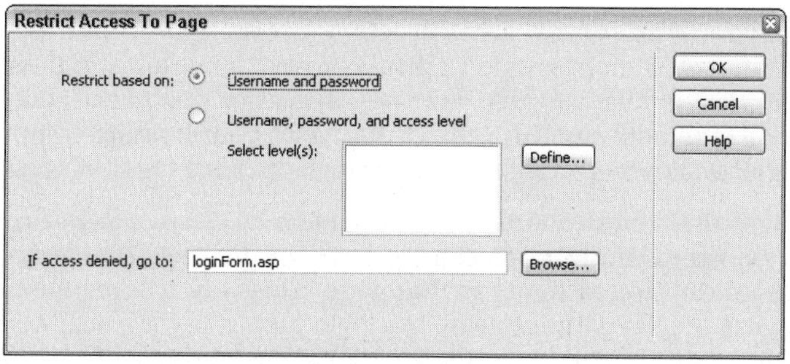

Figure 15-3:
The Restrict Access to Page dialog box.

You can open the Server Behaviors panel by choosing Window⇨Server Behaviors.

3. **Select Restrict Based on Username and Password.**

4. **In the If Access Denied, Go To box, type the name of your login page.**

   I used `user_auth.asp`. When users try to access this page directly, they're sent to `user_auth.asp` to log in before they can see this page.

5. **Click OK.**

6. **Press F12 to preview the page in your default browser.**

   Instead of the Employee Directory page, you see the user login page. Type a valid username and password to view the employee directory.

Securing Sensitive Information on Your Web Site

You can take security measures that help make your sensitive information more secure on the Web (some steps are for more advanced users):

- ✔ **Carefully choose the passwords you use.** Especially choose carefully for your FTP, database, and the admin login area of your Web site. Too often people use common words, names, and number combinations as passwords that are easy for hackers to figure out. An effective password consists of mixed letters and numbers — the more random the better — and is also a mix of uppercase and lowercase letters whenever possible.

- ✔ **Protect your development machine.** Many Web site break-ins are inside jobs, where someone from within the company obtains the sensitive information because he or she has access to the Web site files. If your development machine is on a network and you must grant access to it, grant only restricted access.

- ✔ **On your Web server, turn Directory Browsing *off.*** Do this so folders without an index page don't display everything that's in them. If you're not the administrator for your Web server or don't know how to do this, ask a technical support representative at your hosting company to either walk you through it or do it for you. It's a fairly simple step.

- ✔ **Pages that require authentication, such as `directory.asp` from the previous example, should have code on the page that kicks out users who didn't log in to get to that page.** This way, if someone happens to access the file without using the login page, they are sent elsewhere (see "Restricting access to pages," earlier in the chapter). One of the easiest ways to do this is with a cookie — of the ASP variety, not chocolate chip! In fact, this is how Dreamweaver's Server Behaviors does it behind the scenes. You can find out more about cookies and ASP in *Beginning Active Server Pages 3.0* by David Buser, et al (published by Wrox Press).

- ✔ **Don't use an Access database for a serious Web site.** Not only is it slow, but stealing the info is simple because it's typically a single file. Even if a malicious person doesn't know SQL, he or she may be able to find the Access file and read it off your Web server. If you are using an Access database, make sure it is stored in a folder outside the root folder of your Web site.

- ✔ **Keep your database on a dedicated machine, away from direct Internet access.** You can buff up database security by allowing only your Web server to access that machine through a local network infrastructure.

- ✔ **Use SSL technology to encrypt sensitive information sent back and forth from the server.** *Secure Sockets Layer* (SSL) is a form of encryption developed originally by Netscape and used by Web servers and Web browsers to exchange sensitive information. You can find more about encryption and SSL at `http://computer.howstuffworks.com/encryption.htm`.

- ✔ **Don't copy and paste complex snippets of code that you found on the Web unless you absolutely trust the source and checked out all the stops.** Some hackers look for sites running this type of widely used code, and those who know its specific vulnerabilities can easily gain access to your machine.

Please keep in mind that the Dreamweaver Login Authentication can be a basic method of restricting access to a page if you follow only the basic steps outlined in this book. An amateur hacker can quite possibly find your database, figure out passwords, or bypass the login page to get to the information he or she wants. If you are building a site that contains sensitive information and are not familiar with Web site security, consider hiring a consultant to advise you. At the very least, read up on the subject so you can get a better understanding of the security risks you may encounter. *Web Security, Privacy and Commerce* by Simson Garfinkel (published by O'Reilly & Associates) provides a thorough look into the subject.

Searching for Database Records

With Dreamweaver, you can create a form to search for records on your database using specific criteria. This is useful if you have a large database. You don't want to make your users read through pages and pages of listings, whether they are employee records, or products, or anything else. Providing a search form allows your users to quickly find the information they want. In this section, you discover a simple way to implement a database search on your dynamic Web site.

Setting up the search page

The search page is the simplest part to set up. All you need is a form with an action that goes to the results page, a form text field, and a Submit button:

1. **Create a new page that contains a form with the fields you want your users to search.**

   Check out Chapter 11 to go over forms in more detail. I used an employee directory database; my text field is *Lname*, which allows my users to search by employee last names.

2. **In the Action field in the Property inspector, enter the name of the results page.**

   See the next section to find out how to create this page. My result page is called *search_results.asp*.

3. **Save this page.**

Setting up the results page

The results page is a little more complex than the search page. The search actually takes place on the results page, behind the scenes on the server, and what you see is only the result of that search. The text field that you determine in the search page is referred to as the *form variable* in the results page. The information you enter in this form is passed on to the results page for the search to take place:

1. **Create a new page that contains a table with a column for each field you want to display in the results.**

2. **Create a connection and a recordset for this page using the database or table from which you want to bring in the results.**

   See Chapters 13 and 14 if you need more detailed information on how to do this.

3. **In the Recordset dialog box (see Figure 15-4), select the appropriate connection and table.**

4. **Next to the Filter drop-down list, select the column that corresponds to the field with which you want your users to search.**

5. **In the drop-down list directly below the Filter drop-down list, select Form Variable. In the text box next to the drop-down list, enter the name of the text field element from your search form.**

6. **In the Sort field, select the field by which you want to sort your results.**

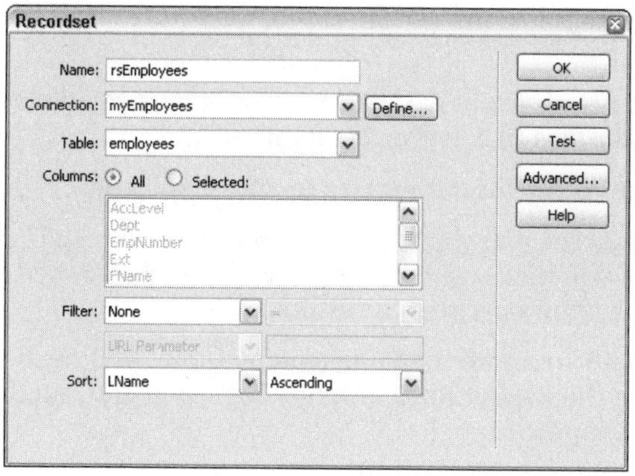

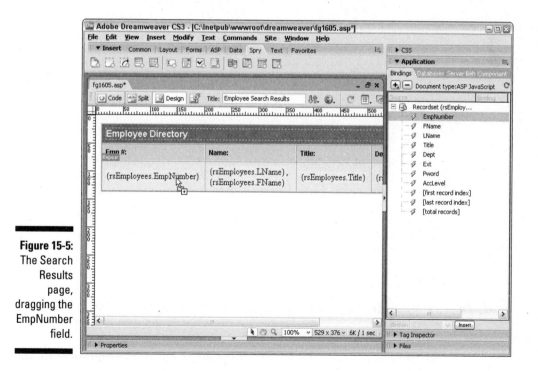

Figure 15-4:
The
Recordset
dialog box
prepared for
search
results.

7. **Click OK.**

8. **Drag each field from your recordset in the Bindings panel to the appropriate column on the table in your results page (see Figure 15-5).**

   Chapter 14 shows you how to drag and drop fields.

Figure 15-5:
The Search
Results
page,
dragging the
EmpNumber
field.

9. **Transfer your pages to the server and open your search page in a browser.**

You find instructions for using Dreamweaver's built-in publishing features to transfer files to a server in Chapter 4.

10. **Try searching for one of the entries in your database.**

The search finds the entry and lists it in your search results page, showing every field you requested on the results page. I searched for *Jackson*, and Figure 15-6 shows my search results.

If you want to return more than one matching row, you need to define a region and use the Repeat Region server behavior. You can find out more about this in Chapter 14.

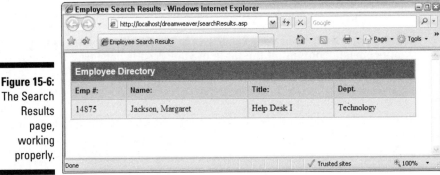

Figure 15-6:
The Search
Results
page,
working
properly.

That's it. Painless, right? This is a database search in its simplest form. The more advanced your understanding of Dreamweaver and the SQL language gets, the more complex you can make your search forms. Users with a basic understanding of SQL can enhance this page to search using multiple criteria, filter search results, sort by various fields, and even display only certain results depending on the access level of the person performing the search.

If you want to find out more about working with databases and SQL, I recommend *Database Development For Dummies* and *SQL For Dummies,* 6th Edition, both by Allen G. Taylor (published by Wiley Publishing, Inc.).

Editing a Database from a Browser

Using forms is also an easy way to perform data-entry tasks on a database without having to open the database application. The person performing those tasks doesn't even need to know how a database works to use the form. All the work is performed right in the browser window. Through the form, a user can add, update, or delete a record from the database.

Suppose that a manager wants to add a new employee and update some information in an employee directory for various employees who just received promotions. Using Dreamweaver, you can create a user-friendly interface where this manager can go to his browser, log in, and make those changes to the database. He can save his changes right there in his browser and view the updated information instantly, all without having to open a database application (such as Access).

You can secure content management pages (such as those discussed in this section) from the public by using the authentication features of Dreamweaver. For more about these authentication features, see the beginning of this chapter.

Adding a record to your database

A record in a database (a row) consists of a complete set of all the fields in the database.

In this section, you use a form to add a record to a database. Before starting, you must create a new dynamic page and connect it to the database you're editing. If you need to refresh your memory on how to do this, see Chapter 13.

After you create your page, you're ready to use the Dreamweaver Record Insertion Form Wizard Data Object. In one easy step, this Data Object Wizard creates a script that allows you to add a record to a database. It also creates the form with which you make the addition.

A *data object* lets you create a more complex function in one easy step.

Follow these steps to add a record using a form:

1. **Open your new page and place the cursor where you want the form to start.**

2. **Choose Insert⇨Data Objects⇨Insert Record⇨Record Insertion Form Wizard.**

   The Record Insertion Form dialog box opens (see Figure 15-7).

3. **Select the appropriate database connection, select the appropriate table from that database, and then enter the name of the page the user is redirected to after the new addition is made.**

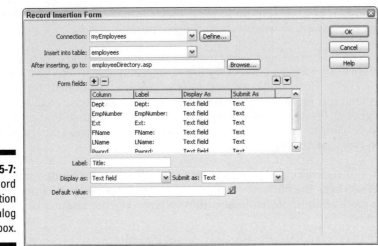

Figure 15-7:
The Record
Insertion
Form dialog
box.

4. In the Form Fields section of the dialog box, verify that all the fields are displayed.

In the Label column, you can change the actual name of the column by clicking a field from the list and editing the Label text. You can also determine what kind of form field (text, radio button, select menu) and what type of formatting (numeric, text, and so on) is used for each field. If any field has a default value, you can define that as well.

If your database table has an auto-number field (a field that the database automatically numbers sequentially for each record), you cannot submit data for that field; it needs to be removed from the Form Fields area.

5. Click OK.

You can now test your page (see Figure 15-8). Simply upload the page to your server, open it in your browser, and enter all the information for a new record. Click the Insert Record button. Your new record shows up in the database.

Upload the Connections folder when you upload your site files to the application server; otherwise, you get an ASP `Include File Not Found` error message.

When you create the database connection (refer to Chapter 13), a Connections folder is added to your site on the local drive. The ASP files in the Connections folder store necessary information that makes your page work correctly with the database. This type of file is typically called an *include file* because its content is referenced by the code in another page. Dreamweaver automatically *includes* the content of this file on any page you create that uses this database connection.

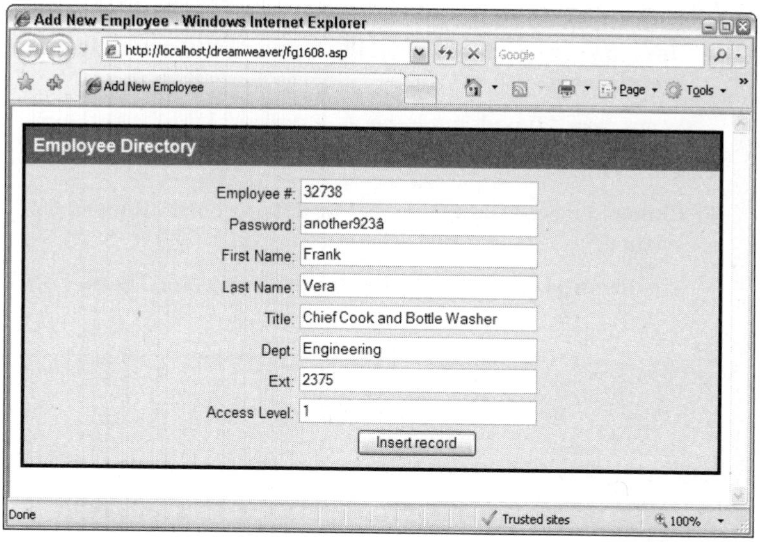

Figure 15-8:
The Record
Insertion
Form in
action.

Updating a record using a browser

To edit, or *update,* a record from a database, you first need to create a search form to search for the record you want to update or a master page list where you can pick out the record. After you find the record, the Update Record form appears, which is where you perform the actual update.

Follow these steps to update an existing record:

1. **On a new page, create a simple search form with a text field element and a Submit button.**

   See the "Searching for Database Records" section, earlier in this chapter, if you need a refresher on creating search forms.

2. **Select the text field on your page, and in the Property inspector, replace *textfield* with a more descriptive name.**

   For example, replace *textfield* with *mysearch.* This name helps differentiate one text field from another on a page that contains multiple fields.

3. **Create a recordset, and filter by the field that you use as your search criteria.**

   I used Employee Number (EmpNumber) as my search criteria.

4. **In the drop-down list directly below the Filter list, select Form Variable. Next to Form Variable, type the name of the text field from your search form.**

   In my case, I typed *mysearch*.

5. **Click OK.**

6. **Choose Insert⇨Data Objects⇨Update Record⇨Record Update Form Wizard.**

   The Record Update Form dialog box opens (see Figure 15-9).

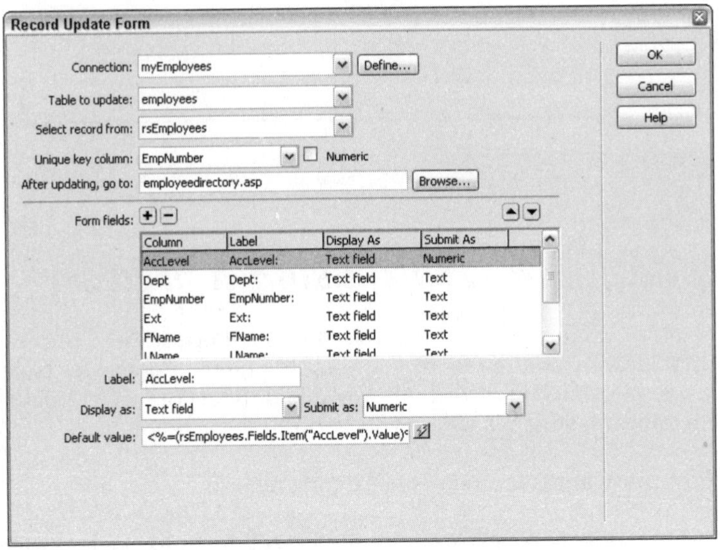

Figure 15-9: The Record Update Form dialog box.

7. **Select the appropriate connection and table.**

8. **In the After Updating, Go To box, type the name of the page you want to display after the update is made.**

   I use `employeeDirectory.asp`, which is my default employee directory page.

9. **In the Form Fields list, make sure that the field labels are correct, or rename them by selecting the label in the list and editing the name in the Label field.**

   The label is what will appear on the update form. You can also rename these fields later by selecting and replacing the text for each field directly on your page in Dreamweaver's design area.

10. **Click OK.**

    A new form appears on your page. You can format the look of the form (font, color, and so on) to make it match the rest of your site.

11. **Select the Server Behaviors panel and click the plus sign (+). Choose Show Region⇨Show Region If Recordset Is Not Empty.**

    This last step ensures that you don't get an error if no recordset matches the criteria you enter in the search field.

    Your Update form is now complete (see Figure 15-10).

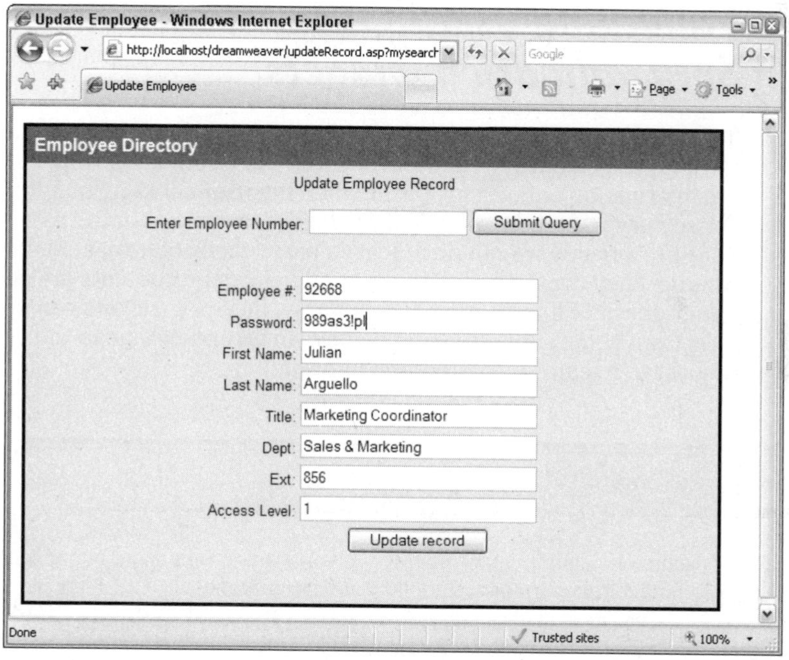

Figure 15-10: The newly created Update form.

You can test the new page by previewing it in your browser. Enter a value that you know exists in that field in your database and click the Submit button. The Record Update form is now populated with the information for that record. You can now make any changes to that record and click the Update Record button to save the changes to the database. The next time you view that record online, the changes appear (see Figure 15-11).

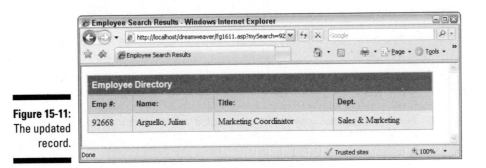

Figure 15-11:
The updated
record.

Validating user input with Spry validation widgets

If you don't want a browser to submit the form unless the fields are properly filled in, you can use Dreamweaver's new Spry validation widgets to validate the information entered by a user when the user clicks a Submit button. These Spry widgets work only if JavaScript is enabled in the user's browser. They are a handy way to do at least a basic check of form fields to see whether they contain valid information before the contents are submitted. If a user doesn't fill in a form field correctly, the Spry widgets can prevent the form from being submitted and display an error message to the user with a request to re-enter or correct the information.

Validating fully

The Spry validation widgets work only if JavaScript is enabled in the browser. To fully validate user forms, you need to have code running on the server that checks the information from each field to make sure it is correct before using the data. Dreamweaver's Spry widgets offer server-side validation only when using ASP.NET or ColdFusion MX 7 pages.

However, if you use ASP.NET validation, the validation is automatically performed on the server and can optionally be performed on the browser as well; the result looks similar to what Spry widgets do, but provides validation even if a browser doesn't support JavaScript or your users have turned JavaScript off in their browsers.

If you want to read more about ASP.NET input validation, go to http://msdn.microsoft.com/library/default.asp?url=/library/en-us/cpgenref/html/cpcontextboxwebservercontrol.asp, but note that the information gets very techie very fast. ColdFusion field validation can be specified to work on either the server or the browser using JavaScript. It requires a bit more work if you want to validate using both methods. You can get more information about developing with ColdFusion at http://www.adobe.com/devnet/coldfusion/getting_started.html.

For the following steps, I assume that you are working with the form created by the Record Update Form Wizard and that you have at least an Employee Number field and a Password field on the form.

To validate form fields with Spry validation widgets, follow these steps:

1. **Open the page that has the Update Record form.**

2. **Select both the Employee Number and Password fields and remember the Text Field names shown in the Property Inspector.**

   You need to name the Spry validation text fields using the same names for each field. In the example form I'm using the field names are *EmpNumber* and *Pword*.

2. **Right-click the Employee number (EmpNumber) and choose Remove Tag <input> from the menu (see Figure 15-12). Then repeat this step selecting the Password field.**

   You will replace these inputs with Spry validation text fields in the next steps.

3. **In the Spry Insert bar, drag a Spry validation text field for the Employee Number (see Figure 15-13).**

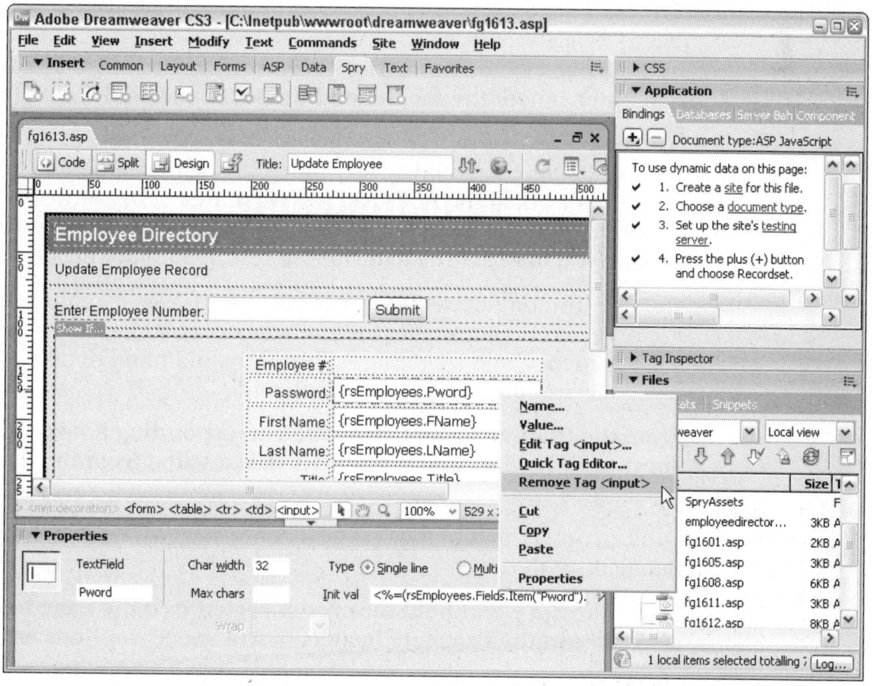

Figure 15-12:
You can remove tag inputs from any field by right-clicking the name and selecting Remove Tag.

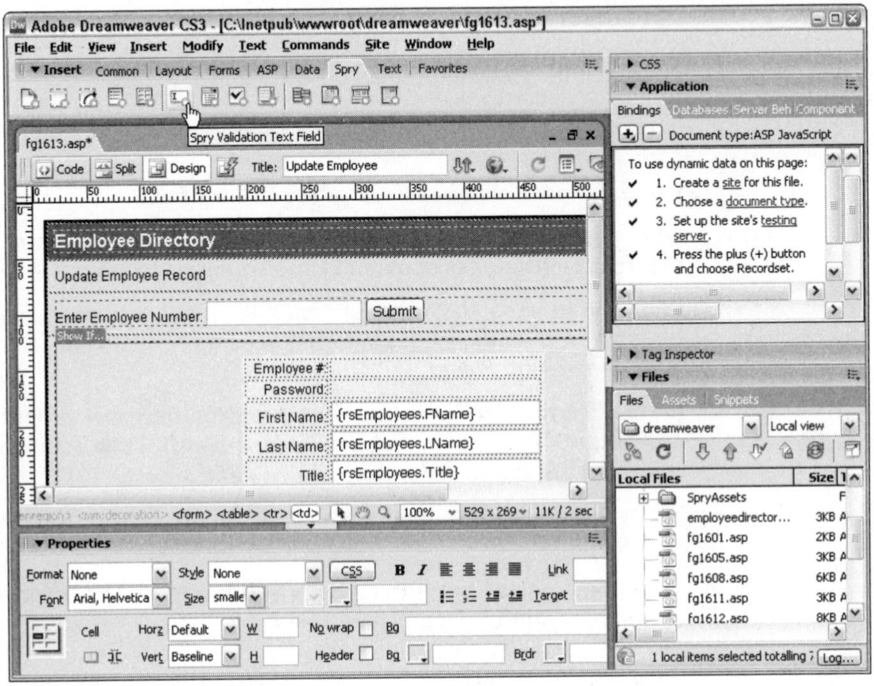

Figure 15-13:
You can
add Spry
validation
fields by
clicking
their icons
in the Spry
Insert bar.

4. **In the ID box of the Input Tag Accessibility Attributes dialog box, type the name of the Employee Number input field from Step 1 (see Figure 15-14).**

   The Input Tag Accessibility Attributes dialog box appears only if you have not disabled the Accessibility attributes in Dreamweaver's Preferences. If the Input Tag Accessibility Attribute dialog box doesn't appear, you *must* set the name of the text field in the Property Inspector.

   You can turn on Accessibility attributes for forms by choosing Edit⇨ Preferences (Dreamweaver Preferences on a Mac), clicking the Accessibility category, and selecting Forms. (You find more details about the form Accessibility options in Chapter 12.)

5. **From the Bindings panel, drag the corresponding Source field into the Spry Input field so that it grabs its initial value from the database (see Figure 15-15).**

   You can open the Bindings panel by choosing Window⇨Bindings Behaviors.

6. **Select the Spry text field that you inserted into the page to display its attributes in the Property inspector and specify options as desired.**

   Make sure that Required is selected. Also, you can change when the Spry widget will validate the input field by selecting Blur (when the user leaves the text field) or Change (anytime the user types something into the text field). Submit is automatically selected because the Spry widget validates the text field before the form is submitted.

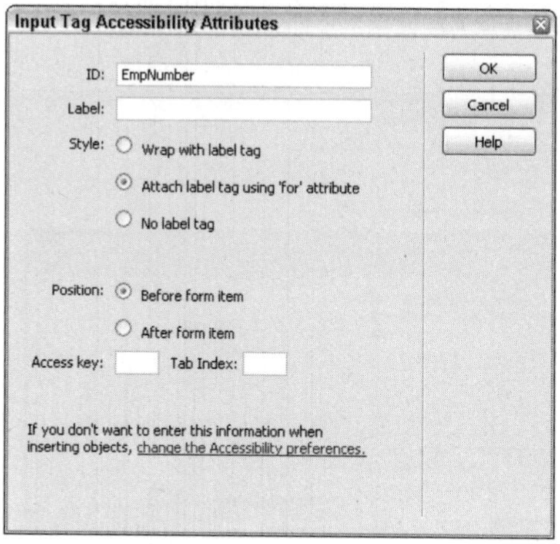

Figure 15-14:
The Input Tag Accessibility Attributes dialog box.

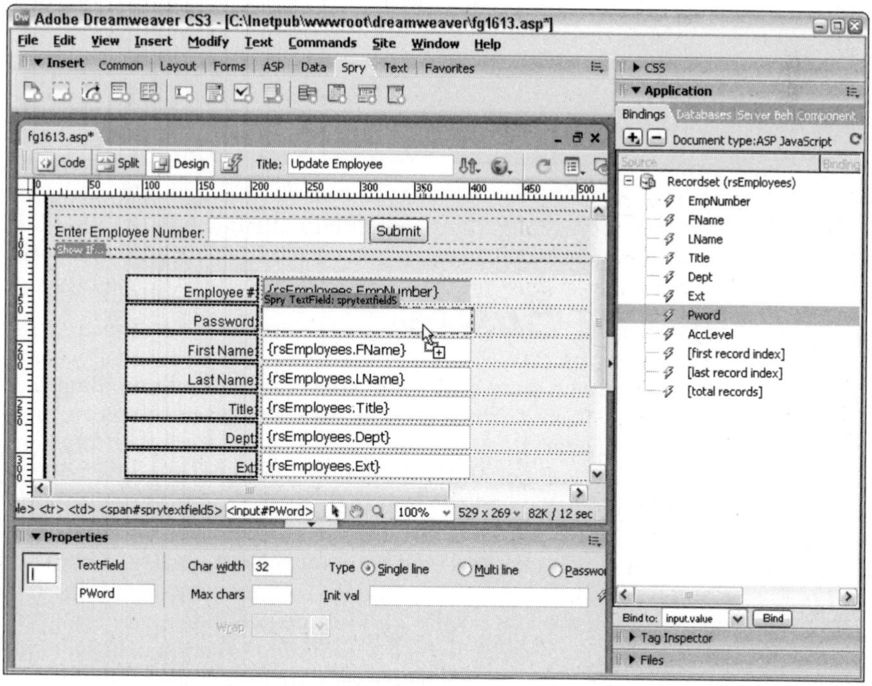

Figure 15-15:
You can use click and drag any Source field from the Bindings panel into an input field.

7. **Repeat Steps 3 through 6 for the Password field.**

   Remember to use the name of the password field from Step 1.

8. **Save the page and preview it to see the validation in action (see Figure 15-16).**

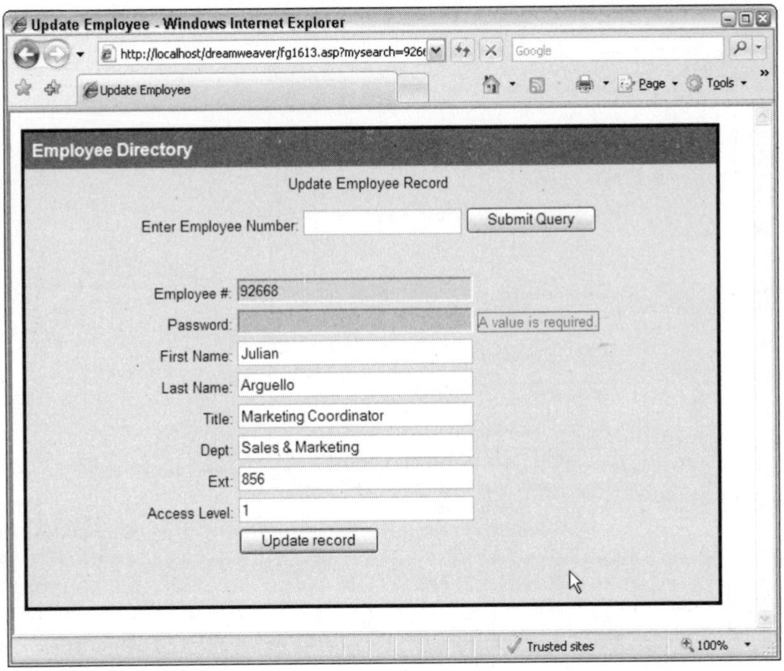

Figure 15-16:
The text to the right of the Password field was generated by the Spry validation widgets because the user did not enter a password.

E-Commerce Basics

Most people who want a Web site are certain about one thing: They want to make money from it. The era of the brochure site is no more, my friends. People hawk everything from fine china to soil from the Holy Land on the Internet (I kid you not about that one). E-commerce helps bring together shoppers and sellers on the Internet.

In the rest of this chapter, I tell you more about what an e-commerce Web site is and what you need to have in place to create one. However, if you're looking for information on how to create an e-commerce site right out of the box with Dreamweaver, stop here. It's not going to happen. I don't know why the powers that be over at Adobe haven't included this feature yet. To be quite frank, I think this is one of the only major flaws I can find with Dreamweaver. You *can* create an e-commerce Web site using Dreamweaver, but it requires an extension, which I go into in just a moment.

What puts the e-commerce into an e-commerce Web site?

An e-commerce Web site, in a nutshell, is a Web site that accepts real-time payments for goods and services. For example, if you're looking for a weight loss supplement, you can go to www.MetabolicNutrition.com, browse offerings in its weight loss product line, and have one shipped to you overnight.

Not all e-commerce Web sites are the same — many companies have built customized tools to aid users in the shopping process. For example, Metabolic Nutrition also allows you to store your shipping information so that you don't have to enter it every time you order. It also has a virtual personal assistant that recommends products based on your health, age, diet, and lifestyle.

The cost of an e-commerce Web site is significantly more than the cost of building a regular Web site because you have to figure in several third-party costs. Here's a quick run-down of the minimal (traditional) e-commerce requirements:

- **A shopping cart:** A shopping cart is a series of scripts and applications that display items from your database, allow users to choose which ones they want, and then collect payment and shipping information. Some Web-hosting accounts come with shopping carts included. A popular one is Miva Merchant (www.miva.com). Various Dreamweaver shopping cart extensions are also worth looking into. For example, PDG Software (www.pdgsoft.com) offers a Dreamweaver extension that provides full integration with PDG's shopping cart with a price tag of about $400 for a lifetime license.

- **A merchant account:** This is literally an account with a bank or a financial institution that allows you to accept credit cards from your clients. Many merchant account providers also offer payment gateways and virtual terminals as a suite, which can save you money and time. Costs and transactions fees vary, as service providers set their own prices. Online Data Corp (www.onlinedatacorp.com) is a good one.

- **A payment gateway and virtual terminal:** A payment gateway is what ties your shopping cart to your merchant account. A virtual terminal is like an electronic bookkeeper and cash register in one — you can view your Web site transactions, issue refunds, and manage orders. A popular Merchant package is offered by PayPal Merchant Services (formerly Verisign's PayFlow). Get more information at www.paypal.com.

- **A secure site certificate:** This encrypts information between your Web site and the client's computer to protect the information from being stolen as you make your purchase online. This is commonly referred to as Secure Sockets Layer (SSL) technology. Verisign and Thawte's 128-bit certificates are popular picks. If you're on a shared Web hosting account, you may be able to share the server's certificate to save money; however, this is often regarded as unprofessional, because the security certificate doesn't display your company name on it — shoppers who check it see your Web hosting company's name instead.

The definition of what a *traditional* e-commerce Web site is continues to change as new technologies and application service providers emerge. Services such as Yahoo! Stores allow you to create a site without purchasing any of the previously mentioned items. PayPal.com offers all-inclusive e-commerce services with free shopping cart tools.

Premade shopping carts and e-commerce systems save you time and money up front, and buying one is the fastest way to get a business online. The downside of using a premade shopping cart is that you often can't make it look like an integral part of your Web site, meaning that you usually have limited control over the graphical elements on shopping-cart–driven pages. Also, most shopping carts use their own databases and give you limited access to the code (because a lot of it may be compiled CGI, which Dreamweaver can't read), so you may run into brick walls when trying to build new features that you didn't buy out of the box.

Considering the investment and risk, many companies prefer to hire a professional programming team to create a system from scratch that looks and functions exactly how they want it to. Amazon.com, for example, has spent millions on its system to make it the incredibly smart and easy-to-use system it is today. But you don't have to break the bank — many successful, custom-built e-commerce Web sites are created for thousands of dollars, not millions.

Adding e-commerce extensions to Dreamweaver

At last count, a few minutes ago, Dreamweaver has 113 e-commerce-related extensions on the Adobe Web site, from stand-alone shopping carts to a PayPal extension that allows your shoppers to pay you using PayPal directly from your Web site.

However, e-commerce is just the proverbial tip of the iceberg when extending Dreamweaver. At the Adobe Exchange Web site, you can download an extension for just about any Web site functionality. In Chapter 10, you find detailed instructions for downloading and installing extensions in Dreamweaver.

Part V
The Part of Tens

The 5th Wave   By Rich Tennant

In this part . . .

The Part of Tens features ten great online resources to help you add more advanced features to your Web pages and ten timesaving tips to help you get the most out of Dreamweaver. You also find ten great Web sites designed in Dreamweaver, to show you what's possible with this Web-design program.

Chapter 16

Ten Resources You May Need

Although Dreamweaver is a wonderful tool for creating Web sites, it can't handle everything you need to put a site online. For example, you can't register a domain name using Dreamweaver, and when you're ready to publish your site, you'll need a Web server. I added this chapter to offer you a handy list of resources that can help you finish your site when you need to go beyond the features in Dreamweaver.

Registering a Domain Name

The address for your Web site is called its *domain name*. It's what visitors need to know to find your Web site. For example, you can visit my Digital Family Web site at `DigitalFamily.com`.

Even before you start building your Web site, I recommend that you register your own domain name. The process is simple, painless, and costs less than $10 per year, but it can take from a few hours to a few days for the domain registration process to be completed.

You can register any domain name that hasn't already been taken by someone else, and you can check to see whether a domain name is already taken for free. Just visit any domain registrar, such as `www.godaddy.com` or `1and1.com`, and enter the domain name you want into the search field on the main page of the registrar's site. If the name you want is no longer available, most registration services will give you a list of recommended alternatives.

Most domain registration services also provide Web hosting services, but you do not have to host your site at the same place where you register the name. You can set up a Web server anywhere you want and then use the domain management settings at your domain registration services to point your name to the server where your Web site is hosted.

When you enter a domain name into a Web browser, everything before the extension (the `.com`, or `.net`, or `.org` part) can be written in uppercase or lowercase, and it will work just fine. However, if you want to go to a specific page within a Web site, such as `www.DigitalFamily.com/videos`, the text that comes after the extension is often case sensitive. Because the part before the `.com` doesn't matter, I find it easier to recognize domain names when they are written with capital letters. So, for example, I use `www.DigitalFamily.com` on my business cards instead of `www.digitalfamily.com`.

Choosing a Web Hosting Service

A *Web server* is a computer with a permanent connection to the Internet and special software that enables it to communicate with Web browsers, such as Internet Explorer, Safari, or Firefox. As a general rule, you create a Web site on your computer's hard drive, using a program such as Dreamweaver, and then transfer the completed site to a Web server when you're ready to publish it on the Internet. If you work at a big company or university, you may be able to access a central server that is owned and operated by your organization. If you're creating a site for yourself or for a smaller business or organization, you'll probably be best served by using a commercial service provider or Web hosting service.

Most commercial service providers have rooms full of computers with really big hard drives, special server software, and special high-speed Internet connections that keep them connected 24/7 (or at least as close to 24/7 as their tech support and backup systems allows). When a service provider sells hosting services, generally it is renting you a section of one of the hard drives on one of its computers and giving you a special password so that only you can get to that section, where you can upload your pages and make them accessible on the Web.

Not all Web hosting services are created equal. Some handle surges in traffic better than others, some offer better security, and some are set up to stream video and audio files. Some are very expensive (costing hundreds or even thousands of dollars per month), and others are highly discounted and can cost as little as a few dollars a month.

In my experience, choosing a Web host is a bit like choosing a long-distance company: You have to study their plans carefully to find the one that's right for you. For example, if you make occasional phone calls but do a lot of international travel, you'll probably want a different cell phone plan than someone who makes hours and hours of calls within the borders of the United States.

With Web servers, the main factors affecting costs are usually how much hard drive space you need, how much traffic you receive, and what level of security you want. Of course, there are also the variables of any service in a competitive market — you may pay extra for big name services or find great discounts if you shop around.

Your best bet is to try a few. Just search for hosting services in Google or another search engine and you'll find dozens of popular options (I hate to recommend one over another, but I've been happy with `Dreamhost.com`).

Here are a few questions you may want to ask as you consider your options.

How much do you charge?

Find out how much hard drive space comes with the basic plan, how much it costs to add more space if you need it, and how much you'll pay for traffic to your site. Unless you get dramatic surges in traffic, or you're hosting huge amounts of content (such as large multimedia files), the basic plans on most big service provider plans are a good place to start; but find out what it will cost to upgrade before you get started.

Do you provide e-commerce services?

Some service providers include great e-commerce systems, but you may be able to use a third-party solution, such as PayPal or a Yahoo! store, no matter what service provider you choose.

How do you provide technical support?

If you run into trouble uploading or maintaining your site, you may need to contact your hosting company to learn more about the specifics of connecting to its Web server.

Some ISPs have knowledgeable technical support staff on call 24 hours a day; others may never answer the phone (especially those with the lowest rates) because they deal with you only by e-mail. Before you sign up for a service, I recommend that you contact the tech support department of the service providers you're considering to see how long it takes each one to respond to your initial questions by phone or e-mail.

Where are you located?

When you look for a Web hosting service, keep in mind that it doesn't need to be in your geographic location. You can send files anywhere on the Internet, so your Web site can be almost anywhere. If you're in a small town or an isolated area where few companies provide Web hosting, you may want to look beyond your neighborhood to find a better deal.

Can I host more than one domain name?

As you compare options, you may notice that some providers charge more for packages that enable you to host multiple domain names. If you are working on multiple Web sites, you may save money by paying for a more expensive hosting service that lets you host multiple domains rather than use a less expensive service for each site you maintain.

Note that there is a difference between hosting multiple domain names that point to different Web sites and pointing two or more domain names to the same site. For example, I registered both www.JanineWarner.com and www.JCWarner.com, but both domain names go to the same site. I was able to set that up at my domain registrar for no extra cost.

Selling Stuff on the Web

There are many ways to sell things online. As I general rule, I recommend that you start simple and add more complex and expensive options after you know that you're going to make money with your site.

At the simple end of the spectrum, you can add a purchase button with the services offered at PayPal.com. Moving up in complexity and price, you can create a shopping system at smallbusiness.yahoo.com/ecommerce/. If you want a more custom solution and your own shopping cart, check out the powerful, highly customizable Dreamweaver extension at http://cartweaver.com/.

Keeping Track of Traffic

Most Web hosting services provide basic log reports and traffic information, but if you want to really know how people are finding your Web site and what they're doing once they get there, consider using a service such as StatCounter.com. You can start with a free, limited level of service at StatCounter, and upgrade for a fee to view more data.

To use the service, you set up an account and copy a bit of code from the site into your Web pages. (It's a simple copy-and-paste procedure you can do using code view in Dreamweaver.) StatCounter then uses that bit of code to track your traffic. Visit `StatCounter.com` for a demo and sample report with all the different kinds of information you can collect, including what search terms someone used to find your site through a search engine. Studying how people use your Web site is one of the best ways to determine how you should continue to develop your content and your design.

Survey Your Visitors

Want to know what your visitors really think? Ask them. You can create a free, online survey at `SurveyMonkey.com` and link to it from your Web site. Survey Monkey makes it easy to create the survey using a Web browser and then automatically tallies the results and presents them in a series of reports and pie charts. It's a great way to impress your board of directors at the next annual meeting.

What Font Is That?

If you've ever tried to identify an unusual font, you know how challenging it can be and you'll likely appreciate the character recognition software offered at `WhatTheFont.com`. Using this free online service, you can upload any graphic or enter the URL to any image on the Web, and the program will analyze the image and try to recognize the font. It's not a perfect system, but even if it can't identify the font, it will try to give you the closest matches it can find. After you do match the font using this service, the site's creators will be happy to sell you the font so you can download it.

Save Time with Templates

If you want more predesigned templates than the ones included in Dreamweaver, use one of the many third-party companies that create and (usually) sell their templates over the Web.

Visit `www.dreamweaver-templates.org` for a long list of sites that offer templates for free or a fee. Just download them and open them in Dreamweaver, and you can start building your Web site around these professionally created templates in no time.

Keep Up with Web Standards at W3.org

If you want to keep up with the latest developments in Web design and make sure you're following standards, there is no better place than W3.org, the official Web site of the organization that sets Web standards. You'll find loads of information on this nonprofit site, including the full specification for HTML, CSS, and much more. You can also test your Web pages by entering the URL into their validation system at: jigsaw.w3.org/css-validator/.

Extend Dreamweaver at Adobe.com

Visit the Dreamweaver Exchange Site at www.adobe.com/cfusion/exchange/index.cfm?view=sn120 to find a vast collection of extensions you can use to add behaviors and other features to Dreamweaver. It's easy to install them using the Extensions Manager, covered in Chapter 10.

While you're at the site, check out Adobe's growing collection of tutorials, updates, and resources, including the new CSS section, where you'll find the latest in CSS hacks, tips, and workarounds.

Dress Up the Address Bar with a Favicon

Have you ever wondered how some sites add a custom graphic to the address bar at the top of browsers such as Internet Explorer? Google adds a capital *G,* Adobe adds its logo, and you can add an image, too. But first you have to get it in the right format.

To convert an image into a Favicon, visit Favicon.com, where you can upload a graphic and have it converted for free. Then just add that image to the root level of your main site folder, and it will automatically display in the address bar of a browser.

Find Out More from Other Web Designers

If you want to keep up with the buzz among top Web designers, visit AListApart.com and you'll find great articles, notes, and tips, updated early and often. Boasting an impressive crew of contributors, the site describes itself as a magazine that "explores the design, development, and meaning of web content, with a special focus on web standards and best practices."

Chapter 17

Ten Timesaving Tips

A ll good Web sites grow and evolve. If you start with a strong design and pay close attention to some basic rules about interface, navigation, and style, you have a better foundation to build on. The following design ideas and Dreamweaver tips can help you save time as you create Web sites that look great for all your visitors.

Design for Your Audience

No matter how technically sophisticated a Web site is or how great the writing, most people notice the design first. Make sure that you leave plenty of time and budget to develop an appropriate and attractive design for your Web site. The right design is one that best suits your audience — and that may or may not mean lots of fancy graphics and animations.

Think about who you want to attract to your Web site before you develop the design. A gaming Web site geared toward teenagers should look very different from a Web site with gardening tips for the semiretired or an online investment site for busy professionals.

A great way to get ideas is to visit other sites designed for your target market, even if they don't offer the same content, products, or services. As you consider design ideas, keep in mind your audience's time constraints, attention span, and goals. If you're creating a site for busy professionals, you may want to include a search engine and lists of links that make it easy to go directly to key information. If you're designing an entertainment destination, your audience may be willing to wait a little longer for animation, video, and other interactive features.

Create a Consistent Design

Most Web sites work best and are easiest to navigate when they follow a consistent design. Case in point: Most readers take for granted that books don't change their design from page to page, and that newspapers don't change headline fonts and logos from day to day. Consistency is one of the primary tools used in books and newspapers to make it easy for readers to distinguish different elements and follow a story or theme.

As you lay out Web pages, keep related items close to one another and be consistent about how you design similar content elements. You want your viewers to instantly understand which pieces of information are related to each other. Distinguish different kinds of information by their

- Design
- Location
- Prominence

This type of organization makes following information visually much easier.

Make sure that similar elements follow the same design parameters, such as type style, banner size, and page background color. Give elements of similar importance the same weight on a page. If you use too many different elements on a page or on the same Web site, you can confuse your viewers.

To ensure a consistent style, define a set of colors, shapes, or other elements that you use throughout the site. Choose two or three fonts for your Web site and use those consistently as well. Using too many fonts makes your pages less appealing and harder to read.

Strive for consistency in your designs — except when you're trying to be unpredictable. A little surprise here and there can keep your Web site alive.

Follow the Three Clicks Rule

The three clicks rule states that no important piece of information should ever be more than three clicks away from anywhere else on your Web site. The most important information should be even closer at hand. Some information, such as contact information, should never be more than one click away. You can make finding information easy for viewers by creating a *site map* (with links to all or most of the pages in your site) and a *navigation bar* — a set of links to all the main sections on your site.

Get a Head Start on Your Designs

Dreamweaver CS3 features many predesigned templates, including an upgraded collection of CSS designs you can edit to create two-column, three-column, and other popular CSS layouts.

You'll also find Starter Pages, which include not only topic-based designs but also text. You may need to edit the text to meet your needs, but if you're creating a common site feature, such as a calendar or product listings, the general text already in place gives you a head start.

When you create a file in Dreamweaver (such as by choosing File⇨New), the New Document window offers you many ways to create a predesigned page, including the following:

- **Template pages:** Choose the Template Page category to open a list of templates types. The options are ASP JavaScript, ASP VBScript, ASP.Net C#, ASP.Net VB, ColdFusion, HTML, JSP, and PHP. Note that all these formats except HTML require programming and require the most advanced features of Dreamweaver. You find more about these options and how they can be used to create database-driven Web sites in Chapters 13, 14, and 15.

- **Layout Designs for Frames:** Choose Framesets to open a collection of predesigned framesets. Because these templates can save you so much time, they're a "must use" feature if you're creating a site that uses frames.

- **CSS-Designed Pages:** Choose from any of the predesigned layouts included in the New Document window under Layout when you create a new file.

- **Predesigned Pages with Text:** Choose Starter Pages to open a list of common page designs that include content you can easily adapt for a wide variety of Web sites.

- **Regular Template Designs:** Choose Page Designs to open a list of basic HTML templates. Although they may seem simple by comparison, these are well-designed pages that can help you get a static Web site up and running with a lot less effort than creating it from scratch.

Split the View

If you like to switch back and forth between the HTML source code and design view in Dreamweaver, you'll appreciate the option to split the window so that you can view both the source code and the page design at the same time. To split the window, choose View⇨Code and Design or click the Show Code and Design Views button, located just under the Insert bar at the top of the workspace.

With the code improvements in Dreamweaver CS3, source code has better color coding and tagging features, similar to those in HTML editors such as HomeSite and BBEdit. Notice as you're working that if you select an image, text, or another element on a page in design view, it is automatically highlighted in code view, a great feature that makes it easier to find your place in the raw code.

Design in a Flash

Flash rocks! Adobe has made Flash better than ever by providing enhanced integration with Dreamweaver, Photoshop, and Fireworks. Flash is a vector-based design and animation program and the tool used to create most of the coolest Web sites on the Net today. Flash makes is possible to create fast-loading images, complex animations, and even video files that dynamically adjust to fit any screen size. Now that the vast majority of Web surfers have the Flash plug-in, Flash has become a standard, and Dreamweaver has made inserting Flash files easier than ever.

You can even create Flash files, such as Flash buttons and Flash text, using Dreamweaver (even if you don't have Adobe Flash). With Dreamweaver's integrated tools, you can customize the button style, text, and other elements of Flash buttons and create cool Flash text effects. Just choose Insert➪Media, select the Flash option you want from the list, and use the dialog box to customize the Flash file and save it to your Web site.

You find detailed instructions for inserting Flash files into Web pages in Chapter 11.

Find Functional Fonts

Designers get so excited when they find out that they can use any font on a Web page. But in reality, your viewers must still have the font on their computers for it to appear. The more common the font, the more likely it is to appear the way you intend. If you want to use a more unusual font, go for it — just be sure that you also include alternatives. The Dreamweaver font list already includes collections of common fonts, and you can create your own font list by choosing Text➪Font➪Edit Font List.

In an effort to make text easier to read on the Web, Adobe and Microsoft have both created fonts especially suited to computer screens. To find out more, visit their Web sites at www.adobe.com and www.microsoft.com, respectively, and search for Web fonts.

Keep Frequently Used Items Handy

Ever wish you could keep all your favorite Dreamweaver features in one convenient place? You can with the Favorites tab.

When you launch Dreamweaver, the Common tab is visible in the Insert bar at the top of the workspace. Click the arrow to the right of it to open it (if it's not open already), and you find a collection of tabs or a drop-down list (depending on how you set up the interface). The Insert bar includes several sections, or tabs, including Layout, Forms, and HTML. At the very end of the Insert bar (or the bottom of the drop-down list) you find the Favorites Insert bar.

Select the Favorites Insert bar and you can customize it with all your favorite feature icons; just right-click (or Control+click) and choose Customize Favorites. Use the Favorites Insert bar as a convenient way to keep all your favorite features handy. You can even change it for special projects that require a series of steps or elements.

Be Prepared for Fast Updates

The Web provides a powerful vehicle for businesses and nonprofit organizations to present their side of any story and get the word out quickly when tragic events, bad press, and other crises arise.

But don't wait for an emergency to find out whether you're prepared to add new information to your Web site quickly, and don't fool yourself into thinking that just because you don't manage a daily Internet newspaper you don't have to worry about speedy updates.

With a little planning and key systems set up in advance, you can be prepared for events that require timely information — whether an international crisis stops air travel, a flood closes your nonprofit, or an embarrassing event makes your CEO cringe and demand that the real story be told as soon as possible.

Most organizations develop Web sites that are updated on a weekly, monthly, or even annual basis. More sophisticated sites may link to databases that track inventory or update product listings in real time, but even high-end sites are often ill-prepared to update special information quickly.

Here are a few precautions you can take to be prepared for timely updates on your site:

- ✔ **Make sure you can send new information to your Web site quickly.** Many Web sites are designed with testing systems that safeguard against careless mistakes, but these systems can add hours, or even days, to the time it takes to add new information to your Web site. Work with your technical staff or consultants to make sure you can update your site quickly if necessary. This may require creating a new section that you can update independently from the rest of the site or that can override the regular update system.

- ✔ **Make updating important sections of your site easy.** Consider building or buying a content management system that uses Web-based forms to post new information to your site. Such a system can be designed to change or add information to a Web page as easily as filling out an online order form. You need an experienced programmer to develop a form-based update system. Many Web consultants offer this kind of service for a reasonable fee. This method works, for example, if you are a real estate agent and need to change listings or if you have a calendar of events. Include password protection so that you control access to the form. As an added advantage, a form enables you to make updates from any computer connected to the Internet, so you can update your Web site even if you can't get back into your office.

✔ **Identify and train key staff to update the site.** With the right systems in place, you do not need to have much technical experience to make simple updates to a site, but your staff needs some instruction and regular reminders. Make sure you also develop a schedule for retraining to ensure that no one forgets emergency procedures. Your most serious emergency could happen tomorrow or may not happen for years to come — you never know — but being prepared pays off in the end.

Back It Up

Make sure you have a system in place to back up your Web site. Always keep a copy of all the files on your server in a separate location and update it regularly to make sure you have the latest version of your site backed up at all times. Even the best Internet service providers sometimes have technical problems, so you should keep a backup of your site where you have easy access to it and can get it back online quickly if something deletes any or all the files you have on the server.

Also keep a backup of your original source files, such as Photoshop images. For example, when you develop images for the Web, you usually start in a program such as Photoshop, creating a high-resolution image that may include layers and other elements. Before the image goes on your Web site, those layers get flattened and the image gets compressed or reduced and converted into a GIF or JPEG. If you ever want to go back and alter that image, you'll want the original source file before it was compressed and the layers were flattened. Whether you create your own images or you hire a professional designer, make sure you develop a system for saving all these original elements and make sure you get the original files from the designer, if possible, so that you have them if you ever need to alter an image later.

Chapter 18

Ten Great Web Sites Designed in Dreamweaver

Dreamweaver is the clear choice of professional Web designers and the program behind many of the best-designed sites on the Web.

The sites in this chapter provide an overview of what you can do with Dreamweaver — and they're all great examples of what's possible on the Web today. Many of the sites take advantage of the latest Web technologies, integrating Flash to create vivid animations. They also use dynamic technologies, such as PHP, to add powerful interactivity.

Review the descriptions to discover what tools the designers used and how Dreamweaver helped them create these Web sites. Then spend some time online, visiting each site to appreciate the full effect of their design, navigation, and other features.

An Artist Showcase

RobinEschner.com

Robin Eschner first turned to Digital Cottage to create a Web site where she could showcase and sell her beautiful paintings, cards, and prints. The site was later redesigned by Mariana Davi Cheng, who created the overall site design and added the rollover effect you see in Figure 18-1.

A simple image-swap creates the rollover feature, drawing attention to links and adding a colorful, interactive element to the page. In the inside pages, Davi created a design that displays several images at once, using a more complex image swap that showcases larger image of each painting when a visitor rolls a cursor over a thumbnail image. (Image rollovers and other behaviors are covered in Chapter 10.)

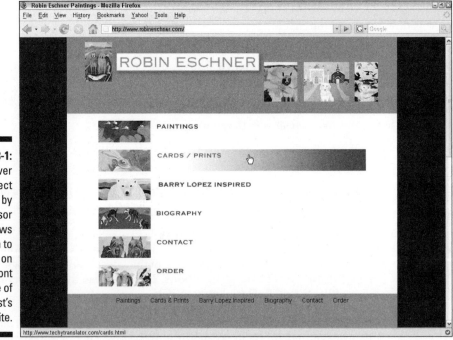

Figure 18-1:
A rollover effect activated by the cursor draws attention to the links on the front page of this artist's Web site.

A Powerful Yoga Site

Poweryoga.com

The soothing yoga site design shown in Figure 18-2 was created by Kathy McCarthy, and the programming that makes this site so powerful was done by Anissa Thompson, using Dreamweaver to create a dynamic site that uses PHP and MySQL. These advanced Web technologies make it possible to connect Web sites to databases and to create administrative tools that make it easy for clients to update their own Web sites. For example, Anissa developed an administrative system that client Chris Fang can use to add workshop descriptions and dates to the site without having to learn Dreamweaver or HTML. Chris simply uses a Web browser, logs into a special page on the site (that is not available to the public), and makes updates by simply filling in a few form fields and pressing a Submit button. The result is a beautiful, richly interactive site that's easy to update. You find an introduction to Dreamweaver's most advanced features in Chapters 13, 14, and 15.

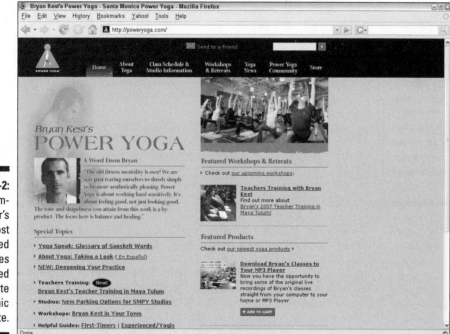

Figure 18-2:
Dream-
weaver's
most
advanced
features
were used
to create
this dynamic
site.

Sage Words on the Web

`sparselysageandtimely.com/blog`

When Pulitzer-prize winning publisher David Mitchell sold his small-town newspaper, *The Point Reyes Light*, he took his column and his years of journalism experience to the Web with a blog that bears the same name he used for his newspaper column, Sparsely Sage and Timely (see Figure 18-3).

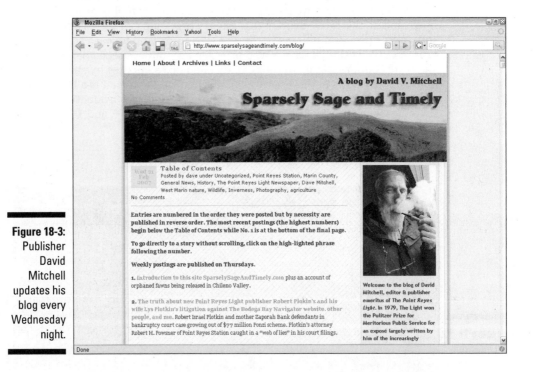

Figure 18-3: Publisher David Mitchell updates his blog every Wednesday night.

When I started out as a journalist many, many moons ago, my first job out of college was at *The Point Reyes Light,* and David and I have remained friends ever since. So it was an honor and a pleasure to help him develop his blog when he finally retired. When David wants to create posts that go beyond the built-in features of WordPress, the program he uses for the blog, I used Dreamweaver to help with formatting. Blogs are an easy way for people like David to make frequent updates to a site without having to learn how to use a program such as Dreamweaver, but that doesn't mean you can't use Dreamweaver's great design features to add a little extra formatting to the design once in while.

The Memory Keeper's Daughter

memorykeepersdaughter.com

Kim Edwards's debut novel, *The Memory Keeper's Daughter,* has been such a runaway success that she and her publisher decided to build a Web site just for the book. The book is a novel about a Midwestern doctor's late-night decision to put his newborn Down syndrome daughter into an institution and hide her existence from his wife and the baby's twin. The book's haunting cover and imagery gave Web designers at Hop Studios a wonderful place to start when creating a companion Web site.

They built the site in Dreamweaver (see Figure 18-4), relying heavily on Dreamweaver's excellent CSS tools and using a Library item to include the code for a third-party traffic-counting tool on every page. The site is rounded out by a Dreamweaver-built contact form that site visitors can use to send e-mail to Kim's publicist. Dreamweaver's template and library features are covered in Chapter 9.

Figure 18-4:
Most authors now develop Web sites to help promote their books and better connect with readers.

Lights, Camera, Multimedia

Studioweasel.com

Director David LaFontaine used Flash video to showcase clips from his latest film project and Dreamweaver's multimedia features to integrate the video files into the pages of the site shown in Figure 18-5. Flash video has a growing audience because the Flash plug-in is so widely distributed, and the Flash video format is an increasingly popular choice among Web designers.

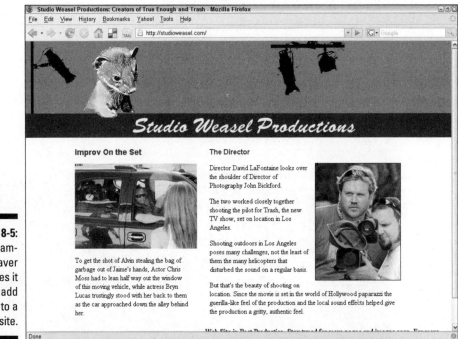

Figure 18-5: Dreamweaver makes it easy to add video to a Web site.

Because Adobe owns both Flash and Dreamweaver, it's easy to insert Flash files into your Web pages and even test the results in the design window. You find out more about working with multimedia and inserting Flash files in Chapter 11.

A Sure Shot of Entertainment

`sureshotentertainment.com`

Rodeo and Wild-West performer Sally Bishop uses her Web site as a calling card when auditioning for film and television and as a showcase for her skills as a horsewoman (see Figure 18-6). This Wild-West–themed Web site was built entirely in Dreamweaver and takes advantage of one of the best of Dreamweaver's built-in tools, Library items. The site's navigation and page footer were built as Library items so that the site can be quickly updated when Sally needs to add a new section.

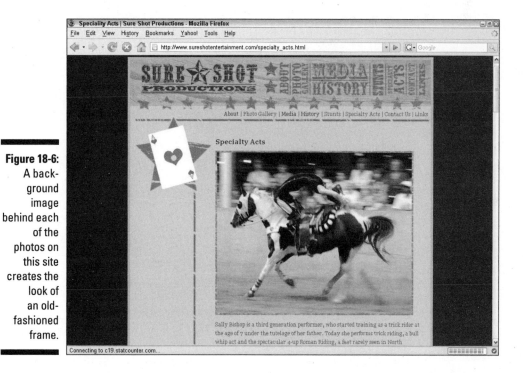

Figure 18-6: A background image behind each of the photos on this site creates the look of an old-fashioned frame.

The site's neatest little code feature occurs with the border around the photos. Using Dreamweaver's built-in CSS tools, Web designers at Hop Studios set a background image and a margin for each photograph. Because the background image is larger than the photo, the background image is visible around the photo, thus creating the wooden border effect. Dreamweaver's CSS features are covered in Chapters 5 and 6.

A Delicious Blog Edited in Dreamweaver

`candyblog.net`

Cybele May's Candy Blog (shown in Figure 18-7) is a tasty treat every day of the week. Her reviews of sugary snacks are humorously written but still serious enough to please any candy connoisseur. Cybele doesn't stop with a simple thumbs up/thumbs down; she includes the hard truth about cost, size, and calories. Paired with her terrific close-up photography, this site is a thorough and entertaining confection all on its own.

Figure 18-7: The design for this candy blog was created in Dreamweaver.

The site was designed and produced by Vancouver-based Hop Studios, whose designers used the project as an excuse to eat a lot of candy while working on it. Ultimately, the site is run using blog software, and Hop Studios' creative director Susannah Gardner faced a specific challenge while creating Candy Blog: They were redesigning Cybele's two other blogs (Fast Fiction and Playwright) at the same time and had to keep costs down. The decision was made early on to use the same layout and design opportunities in all three blogs. This meant, for example, that the logo for each blog would be different but would take up the same amount of space and be in the same location.

Dreamweaver's CSS menus were crucial in making this efficiency work at the code level. Hop Studios set up a single template for the blogs, and then essentially created three flavors of style sheet styles. Applied selectively, they make the same page transform into three different looking blogs. From Dreamweaver, the HTML templates and CSS were moved into blog software, and the result is the sweet sensation that is Candy Blog!

Showcasing a Portfolio

`christophernoxon.com`

Author and freelance journalist Christopher Noxon has had a portfolio Web site showcasing his work for some time, but in 2006 he decided to get serious about it. What he really wanted, he decided, was a Web site with design and organization that matched the quality of the writing it contained. And why not also use it as a place to highlight his artwork, from photos to sketches?

The Web site redesign (shown in Figure 18-8) was undertaken by Hop Studios, who also produced the Web site for Christopher's book *Rejuvenile: Kickball, Cartoons, Cupcakes and the Reinvention of the American Grown Up* (`www.rejuvenile.com`).

Figure 18-8: Dreamweaver is an ideal tool for creating online portfolios and other showcase sites.

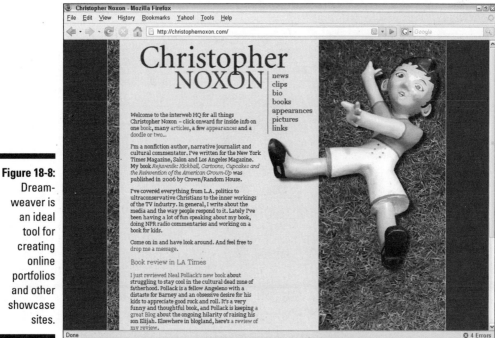

It was important to Christopher that the new site also reflect the variety and sense of humor that characterizes his writing, and Hop Studios worked with Christopher to create a different treatment for each of the site's sections. Dreamweaver was instrumental in this incremental design process. Hop Studios designed and built the templates for each section in Dreamweaver, which Christopher previewed and tweaked before the code was migrated into a content management system.

My Growing Digital Family

`DigitalFamily.com`

Know someone who needs a simple solution to creating a family Web site, photo album, or blog? You'll find free tutorials and lessons at DigitalFamily.com (shown in Figure 18-9). You'll also find more tutorials on Dreamweaver and other professional Web design tools. I designed this site to help my friends and family create Web sites for weddings, new babies, reunions, or any of the seemingly unlimited number of personal uses that have become popular on the Internet. Over the years, it has grown to also include tips and tutorials for more professional designers who use programs like Dreamweaver.

Figure 18-9:
The Digital Family Web site was designed with Dream-weaver templates.

DigitalFamily.com is an example of how many authors, like myself, are creating Web sites to complement their books and provide updated information between revisions. It should be no surprise that I used Dreamweaver to create this site, relying heavily on the template features to make adding pages fast and easy, as well as to maintain a consistent design theme throughout the site. You discover how to design templates in Chapter 9 and how to use other site management features in Chapter 4.

Yours Truly

JCWarner.com

I use my own Web site at JCWarner.com as a personal portfolio and online profile (see Figure 18-10). I recommend that every professional consider building a site like this these days, even if your bio already appears on another Web site.

Figure 18-10:
My own Web site was, of course, built with Dreamweaver.

My site was originally built using HTML tables, a layout option that has long been popular on the Web, but today if you look at the code behind my pages, you'll see that it's designed completely with CSS, using div tags, unordered lists, and other basic HTML to organize the content. The result is a site that is highly accessible and easy to manage and update. (CSS is covered in Chapters 5 and 6.) And I use Dreamweaver to make all the additions, updates, and changes to my site.

Index

BUSINESS, CAREERS & PERSONAL FINANCE

0-7645-9847-3   0-7645-2431-3

Also available:
- Business Plans Kit For Dummies
  0-7645-9794-9
- Economics For Dummies
  0-7645-5726-2
- Grant Writing For Dummies
  0-7645-8416-2
- Home Buying For Dummies
  0-7645-5331-3
- Managing For Dummies
  0-7645-1771-6
- Marketing For Dummies
  0-7645-5600-2

- Personal Finance For Dummies
  0-7645-2590-5*
- Resumes For Dummies
  0-7645-5471-9
- Selling For Dummies
  0-7645-5363-1
- Six Sigma For Dummies
  0-7645-6798-5
- Small Business Kit For Dummies
  0-7645-5984-2
- Starting an eBay Business For Dummies
  0-7645-6924-4
- Your Dream Career For Dummies
  0-7645-9795-7

HOME & BUSINESS COMPUTER BASICS

0-470-05432-8   0-471-75421-8

Also available:
- Cleaning Windows Vista For Dummies
  0-471-78293-9
- Excel 2007 For Dummies
  0-470-03737-7
- Mac OS X Tiger For Dummies
  0-7645-7675-5
- MacBook For Dummies
  0-470-04859-X
- Macs For Dummies
  0-470-04849-2
- Office 2007 For Dummies
  0-470-00923-3

- Outlook 2007 For Dummies
  0-470-03830-6
- PCs For Dummies
  0-7645-8958-X
- Salesforce.com For Dummies
  0-470-04893-X
- Upgrading & Fixing Laptops For Dummies
  0-7645-8959-8
- Word 2007 For Dummies
  0-470-03658-3
- Quicken 2007 For Dummies
  0-470-04600-7

FOOD, HOME, GARDEN, HOBBIES, MUSIC & PETS

0-7645-8404-9   0-7645-9904-6

Also available:
- Candy Making For Dummies
  0-7645-9734-5
- Card Games For Dummies
  0-7645-9910-0
- Crocheting For Dummies
  0-7645-4151-X
- Dog Training For Dummies
  0-7645-8418-9
- Healthy Carb Cookbook For Dummies
  0-7645-8476-6
- Home Maintenance For Dummies
  0-7645-5215-5

- Horses For Dummies
  0-7645-9797-3
- Jewelry Making & Beading For Dummies
  0-7645-2571-9
- Orchids For Dummies
  0-7645-6759-4
- Puppies For Dummies
  0-7645-5255-4
- Rock Guitar For Dummies
  0-7645-5356-9
- Sewing For Dummies
  0-7645-6847-7
- Singing For Dummies
  0-7645-2475-5

INTERNET & DIGITAL MEDIA

0-470-04529-9   0-470-04894-8

Also available:
- Blogging For Dummies
  0-471-77084-1
- Digital Photography For Dummies
  0-7645-9802-3
- Digital Photography All-in-One Desk Reference For Dummies
  0-470-03743-1
- Digital SLR Cameras and Photography For Dummies
  0-7645-9803-1
- eBay Business All-in-One Desk Reference For Dummies
  0-7645-8438-3
- HDTV For Dummies
  0-470-09673-X

- Home Entertainment PCs For Dummies
  0-470-05523-5
- MySpace For Dummies
  0-470-09529-6
- Search Engine Optimization For Dummies
  0-471-97998-8
- Skype For Dummies
  0-470-04891-3
- The Internet For Dummies
  0-7645-8996-2
- Wiring Your Digital Home For Dummies
  0-471-91830-X

* Separate Canadian edition also available
† Separate U.K. edition also available

Available wherever books are sold. For more information or to order direct: U.S. customers visit www.dummies.com or call 1-877-762-2974.
U.K. customers visit www.wileyeurope.com or call 0800 243407. Canadian customers visit www.wiley.ca or call 1-800-567-4797.

SPORTS, FITNESS, PARENTING, RELIGION & SPIRITUALITY

0-471-76871-5

0-7645-7841-3

Also available:
- Catholicism For Dummies
  0-7645-5391-7
- Exercise Balls For Dummies
  0-7645-5623-1
- Fitness For Dummies
  0-7645-7851-0
- Football For Dummies
  0-7645-3936-1
- Judaism For Dummies
  0-7645-5299-6
- Potty Training For Dummies
  0-7645-5417-4
- Buddhism For Dummies
  0-7645-5359-3

- Pregnancy For Dummies
  0-7645-4483-7 †
- Ten Minute Tone-Ups For Dummies
  0-7645-7207-5
- NASCAR For Dummies
  0-7645-7681-X
- Religion For Dummies
  0-7645-5264-3
- Soccer For Dummies
  0-7645-5229-5
- Women in the Bible For Dummies
  0-7645-8475-8

TRAVEL

0-7645-7749-2

0-7645-6945-7

Also available:
- Alaska For Dummies
  0-7645-7746-8
- Cruise Vacations For Dummies
  0-7645-6941-4
- England For Dummies
  0-7645-4276-1
- Europe For Dummies
  0-7645-7529-5
- Germany For Dummies
  0-7645-7823-5
- Hawaii For Dummies
  0-7645-7402-7

- Italy For Dummies
  0-7645-7386-1
- Las Vegas For Dummies
  0-7645-7382-9
- London For Dummies
  0-7645-4277-X
- Paris For Dummies
  0-7645-7630-5
- RV Vacations For Dummies
  0-7645-4442-X
- Walt Disney World & Orlando
  For Dummies
  0-7645-9660-8

GRAPHICS, DESIGN & WEB DEVELOPMENT

0-7645-8815-X

0-7645-9571-7

Also available:
- 3D Game Animation For Dummies
  0-7645-8789-7
- AutoCAD 2006 For Dummies
  0-7645-8925-3
- Building a Web Site For Dummies
  0-7645-7144-3
- Creating Web Pages For Dummies
  0-470-08030-2
- Creating Web Pages All-in-One Desk
  Reference For Dummies
  0-7645-4345-8
- Dreamweaver 8 For Dummies
  0-7645-9649-7

- InDesign CS2 For Dummies
  0-7645-9572-5
- Macromedia Flash 8 For Dummies
  0-7645-9691-8
- Photoshop CS2 and Digital
  Photography For Dummies
  0-7645-9580-6
- Photoshop Elements 4 For Dummies
  0-471-77483-9
- Syndicating Web Sites with RSS Feeds
  For Dummies
  0-7645-8848-6
- Yahoo! SiteBuilder For Dummies
  0-7645-9800-7

NETWORKING, SECURITY, PROGRAMMING & DATABASES

0-7645-7728-X

0-471-74940-0

Also available:
- Access 2007 For Dummies
  0-470-04612-0
- ASP.NET 2 For Dummies
  0-7645-7907-X
- C# 2005 For Dummies
  0-7645-9704-3
- Hacking For Dummies
  0-470-05235-X
- Hacking Wireless Networks
  For Dummies
  0-7645-9730-2
- Java For Dummies
  0-470-08716-1

- Microsoft SQL Server 2005 For Dummies
  0-7645-7755-7
- Networking All-in-One Desk Reference
  For Dummies
  0-7645-9939-9
- Preventing Identity Theft For Dummies
  0-7645-7336-5
- Telecom For Dummies
  0-471-77085-X
- Visual Studio 2005 All-in-One Desk
  Reference For Dummies
  0-7645-9775-2
- XML For Dummies
  0-7645-8845-1

HEALTH & SELF-HELP

0-7645-8450-2   0-7645-4149-8

Also available:
- Bipolar Disorder For Dummies
  0-7645-8451-0
- Chemotherapy and Radiation
  For Dummies
  0-7645-7832-4
- Controlling Cholesterol For Dummies
  0-7645-5440-9
- Diabetes For Dummies
  0-7645-6820-5* †
- Divorce For Dummies
  0-7645-8417-0 †

- Fibromyalgia For Dummies
  0-7645-5441-7
- Low-Calorie Dieting For Dummies
  0-7645-9905-4
- Meditation For Dummies
  0-471-77774-9
- Osteoporosis For Dummies
  0-7645-7621-6
- Overcoming Anxiety For Dummies
  0-7645-5447-6
- Reiki For Dummies
  0-7645-9907-0
- Stress Management For Dummies
  0-7645-5144-2

EDUCATION, HISTORY, REFERENCE & TEST PREPARATION

0-7645-8381-6   0-7645-9554-7

Also available:
- The ACT For Dummies
  0-7645-9652-7
- Algebra For Dummies
  0-7645-5325-9
- Algebra Workbook For Dummies
  0-7645-8467-7
- Astronomy For Dummies
  0-7645-8465-0
- Calculus For Dummies
  0-7645-2498-4
- Chemistry For Dummies
  0-7645-5430-1
- Forensics For Dummies
  0-7645-5580-4

- Freemasons For Dummies
  0-7645-9796-5
- French For Dummies
  0-7645-5193-0
- Geometry For Dummies
  0-7645-5324-0
- Organic Chemistry I For Dummies
  0-7645-6902-3
- The SAT I For Dummies
  0-7645-7193-1
- Spanish For Dummies
  0-7645-5194-9
- Statistics For Dummies
  0-7645-5423-9

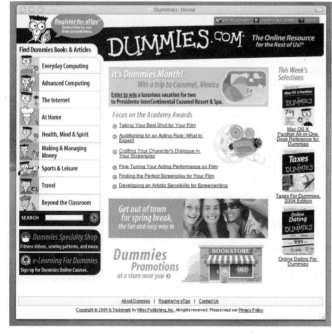

Get smart @ dummies.com®

- **Find a full list of Dummies titles**
- **Look into loads of FREE on-site articles**
- **Sign up for FREE eTips e-mailed to you weekly**
- **See what other products carry the Dummies name**
- **Shop directly from the Dummies bookstore**
- **Enter to win new prizes every month!**

* Separate Canadian edition also available
† Separate U.K. edition also available

Available wherever books are sold. For more information or to order direct: U.S. customers visit www.dummies.com or call 1-877-762-2974.
U.K. customers visit www.wileyeurope.com or call 0800 243407. Canadian customers visit www.wiley.ca or call 1-800-567-4797.

Do More with Dummies

Instructional DVDs • Music Compilations
Games & Novelties • Culinary Kits
Crafts & Sewing Patterns
Home Improvement/DIY Kits • and more!

Check out the Dummies Specialty Shop at www.dummies.com for more information!

WILEY